Apprenticeship in Early Modern Europe

This is the first comparative and comprehensive account of occupational training before the Industrial Revolution. Apprenticeship was a critical part of human capital formation, and, because of this, it has a central role to play in understanding economic growth in the past. At the same time, it was a key stage in the lives of many people, whose access to skills and experience of learning were shaped by the guilds that trained them. The local and national studies contained in this volume bring together the latest research into how skills training worked across Europe in an era before the emergence of national school systems. These essays, written to a common agenda and drawing on major new data sets, systematically outline the features of what amounted to a European-wide system of skills education, and provide essential insights into a key institution of economic and social history.

Maarten Prak is Professor of Social and Economic History at Utrecht University. His wide collection of writings includes *Citizens without Nations: Urban Citizenship in Europe and the World, c. 1000–1789* (2018).

Patrick Wallis is Professor of Economic History at the London School of Economics and Political Science. His many publications include *Medicine and the Market in England and Its Colonies, c. 1450–c. 1850* (2007), co-edited with Mark S. R. Jenner, and he currently edits the *Economic History Review.*

Apprenticeship in Early Modern Europe

Edited by

Maarten Prak

Universiteit Utrecht, The Netherlands

Patrick Wallis

London School of Economics and Political Science

CAMBRIDGE
UNIVERSITY PRESS

CAMBRIDGE
UNIVERSITY PRESS

University Printing House, Cambridge CB2 8BS, United Kingdom

One Liberty Plaza, 20th Floor, New York, NY 10006, USA

477 Williamstown Road, Port Melbourne, VIC 3207, Australia

314–321, 3rd Floor, Plot 3, Splendor Forum, Jasola District Centre, New Delhi – 110025, India

79 Anson Road, #06–04/06, Singapore 079906

Cambridge University Press is part of the University of Cambridge.

It furthers the University's mission by disseminating knowledge in the pursuit of education, learning, and research at the highest international levels of excellence.

www.cambridge.org
Information on this title: www.cambridge.org/9781108496926
DOI: 10.1017/9781108690188

© Cambridge University Press 2020

First published 2020

Printed in the United Kingdom by TJ International Ltd, Padstow Cornwall

A catalogue record for this publication is available from the British Library.

Library of Congress Cataloging-in-Publication Data
Names: Prak, Maarten Roy, 1955– editor. | Wallis, Patrick, editor.
Title: Apprenticeship in early modern Europe / edited by Maarten Prak, Patrick Wallis.
Description: Cambridge ; New York, NY : Cambridge University Press, 2020. | Includes bibliographical references and index.
Identifiers: LCCN 2019027820 (print) | LCCN 2019027821 (ebook) | ISBN 9781108496926 (hardback) | ISBN 9781108690188 (epub)
Subjects: LCSH: Guilds – Europe – History. | Apprenticeship programs – Europe – History. | Europe – Economic conditions.
Classification: LCC HD6473.E85 A66 2020 (print) | LCC HD6473.E85 (ebook) | DDC 331.25/92209409031–dc23
LC record available at https://lccn.loc.gov/2019027820
LC ebook record available at https://lccn.loc.gov/2019027821

ISBN 978-1-108-49692-6 Hardback

Contents

Tables

Figures

    * Maps produced by Iason Jongepier, GIStorical Antwerp
(UAntwerp/Hercules Foundation)

Contributors

ANNA BELLAVITIS is Professor of Early Modern History at the Groupe de Recherche d'Histoire, University of Rouen, France.

RICCARDO CELLA is a researcher at the Groupe de Recherche d'Histoire, University of Rouen, France.

GIOVANNI COLAVIZZA is Assistant Professor of Digital Humanities at the University of Amsterdam, the Netherlands.

CLARE HARU CROWSTON is Professor of History at the History Department of the University of Illinois at Urbana Champaign, USA.

ANNELIES DE BIE is Head of Training Associate Degrees, Department of Science and Technology, Artesis Plantijn University College Antwerp, Belgium.

RAOUL DE KERF is an independent scholar affiliated with the History Department of the University of Antwerp, Belgium.

BERT DE MUNCK is professor at the History Department of the University of Antwerp, Belgium.

CLAIRE LEMERCIER is CNRS research professor of History at the Center for the Sociology of Organizations, Sciences Po in Paris, France.

VICTORIA LÓPEZ BARAHONA is post-doctoral researcher at the Grupo Taller de Historia Social, Department of Early Modern History, Autonomous University of Madrid, Spain.

JOEL MOKYR is Robert H. Strotz Professor of Arts and Sciences and Professor of Economics and History at Northwestern University, USA.

JOSÉ ANTOLÍN NIETO SÁNCHEZ is professor at the Department of Early Modern History, Autonomous University of Madrid, Spain.

MAARTEN PRAK is Professor of Social and Economic History at the Department for History and Art History of Utrecht University, the Netherlands.

REINHOLD REITH is Professor of Social and Economic History at the History Department of the Universität Salzburg, Austria.

RUBEN SCHALK is post-doctoral researcher at the Department for History and Art History of Utrecht University, the Netherlands.

GEORG STÖGER is post-doctoral researcher at the History Department of the University of Salzburg, Austria.

MERJA UOTILA is post-doctoral researcher at the Department of History and Ethnology of the University of Jyväskylä, Finland.

PATRICK WALLIS is Professor of Economic History at the Department of Economic History of the London School of Economics, UK.

BEATRICE ZUCCA MICHELETTO is Marie Skłodowska-Curie Fellow at the Faculty of History, University of Cambridge, UK.

Introduction: Apprenticeship in Early Modern Europe

Maarten Prak and Patrick Wallis

Apprenticeship is one of Europe's most enduring institutions. For at least 800 years, young people have gained the experience and knowledge needed to carry out a wide range of skilled jobs through formal agreements with employers in which they exchange labour for training. Today, the significance of apprenticeship for the supply of an able and effective labour force in industry is widely accepted. It is, for example, commonly seen as one of the underlying explanations for the continued success of German manufacturing. This advantage is so generally accepted that the desirability of restoring, reintroducing or expanding apprenticeship has been a political commonplace for decades in the United States, United Kingdom and other countries struggling to maintain global competitiveness and anxious about the quality of their young workers.[1] Historically, the advantages offered by apprenticeship have been put forward as partial explanations for several of the most significant divergences in the wealth and character of nations, from the Great Divergence between Europe and China, to the emergence of the 'Varieties of Capitalism' observed across the Western World, to the Industrial Revolution itself.[2]

Apprenticeship has mattered historically not just because of its connection to human capital, but because of its importance to our understanding of rights. In the period before national citizenship, one of the key local citizenship rights was the right to work – to exercise a particular occupation or trade. The right to work was frequently linked to guild membership, and guild membership was, in many parts of Europe, linked

---

[1] K. Thelen, *How Institutions Evolve: The Political Economy of Skills in Germany, Britain, the United States, and Japan* (Cambridge: Cambridge University Press, 2004).

[2] M. Prak and J. L. van Zanden (eds.), *Technology, Skills and the Pre-modern Economy in the East and the West* (Leiden: Brill, 2013); P. A. Hall and D. Soskice (eds.), *Varieties of Capitalism: The Institutional Foundations of Competitive Advantage* (Oxford: Oxford University Press, 2001), esp. chs. 1 and 2; R. C. Allen, *The British Industrial Revolution in Global Perspective* (Cambridge: Cambridge University Press, 2009), ch. 10; J. Mokyr, *The Enlightened Economy: An Economic History of Britain, 1700–1850* (New Haven, CT: Yale University Press, 2009), 117–21; J. Humphries, *Childhood and Child Labour in the British Industrial Revolution* (Cambridge: Cambridge University Press, 2010), ch. 9.

to apprenticeship.[3] The effect was akin to a modern professional monopoly or occupational licensing regime, in establishing a barrier around a sector, defining access at least in part by technical ability, and leaving most of the control over entry to the members of the occupation itself.[4] Those who wished to be goldsmiths in Antwerp, bakers in Paris or metalworkers in Sheffield usually had to serve a period of training with an existing 'master' of the trade.[5] Other paths to these rights existed, especially for the sons of existing masters. But in most guilds, incomers supplied the majority of new masters, and they had qualified – in large part – through their apprenticeships. In what we might think of as the great age of the guilds, a period from the fifteenth to the eighteenth century when urban economies across Europe saw a wave of incorporation that expanded the number and extent of craft guilds, apprenticeship often possessed a doubled nature, as a source of both skills and rights.

Its centrality to both human capital and occupational rights meant that apprenticeship was a key ingredient in two major developments that fundamentally altered Europe during the three or four centuries before industrialisation. First, economically, European crafts were transforming the quality and quantity of their output in the centuries before the Industrial Revolution started to kick in. During what we might call the Industrial Evolution, between roughly 1400 and 1800, European industrial producers achieved a small miracle. Many of their products became

---

[3] For surveys on apprenticeship and craft guilds, see B. De Munck, *Technologies of Learning: Apprenticeship in Antwerp Guilds from the 15th Century to the End of the Ancien Régime*, Studies in European Urban History (1100–1800), vol. 11 (Turnhout: Brepols, 2007); B. De Munck, S. L. Kaplan and H. Soly (eds.), *Learning on the Shop Floor: Historical Perspectives on Apprenticeship* (Oxford: Berghahn, 2007); S. R. Epstein and M. Prak (eds.), *Guilds, Innovation and the European Economy, 1400–1800* (Cambridge: Cambridge University Press, 2008); I. A. Gadd and P. Wallis (eds.), *Guilds and Association in Europe, 900–1900* (London: Centre for Metropolitan History, 2006); A. Kluge, *Die Zünfte* (Stuttgart: Franz Steiner, 2007); J. Lucassen, T. De Moor and J. L. van Zanden (eds.), *The Return of the Guilds*, supplement 16, *International Review of Social History* 53 (Cambridge: Cambridge University Press, 2008); S. Ogilvie, *The European Guilds: An Economic Analysis* (Princeton, NJ: Princeton University Press, 2019); M. Prak, C. Lis, J. Lucassen and H. Soly (eds.), *Craft Guilds in the Early Modern Low Countries: Work Power and Representation* (Aldershot: Ashgate 2006); M. Sonenscher, *Work and Wages: Natural Law, Politics, and the Eighteenth-Century French Trades* (Cambridge: Cambridge University Press, 1989).

[4] See also the perceptive remarks about guild 'monopolies' in G. Richardson, 'A tale of two theories: Monopolies and craft guilds in medieval England and modern imagination', *Journal of the History of Economic Thought* 23 (2001), 217–42.

[5] R. De Kerf, 'De circulatie van technische kennis in het vroegmoderne Antwerpse ambachtswezen, 1500–1800 (casus kuipers en edelsmeden)', PhD thesis, University of Antwerp, 2014; S. L. Kaplan, *The Bakers of Paris and the Bread Question, 1700–1775* (Durham, NC: Duke University Press, 1996), ch. 7; J. Unwin, 'Apprenticeships and Freedoms: The computer analysis of the records of the Cutlers' Company in Sheffield', *Local Historian* 25 (1995), 194–208.

increasingly sophisticated, while at the same time the prices of those products were decreasing spectacularly. As a result, many industrial products that were only accessible to the richest class of people in 1400, were available to ordinary people by 1800. Moreover, these cheap 'populuxe' goods of the eighteenth century were often of a higher quality than their very expensive predecessors of the Middle Ages.[6] In the absence of breakthrough innovations or large capital investment in most industries, we must assume that labour inputs were largely responsible for this remarkable achievement. Apprenticeship was the mechanism that shaped the quality and quantity of those labour inputs in many industries.

Second, during the centuries covered by this book, Europe's total population more or less doubled, as did the percentage of that population living in towns and cities. Europe's urban population therefore quadrupled.[7] More or less simultaneously, cities transformed their citizenship regimes.[8] Citizenship emerged as a formal status, providing economic, social and political rights. In many of these towns and cities, guilds were represented in local government, but even when they were not, 'honourable' work, i.e. work that was incorporated, and civic status became mutually dependent.[9] Apprenticeship thus emerged as one of the main gateways into urban privileges and duties.

While its doubled nature underlines the significance of apprenticeship, it has also contributed substantially to the uncertain state of historical evaluations of apprenticeship today, as different scholars have read off quite different implications from the actions of guilds, the behaviour of apprentices and the interest or disinterest paid by the state towards training. As will be discussed, apprenticeship has been swept up in debates over the benefits and harms of guilds and other pre-modern economic institutions that form part of a wider conversation about exclusion, inequality and social capital.[10] While of tremendous importance, this has at times amounted to a clash of ideal types that neglect the

---

[6] C. Fairchilds, 'The production and marketing of populuxe goods in eighteenth-century Paris', in: J. Brewer and R. Porter (eds.), *Consumption and the World of Goods* (London: Routledge, 1998), 228–48; M. Kelly and C. O'Grada, 'Adam Smith, watch prices, and the Industrial Revolution', *Quarterly Journal of Economics* 131 (2016), 1727–52.

[7] J. de Vries, *European Urbanization, 1500–1800* (London: Methuen, 1984), 36, 39.

[8] M. Prak, *Citizens without Nations: Urban Citizenship in Europe and the World* (Cambridge: Cambridge University Press, 2018), ch. 1.

[9] Classic description in M. Walker, *German Home Towns: Community, State, and General Estate 1648–1871* (Ithaca, NY: Cornell University Press, 1971), ch. 3; also J. R. Farr, *Hands of Honor: Artisans and Their World in Dijon, 1550–1650* (Ithaca, NY: Cornell University Press, 1988).

[10] S. R. Epstein, 'Craft guilds in the pre-modern economy: A discussion', versus S. Ogilvie, 'Rehabilitating the guilds: A reply', both in *Economic History Review* 61 (2008), 155–74 and 175–82, epitomises this debate.

diversity of apprenticeship across Europe. It is with an eye to achieving much needed clarity about apprenticeship in its own right that this book has been written.

The chapters in this book examine the different forms which apprenticeship took across Europe between the sixteenth and nineteenth century. Like most institutions, apprenticeship is both universal – to the extent that anthropologists repeatedly identify versions of it in traditional and modern societies – and highly particular.[11] Our central concern is to trace what aspects of apprenticeship were common across the continent and which were distinctive to particular cities and regions. This comparative strategy aims to achieve a better understanding of the regularities of apprenticeship, some of which might even be independent from temporal contexts, and of the dimensions that varied across time and space and therefore suggest options, or menus, that were combined in distinct ways in different localities. Such menus will each have their advantages and disadvantages, in terms of recruitment and of learning outcomes. The sort of comparative historical analysis offered by this book therefore creates the possibility of using historical trajectories as laboratories of the long-term effect of institutional variation.[12]

Despite historians' long-standing acceptance of the importance of apprenticeship, this systematic comparison across nine European nations and cities is an exercise that has not previously been attempted. That it has become feasible now is a reflection of a dramatic growth in the scale of available evidence on the practice of apprenticeship, as a result of the digitisation of materials from across Europe, and a revival of scholarly work on the history of apprenticeship. Therefore, it is now possible to examine the realities of training alongside the norms and regulations that were the conventional focus of earlier studies of apprenticeship.

Theories of Apprenticeship

Thinking about apprenticeship has long been shaped by a pair of powerful theories that identify the institution as a solution to two of the basic problems that emerge from the human life cycle. The longest-standing, reaching back to the early modern period in many ways, analyses

---

[11] M. W. Coy (ed.), *Apprenticeship: From Theory to Method and Back Again* (Albany: State University of New York Press, 1983); S. S. Obido, 'Skill acquisition through indigenous apprenticeship: A case study of the Yoruba blacksmith in Nigeria', *Comparative Education* 31 (1995), 369–83; T. H. J. Marchand, *Minaret Building and Apprenticeship in Yemen* (Richmond: Curzon, 2001); Marchand, *The Masons of Djenné* (Bloomington, IN: Indiana University Press, 2009).

[12] B. van Bavel, 'History as a laboratory to better understand the formation of institutions', *Journal of Institutional Economics* 11 (2015), 69–91.

apprenticeship as a mechanism to manage adolescence. The majority of apprentices lived with people other than their parents, who had handed over the authority to govern their children's behaviour to the master. By locking youths into patriarchal household structures outside the birth family, it secured them (or restricted their independence) during a potentially 'dangerous' period of life and instilled positive and productive cultural values. This is essentially a response to a sociocultural challenge.

Most apprentices were adolescents and, as this theory would suggest, part of their education was thus not so much concerned with their future jobs, but with life itself. Evidence for the importance of social regulation is widespread. Ensuring due respect, reproducing social order, instilling values and suppressing disorderly exuberance were the focus of many apprenticeship regulations, while breaches of domestic order were frequent sources of conflicts between master and apprentice.[13] In 1640, the Aldermen of the City of London ruled that an apprentice would be eligible for citizenship if he could present himself 'with the hair of his head cut in a decent and comely manner'.[14] In post-Reformation German towns, youngsters of illegitimate birth were excluded from apprenticeship.[15] In 1632, an Antwerp apprentice was sent away by his master when he refused to look after the shop while his master and mistress were out.[16] As these examples suggest, it is therefore arguable that, socially, apprenticeship offered a framework 'through which people in a wide range of occupations were indoctrinated into a common set of religious and cultural values'.[17]

The economic problem is also one of transition: how to change unskilled young workers into skilled artisans? Behind this looms the larger issue of the formation of human capital. Increasingly, human capital is recognised as one of the most important assets of any society.[18] Its

---

[13] B. De Munck and H. Soly, 'Learning on the shop floor" in historical perspective', in: De Munck, Kaplan and Soly (eds.), *Learning on the Shop Floor*, 20–23; Humphries, *Childhood and Child Labour*.

[14] S. R. Smith, 'The London apprentices as seventeenth-century adolescents', *Past and Present* 61 (1973), 151.

[15] M. R. Boes, '"Dishonourable" youth, guild, and the changed world view of sex, illegitimacy, and women in late-sixteenth-century Germany', *Continuity and Change* 18 (2003), 345–72.

[16] B. De Munck, 'In loco parentis? De disciplinering van leerlingen onder het dak van Antwerpse ambachtsmeesters (1579–1680)', *Tijdschrift voor Sociale en Economische Geschiedenis* 1 (2004), 15.

[17] C. Brooks, 'Apprenticeship, social mobility and the middling sort, 1500–1800', in: J. Barry and C. Brooks (eds.), *The Middling Sort of People: Culture, Society and Politics in England, 1550–1800* (Houndmills: Macmillan, 1994), 83.

[18] R. J. Barro, 'Human capital and economic growth', *American Economic Review* 91/2 (2001), 12–17; also U. Sunde and T. Vischer, 'Human capital and growth: Specification matters', *Economica* 82 (2015), 368–90, and E. A. Hanushek, G. Schwerdt, S. Wiederhold and

creation is, however, a challenge in its own right. Much of this has to do with the distribution of costs and benefits involved in training.

By enabling young workers to obtain the training they need to carry out skilled jobs, apprenticeship offers a solution to one of the key economic problems that affect labour markets. As Joel Mokyr discusses in Chapter 1, economists thinking about training distinguish between general and specific skills. Firms, they argue, will only invest in teaching workers 'firm-specific' skills; workers have to fund their own acquisition of general skills. It turns out that firm-specific skills are quite narrowly defined: skills that are *only* useful to that firm. If they could be useful elsewhere, the firm will not be able to recover its investment. If firms provide workers with instruction in more general skills – training them to weld, to keep accounts, to use a lathe – then they will be hard-pressed to gain any return from their investment or to even cover their own costs. A firm could try to pay the workers it trained less than their market wage. But then the worker will have every reason to move to another employer, who will pay them a wage that reflects their enhanced productivity. This problem is more acute in theory than practice, as frictions exist in labour markets and workers and firms both value the information and future career options that training generates.[19] But the basic issue remains: because they will reap the benefits of their skills, it is workers (or their families) who need to fund the majority of their training.

Vocational training presents a further challenge when compared to academic education. Many occupational skills demand elements of practice that need to be learned 'on the job'.[20] In short, these skills can only be gained within workplaces, creating problems of scale and access that are apparent in the much lower ratio of apprentices to masters compared to the ratio of students and teachers achieved by schools. The problem is compounded if we recognise that relatively few ordinary families had much money to spare to pay a firm to train their children. Certainly, many would struggle to pay up front for instruction. Young people, in their own right, usually lack either the capital or the credit to raise money to purchase training. Apprenticeship slices through this problem by offering firms a way to recover the cost of training, and the youth a way to fund their learning. Apprenticeship fixes a term of employment during which

L. Woessmann, 'Returns to skills around the world: Evidence from PIAAC', *European Economic Review* 73 (2015), 103–30.

[19] W. Smits and T. Stromback, *The Economics of the Apprenticeship System* (Cheltenham, Edward Elgar, 2001).

[20] D. Guile and T. Griffiths, 'Learning through work experience', *Journal of Education and Work* 14 (2001), 113–31; R. Cowan, P. A. David and D. Foray, 'The explicit economics of knowledge codification and tacitness', *Industrial and Corporate Change* 9 (2000), 211–53.

training will occur, and the apprentice will labour for her or his master. By giving up their right to change job – and thus to capitalise on their new-found skills – apprentices are able to fund their training through the sweat of their brow.

These two theories, one social, the other economic, offer compelling visions of an ideal type of apprenticeship. They are not, obviously, mutually exclusive, though they each suggest a different functional explanation, on one side sustaining social order, on the other increasing productivity, that may lay behind the institution. When applied historically, both, however, leave us open to the risk that we infer the efficiency of an institutional framework from its existence and durability.[21] Where power and money are at stake, abuse can never be far away. Critics of apprenticeship, and more specifically of the guilds that regulated apprenticeship in most countries, have highlighted the potentially exploitative character of apprenticeship. They have pointed out, for example, that the variations in the length of the terms apprentices served suggest that in many places guilds were keeping apprentices longer than was strictly necessary to learn the skills they needed, with the purpose of exploiting this cheap source of labour. It has also been claimed that the existence of alternative mechanisms of learning suggests that the guilds' 'monopoly' over training was really designed to regulate the in-flow of skilled workers, with the aim of driving up the price of their labour.[22] In a similar vein, historians of early modern Europe's patriarchal households have made clear the, at times, brutal and oppressive texture of life faced by some subordinate members.[23]

The degree of abstraction and the essential functionalism of these ideas is the source of their power, but should also give us pause for thought. While they suggest powerful explanations for the basic purpose of apprenticeship, they do so in ways that are – by definition – hard to test.

[21] S. Ogilvie, "Whatever is, is right?" Economic institutions in pre-modern Europe', *Economic History Review* 60 (2007), 649–84.

[22] S. Ogilvie, *State Corporatism and Proto-Industry: The Württemberg Black Forest, 1580–1797* (Cambridge: Cambridge University Press, 1997), 140–47, 157–61; see also J. Lane, *Apprenticeship in England, 1600–1949* (London: UCL Press, 1996), ch. 10; B. De Munck, *Technologies of Learning*, ch. 2; A. Caracausi, 'Beaten children and women's work in early modern Italy', *Past and Present* 222 (2014), 118–19.

[23] The classic account is in R. Darnton, *The Great Cat Massacre, and Other Episodes in French Cultural History* (London: Penguin, 1984), ch. 2. See also M. Mitterauer, *The European Family: Patriarchy to Partnership from the Middle Ages to the Present* (Oxford: Blackwell, 1982; orig. *Vom Patriarchat zur Partnerschaft: Zum Strukturwandel der Familie*, 1977); D. I. Kertzer and M. Barbagli (eds.), *The History of the European Family*, vol. 1: *Family Life in Early Modern Times, 1500–1789* (New Haven: Yale University Press, 2003); as well as B. De Munck, 'From brotherhood community to civil society? Apprentices between guild, household and the freedom of contract in early modern Antwerp', *Social History* 35 (2010), 1–20, and De Munck, *Technologies of Learning*, chs. 5–6.

Identifying the balance between order, productivity and rents in any specific context surely offers an important agenda for any history of apprenticeship. However, it is necessary to look beyond this debate, to pay heed to other, equally fundamental historical questions about the significance, impact and development of apprenticeship within the societies and economies in which it existed. For example, how was apprenticeship created, sustained and extended? How was it perceived and evaluated? Where did it thrive and when did it wither? Answering such questions requires us to open the black box of apprenticeship to ask what were the specific institutions – the rules of the game – that constituted this form of training. In thinking about the history of apprenticeship, we must also take a further step away from seeing it as a single, homogenous structure that worked in the same way across the continent and over time. In short, we need to ask: was apprenticeship one system or many?

Institutions of Training

In the late Middle Ages and early modern period, apprenticeship possessed a particular economic and political position that marks it out from what came later. While in many prominent contexts apprenticeship was tied into formal systems of certification for occupations backed up by local or central regulation, the state was not yet involved in vocational training to any meaningful degree. The combination of subsidised classroom instruction with on-the-job training that characterises modern-day apprenticeship did not exist until the late nineteenth century. Nor, of course, could apprenticeship yet obtain its purpose from serving the interests of the large, managerially led firm. If anything, the growth in the scale of economic organisation was one of the shocks of industrialisation that initially weakened apprenticeship in the nineteenth century.

The distinction from earlier periods is weaker. Much of the institutional framework around apprenticeship developed by guilds and cities had taken shape over the twelfth to sixteenth centuries.[24] It grew in scale, but changed little in nature. Yet in at least one dimension early modern apprenticeship did experience a major development: that of a much enlarged set of welfare institutions that, in various ways, provided forms of apprenticeship to poor children to set them onto a productive trajectory, albeit rarely one that would lift them far up the social ladder.

---

[24] For the early history, S. A. Epstein, *Wage Labor and Guilds in Medieval Europe* (Chapel Hill: University of North Carolina Press, 1991); K. Wesoly, *Lehrlinge und Handwerksgesellen am Mittelrhein: Ihre soziale Lage und ihre Oranisation vom 14. bis ins 17. Jahrhundert* (Frankfurt/Main: Kramer, 1985).

Across early modern Europe, apprenticeship was primarily and initially a private legal agreement between the master and the apprentice and/or the apprentice's family, depending on their age and norms on the legal agency of minors. In some regions and centres, the apprenticeship agreement had acquired a public element by the sixteenth century, through registration requirements or specifications about the terms of contracts. This public element was exercised at the local, usually occupational, level by guilds or cities. One of the central distinctions between early modern apprenticeship and its modern equivalent is the universality of state involvement, as governments have tied funding to the acceptance of regulation since the early twentieth century. Except in England, where it was regulated nationally from the sixteenth century, central governments were happy to leave local institutions in charge of apprenticeship.[25]

The framework in which contracting took place varied over Europe. Broadly speaking, three traditions can be distinguished: notarial; city or guild-registered; and purely private. In notarial systems, such as France, Madrid and the Southern Netherlands, apprenticeship contracts were arranged privately by notaries, who brokered contracts and recorded them. In city or guild systems, seen in Dutch, English, Italian and Finnish towns and cities, contracts were also arranged privately, but were registered with guilds or city authorities, providing both a record of the contract and ensuring that they met local rules. Finally, a large number of apprenticeships were simply agreed between the youth's family and the master; as areas without guilds outnumbered those with guilds, these were probably the most common – though also the ones that are least understood. These systems could overlap: in Spain and the Southern Netherlands, some apprenticeships were registered by notaries, while others were settled orally. An important question is how these different contracting regimes may, or may not, have affected the content and quality of the training, or its accessibility.

The exchange at the centre of all apprenticeship contracts was for the apprentice to work for the master for a fixed period, during which time the master would teach them their trade and usually accommodate them in his or her home.[26] The core pair of commitments to work and train was rarely glossed much beyond this. What was to be taught was never

[25] Lane, *Apprenticeship in England*, 2–8.

[26] For examples of apprenticeship contracts, see Lane, *Apprenticeship in England*, 249–51; also C. H. Crowston, *Fabricating Women: The Seamstresses of Old Regime France, 1675–1791* (Durham, NC: Duke University Press, 2001), 301–05; Kluge, *Die Zünfte*, 154–55; C. Minns and P. Wallis, 'The price of human capital in a pre-industrial economy: Premiums and apprenticeship contracts in 18th-century England', *Explorations in Economic History* 50 (2013), 335–50.

specified in detail, and only rarely defined beyond the generic reference to the master's trade. Clearly, contemporaries recognised the impossibility of seeking to define the contents of such an open-ended process: no details were included of the curriculum, standards or elements of technique that were involved.

Yet many of the other elements of apprenticeship contracts were open to negotiation. How much would the master or apprentice pay each other? Where should the apprentice live? Who supplied their food or clothing? How long should the contract last? Who paid for their care if they fell ill? The extent to which these issues were fixed in the contract varied between regions of Europe. Some areas tended towards including greater detail in contracting, with specific clauses about the apprentices' treatment, tasks and discipline. Unsurprisingly, this often went alongside the use of notaries.

Whether verbose or terse in format, the central issue behind these secondary features of apprenticeship contracts was balancing the supply and demand for training by adjusting the amount that a master earned from taking and training an apprentice against the size of the wage that the youth received. On the one hand, parents and apprentices could give the master fees in cash, agree to extended terms or take on the cost of clothing, feeding or – in a step that reshaped the relationship of master and apprentice in fundamental ways and remained relatively uncommon across Europe before the nineteenth century – housing the youth themselves. On the other, masters might offer wages, promise to release the apprentice early or offer to give him or her an end of contract payment in cash or kind. One would expect to find that where training was scarce relative to demand, as occurred most often in lucrative occupations such as overseas trade, masters wanted to be paid substantial amounts to take an apprentice. Where apprentices were most productive and demand for them was high, they could sometimes demand reasonable cash wages. Like other parts of the labour market, the level of the apprentice's wage was the key variable. Unlike most other agreements, much (sometimes all) of the apprentice's wage was received in kind: in bed and board.

Finally, the timing of exchange mattered because by deferring payments to particular points in the term of an apprenticeship both parties could build in a mechanism to encourage compliance. This is most obvious in the cash and tools that masters sometimes promised to give their apprentices at the end of their term. A similar intent is apparent when apprentices' families split fees to masters over several years to reduce the risk that they would default on their obligations.

As markets changed, cities boomed or regions stagnated, the balance shifted and terms changed. The challenge is to find out if different conditions applied in different parts of Europe, leading to distinct patterns in the mixture between learning and work.

The Apprentice

In early modern Europe's towns and cities, apprentices were a large and important group. Perhaps 2–5 per cent of the population of most larger cities were apprentices. As a share of the male labour force, apprentices were even more important: perhaps one in five workers in some trades were apprentices. Apprentices were somewhat less common in regions such as Italy, where masters were not expected to indenture their own sons.[27]

Who were the apprentices of early modern Europe? Most obviously, these were young people.[28] But they were teenagers for the most part, not small children. Apprenticeship occupied the second half of youths' teenage years. One implication of this is that, unlike today, many would already have been working for some time before starting their apprenticeship. Another is that most apprentices would finish at around 20 years old, much as they still do in many parts of Europe today. There was much variation around these averages. Some is explicable by the needs of occupations. Where strength was essential, as for smiths, apprentices might be older, for example.

Apprentices who were very young (and very old) were relatively rare. But they are an important signal about the inherent flexibility of apprenticeship. It could be used to provide employment and maintenance for small children. These were often poor children, and were frequently placed by welfare institutions rather than their families, as in England's parish poor law. These young apprentices often served longer terms. Alternatively, apprenticeship contracts could be written to supply advanced instruction for journeymen who had already served one term of service.

Most apprentices were also male. After the Middle Ages, female apprentices were formally banned by some urban guilds in Spain, Germany, Italy and the Low Countries.[29] Women were squeezed out of guild trades in these countries, and female masters only survived in

---

[27] For detailed estimates, see pp. 47–9, 142–3, 178–80, 192–3, 255–9, 286–9.

[28] I. Krausman Ben-Amos, *Adolescence and Youth in Early Modern England* (New Haven, CT: Yale University Press, 1994), chs. 4–5; De Munck, *Technologies of Learning*, 178–81; Humphries, *Childhood and Child Labour*, ch. 9; P. Wallis, C. Webb and C. Minns, 'Leaving home and entering service: The age of apprenticeship in early modern London', *Continuity and Change* 25 (2010), 377–404.

[29] Specific examples are discussed on pp. 70–1, 84, 141–2, 171, 226, 230.

unincorporated occupations, such as dressmaking, lacemaking and cloak-weaving. But even where no gender bar was in place, female apprentices were rare, and those that are observed were mostly concentrated in a small group of textile-related trades. Among women, the share entering formal apprenticeships was far outweighed by the share who learned trades within the family workshop, as wives and daughters of artisans. Guild rules thus reinforced a wider norm about gender and apprenticeship.[30]

Beyond these very broad commonalities of age and gender, apprentices were a diverse group. Across Europe, they were drawn from a broad social range, which encompassed rich and poor. It looks as if accessing apprenticeship was harder for children from poor families, but that at least some succeeded, sometimes with the help of orphanages and other welfare institutions. For middling and wealthy families, apprenticeship was the necessary mechanism to place a child into a prosperous career. Perhaps the only group who do not seem to have used apprenticeship was the high nobility.

Apprentices also came from a wide geographical space.[31] The security of housing and subsistence within a long-term contract made apprenticeship a common channel for migration, but this was not always the case. Cycles of migration into apprenticeship may have reflected economic conditions. One consequence of this migratory tendency was that many apprentices were training with masters with whom they had no family tie.[32] Apprenticeship allowed youths to bridge the boundaries of their own kinship group and seek opportunities in places and occupations that lay outside their own family networks. This is, of course, one of the obvious reasons for the formalisation of the training contract itself –

---

[30] See C. Crowston, 'Women, gender and guilds in early modern Europe: An overview of recent research', in: Lucassen, De Moor and van Zanden (eds.), *Return of the Guilds*, 30–34; also K. Snell, *Annals of the Labouring Poor: Social Change and Agrarian England 1660–1900* (Cambridge: Cambridge University Press, 1985), ch. 6; B. Hill, *Women, Work and Sexual Politics in Eighteenth-Century England* (Oxford: Blackwell, 1989), ch. 6; D. Simonton, 'Apprenticeship: Training and gender in eighteenth-century England', in: M. Berg (ed.), *Markets and Manufacture in Early Industrial Europe* (London: Routledge, 1991), 227–58; I. Krausman Ben-Amos, 'Women apprentices in the trades and crafts of early modern Bristol', *Continuity and Change* 6 (1991), 227–52; M. G. Athenas, 'Handlungsspielräume von Kölner Zunfthandwerkerinnen in der Frühen Neuzeit', in: E. Jullien and M. Pauly, *Craftsmen and Guilds in Medieval and Early Modern Periods*, VSWG Beiheft 235 (Stuttgart: Franz Steiner, 2016), 133–34.

[31] M. Prak, C. Crowston, B. De Munck, C. Kissane, C. Minns, R. Schalk and P. Wallis, 'Access to the trade: Monopoly and mobility in European craft guilds, 17th and 18th centuries', *Journal of Social History* 53 (2020), Data Appendix.

[32] Lane, *Apprenticeship in England*, 54–60; De Munck, *Technologies of Learning*, ch. 5; T. Leunig, C. Minns and P. Wallis, 'Networks in the pre-modern economy: The market for London apprenticeships, 1600–1749', *Journal of Economic History* 71 (2011), 413–43.

within families, agreements can be informal as they are underpinned by strong and durable ties – and this was one of the key advantages of the system within the highly fragmented, small-scale economy of early modern European manufacturing and services.

It is clear that, despite this commonly being assumed, apprenticeship did not sharply decline or disappear with the end of the Ancien Régime.[33] Yet there can be little doubt that it was changing. Two aspects of this development deserve to be teased apart, to the extent that this is possible. The first is the change – and often the decline – in the use of apprenticeship that occurred across Europe as specialisation within economies increased, large firms began to emerge and industrialisation gathered pace. The second is the effect of the abolition or attenuation of guild control that occurred at different times between the early eighteenth and late nineteenth centuries. Where guild controls were withdrawn patterns of apprenticeship changed, as the removal of guild rules encouraged greater variation in the structure of agreements.

The effect of these changes in the longer term was a more focused and restricted use of apprenticeship by the late nineteenth century in much of Europe. In some occupations, apprenticeships remained the main channel through which training was obtained; this was particularly important in trades where firms took on the provision of training within a longer-term career structure. Philips in the Netherlands offers one example. In some places, however, apprenticeship became hollowed out, losing its instructional element and becoming simply a framework for child labour. The textile factories of England are the obvious illustration of this. In others, expectations for apprenticeship dwindled.

There is a striking commonality in the timing of what might be seen as the late nineteenth-century crisis in apprenticeship across Europe.[34] This is most clearly visible in the Northern Netherlands. The extremely unstable and brief contracts experienced by Amsterdam orphans in the early 1900s, whose terms averaged six months and which ended abruptly as work dried up or the apprentice ran off, are a stark contrast to the more durable agreements that existed a century earlier. Yet England and France both appear to have been experiencing similar conditions at this time, with complaints about the unstable employment and limited

---

[33] A. Steidl, 'Silk weaver and purse maker apprentices in eighteenth- and nineteenth-century Vienna', in: De Munck, Kaplan and Soly (eds.), *Learning on the Shop Floor*, 133–57; S. L. Kaplan and Ph. Minard (eds.), *La France: Malade du corporatisme? XVIIIe–XXe siècle* (Paris: Belin, 2004); J. Humphries, 'Rent-seeking or skill creating? Apprenticeship in early industrial Britain', in: P. Gauci (ed.), *Regulating the British Economy, 1660–1850* (Farnham: Ashgate, 2011), 235–58.

[34] See particularly Chapter 7 on the Northern Netherlands and Chapter 10 on France, in this book.

training of young workers abounding – prompting several of the earliest historical studies of early modern apprenticeship. In the wake of this period, states established a new set of institutional structures that reshaped apprenticeship into a subsidised blend of schooling and work that continues in some form in most countries of Europe today, albeit with differing degrees of popularity.[35]

Apprenticeship and Welfare

The ubiquity of apprenticeship as the main mode of entry into most skilled manufacturing occupations and many roles in trade and retail meant that apprentices were necessarily recruited from across the social spectrum, just as the demographic imbalance between town and country meant that a flow of youths from farming families were an integral part of the survival of Europe's urban landscape. Alongside these persistent shared patterns across the continent, a significant development, rooted in the early evolution of welfare provison, was changing the nature of apprenticeship in Europe.

Apprenticeship was seen as a potential solution to poverty across early modern Europe. The authors of schemes for institutionalised welfare, in particular, often pinned their ambition to raise paupers into productive citizens on some form of apprenticeship.[36] This idea became widespread across Europe between the sixteenth and eighteenth centuries and increasingly found concrete manifestation, particularly in urban centres. To some extent this was not new. In the Netherlands, city orphanages had always seen apprenticeship as the natural destination for the children of deceased burghers. Turin's hospitals for paupers, such as the *Albergo di Virtu*, had emphasised training for young people in the sixteenth century. But there was a substantial growth in the number and often the scale of these institutions, and internal, institutional training became more common.[37]

---

[35] Thelen, *How Institutions Evolve*, 39–40, 94–95; M. Busemeyer and C. Trampusch (eds.), *The Political Economy of Collective Skill Formation* (Oxford: Oxford University Press, 2012), 101–25; R. Schalk, *Splitting the Bill: Matching Schooling to Dutch Labour Markets, 1750–1920* (Amsterdam: Boom, 2015), ch. 3.

[36] H. Cunningham, *The Children of the Poor: Representations of Childhood since the Seventeenth Century* (Oxford: Blackwell, 1991), 30–31; S. Cavallo, 'Conceptions of poverty and poor-relief in Turin in the second half of the eighteenth century', in: S. Woolf (ed.), *Domestic Strategies: Work and Family in France and Italy 1600–1800* (Cambridge: Cambridge University Press, 1991), 148–99; Lane, *Apprenticeship in England*, ch. 4; R. Schalk, 'From orphan to apprentice: Apprenticeship careers and contract enforcement in the Netherlands before and after the guild abolition', *Economic History Review* 70 (2017), 730–57.

[37] See Chapter 3 (Turin), pp. 95–101 and Chapter 7 (Northern Netherlands), p. 191.

For pauper children, apprenticeship or training was often entered when they were younger than private apprentices, and it focused on low-end jobs.[38] Putting poor children to work for long hours, in conditions of severe discipline, at simple tasks such as spinning hardly sounds like an investment in human capital. Yet some of these institutions were more ambitious. Some even provided easier access into the guild, with lower fees and shorter times spent as journeymen. The effect of the growth of pauper apprenticeship and institutions was not necessarily hostile to guild apprenticeship, in short. But it generated new alternatives for the process of training, and – at least at the lower end of the labour market – must have put pressure on demand for private apprenticeship.

Learning and Living as an Apprentice

In contrast to the detail available to us about contracts, all too little is known about how apprentices learned their trade.[39] The near invisibility of training is a natural outcome of several factors: the scarcity of any written records about this aspect of society; the sheer ordinariness and unremarkable nature of most productive processes; and the tacit, unspoken character of many occupational skills. Failures of training do feature frequently in records of disputes between masters and apprentices, but these rarely show us much of the process of learning beyond debates over what types of work were or were not appropriate. Trial and error mattered, to be sure. And even though performing non-craft-related tasks might at times be a cause for complaint, it seems that in most places apprenticeship could include a wide range of work alongside tasks that were obviously related to the occupation being learned. Domestic duties, helping gather the harvest, fetching and carrying were all part of the myriad of chores that went along with the opportunity to practise one's skill. Beyond the trade, apprentices also learned how to be artisans and – in towns – to be citizens. Their transformation was signalled in western Finland by adopting a craft surname – such as Sax (scissors) for tailors.

We can see the trajectory of youths through apprenticeship more clearly than we can the changes that they underwent as workers and people. And when we look at apprentices' progression through their terms we find that, in much of Europe, the agreement between master and youth was markedly more flexible in practice than the text of contracts suggests.

---

[38] E. van Nederveen Meerkerk and A. Schmidt, 'Between wage labor and vocation: Child labor in Dutch urban industry, 1600–1800', *Journal of Social History* 41 (2008), 717–36.

[39] P. Wallis, 'Apprenticeship and training in premodern England', *Journal of Economic History* 68 (2008), 848; M. Prak, 'Painters, guilds and the art market during the Dutch Golden Age', in: Epstein and Prak (eds.), *Guilds, Innovation*, 155–56; this volume, pp. 88, 157–9, 177–8, 225–9.

Apprentices could and did move to new workshops or abandon their training entirely. Some shifted trade. Some slipped into crime. Some died. Apprentices worried they were not receiving enough training, that they were wasting time on trivial activities, chores and unrelated work, or that they were being beaten too harshly or fed too little. For their part, masters could eject the unwanted. These adjustments were not costless. But they were not rare.[40]

Given that abandoning a contract often meant giving up on the opportunity to enter a guild, the price might seem prohibitive. But that argument neglects the reality that most apprentices had little chance of becoming members of guilds in the first place. Only a small share of apprentices would ever become masters. Others would have become masters in other cities, but even if we adjust for that perhaps one in five apprentices reached mastership. Most apprentices remained journeymen or shifted to a different line of work. The ideal typical path from apprentice to journeyman to master was a mirage for most youths. A full appreciation of how apprenticeship fit into the life-course of artisans and others can probably only be achieved by looking at apprentices and journeymen together, and at present the latter remain a remarkably neglected topic in social history.

Craft Guilds and Apprenticeship

Where they existed, guilds were often involved in regulating apprenticeship. This was not a universal. Some guilds ignored apprenticeship. In Italy, only half of guilds introduced any apprenticeship rules, for example.[41] Other guilds only introduced a limited number of regulations.

The rules that guilds imposed on apprenticeship usually focused on four areas: (1) compulsory registration of apprentices; (2) setting requirements for the minimum length of their service, their age, their gender or their social or geographical background; (3) specifying maximum limits on the numbers that could work for one master; and (4) preventing

---

[40] P. Wallis, 'Labor, law and training in early modern London: Apprenticeship and the City's institutions', *Journal of British Studies* 51 (2012), 791–819; R. Schalk, P. Wallis, C. Crowston and C. Lemercier, 'Failure or flexibility? Apprenticeship training in pre-modern Europe', *Journal of Interdisciplinary History* 48 (2017), 131–58; also Sonenscher, *Work and Wages*, 109–10; Wallis, 'Apprenticeship and training'; C. Minns and P. Wallis, 'Rules and reality: Quantifying the practice of apprenticeship in early modern England', *Economic History Review* 65 (2012), 556–79.

[41] L. Mocarelli, 'Guilds reappraised: Italy in the early modern period', in: Lucassen, De Moor and van Zanden (eds.), *Return of the Guilds*, 175–76.

masters poaching each other's apprentices – for example, masters could not hire one another's apprentices without permission in Turin and London. It is hard to see these rules as designed to ensure the quality of training.[42] At most one could imagine that minimum term lengths meant that inexperienced workers were kept out of labour markets, but there is little evidence that this – rather than arbitrarily slowing entry – was their intent or their effect. Rather, these rules were mainly designed to prevent concentration of labour – and inequalities in firm size – that would expand the divisions between masters, and to protect journeymen from facing a rapid influx of competition in the labour market.[43] In short, guild rules were consciously created to add friction into competitive markets for labour and products. As such, they might be tightened or loosened in response to economic pressure and political circumstances.

Very few parts of Europe had guilds that set regulations to encourage masters and apprentices to comply with their contracts. Very few established a formal system to resolve disputes. Very few examined apprentices at the end of their training to provide a quality check. It is true that some guilds did do more, but these were exceptions. For the most part, the importance of guilds in contract *enforcement*, a hypothesis that has been widely discussed in recent studies, was more limited.[44]

Guild regulation was much tighter on entry to mastership than apprenticeship. Who could become a master and how was a crucial question. This process influenced apprenticeship. Serving an apprenticeship was frequently one requirement for new masters, especially for those whose fathers were not masters. Some guilds expected masters to prove their skills by creating 'masterpieces'. But the degree to which this kind of test was a general phenomenon has frequently been exaggerated.[45] More importantly, the masterpiece was *not* an examination to test what had been learned during apprenticeship. It usually followed several years in which the aspiring master had been working as a journeyman.

Despite the attention that guilds have attracted, it was the city or sometimes the state itself that offered the chance of recourse to masters

---

[42] B. De Munck, 'Skills, trust, and changing consumer preferences: The decline of Antwerp's craft guilds from the perspective of the product market, c. 1500–c. 1800', *International Review of Social History* 53 (2008), 210–15.

[43] De Munck, *Technologies of Learning*, 59–68.

[44] De Munck and Soly, '"Learning on the shop floor"', 10–13; also S. R. Epstein, 'Craft guilds, apprenticeship, and technological change in pre-industrial Europe', *Journal of Economic History* 53 (1998), 684–713; Wallis, 'Apprenticeship and training'; B. De Munck, 'Gilding golden ages: Perspectives from early modern Antwerp on the guild debate, c. 1450–c. 1650', *European Review of Economic History* 15 (2011), 227–32; Schalk, 'From orphan to apprentice'.

[45] De Munck, 'Skills, trust'.

or apprentices whose contracts were imperilled. In fact, in most urban centres, the centre of formal enforcement of apprenticeship contracts was outside the guilds.

Courts across Europe heard complaints from both apprentices and masters that focused on a cluster of key issues: was sufficient training being given; was the apprentice getting enough food or suitable accommodation; were they being beaten excessively or mistreated; had they run away or left without permission; were they abusing the master or mistress or behaving badly?[46] And these courts usually had the power to dissolve contracts or discipline one or the other party, if reconciliation – usually the first goal of most early modern dispute mechanisms – failed. In providing legal mechanisms to settle differences, Europe's states and cities may have contributed substantially to the viability of apprenticeship, and this institutional endowment provides one of the distinctive features of training in the west.

About This Book

This chapter has sought to pull together some of the ideas about apprenticeship proposed in the literature. In the chapters that follow, our concern has been to identify the presence or absence of regional or national differences, and to isolate distinctive elements of the structures of apprenticeship as it existed in early modern and early industrial Europe. To achieve this, experts from almost all corners of Europe have been asked to describe and analyse the local or national system of apprenticeship that they know from close up. The chapters therefore offer a mixture of new data and surveys of existing materials. Writing their chapters, the authors have responded to a common set of questions, the outline of which corresponds to the topics raised in this Introduction. Joel Mokyr, in Chapter 1, analyses the institution of apprenticeship from the perspective of Economics theory.

With the chapters addressing a coherent set of issues and questions, the Conclusion combines the results of these local and national studies. It tries to provide an answer to the central question of this book: was there

---

[46] H. Deceulaer, 'Guilds and litigation: Conflict settlement in Antwerp (1585–1796)', in: M. Boone and M. Prak (eds.), *Statuts individuels, statuts corporatifs et statuts judiciaires dans les villes européennes (moyen âge et temps modernes)* [Individual, corporate and judicial status in European cities (late Middle Ages and early modern period)] (Louvain: Garant, 1996), 171–208; Wallis, 'Labor, law and training'; A. Caracausi, 'A reassessment of the role of guild courts in disputes over apprenticeship contracts: A case study from early modern Italy', *Continuity and Change* 32 (2017), 85–114.

such a thing as a European system of apprenticeship, or were there several such regimes existing next to each other, as is often posited for the modern era?

The chapters that follow were all especially commissioned for this book and all appear here for the first time in print. They draw on extensive earlier work as well as new projects undertaken by our authors. The chapters were first presented in a workshop at Utrecht University on 3 and 4 July 2016. This workshop was held in the context of the bEUcitizen project that was funded by the European Commission in the context of its 7th Framework Programme (grant number 320294). Apart from the authors, the workshop was also attended by Feike Dietz, Steven L. Kaplan, Nina Lerman, Philippe Minard, Elise van Nederveen Meerkerk, Margaret Pelling, Sandra de Pleijt, Àngels Solà Parera and Karine Van der Beek, whose critical reflections have helped sharpen our thoughts and arguments.

1   The Economics of Apprenticeship

Joel Mokyr

Introduction

The subject of apprenticeship, one of the more enduring of all economic arrangements, has received more attention from economic historians and the economics profession at large in recent years.[1] Yet, compared, say, with issues such as the economics of slave labor or the rise of formal human capital and literacy, apprenticeship – the mechanism through which practical skills were transferred from generation to generation – has not been the subject of much research before 2000. Even in the literature that has revised and criticized the old view of the guilds as a pure redistributive institution and an impediment to efficiency and technological progress, apprenticeship was often mentioned but was eclipsed by other issues such as exclusionary rent-seeking and allocative efficiency. There were some exceptions in specific cases, but in proportion to its importance and prevalence, the institution remained strangely under-researched until recently.[2] This is now changing, in large part through the pioneering work of a number of scholars on apprenticeship in Canada and Europe such as Gillian Hamilton, Bert De Munck, and Patrick Wallis, among others.[3]

---

[1] The comments and suggestions of David De la Croix, Morgan Kelly, Cormac Ó Gráda, Maarten Prak, and Patrick Wallis on an earlier draft are acknowledged with gratitude. A longer version of this essay with detailed footnotes can be found at www .faculty.econ.northwestern.edu/faculty/mokyr.

[2] O. J. Dunlop, 'Some aspects of early English apprenticeship', *Transactions of the Royal Historical Society*, third series, 5 (1911), 193–208; O. J. Dunlop, *English Apprenticeship and Child Labor* (New York: MacMillan, 1912); B. Elbaum, 'Why apprenticeship persisted in Britain but not in the United States', *Journal of Economic History* 49 (1989), 337–49; J. Lane, *Apprenticeship in England 1600–1914* (Boulder, CO: Westview Press, 1996); G. Hamilton, 'Enforcement in apprenticeship contracts: Were runaways a serious problem? Evidence from Montreal', *Journal of Economic History* 55 (1995), 551–74; G. Hamilton, 'The decline of apprenticeship in North America: Evidence from Montreal', *Journal of Economic History* 60 (2000), 627–64.

[3] B. De Munck, *Technologies of Learning: Apprenticeship in Antwerp Guilds from the 15th Century to the End of the Ancien Régime* (Turnhout: Brepols, 2007); B. De Munck, 'From brotherhood community to civil society? Apprentices between guild, household and the

The new research has been directed primarily at economic and social historians; the important implications of apprenticeship for issues in economic growth, the economics of innovation and technological diffusion, labor economics, and the new institutional economics, need to be spelled out in some detail, which is what this chapter will attempt to do. As the other chapters in this volume amply attest, a great deal of new information has been unearthed in recent years about the actual workings of apprenticeship in the past. At the same time, economics provides a set of analytical tools that offer a theoretical framework to interpret the new data. These tools are both microeconomic and macroeconomic. In terms of microeconomics, one issue concerns contracts, that is, analyzing the transaction between the supplier of training (the master) and the customer (the apprentice and his family). Other microeconomic themes of interest connect directly to the organization of the industry and the use of apprenticeship as a barrier to entry and the structure of pre-modern urban labor markets, as apprentices and journeymen were a form of *un*proletariat before the Industrial Revolution.

Human capital theory suggests that investment in education is one of the most important human activities that determines lifetime outcomes on the microeconomic level and the economic performance of society on the macro level. An analysis of apprenticeship involves the intergenerational transmission of technical skills. These skills constituted a special form of human capital, a set of recipes often referred to as the "secrets of the trade," a *savoir faire* that determined how goods and services were to be produced and who would be allowed to engage in it. The economics of knowledge stresses the important distinction between codifiable and tacit knowledge.[4] Much of the knowledge imparted to apprentices was *tacit* knowledge, which could not be obtained from textbooks or encyclopedias and was not taught in schools. The only way for a young lad to become a barber, a cooper, or a cabinetmaker was through direct contact with, and imitation of, people who already possessed the requisite competence

---

freedom of contract in early modern Antwerp', *Social History* 35 (2010), 1–20; B. De Munck, 'Corpses, live models, and nature: Assessing skills and knowledge before the Industrial Revolution (case: Antwerp)', *Technology and Culture* 51 (2010), 332–56; P. Wallis, 'Apprenticeship and training in premodern England', *Journal of Economic History* 68 (2008), 832–61; P. Wallis, 'Labor, law, and training in early modern London: Apprenticeship and the City's institutions', *Journal of British Studies* 51 (2012), 791–819. Economists, too, are gradually recognizing its importance, e.g. W. Smits and Th. Stromback, *The Economics of the Apprenticeship System* (Cheltenham: Edward Elgar, 2001); D. De la Croix, M. Doepke and J. Mokyr, 'Clans, guilds, and markets: Apprenticeship institutions and growth in the pre-industrial economy', *Quarterly Journal of Economics* 133 (2018), 1–70.

[4] D. Foray, *The Economics of Knowledge* (Cambridge, MA: MIT Press, 2004), especially 71–90.

and were willing and able to teach it.[5] In terms of more aggregative analysis, apprenticeship was a major factor in the determination of the rate and quality of human capital formation. Beyond that, masters acted *in loco parentis* and apprenticeship was a major part of socialization and the intergenerational transmission of culture and norms, a topic that has recently become quite interesting to economists.[6] Here the interests of the two disciplines clearly are conjoined, and interdisciplinary research is promising.[7]

Moreover, apprenticeship should also be analyzed through the prism of the new institutional economics pioneered by Douglass North. The market for apprenticeship, like all markets, depended on a set of institutions that determined how the contracts were enforced, how effective the training was, whether innovation was encouraged, and what it implied for the status of masters and apprentices. The institutions governing apprenticeship thus represent a prime example of a set of Northian "rules of the game" that determined economic outcomes. In its regulation, formal (that is to say, government) institutions coexisted and overlapped with private arrangements and corporate bodies and underlay pre-modern non-agricultural labor markets.

Finally, I will turn to the issue of economic growth and the Industrial Revolution, and argue that the work of economists implies a central role for apprenticeship in the questions regarding the sources of the "Great Enrichment" in Europe. An obvious reason for its significance in the growth literature is the observed differences in technological capabilities in different economies, with far-reaching consequences for economic performance. In the case of the British Industrial Revolution, for instance, it has been argued that the level of skills of British workers was higher than elsewhere largely due to its superior and flexible institutions of training youngsters.[8]

[5] J. R. Harris, 'Skills, coal and British industry in the eighteenth century', in: Harris, *Essays in Industry and Technology in the Eighteenth Century* (Aldershot: Ashgate/Variorum, 1992), 33 called the tacit knowledge in the iron industries 'unanalyzable pieces of expertise' and 'the knacks of the trade,' but it was equally true in many service industries; see J. R. Farr, *Artisans in Europe, 1300–1914* (Cambridge: Cambridge University Press, 2000), 34.

[6] A. Bisin and Th. Verdier, 'The economics of cultural transmission and socialization', in: J. Benhabib, A. Bisin and M. O. Jackson (eds.), *Handbook of Social Economics*, vol. 1A (Amsterdam: North-Holland, 2011), 339–416.

[7] De Munck, *Technologies of Learning*, 4–5.

[8] M. Kelly, J. Mokyr and C. Ó Gráda, 'Precocious Albion: A new interpretation of the British Industrial Revolution', *Annual Review of Economics* 6 (2014), 363–89; J. Humphries, 'English apprenticeships: A neglected factor in the first Industrial Revolution', in: P. A. David and M. Thomas (eds.), *The Economic Future in Historical Perspective* (Oxford: Oxford University Press, 2003), 73–102; N. Ben Zeev, J. Mokyr and K. van der Beek, 'Flexible supply of apprenticeship in the British Industrial Revolution', *Journal of Economic History* 77 (2017), 208–50.

The Industrial Revolution did not lead to the end of apprenticeship. In many economies one-on-one training is still very widely practiced. Despite the abolition of the English Statute of Apprentices and Artificers in 1814, apprenticeship remained of central importance in the British textile engineering sector, one of the high-tech sectors of the day.[9] Moreover, while in our time apprenticeship has been partially supplanted by formal instruction in vocational and professional schools, the personal, one-to-one transmission of knowledge and hands-on experience is still felt to be of substantial importance, complementing rather than replacing more formal forms of instruction.[10]

Tacit Knowledge and Personal Teaching

One way to look at apprenticeship is as a personal and direct way of passing tacit skills and competence from master to pupil. Skills have been described by Michael Polanyi in his classic work on the topic as "the observance of a set of rules not known to the person following them."[11] Tacit knowledge of any kind is likely to be transmitted through personal contact: by observation, memorization, and imitation. Hence, Polanyi argued, "An art which cannot be specified in detail cannot be transmitted by prescription, since no prescription for it exists. It can be passed on only by example from master to apprentice. This restricts the range of diffusion to that of personal contacts, and accordingly craftsmanship tends to survive in closely circumscribed local traditions."[12] One corollary is that many high-skilled crafts were located in urban areas; rural manufacturing – while widespread – was mostly low-skill.[13] In the modern age, it is common to think of codified and tacit knowledge as complements in which a hands-on personal relation supplements formal course work. Not so before the Industrial Revolution: formal instruction in the

---

[9] G. Cookson, *The Age of Machinery: Engineering the Industrial Revolution, 1770–1850* (Woodbridge: Boydell Press, 2018), 236. As late as 1925, there were 315,000 apprentices and 110,000 'learners' in Great Britain; see Smits and Stromback, *Economics,* 20.

[10] In Germany today almost 60% of young people train as apprentices, compared with less than 5% in the United States. Apprenticeship occurs not just in manufacturing but in banking, IT, and hospitality. In experimental sciences, postdoctoral training – a form of apprenticeship – is still required; e.g. T. Jacoby, 'Why Germany is so much better at training its workers,' *The Atlantic,* 16 October 2014, www.theatlantic.com/business/arc hive/2014/10/why-germany-is-so-much-better-at-training-its-workers/381550/.

[11] M. Polanyi, *Personal Knowledge: Towards a Post-Critical Philosophy* (Chicago: University of Chicago Press, 1962), 49.

[12] Ibid., 53.

[13] P. Desrochers, 'Geographical proximity and the transmission of tacit knowledge', *Review of Austrian Economics* 14 (2001), 26 provides data for our time, but his argument holds *a fortiori* for medieval and early modern Europe.

majority of trades and occupations was rare. Only in law, medicine, and religion was there formal training in schools and universities. Artisans, both in manufacturing and in services, were taught the secrets of the trade by associating with a master with whom they spent their adolescent years.

How the transmission of knowledge took place exactly is not always easy to establish and was likely to depend on the idiosyncratic characteristics of individual masters and the special characteristics of the techniques taught. Most studies concede that little is known regarding the actual learning process, but Schalk speaks for the consensus when he surmises that skills were picked up primarily through imitation and learning by doing.[14] The costs were the master's time as well as the raw materials used up in the less-than-successful products produced by the apprentice. An interesting formulation is suggested by Steffens suggesting that skill transmission took place through apprentices "stealing with their eyes" – meaning that they learned mostly through emulation, observation, and experimentation. Goody suggests that most learning comes from "monitored participation," a form of learning by doing in which the apprentice was allowed to carry out increasingly more complex tasks.[15] Apprentices learned by being "inserted into the production process" from the start and in the absence of any serious epistemic base of the techniques in use, learning by doing and emulation were clearly central in the process.[16] The tasks to which apprentices were put at first, insofar as they can be documented at all, seem to have consisted of menial assignments such as making deliveries, cleaning, and guarding the shop. Only at a later stage would an apprentice be trusted with more sensitive tasks involving valued customers and expensive raw materials.[17]

Contracts and the Nature of Apprenticeship

To start an apprenticeship, some kind of agreement had to be made between the two parties. In the absence of any formal and detailed description of what and how the youngster would be taught, the contract between him and his guardian on one side and the master on the other must be regarded as an archetypal incomplete contract. Unlike the standard incomplete contract model in economics, in which the main issue is the inability to specify all contingencies ex ante, in the case of

---

[14] R. Schalk, 'Apprenticeships with and without Guilds', Chapter 7 in this volume.

[15] S. Steffens, 'Le métier volé: Transmission des savoir-faire et socialization dans les métiers qualifiés au XIXe siècle', *Revue du Nord* 15 (2001), 131; E. Goody, 'Learning, apprenticeship, and the division of labor', in: M. W. Coy (ed.), *Apprenticeship: From Theory to Method and Back Again* (Albany: SUNY Press, 2001), 289.

[16] De Munck, *Technologies of Learning*, 4, 9.   [17] Lane, *Apprenticeship in England*, 77.

apprentice indentures the exact nature of the service to be exchanged was itself vague. Even when some contracts were written by public notaries and contained details of the mutual expectations, the full details could not be specified ex ante, nor could they be observed with much accuracy ex post, due to the tacit nature of the service provided.[18] Both the diligence and motivation of the pupil and the effort put in by the master were matters of discretion. The parents and guardians had to trust the master that he would teach properly; without such trust, the contract could not be viable. Moreover, the contract was normally concluded and signed by the parents, and when a tuition fee or "premium" was paid, this normally came out of their funds. Hence there was another agency problem, in that the main subject of the contract, the youngster himself, was usually not a party to the negotiation. In that regard an indenture contract between an apprentice and a master in early modern Europe was similar to the implicit contract between a student and a college in our time. The difference is that each apprentice–master relation was a non-repeated, personal, and unique interaction. Furthermore, the number of apprentices per master was small, so the informational difficulties were amplified and the possibilities for opportunistic behavior on either side were considerable.

Most of the economics literature on incomplete contracts is of little help here, since the solutions proposed there, such as the integration of firms to resolve hold-up situations or an ownership assignment that may incentivize both sides, seem irrelevant to this particular question. What is more, the information about the realized transaction was asymmetric in two ways. First, even if the two sides could observe the outcome perfectly themselves, it may have been impossible to convey this information to third parties asked to adjudicate disputes, that is, "incompleteness arises because states of the world, quality and actions are observable (to the contractual parties) but not verifiable (to outsiders)" – such as courts.[19] But in this case one of the sides to the contract – the apprentice – was *by definition* underinformed about the material to be taught (and his parent or guardian, often the signatory on the contract, absent from the scene), and the incompleteness was compounded by an informational asymmetry between the contracting parties.[20] To make things worse, the apprenticeship contract was non-repeatable and had a clear-cut termination date after which the relationship was resolved, which made opportunistic behavior especially attractive as the contract came to an end.

[18] De Munck, *Technologies of Learning*, 42.
[19] O. Hart, 'Incomplete contracts', in: S. N. Durlauf and L. E. Blume (eds.), *The New Palgrave Dictionary of Economics*, 2nd edition, online version, unpaginated.
[20] Smits and Stromback, *Economics*, 41–2.

The contract between master and apprentice was subject to what is known as the credible commitment problem, which occurs widely in contract theory and political economy.[21] The issue is basically this: if the apprentice or his guardian could advance the full cost of his training at the outset, this would be obviously desirable for the master. But when the apprentice was impecunious, and credit markets unavailable for this purpose, the best way to cover the master's cost was to have the apprentice commit to work for him when the training had advanced, thus securing a flow of cheap skilled labor for the master in compensation for his teaching efforts.[22] From the point of view of incentivizing the master to teach properly, this makes sense: the productivity of the apprentice as employee depended on how skilled he was when the time came. The commitment problem, however, meant that while the apprentice or his guardian could promise from the outset to supply this work, when the time came he had no incentive to do so, and instead might shirk in his work or abscond carrying in his head the human capital he had accumulated.[23] As the master knew this, the apprentice could not credibly commit to providing the work and the entire apprenticeship system might unravel. The contract was therefore not self-enforcing. Smits and Stromback, after showing when the contract might be stable, note that neither the effort exerted by the apprentice nor the quality of instruction were contractable, and so the credible commitment problem remains.[24]

The exchange between master and apprentice thus typically involved two bundled services: the master taught the apprentice the skills and secrets of the trade, which involved his time and the time of his employees, as well as the tools and raw materials that were used up in the instruction process. Moreover, in most documented cases, the apprentice was provided room and board by the master and in many cases he was socialized in other subjects, such as piety, literacy, and good manners.[25] As in most educational markets, the training involved not just the actual transmission of knowledge but also a formal stamp of approval at the end of the training that permitted the trainee to practice

---

[21] For a good summary, see D. Acemoglu and J. Robinson, *Economic Origins of Dictatorship and Democracy* (Cambridge: Cambridge University Press, 2006), 133–36.

[22] See e.g. S. A. Epstein, *Wage Labor and Guilds in Medieval Europe* (Chapel Hill: University of North Carolina Press, 1995), 143–44.

[23] The hard-to-observe effort exerted by the apprentice working for his master is at the core of the principal–agent models that analyze such contracts, as Adam Smith already noted: *The Wealth of Nations*, ed. E. Cannan (Chicago: University of Chicago Press, 1976), pt. I, 137.

[24] Smits and Stromback, *Economics*, 77, 88–89.

[25] For examples on the demand of apprentices for literacy skills, see M. Davies and A. Saunders, *The History of the Merchant Taylors Company* (Leeds: Maney Publishing, 2004), 109.

the trade, hopefully eventually as a master himself. It was thus a complex transaction on both sides, and it is easy to see what could go wrong.

An example from mid-thirteenth-century France serves as an illustration. In one contract, from Arras, a mother (probably a widow) apprenticed her son to a weaver for four years and basically guaranteed his good behavior.[26]

Be it known to present and future aldermen that Ouede Ferconne apprentices Michael, her son, to Matthew Haimart on security of her house, her person, and her chattels, and the share that Michael ought to have in them, so that Matthew Haimart will teach him to weave in four years, and that he (Michael) will have shelter, and learn his trade there without board. And if there should be reason within two years for Michael to default she will return him, and Ouede Ferconne, his mother, guarantees this on the security of her person and goods. And if she should wish to purchase his freedom for the last two years she may do so for thirty-three solidi, and will pledge for that all that has been stated. And if he should not free himself of the last two years let him return, and Ouede Ferconne, his mother, pledges this with her person and her goods. And the said Ouede pledges that if Matthew Haimart suffers either loss or damage through Michael, her son, she will restore the loss and damage on the security of herself and all her goods, should Michael do wrong.

This example may create a mistaken idea of uniformity; in fact there was great variety in the nature of these contracts. In fourteenth-century Montpellier, for example, out of 126 surviving contracts, 48 were signed by the apprentice himself, so that nobody could vouchsafe or place a bond for their good behavior and ability to learn the trade.[27] In some cases, the apprentice had to pay a premium and separately for his room and board; in others, the money flowed in the other direction and he received a wage. In a way, the apprenticeship market resembled the marriage market: depending on the economic circumstances, traditions, and the way the matching operated, money could flow from the bride side to the groom side or the reverse.[28]

From a purely theoretical point of view, it might thus have been logical for apprenticeship to take place within families, in which fathers taught their sons. The agency and enforcement problems would have been much reduced. In fact, in agriculture – that is, the majority of workers in pre-

---

[26] G. Espinas and H. Pirenne (eds.), *Recueil de Documents Relatifs à l'Histoire de l'Industrie Drapière en Flandre* (Brussels: Académie Royale de Belgique, 1906), vol. 1, 121. For earlier examples, see C. Hawkins, *Roman Artisans and the Urban Economy* (Cambridge: Cambridge University Press, 2016), 109–10.

[27] K. L. Reyerson, 'The adolescent apprentice/worker in medieval Montpellier', *Journal of Family History* 17 (1992), 358.

[28] G. Hamilton, 'The market for Montreal apprentices: Contract length and information', *Explorations in Economic History* 33 (1996), 505–07.

Industrial Revolution Europe – this was predominantly the case, and formal apprenticeship was rare (although teenage farm servants must have had some similar characteristics to apprentices). In urban occupations – both artisanal and commercial – fathers teaching their sons was fairly unusual, Alessandro Scarlatti, Johann Sebastian Bach, and Leopold Mozart notwithstanding.[29] By the seventeenth century, apprentices trained by relatives were a distinct minority, estimated in London to be somewhere between 7% and 28%.[30] Training within the extended family or clan was less common in Europe, because the nuclear family had become the norm from the early Middle Ages on, although relatives remained an option.[31] It can be shown that if apprentices could select from a wide array of unrelated masters, technological progress was faster than if he was limited to family members.[32]

Given that the contractual relation between master and apprentice can thus be seen as the mother of all incomplete contracts, one wonders how various past societies solved the threat of opportunistic behavior on both sides. There were countless margins at which things could go wrong, and they often did. The incentives simply did not line up. Even a competent teacher might skimp on the board and room, or humiliate and beat up his pupil.[33] The apprentice, as noted, might learn the secrets of the trade quickly and then abscond, or he might learn very slowly and thus be an unproductive worker. The relationship was by its nature asymmetric, but it became progressively more symmetric as the apprentice acquired the skills of the trade.[34] Yet it was in the interest of the master to keep the asymmetry as long as possible, since it was this asymmetry that allowed him to control his worker and thus draw rents from the apprentice's labor. It also delayed the appearance of another potential competitor in the local market.

---

[29] Reyerson, 'The adolescent apprentice', 357.

[30] T. Leunig, C. Minns and P. Wallis, 'Networks in the premodern economy: The market for London apprenticeships, 1600–1749', *Journal of Economic History* 71 (2011), 42; M. Prak, 'Mega-structures of the Middle Ages: The construction of religious buildings in Europe and Asia, c. 1000–1500', in: M. Prak and J. L. van Zanden (eds.), *Technology, Skills and the Pre-modern Economy* (Leiden: Brill, 2013), 153; see also Goody, 'Learning', 239. Fragmentary evidence for the Roman period indicates the likelihood that even in antiquity artisans commonly sent their sons to be trained with others: Hawkins, *Roman Artisans*, 198–202.

[31] Epstein, *Wage Labor*, 105–06.

[32] De la Croix, Doepke and Mokyr, 'Clans, guilds, and markets'.

[33] The awful experiences of the printer's apprentices in Paris in the later 1730s described in R. Darnton, *The Great Cat Massacre and other Episodes in French Cultural History* (New York: Basic Books, 1984), 75 may be an extreme example.

[34] H. Buechler, 'Apprenticeship and transmission of knowledge in La Paz, Bolivia', in: Coy (ed.), *Apprenticeship*, 44.

Institutions and Apprenticeship

It is thus perhaps surprising to the economist that apprenticeship worked at all, let alone its longevity and ubiquity. Some kind of institution was needed to enforce the contract between master and apprentice. In the absence of such an institution, opportunistic behavior would doom apprenticeship and limit it to the nuclear family. Over time, implicit and formal local institutions evolved that created conditions in which contractual relations for training could be carried out in an effective manner and resolve the threats of moral hazard and opportunistic behavior. Local governance was usually involved. After all, there was a collective interest at stake, since external economies and economies of agglomeration meant that the entire community had an interest in the preservation of certain specialized skills and the reputational rents that came with it.[35] However, this collective need does not, by itself, explain why certain institutions arose that made the institution work. Indeed, in the United States the absence of a guild tradition and high mobility made third party enforcement of apprenticeship contracts impracticable and the "market for apprenticeship" virtually disappeared.[36]

Three types of institutions emerged that carried out the task of enforcing and supervising the apprentice–master relationship and made it work. Perhaps the most important one is the hardest to observe: personal reputation. In an urban environment, in which transactions were repeated and in which people knew one another through a variety of channels, maintaining one's reputation as an honorable and trustworthy person was extraordinarily valuable. The economics of such network relations are well-understood.[37] The idea is fairly simple: Suppose two agents face one another in two spheres, for instance a master training an apprentice, whose father served with the master in a local institution or was socially connected to his customers. If the master cheated the apprentice by shirking in his teaching duties or mistreated him, it could entail reputational damage and thus punishment in the other spheres. Thus, the possibility of punishment in one game may be used to induce cooperation in the other. Knowing this, the master would be incentivized to refrain from opportunistic behavior. What was true for the master would be equally true for the apprentice: misbehavior might threaten to damage

[35] Reyerson, 'The adolescent apprentice', 360.
[36] Elbaum, 'Why apprenticeship persisted'; B. Elbaum and N. Singh, 'The economic rationale of apprenticeship training: Some lessons from British and US experience', *Industrial Relations: A Journal of Economy and Society* 34 (1995), 593–622.
[37] G. Spagnolo, 'Social relations and cooperations in organizations', *Journal of Economic Behavior and Organizations* 38 (1995), 1–25.

his reputation as a trustworthy person as well as lead to sanctions on his family.

This insight is an example of how trust emerged through social networking and its effect on the efficiency of the apprenticeship market. When trust can be transferred from a social relationship into an economic one it can sustain cooperative outcomes in which exchange can take place and disputes are resolved even without strict contract enforcement by a third party such as courts or arbiters.[38] It is this kind of environment, whether or not one wants to refer to it as "social capital," that created the possibility of cooperation even when standard behavior in finite games would suggest that opportunism and dishonest behavior might have been a dominant strategy. To work effectively, however, the environment needed to be stable and fairly limited in size and mobility low, so that information networks could operate effectively. The more dynamic and sophisticated the economy, the less these conditions obtained.[39]

For that reason, more formal institutions involving third-party enforcement were needed to supervise the training and arbitrate between master and apprentice when disputes arose. There were many variations on the basic theme that some respectable local third party, such as a Justice of the Peace, was needed to arbitrate and settle out of court the frequent disputes that arose between master and apprentice.[40] Going to a formal court of law was possible in many countries, but given the cost and uncertainty of the outcome and the long duration of lawsuits, it must have been a *pis aller* (though some courts employed speedier and less costly arbitration and reconciliation procedures). Much of the negotiation between the master and the apprentice and his family must have taken place in the "shadow of the law" suggested by scholars in Law and Economics.[41] In many cases, then, the combination of the fear of reputational damage and the possibility of legal action were often enough to make the apprenticeship system work. In some cases special organizations (such as the *neringen* in the Netherlands) set up by city government regulated the trade, including apprenticeship.[42] In other cases, the

---

[38] See for example, E. A. Posner, *Law and Social Norms* (Cambridge, MA: Harvard University Press, 2000).

[39] Hamilton, 'Decline', especially 650–56.

[40] M. G. Davies, *The Enforcement of English Apprenticeship: A Study in Applied Mercantilism, 1563–1642* (Cambridge, MA: Harvard University Press, 1956), 207–08.

[41] R. Cooter, S. Marks and R. Mnookin, 'Bargaining in the shadow of the law: A testable model of strategic behavior', *Journal of Legal Studies* 11 (1982), 225–51; also P. Rushton, 'The matter in variance: Adolescents and domestic conflict in the pre–industrial economy of Northeast England, 1600–1800', *Journal of Social History* 25 (1991), 102.

[42] K. Davids, *The Rise and Decline of Dutch Technological Leadership* (Leiden: Brill, 2008), vol. 2, 385.

masters set up a number of clever contractual devices that made it less attractive for apprentices to abscond before fully serving their term. The up-front premium that would be forfeited and a promise of a cash payment upon completion were some of the contractual devices used to prevent the premature ending of the contract.[43]

The third type of institution for making apprenticeship work is the best known: the craft guild. The history of apprenticeship and the history of the craft guild are intertwined and overlapping. Yet they are conceptually quite separate, and apprenticeship, being the more universal of the two, should be in a different category. While craft guilds of some kind existed all over the world, many – but not all – European guilds actively regulated and controlled apprenticeship.[44] When the guilds were abolished in France, many expressed concern about the future of apprenticeship.[45] More recent work casts some doubt on how widely guilds were engaged in explicitly enforcing the terms of the contract. In a conflict between a master (and thus a member of the guild) and an apprentice (who was not), it was unlikely that the apprentice would prevail if the guild was called on to arbitrate.[46] This asymmetry would explain why eventually local officials and courts became increasingly involved in contract enforcement, creating conditions in which the market for apprenticeship could operate relatively freely and effectively. In a study of eighteenth-century northern England conflicts between masters and apprentices and servants, it was found that in the cases that went before the courts, the apprentice was usually the plaintiff, "while the companies [guilds] offered the masters sufficient scope for correcting their apprentices, the latter had to appeal to the mercy of the more public forum of the quarter sessions to obtain justice."[47]

Yet there is too much evidence pointing to the guilds being closely associated with regulating apprenticeship to dismiss altogether their role in making the institution work properly. This was especially true when the effective power of local government, to say nothing of "the state," was limited. In many cases, apprentices had to pay a special fee (known as *Lichtgeld* in Germany) to the guild to start their term, and it stands to reason that this fee was for the supervisory functions that the guild

[43] Hamilton, 'Enforcement'.
[44] The canonical statement is by S. R. Epstein, 'Transferring technical knowledge and innovating in Europe, c. 1200–c. 1800', in: Prak and van Zanden (eds.), *Technology, Skills*, 31–32; also S. L. Kaplan, *The Bakers of Paris and the Bread Question* (Durham, NC: Duke University Press), 199.
[45] M. Fitzsimmons, *From Artisan to Worker: Guilds, the French State, and the Organization of Labor, 1776–1821* (Cambridge: Cambridge University Press, 2010), 46, 144–46.
[46] Summarized by M. Prak and P. Wallis, 'Introduction', in this volume.
[47] Rushton, 'Matter in variance', 92.

exerted.[48] A stylized version of the evolution of apprenticeship suggests that guilds were central in creating the institution in the first place in medieval Europe, and eventually the "market" (backed by the enforcement power of courts and similar third-party enforcement institutions) took over. In reality, the two systems overlapped, cooperated, and reinforced one another.[49]

European guilds were a classic example of a "corporation" (which is the term used for guild in French) in that they consisted of people who shared a common economic interest and occupation, but who were typically not related.[50] Precisely because they were a form of social capital, in which people met and exchanged information, guilds created the networks that supported reputation mechanisms that may have been the most effective way in which most contracts were enforced. As in many models of collective action, each master had a strong incentive to free ride and "renege," unless a penalty was likely. A master who systematically exploited and mistreated his apprentices might gain an advantage over his competitors. The same would be true for a master who poached the trained apprentices from a colleague before they had fully repaid their training cost. Improper training could lead to the production of shoddy goods and would create an externality by harming the reputation for quality of the entire town.[51] The craft guild was one institution that curbed such opportunistic behaviors. The many social and professional joint activities bound up in the guild created the kind of phenomenon captured in Spagnolo's model – the costs of opportunistic behavior could come from a very different corner than where the benefits were.[52]

Guilds, Apprentices, and Markets

Did the role of craft guilds in regulating apprenticeship affect efficiency and the pace of innovation? The debate between those scholars who on balance see craft guilds as a positive force in the intergenerational transmission and accumulation of skills and those who see them primarily as an encumbrance to the development of human capital and well-functioning markets will not easily be decided. It concerns a three-dimensional

---

[48] R. Reith, 'Apprentices in the German and Austrian crafts in early modern times: Apprentices as wage earners?', in: B. De Munck, S. L. Kaplan and H. Soly (eds.), *Learning on the Shop Floor: Historical Perspectives on Apprenticeship* (New York: Berghahn Books, 2007), 182. Schalk, 'Apprenticeships with and without Guilds'.

[49] For example, G. Colavizza, R. Cella and A. Bellavitis, 'Apprenticeship in Early Modern Venice', Chapter 4 in this volume.

[50] A. Greif, 'Family structure, institutions, and growth: The origins and implications of Western corporations', *American Economic Review* 96 (2006), 308–12.

[51] Reyerson, 'The adolescent apprentice', 360.   [52] Rushton, 'Matter in variance'.

complex phenomenon that stretched over many centuries, a large number of different occupations, and countless localities.

As argued above, guilds were not the only mechanism to enforce and arbitrate apprenticeship contracts; and guilds, moreover, had many other functions unrelated to training. A guild system was thus neither necessary nor sufficient for the emergence of effective apprenticeship institutions.[53] When other methods of contract enforcement were effective, apprenticeship could function without them. Conversely, completing a guild-mandated apprenticeship did not guarantee a mastership.[54]

Nonetheless, the guilds were an institution that could help overcome some inherent market failures that might have led to less and lower-quality human capital accumulation. They set rules to minimize the incentives for apprentices to engage in opportunistic behaviors. Perhaps the most obvious way was by solving the apprentice's commitment problem discussed above. With the power and authority of the guild behind him, the master could feel that the chances of opportunistic behavior were much lower, since an apprentice who departed before fulfilling the terms of his contract could be denied becoming a master or even employment altogether, or otherwise punished. The guilds had the power to enforce compliance with the contract through a variety of sanctions they could impose on wayward apprentices, including "compulsory membership, blackballing, and boycott."[55] Yet, as Adam Smith was the first to point out, guilds used limitations on apprenticeship as a way of generating rents for their members.[56] One complaint is that the uniform length of the apprenticeship term imposed by guilds was an inefficient one-size-fits-all kind of measure, and may have served more as a barrier to entry than as an efficient way of teaching youngsters.[57] That said, the specified duration of the term varied from skill to skill and they were a way of ensuring that the master could expect some labor services at the later stages of the apprentice's term. After all, all educational institutions have imposed some kind of uniform duration standard on students, including modern universities.

---

[53] S. Ogilvie, *The European Guilds: An Economic Analysis* (Princeton, NJ: Princeton University Press, 2019), ch. 7. See also, Hamilton, 'The market', 498.

[54] De Munck, *Technologies of Learning*, 41.

[55] S. R. Epstein, 'Craft guilds, apprenticeship and technological change in pre-industrial Europe', in: S. R. Epstein and M. Prak (eds.), *Guilds, Innovation and the European Economy, 1400–1800* (Cambridge: Cambridge University Press, 2008), 61.

[56] Smith, *Wealth of Nations*, pt. I, 133. U. Pfister, 'Craft guilds, the theory of the firm, and early modern proto-industry', in: Epstein and Prak (eds.), *Guilds, Innovation*, 27 has asserted that the exclusionary rents generated by guilds were necessary to correct for the underinvestment in human capital implied by the market failures in human capital formation.

[57] Ogilvie, *European Guilds*, ch. 7.

The advantage of a guild-enforced contract system was above all in supporting a system in which kinship was not the chief organizing principle of intergenerational transmission of skills. For one thing, innate abilities differed from father to son, and it seems obviously desirable that the son of a carpenter could become a notary and vice versa. More generally, however, what a non-kinship based system implies is that apprentices could choose a master able to teach them the best techniques extant, and that in principle they could learn from more than one master. De Munck refers to the custom of apprentices to roam from one workshop to the other as "shopping."[58] A number of the chapters in this volume provide evidence of apprentices changing masters, and while it probably was not a very common phenomenon, it may have played a disproportionate role in diffusing best-practice techniques. In many documented cases apprentices were "turned over" to another master – according to one calculation this was true of 22% of all apprentices in England who did not complete their term.[59] Estimates for tailors' apprentices in late medieval England who did not complete their terms have gone as high as two-thirds.[60] There could be many reasons for this, of course, including the master falling sick or becoming otherwise indisposed. But at least some apprentices might also have discovered midway through their training that their master did not teach them best-practice techniques or that the trade they were learning was not as suitable to them or as remunerative as some other and switched to a different master.[61]

Within the formal stipulations, however, apprenticeship systems could show surprising flexibility. In England, the formal length of the contract (stipulated by the 1563 Statute) was perhaps more of a guideline than a binding constraint.[62] The flexibility of the guild system varied considerably across Europe, but nowhere in Europe was the institution as rigid as the written record suggests.[63] Still, it is no accident that economies in which such flexibility was more pronounced and apprenticeship was regarded as a "market" in which the terms between master and apprentice were negotiable were more dynamic and experienced more growth in productivity.

---

[58] De Munck, *Technologies of Learning*, 50.

[59] Wallis, 'Apprenticeship and training', 842–43.

[60] Davies and Saunders, *History of the Merchant*, 55; See also B. De Munck and H. Soly, 'Learning on the shop floor in historical perspective', in: De Munck, Kaplan and Soly (eds.), *Learning on the Shop Floor*, 9–10.

[61] But see R. Schalk, 'From orphan to artisan: Apprenticeship careers and contract enforcement in the Netherlands before and after the guild abolition', *Economic History Review*, 70 (2017), 737.

[62] Wallis, 'Apprenticeship and training'.   [63] Prak and Wallis, 'Introduction'.

The archetypical example for this kind of flexibility was the Northern Netherlands. In his authoritative work on Dutch technological progress, Karel Davids acknowledges that guilds "supplied facilities for the training and education of skilled workers."[64] Yet he shows convincingly that many of the formal restrictions that guilds imposed on apprentices were enforced with a wink and a nod. An example is the "master piece," a kind of proof of competence that apprentices who had completed their term were supposed to submit. These tests of competence, in Davids's words, "were characterized by a certain "open-endedness", which left room for innovation within the margins of a broad, liberal formula."[65] Moreover, some of the craft guilds could force youngsters to take formal classes in drawing or mathematics if this was deemed a necessary complement to their proper training.[66]

Apprenticeship, Labor Markets, and the Distribution of Income

Pre-Industrial Revolution economies differed from modern ones in many crucial ways, not least of them the way income was distributed between labor and non-labor and the blurry lines between firms and households. While in much of Europe land rents accrued largely to a well-defined class of landowners few of whom worked, in the non-agricultural economy the typical "firm" was a self-employed artisan in a workshop, often in or adjacent to his home. The distinction between household and firm, so fundamental to modern economics, was thus far from sharp. The main reason that so many of the apprentices received room and board was that it was natural for them to become part of the master's production unit, which coincided with the household.

Master artisans produced two products jointly: the goods or services that they supplied, and the human capital of the youngsters that was created while being trained in his workshop. Training apprentices meant that the master artisan was producing his own replacement but also possibly his own future competitors.[67] In a large competitive industry, these direct effects are very small (since the apprentices trained by one single master competed with all craftsmen in that product line in the area), but he produced an externality for the entire industry. To be sure, as long as a master just replaced himself, the number of artisans remained the same. But given that the average apprenticeship length was

---

[64] Davids, *Rise and Decline*, vol. 2, 423.
[65] See also De Munck, *Technologies of Learning*, 78–79.
[66] Davids, *Rise and Decline*, vol. 2, 382, 486.   [67] Epstein, *Wage Labor*, 109.

perhaps four years plus two more years of journeymanship, each artisan had the potential to train far more apprentices than was needed for his replacement even if he just had one at a time.[68] The much maligned restriction on the number of apprentices that each artisan was allowed to take could be seen as a collective-action mechanism to prevent such an outcome.

In some instances, such as the case of Utrecht documented by Schalk, only a small percentage of apprentices became masters, so the threat of more competition was dealt with in other ways.[69] What happened to those apprentices who did not become masters? Given urban mortality rates, it is certain that many of them died. Others never attained master status and found employment as long-term free journeymen, basically skilled laborers. Given that apprenticeship was an urban institution, it also seems plausible that urban training supplied some artisans to the countryside, where people could work in their trades without the restrictions – guild-driven or otherwise – that urban institutions imposed on them. In times of economic boom, masters had a strong incentive to take on a number of apprentices and journeymen.

Indeed, much evidence suggests that the work that apprentices and journeymen carried out for their master was not a corollary of a transaction in which the main exchange was the acquisition of human capital, but in many cases an indispensable source of wage labor in the artisanal economies of pre-Industrial Revolution European manufacturing. In large part this must have been because other forms of wage labor in much of urban Europe were hard to come by.[70] The obvious smoking guns here are that in many cases apprentices were paid in cash in addition to receiving instruction, room, and board. Moreover, in the early fourteenth century, when labor supply had increased due to population growth, masters were able to demand more from their trainees and give them less.[71]

In terms of economic analysis, the apprenticeship contract can be depicted as a continuum in the flows of resources between master and apprentice: on the one extreme it was purely a transaction involving the transmission of human capital, in which the master taught and the apprentice learned; in such cases a premium would be paid, or the

[68] Ogilvie, *European Guilds*, tables 7.4 and 7.5.

[69] Schalk, 'Apprenticeships with and without guilds'; J. Humphries, *Childhood and Child Labour in the British Industrial Revolution* (Cambridge: Cambridge University Press, 2010), 286.

[70] The pioneering paper that focused on apprenticeship as a labor market relation is Reith, 'Apprentices in the German and Austrian crafts'.

[71] Epstein, *Labor Markets*, 216–20.

equivalent in labor services. On the other extreme, apprenticeship could be a pure wage-labor contract under a different name.[72] In the latter cases, the worker learned little or nothing, and expected to be paid. Every apprentice in Europe found himself somewhere on this scale – most of course somewhere between the two extremes, when they learned and worked simultaneously, with the weights shifting toward the latter as the contract reached the end of the term. How important was the labor-market relation relative to knowledge transfer? Ogilvie's compilation of scores of disparate sources can be used to document this phenomenon. In a survey of sources taken from all over Europe, spanning over half a millennium, she shows that over half of all apprentices were paid a wage and that the phenomenon was widespread.[73] The bargaining position of apprentices and their chances of finding employment in their occupation in the same location varied over time depending on the conditions of demand and supply in the labor market.[74]

In a competitive model, with well-informed agents, an equilibrium condition would be that both master and apprentice broke even, and that the condition of zero excess profit obtained. This kind of model is deployed by Hamilton for Montreal, but the assumptions she has to make for it to hold are rather strong, including free exit and entry into a market in which one side only bought the service once, and the other a small number of times. Still, the conditions imply that term length should have varied positively with the net payment to the apprentice (wages plus payment in kind) and training costs across contracts and negatively with the expected quality of the apprentice, which is what her empirical results show.[75] This labor market was affected by the growing division of labor: the finer the division of labor, the simpler the tasks and the easier it would be to get an untrained beginner to be productive (even though the master himself had to acquire supervisory and managerial skills).[76] As markets expanded, the division of labor became finer and the demand for unskilled labor increased even if the workers were termed "apprentices." The closer the relationship was to one of pure wage labor as opposed to training, the less reluctant the master was to take on more apprentices.

---

[72] Colavizza, Cella and Bellavitis, 'Apprenticeship in Early Modern Venice', suggest outright that it is possible that masters were using apprenticeships as a form of labor contract.
[73] Ogilvie, *European Guilds*, table 7.10; also Schalk, 'Apprenticeships with and without guilds', and Humphries, *Childhood*, 235, 276–77.
[74] Reith, 'Apprentices in the German and Austrian crafts', 189.
[75] Hamilton, 'The market'.
[76] M. Kelly and C. Ó Gráda, 'Adam Smith, watch prices, and the Industrial Revolution', *Quarterly Journal of Economics* 131 (2016), 1727–52.

On the labor-supply side, it is worth pointing to the growth in the demand for market-purchased products associated with the Industrious Revolution in early modern Europe; while not much has been made of the growth of teenage labor in the seventeenth and eighteenth centuries in this literature, it stands to reason that once the emphasis shifts from individual income to household income, the demand for market-purchased goods created an impetus by parents to send their children to work and bring home their wages. In half the households surveyed in late-eighteenth-century England, children contributed to income.[77] This meant that in the process they acquired useful skills, through learning by doing and socialization by employers. For the textile workers who came under pressure due to mechanization, children often ended up as pauper apprentices, which may still have given them a chance to acquire valuable skills.[78]

Apprenticeship, Skills, and the Great Enrichment

Human capital stories have not been central in the literature on the Great Divergence or the Great Enrichment.[79] In large part that is because much of the historical literature has focused on two indicators of human capital: literacy and years of schooling. Yet, before 1750, it is far from clear how valuable literacy was in the artisanal workplace outside some obvious service occupations such as clerks, notaries, teachers, and priests.[80] It is therefore not all that surprising that Britain could be the technological leader in the Industrial Revolution even when it scored somewhat in the middle of the pack as far as literacy is concerned.[81] A more recent work on the Great Divergence surveys the literature and tends to be skeptical of most human capital measures that explain the difference between West

---

[77] J. de Vries, *The Industrious Revolution: Consumer Behavior and the Household Economy, 1650 to the Present* (Cambridge: Cambridge University Press, 2008), 217.

[78] Humphries, *Childhood*, 45–46; S. Horrell, J. Humphries and H.-J. Voth, 'Destined for deprivation: Human capital formation and intergenerational poverty in nineteenth-century England', *Explorations in Economic History* 38 (2001), 358–60.

[79] The notable exception is the economist O. Galor, *Unified Growth Theory* (Princeton, NJ: Princeton University Press, 2011), 30–46. For an introduction to this literature, see J. Mokyr, 'Human capital, useful knowledge, and long-term economic growth', *Economia Politica*, 30 (2013), 251–71.

[80] Economists have suggested that it was the commercial rather than the manufacturing aspect of artisanal work that required literacy and numeracy: M. Kelly and C. Ó Gráda, 'Artisanal skills, apprenticeship, and the English Industrial Revolution: Prescot and Beyond', unpublished working paper, 2017.

[81] D. Mitch, 'The role of education and skill in the British Industrial Revolution', in: J. Mokyr (ed.), *The British Industrial Revolution: An Economic Perspective*, 2nd edition (Boulder, CO: Westview Press, 1999), 241–79; D. Mitch, *The Rise of Popular Literacy in Victorian England* (Philadelphia: University of Pennsylvania Press, 1992).

and East.[82] All the same, many scholars have not only made that connection, but argued that artisanal competence was the main factor that drove the Great Enrichment. Epstein goes so far as to shrug off all formal learning as largely irrelevant before the Industrial Revolution and sees improvements in artisanal skills and their successful dissemination as the key to technological progress.[83]

Skills and technological competence were crucial to economic progress. That does not mean that nothing else was; history does not live by one-line explanations. Artisans *by themselves* were limited in how much and how radically they could innovate, as they were taught a set of skills by their masters. Artisans were trained to make things that they had not invented and did not usually design, reproducing a given design over and over. Was innovation possible in such a system? In many cases the rules of the guilds or other ways in which resistance to innovation could show up imposed obstacles to craftsmen who thought out of the box. And yet many of the great inventors of the Industrial Revolution were trained as craftsmen and in some sectors learning by doing and a growing division of labor could lead to sustained productivity growth. Still, without a growing understanding of the natural laws and regularities that underlay the techniques (the epistemic base), the trial-and-error methods of artisanal innovation would inexorably have run into diminishing returns.[84] As early as the eighteenth century, scientific knowledge and methods were crucial to technological progress in a substantial number of areas.[85] The root of Europe's rapid technological progress was neither artisanal skills alone nor scientific advances by themselves, but the synergistic complementarity of the two.

---

[82] K. Davids, *Religion, Technology and the Great and Little Divergences* (Leiden: Brill, 2012), 60–74.

[83] Epstein, 'Transferring,' especially 53, 67. D. McCloskey, *Bourgeois Dignity: Why Economics Can't Explain the Modern World* (Chicago: University of Chicago Press, 2010), 355–65; D. McCloskey, *Bourgeois Equality: How Ideas, Not Capital or Institutions, Enriched the World* (Chicago: University of Chicago Press, 2016), 505–06 also dismisses formal science as a major factor in economic growth before 1900. M. Berg, 'The genesis of useful knowledge', *History of Science* 45 (2007), 123–34 does not dismiss formal knowledge as Epstein does, but clearly feels that by stressing concepts like the Industrial Enlightenment, my book *Gifts of Athena* did not show a full appreciation for the role that artisanal knowledge played in bringing about the expansion of useful knowledge, and how the mobility of tacit knowledge through traveling craftsmen led to continuous improvement; J. Mokyr, *The Gifts of Athena* (Princeton, NJ: Princeton University Press, 2002).

[84] Mokyr, Gifts of Athena, 31–32.

[85] D. Wootton, *The Invention of Science: A New History of the Scientific Revolution* (London: Allen Lane, 2015), 476–508; J. Mokyr, *A Culture of Growth: The Origins of the Modern Economy* (Princeton, NJ: Princeton University Press, 2016), 270–73.

In terms of artisanal skills, Asia in 1500 was still in many ways ahead of Europe, and it was the fine work of Asian craftsmen that made Europeans desire Chinese ceramics, Indian cotton goods, Persian carpets, and similar high-end goods. Yet in the centuries that followed, European skills caught up, and they learned to make the Asian goods they desired, and then learned to make them better and cheaper than the Asians ever could. Without a flexible and open apprenticeship system that responded to demand and in which the high mobility of workers was normal, such a growth in prescriptive knowledge would not have happened. Footloose young apprentices and journeymen played an important role not only by disseminating best-practice techniques but also by creating a competitive environment in which creative artisans whose ideas were not welcome at home could move elsewhere.[86] In contrast, technology in Asia, with some exceptions, seemed to have been stuck in place, if often at a high level, and lacked the dynamism of Europe. Flexibility was key: "skilled" workers who were experts in the old technology would do little for a Watt, a Smeaton, or a Fairbairn, because innovation implied that the old competences were often outdated. New skills, or new combinations of old skills, were needed, and a rigid system of one master–one apprentice, teaching old and tried methods, would not do. Successful entrepreneurs, such as the Yorkshire textile-machine makers, were hiring well-trained artisans, and were able to make them do things they never did before.[87]

What was it that led up to the Industrial Revolution and allowed it to become the starting point of sustained technological progress and economic growth instead of just another efflorescence? The cheek-by-jowl growth in *both* the competence of European artisans and insights of *savants* studying natural philosophy that laid out the rules and regularities that made their techniques work was key to Europe's success. Brilliant technical ideas without the workmanship and materials to build them from blueprints would suffer the fate of Leonardo's sketches. The apprenticeship system provided Europe with the mechanics, metalworkers, carpenters, instrument makers, and engineers that could execute and scale up the novel designs and turn them into reality. Mechanics trained as metalworkers, millwrights, carpenters, wheelwrights, and clockmakers were in high demand in the textile machinery sector during the Industrial Revolution (even if the skills did not always carry over easily). Skills acquired through apprenticeship in one industry were of great use elsewhere as long as the workers had the mental

---

[86] M. Belfanti, 'Guilds, patents, and the circulation of technical knowledge', *Technology and Culture* 45 (2004), 569–89; Berg, 'The genesis'.
[87] Cookson, *Age of Machinery*.

agility to continue on-the-job learning after their apprenticeship was completed and to adapt to the needs of the new techniques.[88] The competitive and open system in Britain was more suited to such needs than the more rigid systems elsewhere.[89]

Economies that had developed a flexible, mobile, and well-functioning system of apprenticeship could thus count on a higher quality of skill supply and experience greater technological dynamism. This was the case in seventeenth-century Netherlands, where in a host of industries, the Dutch developed technological leadership based on their widely acknowledged expertise.[90] By the eighteenth century, the advantage had shifted to Britain. The French chemist and politician, Jean-Antoine Chaptal was one of many who recognized the importance of tacit knowledge in Britain's precociousness when he pointed out that a central part of British know-how was what he called *tours de main* (tricks) and habits that were the soul of industry. Neither he nor his economist compatriot Jean-Baptiste Say ever spelled out how and why it was that Britain could count on the "superiority of its workmen" (as Say put it).[91] But skills were learned, not transmitted genetically, and as Humphries has emphasized in her seminal paper on the topic, without a better recognition of the efficiency of the system that produced these skills, we will not fully understand Britain's leadership.[92]

Can the difference between Britain and the Continent be generalized to the difference between Europe and Asia? We know all too little about how apprenticeship was organized in the East. Most of what we know supports the argument that elsewhere in the world the family still played a much larger role than it did in Europe.[93] One of Europe's unsung advantages recently stressed by economists was that professional and local corporations and organizations replaced kin-based cooperation.[94] There were

---

[88] Ibid., 227.   [89] Ben Zeev, Mokyr and van der Beek, 'Flexible supply.'

[90] K. Davids, 'Guilds, guildsmen and technological innovation in early modern Europe: The case of the Dutch Republic', Economy and Society in the Low Countries Working Papers, no. 2, 2003; K. Davids, 'Apprenticeship and guild control in the Netherlands, c. 1450–1800', in: De Munck, Kaplan and Soly, (eds.), *Learning on the Shop Floor*, 65–84.

[91] J.-A.-C. Chaptal, *De l'Industrie française* (Paris: chez Antoine-Augustin Renouard, 1819), vol. 2, 430; J.-B. Say, *A Treatise on Political Economy*, 4th edition (Boston: Wells and Lilly, 1821, orig. 1803), vol. 1, 32–33. Darnton, *Great Cat Massacre*, 114–15 has described Montpellier in the mid-eighteenth century as a place in which the products and the scale of production had been static for two centuries.

[92] Humphries, 'English apprenticeships', 74.

[93] J. L. van Zanden, *The Long Road to the Industrial Revolution: The European Economy in a Global Perspective, 1000–1800* (Leiden: Brill, 2009), 165; M. Prak and J. L. van Zanden, 'Technology and human capital formation in the East and West before the Industrial Revolution', in: Prak and van Zanden (eds.), *Technology, Skills*, 15.

[94] Greif, 'Family structure'; A. Greif and G. Tabellini, 'The clan and the corporation: Sustaining cooperation in China and Europe', *Journal of Comparative Economics* 45 (2017), 1–35.

guilds in China, but much more than in Europe they were dominated by common ancestry. Chinese guild regulations often specifically postulated that only family members could learn the trade.[95] In contrast with Europe, the ancient tradition of a close association between kinship (common origin) and training remained intact. In early-twentieth-century southern China it was reported that "not only were the elders of the town the heads of the clan but the entire industry was organized and monopolized by the clan."[96] Even fewer details are known about India, though one scholar assures us that "with few exceptions, the apprentices were members of the household and that the family was the main vehicle of training."[97] While there was a noticeable gap between Britain and much of the Continent in the eighteenth century, this gap proved fairly easy to close in the years after 1815. The gap between western Europe and the rest of the world was much larger.

Recent arguments explaining the Great Enrichment through institutions and culture include the notions that the European state became somehow more inclusive or open access, that a bourgeois ethics arose, and the rise of the Republic of Letters created a more effective market for ideas.[98] What should not be left out is that a mixture of private-order and local government institutions were able to set up a system of professional training that provided the flexibility and the openness to new ideas that allowed Europe to develop a cadre of high-quality craftsmen who could turn blueprints into actual working models of machines and then scale them up and produce them with low levels of engineering tolerance. Once built, these mechanics could install, operate, and maintain the machinery that embodied the new technology. Apprenticeship in Europe, with all its flaws, worked well enough. One part of this success was because apprentices and journeymen had far more choice in whom to study with, because they were not limited to masters to whom they were related. As long as that choice was substantial, best-practice techniques could diffuse faster, and productivity grew.[99] To show this in formal models, economists have to make some rather

---

[95] C. Moll-Murata, 'Guilds and apprenticeship in China and Europe: The Jingdezhen and European ceramics industries', in: Prak and van Zanden (eds.), *Technology, Skills*, 234; H. B. Morse, *The Gilds of China: With an Account of the Gild Merchant or Co-hong of Canton* (London: Longmans, Green and Co., 1909), 33.

[96] D. Macgowan, 'Chinese guilds or chambers of commerce and trades unions', *Journal of the North-China Branch of the Royal Asiatic Society* 21 (1888–89), 181; J. S. Burgess *The Guilds of Peking* (New York: Columbia University Press, 1928), 71.

[97] T. Roy, 'Apprenticeship and industrialization in India, 1600–1930', in: Prak and van Zanden (eds.), *Technology, Skills*, 71, 77.

[98] These are but three hypotheses advanced by recent scholars: D. Acemoglu and J. Robinson, *Why Nations Fail: The Origins of Power, Prosperity, and Poverty* (New York: Crown, 2012); McCloskey, *Bourgeois Equality*; Mokyr, *Culture of Growth*.

[99] De la Croix, Doepke, and Mokyr, 'Clans, guilds, and markets'.

strong assumptions to reach precise conclusions. Relaxing these assumptions, however, only makes the results stronger, if less tractable.

To sum up, the Great Enrichment or the onset of modern economic growth is by all accounts an over-determined phenomenon. It has been explained by many scholars, through geography, politics, culture, religion, demography, and luck. To that list we must add something prosaic and down to earth: technological competence, a practical savoir faire of making things through the right combination of materials, workmanship, and a drive to do things right. Techniques are "prescriptive knowledge," that is, a set of recipes that describe how to produce a good or service. Because the recipe is always incomplete, to carry out these instructions requires competence, a specific form of tacit knowledge. This competence is not hardwired into humans, it has to be acquired at an early age under the right circumstances. It had little to do with schooling and literacy and most of the time it was independent of a theoretical understanding of why the techniques worked. Competence required a natural dexterity as well as learned tricks and procedures that were transmitted intergenerationally, that is, taught. The institution that took care of that was apprenticeship, and its crucial role in economic history merits the belated attention and research effort that it has received since 2000. Like all institutions, its form and functionality differed greatly among different societies, and these differences mattered to the outcomes.

2 Artisan Apprenticeship in Early Modern Madrid

Victoria López Barahona and José Antolín Nieto Sánchez

Learning on the shop floor was a reality for a host of European apprentices throughout the early modern age.[1] Madrid was no exception. In this chapter we explore the artisan apprenticeship system in the capital of the Spanish monarchy from 1540 to 1830. We have chosen a broad chronological context and a wide range of crafts, which makes this contribution unique in the field of Spanish historiography on apprenticeship.[2] Our focus on crafts responds to three main factors: the relevance that skills and their transmission had for the artisans' ethos and practice, the fact that artisan trades employed more people than commerce in Madrid, and the role that crafts played in shaping formal apprenticeship, a reason why they have left more traces in the archives than any other occupational sector.

---

[1] B. De Munck, S. L. Kaplan and H. Soly (eds.), *Learning on the Shop Floor: Historical Essays on Apprenticeship* (New York: Berghahn, 2007). The research for this chapter was conducted in the context of several projects funded by the Spanish Ministry of Economy: *Nuevas perspectivas en la Historia Social en la ciudad de Madrid y sus áreas de influencia en época moderna* (HAR 2014–53298-C2-2-P); and *Nuevas perspectivas de Historia Social en los territorios hispánicos del Mediterráneo occidental en la Edad Moderna* (HAR2014-53298-C2-1-P). We are very grateful to Juan Carlos Zofio and José Luis Hernánz for their help with the documentary search, and to James Amelang who kindly revised the English version.

[2] Early modern apprenticeship has hardly been explored by Spanish historians, who have hitherto concentrated on short-term and single-trade approaches. See M. C. Heredia, *Estudio de los contratos de aprendizaje artístico en Sevilla a comienzos del siglo XVIII* (Sevilla: Diputación Provincial, 1974); F. J. Lorenzo, 'El aprendizaje de los oficios artesanos en la Zamora del siglo XVI', *Studia Histórica* 6 (1988), 449–64; A. Muñoz, 'La infancia robada: Niños esclavos, criados y aprendices en la Almería del Antiguo Régimen', in: M. D. Martínez (ed.), *Los marginados en el mundo medieval y moderno* (Almería: Instituto de Estudios Almerienses, 2000), 56–68; J. A. Mingorance, 'Los contratos de aprendizaje en la documentación notarial de Jerez de la Frontera a fines del Medievo y comienzos de la Edad Moderna', *Revista de Historia de Jerez* 7 (2001), 11–35. A broader chronological view is found in J. A. Nieto and J. C. Zofio, 'El acceso al aprendizaje artesano en Madrid durante la Edad Moderna', in: S. Castillo (ed.), *Mundo del trabajo y asociacionismo en España: Collegia, Gremios, Mutuas, Sindicatos*, addenda(Madrid: Asociación de Historia Social, n.d.).

Apprenticeship was an important factor in the reproduction and regulation of artisan work, an essential – though not exclusive – instrument of human capital formation. In eighteenth-century Spain, the major critics of guild apprenticeship were the political and intellectual class known as the Enlightened (*Ilustrados*). They thought that the guilds' skill transmission was flawed because it was tacit, devoid of formal rules and acquired by sheer imitation or learning-by-doing. Moreover, in their view, the masters' only concern was to extend the apprentices' services in order to retain a cheap labour force that could be occupied in menial tasks.[3] These elites do not seem to have grasped that technical knowledge was the property of the master, and the apprenticeship contract was an agreement to transfer it in exchange for money or labour, like in many other parts of Europe.[4] On entering the workshop apprentices did not expect the master to be a pedagogue, but someone who could oversee, approve of or correct the work in progress. In other words, they expected to get experience. Moreover, artisan apprenticeship was contemplated by the poorer families of the city as an optimal way to guarantee a better future to their offspring, who were fatherless in significant numbers.

Artisan apprenticeship, in general, attracted a good number of young people from the cities' rural surroundings, as has been shown for sixteenth-century Toro, Zamora and Valladolid (in Old Castile) and eighteenth-century Barcelona.[5] In Madrid, apprenticeship faced the challenge of a population dominated by adult males. The city did not attract apprentices from elsewhere in sufficient numbers to reverse this demographic trend and, overall, to become the mainstay of the reproduction of the trades. Yet, apprenticeship remained a key element in the transmission of know-how.

Our objective is to sketch out the main characteristics of artisan apprenticeship in early modern Madrid, trace its changes and continuities over

---

[3] P. Rodríguez de Campomanes, *Discurso sobre la educación popular de los artesanos y su fomento* (Madrid: Imprenta de D. Antonio de Sancha, 1775), 92. This criticism turned more severe from 1780, and was backed by contemporary famous playwrights like Nicolás Fernández de Moratín. For broader discussion, see J. A. Nieto, *Artesanos y mercaderes: Una historia social y económica de Madrid, 1450–1850* (Madrid: Fundamentos, 2006).

[4] B. De Munck and H. Soly, '"Learning on the shop floor" in historical perspective', in: De Munck, Kaplan and Soly (eds.), *Learning on the Shop Floor*, 14–15.

[5] Lorenzo, 'El aprendizaje de los oficios'; F. J. Lorenzo Pinar, *El aprendizaje de los oficios artesanos en la ciudad de Toro durante el siglo XVI* (Zamora: Instituto de Estudios Zamoranos Florián de Ocampo, 2009); B. Bennasar, *Valladolid en el Siglo de Oro* (Valladolid: Ámbito, 1983), 216–21; M. Arranz and R. Grau, 'Problemas de inmigración y asimilación en la Barcelona del siglo XVIII', *Revista de Geografía* 4 (1970), 71–80; B. Moreno, 'El aprendiz de gremio en la Barcelona del siglo XVIII', *Áreas* 34 (2015), 63–75; À. Solà and Y. Yamamichi, 'Del aprendizaje a la maestría: El caso del gremio de *velers* de Barcelona, 1770–1834', *Áreas* 34 (2015), 77–91.

time, and check whether it fits into any of the three best-known European apprenticeship models, namely: the British model, characterised by early and vigorous state regulation; the French model, which shows guilds often acting as representatives in indenture contracts; and that of Germany and the Low Countries, where guild officers appear to have exerted direct control over the agreements.[6]

Madrid was the largest city in Spain. Its population grew from 130,000 in 1630 to 190,000 in 1800. Its industrial fabric possessed a remarkable complexity and variety despite the absence of leading industries, a role which textiles played elsewhere. However, the shortcomings in Madrid's productive structure cannot overshadow the effects of the establishment of the royal court in 1561, which fostered the development of a secondary sector based on building, luxury and finishing trades, which we have referred to elsewhere as the 'capitaline triad'. This side of the economy was based on demand from courtiers, bureaucrats, rentiers, clerics and tradesmen, whose incomes were drawn from around the nation but were spent in the city on the products of local producers. At the same time, servants and the families of artisans or dealers represented an elastic source of demand that also provided stimulus to Madrid's workshops.[7]

To look into the practice of artisan apprenticeship we used notarial records.[8] Our main data set contains 4,579 indenture contracts that have been gathered from the Historical Archive of Notary Protocols of Madrid. The sample shows a remarkable gender gap, as only 1.28% of indentures involved girls. This is not surprising given that, in early modern Madrid, women were banned from formal apprenticeship in many crafts, especially from the seventeenth century.

In Madrid, artisans' apprenticeship contracts could either be settled orally or formalised by a notary. Both were enforceable, although the latter gave more security to the parties involved. This was as true in the crafts – whether organised in guilds or not – as in the subsidised private

---

[6] M. Prak, 'Moral order in the world of work: Social control and the guilds in Europe', in: H. Roodenburg and P. Spierenburg (eds.), *Social Control in Europe: 1500–1800* (Columbus: Ohio State University Press, 1992), vol. 1, 179–80.

[7] J. M. López (ed.), *El Impacto de la Corte en Castilla: Madrid y su territorio en la época moderna* (Madrid: Siglo XXI/EUROCIT, 1998); J. C. Zofío, *Gremios y artesanos en Madrid, 1550–1650: La sociedad del trabajo en una ciudad cortesana preindustrial* (Madrid: CSIC/Instituto de Estudios Madrileños, 2005); Nieto, *Artesanos y mercaderes*, 418–19.

[8] Other Spanish studies based on this source are S. Villas, *Los gremios malagueños, 1700–1746* (Malaga: Universidad de Málaga, 1982); P. Buchbinder, *Maestros y aprendices: Estudio de una relación de producción (España, siglos XVI–XVIII)* (Buenos Aires: Biblioteca Biblos, 1991); Lorenzo Pinar, *El aprendizaje*; C. Hernández, 'Trabajo y curso de vida: Los aprendices artesanos y el servicio doméstico femenino (Albacete, 1636–1787)', unpublished paper submitted to *Congreso de la Asociación Española de Demografía Histórica*, Albacete, 2013.

factories promoted by the state through the Royal Chamber of Commerce from 1679 onwards. Another channel of formal apprenticeship which will be examined here was also state sponsored and mediated by charity schemes. It consisted of a network of so-called *escuelas* (schools), which mushroomed in the last third of the eighteenth century in the barrios of the city, intended to train pauper children and youths, especially girls, in textile crafts. As written contracts were not used in this case, we have drawn evidence from the documentation of the Royal Chamber of Commerce, the Royal Economic Society of Madrid and the city's Charity Boards, kept in the National Historical Archive and the General Archive of Simancas.

In quantitative terms, apprenticeship in Madrid bears no comparison to London, which hosted 15,000 in 1600, nor even to eighteenth-century Valencia, where 14,544 apprentices entered the 'major silk art'. The census records 1,592 apprentices in 1757, escalating to 2,716 in 1797. These figures indicate that apprentices comprised 16% of the male artisans whose occupational title can be identified for these years.[9] However, the number of apprentices identified in the census should be seen as a bare minimum, given that non-guild, state-sponsored and illegal forms of apprenticeships are not recorded, nor did the census count masters training their own sons, which was never formalised as an apprenticeship in Madrid, unlike in some parts of Europe. Thus, the evidence available only allows us to examine the tip of Madrid's apprenticeship iceberg.

The discussion is divided into three parts. The general characteristics of Madrid's industry and skill transmission will be examined first. Second, we shall concentrate on a number of topics related to the structure of apprenticeship: the age and birthplace of the apprentices, the occupation of their parents, and the duration and the conditions of service, that is, the terms of the transaction between the master and the apprentice's representative. The third part will focus on female apprenticeships and gender differences over time.

Industry and Apprenticeship in Madrid

Throughout the early modern period, Madrid's industries were largely dominated by artisan producers whose businesses, very often, were small independent family enterprises, largely unaffected by market fluctuations. Madrid's industrial activity, whose greatest source of added value

---

[9] Only male apprentices were registered: Archivo Histórico Nacional (hereafter AHN), *Fondos Contemporáneos, Ministerio de Hacienda* (lib. 7463 bis); and *Census of 1797*.

was the high level of skill of the artisans, did not stimulate an influx of merchant capital and the emergence of capitalist-like labour relations. Nevertheless, the space for new organisational and labour arrangements was not as narrow as it might have appeared. The structure of Madrid's industries was adapted to the unique conditions facing a city hosting the Spanish court, which necessitated a certain degree of flexibility including recourse to labour subcontracting. The urban workshop that emerged in this context therefore combined salary-based work with a hard core of labour embedded in family units.

These workshops, whether supervised by guilds or not, were the sites of most apprenticeships, although only a few workshops accounted for the majority of apprentices. The evidence also indicates that Madrid not only did not try to maintain a closed labour market, but that artisans from elsewhere found it worthwhile to travel there to work and later take the exam to become masters. During the period 1700–1836 almost two out of three new masters (56.1%) were born outside Madrid, although they did come from towns elsewhere in Spain. The capital had become a registry office for several crafts, and a place of reference for obtaining a formal qualification for many artisans from across the country.[10]

The number of trades organised in guilds in Madrid increased over time. In 1757, Madrid had 62 guilds out of which 49 were crafts and 13 were trades. The census carried out that year registered 15,963 artisans, mostly male, of whom 9,567 (60%) were members of a corporation. The numbers grew thereafter, especially in key occupations such as wood-work, tailoring, hat-making, locksmithing, silversmithing and printing. Towards the close of the eighteenth century, artisans accounted for over 50% of Madrid's workforce, due in part to a downturn in construction.[11] The growth of state-subsidised textile factories and informal textile work-shops, led mostly by women, had also led to an additional 1,500 workers engaged in textile handicrafts in 1797. The censuses point to an average of one apprentice for every two masters, which means that the number of apprentices being recruited was not sufficient to replace the vacancies left by journeymen transiting to mastership. At the end of the century the total number of artisans had increased at an annual rate of 1.43%, with the number of masters growing at 1.52% per annum (from 3,114 to 5,696),

---

[10] J. A. Nieto, 'El acceso al trabajo corporativo en el Madrid del siglo XVIII: Una propuesta de análisis de las cartas de examen gremial', *Investigaciones de Historia Económica* 9 (2013), 97–107; J. A. Nieto and J. C. Zofío, 'The return of the guilds: A view from early modern Madrid', *Journal of Social History* 50 (2016), 247–72.

[11] On the reproduction of trades in Madrid, J. A. Nieto and Á. París, 'Transformaciones laborales y tensión social en Madrid, 1750–1836', *Encuentros Latinoamericanos* 6 (2012), 210–74; Nieto and Zofío, 'Return of the guilds'; Nieto, 'El acceso al trabajo corporativo'.

the journeymen at 1.50% (from 4,809 to 8,726) and the apprentices at the lower rate of 1.34%.[12]

Unlike London, Madrid did not serve as a model for other towns in Spain. Nor did Castile develop a national apprenticeship system. Rather, each trade followed its own rules.[13] State regulation of apprenticeship was as slack as it was of artisans' wages and production in general. In regard to apprenticeship, guild regulations show remarkable differences among trades. The 20 ordinances we have found, all dating from the eighteenth century, usually stipulate the duration of the service, which ranged from two years for chocolate grinders to seven years for harness-makers and saddle-makers, though no minimum terms were established. Very rarely did guilds regulate the age of entry to apprenticeship or the age at which the apprentice should finish their term. The glaziers ruled that apprentices under nine years old should not be employed, while the bookbinders did not permit an apprentice to become journeyman until he was 20 years old.

Some ordinances limit the number of apprentices each master was permitted to employ, although other sources indicate that this rule was not always complied with. Hemp-makers could not have over four, braid-makers, harness-makers and saddle-makers, over two, while bookbinders and glaziers were only allowed one apprentice on the grounds that, otherwise, it would be detrimental to the journeymen. The braid-makers' prohibition against paying an advanced apprentice the same wages as a journeyman was seemingly aimed at avoiding competition between these two categories of workers, but it also suggests that, at least in some trades, journeymen gained certain leverage over guilds' ordinances.

The locksmiths explicitly forbade both apprentices and journeymen to work for clock-makers, bridle-makers and the like. Other guilds regulated the mobility of apprentices by prohibiting their transfer from one workshop to another and fining masters who took another's apprentice without the former master's approval. These rules were meant to prevent, seemingly with little success, child labour from being monopolised by one or two masters, so that the traditional ideal of economic equality among the guild members could be preserved.

Unlike the Low Countries and Germany, where guilds closely controlled indenture contracts, in Madrid indentures were considered private agreements about which guild regulations had little to say. This is probably the reason why most of the ordinances we have explored omit some important aspects of apprenticeship. Indenture contracts help us to fill these gaps. Sixteenth and seventeenth-century indentures indicate that, in some crafts, the occupational hierarchy did not yet contain the intermediary category of journeyman, with masters and apprentices being the two main categories of worker in some trades. It seems that the tripartite hierarchy was consolidated sometime during the second half of the seventeenth century. Indentures in general also show that, until the end of the seventeenth century, apprentices in some guild and non-guild trades had to pass an exam at the conclusion of their services, as had journeymen in all trades to achieve mastership. Some contracts for carvers, cabinetmakers and chandlers compel the master to pay the apprentices' exam fees, while barbers and dyers only refer to the master's obligation to make sure the apprentice acquired sufficient skills to pass the exam.

In both guild and non-guild trades, examiners were appointed by both parties: the apprentice's master and his representative.[14] These examiners were usually masters, journeymen or other experts. Only the indenture contracts signed by confectioners, braid-makers, doublet-makers, carpenters, carvers and glovers reveal that the guild's overseers had a leading role in evaluating the apprentices' exams. Unfortunately, we do not know exactly what these examinations consisted of. As mentioned, ordinances seldom regulate this common practice, which was generally abandoned in the later part of the seventeenth century and as late as 1724 for carpenters. Apprentices' exams reappear in some crafts at the end of the eighteenth century, influenced by the state's reformist plan on apprenticeships, but we find very few ordinances that regulate examination fees. The wig-makers, for example, fixed it at 20 *reales*, while the braid-makers only stipulate that the master should cover the cost of the piece the apprentice was due to make.

Several guilds granted some privileges to masters' sons. The locksmiths' ordinances, for example, exempted them from the obligation to complete the four-year apprenticeship, and the exam fees were reduced for them. Among the glaziers of doors and windows, masters' sons and orphans were permitted to enter apprenticeship when they were younger than nine years old, which was the minimum age established in their ordinances. Conversely, some other guilds made clear in their statutes that no privileges should be granted to the masters' offspring. Foundry-

---

[14] A precedent for the apprentices' exams can be found in the General Ordinances of Cloths issued in 1511 for the entire territory of Castile. In this case, exams had to be implemented at the end of each year of service. See Buchbinder, *Maestros y aprendices*, 33–34.

workers and confectioners, for example, emphasised that masters' sons should complete the apprenticeship term, arguing that this was a necessary condition to become fully skilled. Although some trades favoured masters' sons, it seems that this trend was not as conspicuous in Madrid as it was in Paris.[15]

Neither the indenture contracts nor the eighteenth-century ordinances show evidence that apprentices who were masters' sons could become masters without passing through the transitional – often permanent – stage of journeymen, not even by marrying a master's widow, a condition that was, on the contrary, very common among journeymen and contemplated by guild ordinances. In general, a journeyman aspiring to mastership had to pass an exam that consisted of making a masterpiece in the presence of examiners appointed by the guild, and, from the mid-eighteenth century, also state officials of the Royal Chamber of Commerce. However, some guild ordinances, such as the locksmiths', stipulated that a journeyman who married the single daughter – and only offspring – of a guild's official could be endowed with the mastership licence without further procedure 'if he proved himself proficient', although we do not know how this proficiency was evaluated.

The city council and the high court of the *Sala de Alcaldes de Casa y Corte* (Hall of Mayors of House and Court) were the institutions that dealt with disputes between masters and apprentices. Indenture contracts make explicit that the parties submit themselves to the jurisdiction of this high tribunal. However, it was not unusual for disputes to be settled beforehand by agreement of the parties, the mediation of the guild officials or, from the last third of the eighteenth century, the mayor of the Barrio.

Guild and non-guild trades' contracts are not formally different. Rather, the distinct aspects of non-guild trades' indentures lie in the higher number of crafts involved, and the more diversified conditions stipulated for the apprentice's service. For example, giving the apprentice the tools of the trade at the end of his term was characteristic of brick-layers, masons and other construction workers, while the employment of female apprentices was a unique trait of certain textile crafts, and mentions of the poverty of the apprentices was a common feature of indentures signed for the Persian-carpet factory.

In eighteenth-century Madrid, both guild and non-guild trades suffered to some degree because of competition from publicly subsidised *fábricas* (factories) producing leather and textile articles on a larger scale

[15] D. Garrioch, *The Making of Revolutionary Paris* (Berkeley: University of California Press, 2002), 31, 69, 80.

(some 40 were functioning in the 1780s).[16] Among the privileges the factories were given was the capacity to employ paupers, mainly children and women supplied to them by charitable schemes and trained in *escuelas* established for that purpose.

The reformist governments of the second half of the eighteenth century advanced an economic and political programme to increase national industrial output and replace imports. This required a substantial increase in the labour supply, to which the craft guilds were deemed an obstacle. To achieve this, the government promoted two alternative apprenticeship systems. On one hand, the Royal Academy of San Fernando received apprentices for artistic crafts, such as painting and sculpting, as an experiment geared to splitting the arts from the crafts.[17] On the other hand, a broader apprenticeship scheme was addressed to those youths excluded from the guilds or not fully integrated into the labour market: the swathe of children and women living in the capital on the edge of subsistence. It has been estimated that around 40% of the working population of the city lived in poverty.[18]

Poor relief and punitive institutions served as the laboratories to create a new kind of training which was meant to yield skilled, disciplined and industrious workers. Under the banner of 'making the poor a useful force', the state sponsored the establishment of factories in various institutions (hospices, orphanages, houses of correction) and *escuelas* in neighbourhoods. Although some isolated experiments can be traced back to the late sixteenth century, it was only in the second half of the eighteenth century that factories were introduced in a wide range of institutions. In 1773, for example, 70% of the 1,450 inmates of the Ave María Hospice in Madrid were employed in textile manufacturing (679 men and 337 women).[19] In 1786, the correctional house of San Fernando, founded in the aftermath of the popular revolt of 1766, had 365 women and girls working in the textile mills installed on the premises.[20]

The uprising of 1766 had provided another important spur to the government to reinforce the mechanisms of control over the impoverished people of the capital, who had been very active in that 'shameful revolution'. Repression was accomplished by channelling younger paupers into a public apprenticeship system based in workshop-schools,

[16] Nieto, *Artesanos y mercadere*, 361 (table 17.1).

[17] This apprenticeship scheme was initially envisaged as taking place alongside that in the workshop, so that the apprentice could combine the latter with evening classes at the Academy: C. Chocarro, *La búsqueda de la identidad: la escultura entre el gremio y la Academia (1741–1833)* (Madrid: Fundación Universitaria Española, 2001).

[18] J. Soubeyroux, 'Pauperismo y relaciones sociales en el Madrid del siglo XVIII, part 1', *Estudios de Historia Social* 12–13 (1980), 2–227; and López (ed.), *El impacto de la Corte*.

[19] Nieto, *Artesanos y mercaderes*, 423.   [20] AHN, *Consejos*, leg. 49,812.

a term that conveys the double purpose of the *escuelas* as both training and production centres. In 1775, the *Sociedad Económica Matritense de Amigos del País* (Madrid Economic Society of the Country's Friends) was founded and soon committed itself to establishing a 'charitable fund' in an orphanage called *Los Desamparados* (the abandoned).[21] This consisted of a woollen-cloth factory where orphans operated the looms and the yarn was provided by the out-work of poor women in the city – who amounted to 700 in 1785.[22]

In order to 'relieve by teaching', the society opened three day workshop-schools for textile handicrafts in various barrios of the city, called *escuelas patrióticas* (patriotic schools). Although at first these were intended for children of both sexes, from the 1780s the documentation of the society only refers to girls. This is hardly surprising given that certain textile crafts (needlework, silk-weaving, lacemaking, embroidering, spinning, etc.) had begun to be deemed better suited to the 'strengths and decency of women', not least because of the lowering of wages. In these patriotic schools the teaching was supplied by mistresses – or, less often, masters – who were examined and hired from among the independent female artisans of the city by the institution. In addition, the *Diputaciones de Caridad* (charity boards), founded in each of the 64 barrios in 1780, were commissioned to relieve those who qualified as 'deserving poor' and to fund – through alms collection – a workshop-school for the poorest girls of their areas. Eventually, 32 so-called *escuelas gratuitas* (free schools) were opened up, one for every two neighbouring barrios.

Some pauper boys did have the opportunity to be apprenticed through this state-sponsored apprenticeship channel, especially those living in orphanages and the hospice, and, less often, they were directed to the workshop-schools belonging to royal or subsidised factories. That notwithstanding, this new apprenticeship scheme was mainly oriented to girls, whether poor or not, as boys were generally sent to the *escuelas de primeras letras* (primary schools) to learn to read and write. Girls made up the large majority of students in the workshop-schools established in the barrios of the city and the so-called spinning schools which supplied the royal or subsidised textile factories, besides being employed in the textile mills established in boarding schools and hospices.

---

[21] This institution housed boys and girls from the foundling house who had reached the age of seven and had not been adopted. The boys were usually settled to apprenticeship with a private master in different trades, under the guardianship of the General Charity Board. These apprenticeships were usually indentured, but are not included in our sample.

[22] On this charitable fund, see C. de Castro, 'Orden público, política social y manufactura en el Madrid de Carlos III', in S. Madrazo and V. Pinto (eds.), *Madrid en la época moderna: Espacio, sociedad y cultura* (Madrid: UAM, 1991), 11–25.

The Structures of Training

In order to examine the age, birthplace and social backgrounds of apprentices, together with the duration and conditions of their services, we have used a sample of 4,579 indenture contracts (Figure 2.1), which are chronologically distributed as follows: 535 indentures from 1540 to 1599 for apprentices in 70 trades; 1,760 in the seventeenth century including 103 trades; 2,171 in the eighteenth century featuring 70 trades, and 109 in the nineteenth century. This sample reveals that the Golden Age of apprenticeship in Madrid began in the seventeenth century, only to decline in the later part of the eighteenth century.

Out of the eighteenth-century sample, we have selected the 25 trades that issued over 20 contracts each (1,823 instruments, which represent 84% of the century total), among which are shoemakers, passementeriers, wig-makers, doublet-makers, carpenters, printers, silversmiths, cabinet-makers, hatters, surgeons, cutlers, locksmiths, tailors, hemp-workers, glovers, braid-makers, chair-and-harness-makers, booksellers, packsaddle-makers, blacksmiths, silk-weavers, stocking-makers and glaziers. These were also the most important trades in quantitative terms, according to the census of arts and trades carried out in 1757. It is an unbalanced sample given that just one craft – passementeriers, i.e. makers of elaborate

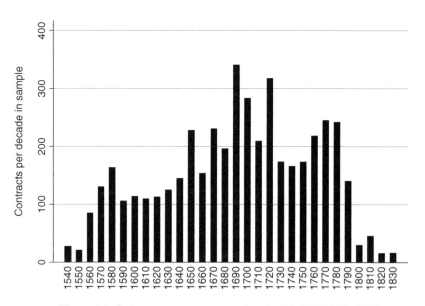

Figure 2.1 Indenture contracts per decade, Madrid 1540–1790

trimmings such as tassels and fringes – generated 506 contracts (27% of the total). But more striking is the scarcity of female indentures in the general sample, which will be examined in the third part of the chapter.

The Age of Entry and the Duration of Apprenticeship

In the second half of the sixteenth century, apprentices in Madrid were between 12 and 18 years old when they started their training, with the average being 14.8. This is a rather young age if we compare it with that of London's apprentices in 1575 (17.4).[23] In the seventeenth century, the average rose to 15.02, with the presence of apprentices under 12 and over 18 growing. In the eighteenth century, the age of entry experienced noticeable fluctuations, but the average remained 15.2, a slight increase from the previous century. Moreover, the number of apprentices who were either younger or older swelled: now 23.1% were under 14; 61% were between 14 and 16; and 16.6% were above 18 years old. The evidence also points to a correlation between the age of entry and the duration of the apprenticeship.

Between 1561 and 1601, apprentices who started at 14–18 years of age were to stay with their masters for an average of four years and four months, varying from the 15-month term of bakers' apprentices to the six years or more served by the carders and artistic craftsmen (Table 2.1).[24] The length of the contract also depended on the family situation of the apprentice. To be represented by a legal tutor rather than a parent made a difference, for example. Such apprentices were likely to be orphans or immigrants and above the average age on entry (15.7). They were also usually indentured for a longer term of service. However, in general, guild ordinances and contracts coincided, with the average term falling between three and four years.[25]

The economic hardships of the seventeenth century led to a widening of the age spectrum at both ends, and longer terms for younger apprentices. In the seventeenth century, young apprentices – those under 14 – were 26.7% of the total and faced the longest contracts. Apprentices over 20 years of age amounted to 6.6% of the total, and had much shorter terms, which usually served to improve their qualifications, as indentures clearly indicate. The eighteenth century saw the same trend, although the

[23] P. Wallis, C. Webb and C. Minns, 'Leaving home and entering service: The age of apprenticeship in early modern London', *Continuity and Change* 25 (2010), 377–404.

[24] A shorter average period of 3.75 years has been estimated for Paris: H. Heller, *Labour, Science and Technology in France, 1500–1620* (Cambridge: Cambridge University Press, 1996), 44.

[25] Zofío, *Gremios y artesanos*, 353–69.

Table 2.1 Entry, duration and completion of apprenticeship, Madrid 1561–1799

Age of entry	1561–99			1600–99			1700–99		
	Cases	Average duration (years)	Average completion age	Cases	Average duration (years)	Average completion age	Cases	Average duration (years)	Average completion age
6.5	–	–	–	1	10.0	16.5	–	–	–
7	–	–	–	3	8.3	15.3	–	–	–
8	–	–	–	3	6.0	14.0	3	6.6	15.6
9	24	5.3	17.3	10	6.7	15.7	6	6.3	16.3
10	32	5.2	18.2	26	6.6	16.6	24	5.8	16.8
11	46	4.7	18.7	33	5.9	16.9	42	5.6	17.6
12	35	4.1	19.1	76	5.9	17.9	116	5.5	18.5
13	42	4.0	20.0	101	5.5	18.5	169	5.2	19.2
14	24	3.4	20.4	210	5.3	19.3	144	5.2	20.2
15	22	3.0	21.0	130	4.8	19.8	107	4.8	20.8
16	–	–	–	114	4.5	20.5	79	4.7	21.7
17	–	–	–	72	4.2	21.2	65	4.2	22.2
18	–	–	–	84	3.4	21.4	22	3.9	22.9
19	–	–	–	21	3.0	22.0	20	3.7	23.7
20	–	–	–	32	3.5	23.5	8	2.6	23.6
21	–	–	–	8	2.3	23.3	5	4.6	26.6
22	–	–	–	5	2.9	24.9	4	3.8	26.8
23	–	–	–	1	3.0	26.0	1	5.0	29.0
24	–	–	–	5	4.5	28.5	6	3.0	28.0
25	–	–	–	3	2.8	27.8	2	2.5	28.5
26	–	–	–	9	2.4	28.4	1	2.0	30.0
28	–	–	–	–	–	–	1	4.0	36.0
32	–	–	–	–	–	–	–	–	–
	225			946			825		

very young no longer show up, while older apprentices became increasingly important. Half of the apprentices whose age of entry is stated in the indentures for this century were 13–15 years old, and the average term was 5.3 years. It seems that the age of entry fell while the period of service grew, varying according to the level of 'advancement' of the apprentice and the time they might have spent in previous workshops. Variations also depended on the level of competition within each trade and conditions in the labour market.

A number of apprentices represented themselves in their contracts. Our seventeenth-century sample contains 63 apprentices who did so: they were over 18 years of age when they started and mostly hailed from other regions, and made up the majority of the older apprentices. Their contracts were often for a very short duration, lasting just months in some instances. These older apprentices mostly aimed to complete or improve their training. The eighteenth-century sample provides fewer examples of apprentices representing themselves (just 23). The average duration of their contracts grew to 3.8 years and the upper age limit of apprenticeships also rose. In eighteenth-century Madrid, many of those entering apprenticeship aged older than 18 paid for their training, which suggests that they appreciated what was taught on the shop floor and the opportunities it could bring in the future.

Between 1670 and 1725, Madrid's guilds adapted to the changes that the seventeenth-century downturn and the War of Succession (1700–13) brought about in the labour market. Notably, waged workers, journeymen, had grown from being a modest complement to family workers into a major part of the workforce in many crafts. Most guilds introduced new ordinances that shortened the apprenticeship term to an average of 2–4 years. Nonetheless, from 1750 conditions tightened for apprentices, due to journeymen's pressure and demands, competition from other trades and the introduction of new organisational forms into production. Masters who hired apprentices who had previously served in another workshop faced penalties. Some guilds even created a registry book to record ancillary workers – albeit no traces of it have been found – and extended the required apprenticeship term from 3–4 years to 5–6 years. Their purpose was to restore internal discipline and safeguard equality within the guild by limiting the number of apprentices that each workshop was permitted. In any case, we are dealing with service terms which do not differ much from the four years and ten months a Parisian apprentice stayed with his master.[26]

---

[26] S. L. Kaplan, 'L'apprentisage à Paris au XVIIᵉ siècle', *Revue d'histoire moderne et contemporaine* 40 (1993), 450–51; see also S. L. Kaplan, 'Réflexions sur la police du monde

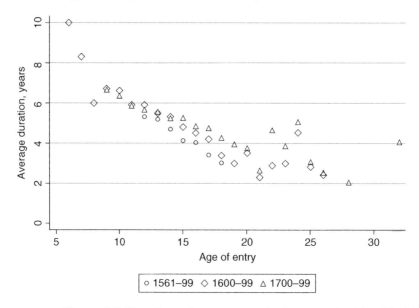

Figure 2.2 Duration of passementeriers' apprenticeship, Madrid 1700–1803

Indentures reveal that crafts followed diverging paths. At the beginning the eighteenth century, the wig-makers contracted apprentices for a 2.5–3-year term. By the second half of the century, it seems that increasing competition from the hairdressers had prompted them to improve their qualification by extending the training period, which rose to 4–6 years. Passementeriers took the opposite path: in the first half of the century, their apprentices had to serve long terms of six and seven years, but they later fell to four years, more in accordance with the guild's minimum period. This change occurred around 1770, when competition from non-guild and more highly capitalised workshops encouraged guild members to use the shorter periods set out in their statutes. Although in the next decade some masters continued signing contracts for five or more years, in the 1790s terms over six years had disappeared (Figure 2.2).

These indentures reveal that the practice of apprenticeship often challenged the norm. Guild regulations set a legal framework which the contracting parties adapted to their own needs, knowing that guild

du travail, 1700–1815', *Revue Historique* 261 (1979), 17–77, and S. L. Kaplan, 'La lutte pour le contrôle du marché du travail', *Revue d'histoire moderne et contemporaine* 136 (1989), 436–79.

overseers very rarely intervened unless a denunciation was made. In a sample of apprentices in four trades (tailors, passementeriers, shoe-makers and harness-makers), in the eighteenth century, the tailors complied with their 1753 ordinances in 35.4% of cases, among harness-makers it was 14.2%, shoemakers 12.2%, and passementeriers 9.6%. This evidence suggests that contracts were negotiated with little reference to guild ordinances, which seem to have been kept in the background as a reference. Indeed, the conditions set out in indentures did not refer to clauses in guild ordinances, but to the custom of the city ('as is customary').

Geographical Origins of Apprentices

We have demonstrated elsewhere that not all artisans who became mas-ters in Madrid were born in the capital.[27] Apprentices' provenances, however, are harder to identify since indentures did not always include their birthplace. In our sample, 62% provide this information. They reveal a different pattern to the mastership entries. Between 1561 and 1606, 31% of apprentices were born in Madrid, rising to 61% in the eighteenth century. It is a considerable increase in the share of apprentices from Madrid, but migrants remained common, with almost 40% of apprentices hailing from elsewhere in Spain in the last half of the eight-eenth century (Table 2.2), although Madrid gains supremacy if we take into account those coming from her hinterland ('Madrid, region').[28]

In the second half of the sixteenth century, the bulk of apprentices came from Old or New Castile. They generally came from small rural commu-nities and the towns of Valladolid and Toledo, while some 3% hailed from abroad.[29] In this period, apprentices reflected the migration to the capital. Thereafter, the seventeenth-century crisis, which Madrid experienced later than other Castilian towns, changed the labour market. In the first half of the century, the capital still attracted artisans from all over the kingdom. Later, the city seems to have ceased to be a worthwhile destination for apprentices from elsewhere, and youths born in Madrid supplied over half of the total. The city's attractiveness fell to its lowest point in the first half of

---

[27] Nieto, 'El acceso al trabajo corporativo'; Nieto and Zofío, 'Return of the guilds'.

[28] Indeed, in the later part of our period Madrid shows remarkable similarities with Vienna, where the majority of apprentices were born in the city and its rural surroundings: J. Ehmer, 'Worlds of mobility: Migration patterns of Viennese artisans in the eighteenth century', in: G. Crossick (ed.), *The Artisan and the European Town* (Aldershot: Ashgate, 1997), 185.

[29] Zofío, *Gremios y artesanos*, 357–60. This pattern diverges from that of sixteenth-century Paris, where 70% of apprentices were born in the city and nearly 30% hailed from the North of the country: Heller, *Labour, Science and Technology*, 44.

Table 2.2 *Apprentices' birthplaces, Madrid 1561–1799*

	1561–99	1600–49	1650–99	1700–49	1750–99
	%	%	%	%	%
Madrid, city	31	37	55	72	61
Madrid, region	15	11	14	7	9
Spain	50	47	30	19	29
Foreign	3	5	1	1	1
N	417	401	669	663	709

the eighteenth century. However, migration to Madrid grew between 1750 and 1800, pushing up the number of outsiders and the diversity of origins among the ranks of the city's apprentices. Madrid was a city that was open to apprentices from all over the country. Only during the first half of the eighteenth century did the proportion of migrants drop below 30%, and it had recovered to reach nearly 40% by the second half of the century. To set this in context, in this period Barcelona drew 60% of its apprentice veil-weavers and 72% of its silk-twisters from other parts of Catalonia.[30]

Apprenticeship did not always guarantee a successful outcome. The question then arises of how many apprentices achieved mastership. Unfortunately, it is impossible, at present, to give a full answer as evidence is only available for a few trades. Between 1750 and 1780, just 9 out of 135 apprentice passementeriers became masters. In other words, over 90% failed. This was a trade whose reproduction relied heavily on both masters' sons and immigrant journeymen and masters, many of whom were French and Catalonian. The passementeriers were not exceptional. Out of 45 carpenters' apprentices indentured from 1723 to 1819, only 5 ended up as masters (11.1%), and a very similar share of the 61 apprentice tailors contracted between 1717 and 1793 made the same step.[31] These very low rates of mastership contrast sharply with evidence from France at the end of the Ancien Régime, where 30% became masters, and

---

[30] B. Moreno, 'El aprendiz de gremio', 69 (and graph 2); À. Solà and Y. Yamamichi, 'Del aprendizaje a la maestría', 82–83 (and graph 2). The figures presented in these articles are quite close to those previously calculated for the entire city of Barcelona, in P. Molas, *Los gremios barceloneses del siglo XVIII* (Madrid: Confederación de Cajas de Ahorros, 1970), 442–43.

[31] A very similar failure rate of 92.7% was estimated in Valencia's 'Major Silk Guild' for the decade of the 1780s: F. Díez, *Viles y Mecánicos: Trabajo y sociedad en la Valencia pre-industrial* (Valencia: Alfons el Magnánim, 1990), 75; and for the veil-makers of Barcelona between 1770 and 1834 (87.5%): Solà and Yamamichi, 'Del aprendizaje a la maestría', 88–89.

with Vienna, where 20%–57% of bookbinders and locksmiths apprentices became masters, respectively.[32] It seems that, in failure figures at least, Madrid was peculiar. As in other European cities, the majority of apprentices completed their services, as suggested by the handful of broken contracts (just 35) in the general sample. However, only a small minority of apprentices reached the highest echelon of their trades. Most would remain in the intermediary category of journeymen.

In sum, the high failure figure, together with the immigration of journeymen from other parts of the kingdom, suggests that apprentices were not the mainstay of guilds' reproduction. In Madrid, the ranks of masters were filled by journeymen who came to the capital to complete their training, obtain their masterships and, in many cases, stay for good.

The Conditions of the Apprenticeship

In the absence of unifying laws or regulations, apprenticeship contracts in Madrid present a great diversity in their form and content. Each craft followed its own particular custom, some differences show up between guild and non-guild trades, but overall they share some common features, such as the apprentice's maintenance, lodging, clothing and health assistance.

Apprentices usually lived with their masters, although under conditions that differed substantially. There were some apprentices whose parents could afford to pay the master for their training and maintenance. Francisco Rodrigo, for example, apprenticed in the seventeenth century, was sent by his parents from a Castilian villa to Madrid in the care of an uncle who was commissioned to place him as an apprentice in the art of painting. Rodrigo's family would pay the master 2,750 *reales* annually and supply clothing and footwear 'of the customary style of the trade'.[33] In our eighteenth-century sample, 3.12% of indentures in 22 trades mention apprentices paying the masters for their training, with a notable concentration among farriers (72.7%) and barber-surgeons (46.5%). However, agreements which balanced the contribution of both parties to the apprentice's maintenance were more common, as were those in which the master provided maintenance while the apprentice contributed to his workforce, often getting an annual payment or a payoff at the end of his service. Some indentures were explicit about the obligation of apprentices to obey their masters – and their wives – in whatever tasks they were ordered to undertake, even if they were not related to the trade.

---

[32] De Munck and Soly, '"Learning on the shop floor"', 9.
[33] The *real* (plural *reales*) was the currency in the Kingdom of Castile.

Table 2.3 *Monetary and non-monetary apprentices' remunerations, Madrid 1600–1836*

	N	Food %	Clothing %	Footwear %	Clean clothes %	Lodging/ bed %	Monetary remuneration %
				Non-monetary remuneration			
1600–49	602	97.6	68.1	67.1	85.4	89.3	1.8
1650–99	1131	96.5	65.7	65.7	85.4	80.6	1.6
1700–49	1141	89.1	57.9	55.3	71.9	67.2	4.3
1750–99	999	86.0	36.7	26.5	55.9	67.6	9.7
1800–36	108	58.3	16.6	12.9	29.6	39.8	31.4
1600–1836	**3981**	**90.9**	**53.8**	**48.0**	**72.6**	**73.7**	**5.3**

Apprenticeship was both a training process and a labour relationship. It represented a substantial tranche of the budget for any artisan enterprise, which masters contemplated as a long-term investment. It was in their interest to keep the apprentice in the workshop in order to retrieve this investment in training; otherwise some other master would garner the benefits of having a skilled worker without having borne the costs.[34] This is made clear as early as 1535 by Alonso de Berruguete, a famous artist, who declared in a lawsuit that 'when an apprentice is settled to learn a craft with a master painter, the first half of the apprentice's service is detrimental to the master because he spends his time in teaching the craft, and the final period is quite profitable ... more worthwhile than the previous two years, say, in a three-year contract'.[35] A similar remark can be found as late as the beginning of the nineteenth century in the ordinances of some guilds, such as the hemp-makers.

Apprentices' wages usually combined payments in kind and cash. Table 2.3 shows the evolution of the share of these two modalities in apprentices' remunerations throughout the period studied. Food, which generally included breakfast, lunch and dinner, together with drink, is the most regular item, and was usually covered by the master. It appears

[34] P. Wallis, 'Apprenticeship and training in premodern England', *Journal of Economic History* 68 (2008), 832–61; R. Reith, 'Apprentices in the German and Austrian crafts in early modern times: Apprentices as wage earners?', in: De Munck, Kaplan and Soly (eds.), *Learning on the Shop Floor*, 179–99.

[35] N. Alonso Cortés, 'Datos para la biografía artística de los siglos XVI y XVII', *Boletín de la Real Academia de la Historia* 80 (1922), 25.

in nine out of ten contracts. However, it progressively loses ground throughout the eighteenth century, and experiences a notable downturn in the final part of the period, when only six out of ten contracts specify the master's obligation to feed his apprentice. Less frequently than food, and equally in decline throughout the period, the provision of clothing as an obligation of the master is included in slightly over half of the contracts.[36]

Indentures contain numerous clauses that aimed to stop apprentices from absconding. Some masters offered incentives such as wage increases and bonuses on productivity. The concerns of the apprentice's representatives, on the other hand, were oriented towards preventing the master abusing the child and ensuring that he would teach him every 'secret of the art' without exceptions. Both parties recognised the shared benefits of complying with the duration agreed in the contract. On completing his term, the apprentice would be able to work anywhere and earn a higher wage, thus improving his position in the labour market.[37] Masters, for their part, would reap enough profit in the second half of the apprentice's term to make up for the expenditures incurred in the early part of the contract. This is why masters took good care to train the apprentices within the period fixed in the contract; it was common that a failed apprenticeship obliged the master to keep the apprentice at his own expense until the youth was fully skilled, paying him a journeyman's wages, or else allocate him to another workshop. This additional period and the final exam that, in some trades, the apprentice had to pass at the end of his term were overseen by experts appointed by both parties.

For those apprentices whose families did not fully fund their training and maintenance, the bulk of remuneration was given in kind, commonly board and lodging, clothing, footwear, laundry and the cure of ailments – usually limited to those not lasting longer than 4–15 days. Table 2.4 shows that food was mentioned in 86% of Madrid's indentures, unlike in London where payments in kind had been in decline since 1600.[38] The remaining items show a wide variation that seems to depend upon the age and parentage of the apprentice as well as the customs of the trade. For example, when the apprentice's representative was a woman (mother, grandmother, sister or aunt), their clothing and its upkeep (darning and washing) were usually her responsibility. Apprentices over the age of 20,

---

[36] Allowing for the different spatial and chronological contexts, this evolution is similar to that established for Montreal by G. Hamilton, 'The decline of apprenticeship in North America: Evidence from Montreal', *Journal of Economic History* 60 (2000), 627–64.

[37] Reith, 'Apprentices in the German and Austrian crafts', 181.

[38] P. Wallis, Chapter 9 in this book.

Table 2.4 *Apprentices' remuneration in kind in 25 trades, Madrid 1690–1834*

	N	Food %	Clothing %	Footwear %	Lodging/ bed %	Clean clothes %
Booksellers	37	92	46	41	68	73
Braid-makers	44	89	68	43	75	75
Cabinetmakers	48	79	10	29	52	77
Carpenters	95	89	47	40	52	60
Carpet-makers	37	35	30	0	35	35
Coach-makers	34	88	88	68	59	71
Cutlers	40	98	70	48	78	80
Doublet-makers	109	95	59	53	54	63
Gilders	30	77	53	53	47	33
Glove-makers	64	83	56	59	44	59
Glaziers	42	81	81	48	69	69
Hatters	38	76	53	34	50	50
Hemp-makers	57	30	25	37	23	25
Locksmiths	43	81	47	37	58	65
Packsaddle-makers	33	94	36	27	73	39
Passementeriers	533	94	51	40	87	71
Printers	38	74	58	42	63	68
Saddle-harness	50	96	68	42	70	58
Silk art	40	80	38	10	73	53
Silversmiths	61	87	25	13	67	72
Shoemakers	117	75	22	55	50	44
Stocking-weavers	50	90	38	20	84	72
Surgeons	45	87	4	4	80	78
Tailors	76	88	51	37	54	64
Wig-makers	195	91	31	15	72	58
All	1956	86	45	37	67	63

on the other hand, were most likely to live elsewhere and often provided for their own maintenance.[39]

The monetary component of the eighteenth-century apprentices' earnings reveals two modalities: a regular payment given at different points during their service (only made explicit in 6% of the sample) and a final endowment, as it was called in Europe, that combined money and goods. Both were modulated by the customs of the trade ('as customary', 'as it is the style and practice'). Nonetheless, in a small number of crafts masters

[39] J. Agua and J. A. Nieto, 'Organización del trabajo: Salario artesano y calendario laboral en el Madrid del siglo XVIII', *Sociología del trabajo* 84 (2015), 69–83.

made payments entirely in cash (hemp-makers) or with part paid in kind, as food (hatters). A changing pattern is evident among the shoemakers, who up to 1770 paid their apprentices in kind and then gradually turned to giving the equivalent in cash. In contracts, payments in cash are generally reckoned in days, and occasionally in weeks or years.

The contents of the payment due to be made to the apprentices at the end of their term is explicit in 56.8% of indentures (Table 2.5). It usually comprised both clothing and cash. Sometimes the clothing could be replaced with an equivalent sum of money, and in some trades the apprentice received a sum to cover the exam fees, or, in others, the tools of the trade, as was the case among shoemakers, glaziers, esparto-makers and frame-carpenters. Some surgeons' contracts stipulate that tools should be given to the apprentice if he was not fully trained at the end of his service. The cash value of payments was usually 200–300 *reales*, and up to 1,000 in the exceptional case of the shoemakers. Although varying by trade, these payments probably gave an incentive for lower-income families to entrust their sons to a master, and, as in other parts of Europe, the composition and size of the payment were closely related to the master's expectations about the apprentice's productivity and the risk of his absconding. In general, final payments became less common over time. The silk-stocking weavers were ahead in abandoning a practice that declined in all crafts from 1800 onwards.

Although throughout the period remuneration in kind remained predominant, in the nineteenth century mixed payments gained ground. For example, in 1830, a master glove-maker agreed that, during the first six months, he should supply the apprentice with board and room, clean clothes and healthcare; during the subsequent 18 months he should add a payment of 2 *reales* a day, rising to 6 *reales* during the last year of service.

The payment system depended on the idiosyncrasies of each trade. Piece rates were not unusual in shoemaking and other crafts whose masters took into account the skills the apprentice might have previously acquired. A number of contracts signed by hatters stipulate that, if the apprentice proved to be dexterous, the master would pay him 1 *real* a day from the start, including holidays; while in some cases, the apprentice would receive an extra bonus if he produced three hats in a day. Cabinetmakers adopted this practice too. In 1823, one master agreed to give his apprentice 1–4 *reales* a day according to the pieces he produced. These payments tended to be concentrated in the later stages of the term or when the contract had been arranged in order to complete the apprentice's training.

Payments depending on workshop's income were common among printers. In these cases, masters and apprentices divided the yearly

Table 2.5 *Apprentices' final payments in 25 trades, Madrid 1690–1835*

Trade	With payment		Type of payment				
	N	%	Money and clothing %	Money only %	Clothing only %	Tools only %	Other %
Bookseller	37	65	14	19	30	0	3
Braid-maker	44	80	34	20	25	0	0
Cabinetmaker	48	71	13	40	19	0	0
Carpenters	95	78	24	27	22	2	2
Carpet-maker	37	38	0	3	35	0	0
Coach-maker	34	100	24	44	32	0	0
Cutler	40	83	5	55	23	0	0
Doublet-makers	109	82	28	28	23	0	2
Gilder	30	50	23	17	10	0	0
Glove-maker	64	73	47	11	16	0	0
Glaziers	42	95	19	45	24	0	7
Hatters	38	50	16	11	24	0	0
Hemp-makers	57	89	7	58	25	0	0
Locksmith	43	79	14	40	23	0	2
Packsaddle-makers	33	82	0	45	27	0	9
Passementeriers	533	35	4	18	11	0	2
Printer	38	63	21	34	8	0	0
Printers	61	69	11	10	46	0	2
Saddle-harness	50	76	22	22	32	0	0
Silk art	40	40	0	10	30	0	0
Shoemakers	117	74	4	43	12	7	9
Stoking weavers	50	48	24	14	10	0	0
Surgeon	45	11	0	2	0	7	2
Tailors	76	80	22	22	33	0	3
Wig-makers	195	31	3	17	10	0	1
All	1956	57	12	24	18	1	2

profits. A contract signed in 1762 stipulated that, during the first two years, the master would give the apprentice a quarter of the earnings obtained, to be raised to a third up to the end of the term.

Tips and other extras were a common part of income for workers in service trades, especially when work was carried out at the customers' households, as was the case for hairdressers. A number of contracts stipulate that any tips given to the apprentice would be held either by the master or the apprentice's tutor. In any case, this income was usually dedicated to helping fund the apprentice's maintenance and clothing. A decent outfit seems to have been appreciated by masters in these trades, as some make explicit: 'a better dressed apprentice may attract more customers'.

Gradually increasing wages over the term appeared to be a common trend in Madrid's apprenticeship system. It was generally the rule that the apprentice would only begin to receive wages after completing the first half of their contract, with a raise during the final period. For example, in 1834, a master hatter agreed to pay 4 *reales* a day for the second semester, 7 during the third semester and 10 until the completion of the service. In this final stretch, the apprentice's wages could equal those of journeymen, as shown in some silversmiths' contracts.

The terms set in indentures were influenced by various factors, among which the social position and family situation of both apprentices and masters played a significant role.[40] There has been a scholarly concern to demonstrate that endogamy was the mainstay of guilds' reproduction. Indeed, father-to-son transmission had some advantages: it reduced costs and effectively allowed masters an additional apprentice beyond the number permitted by guild ordinances. Guilds in Madrid favoured this practice, granting privileges to masters' sons. However, whether this was a generalised and always advantageous practice remains moot. As David Garrioch's research on eighteenth-century Paris has revealed, the sons of successful masters did not follow in their fathers' steps and tended to marry women from outside the trade.[41] Upward social mobility would sometimes be preferred to preserving a family tradition. Besides, should a master in a declining trade want to engage his son in it?

In the case of Madrid, a son who trained in his father's workshop was not subject to an indenture. Thus, the actual incidence of sons following their

---

[40] S. Cerutti, 'Group strategies and trade strategies: The Turin Tailors' Guild in the late seventeenth and early eighteenth centuries', in: S. Woolf (ed.), *Domestic Strategies: Work and Family in France and Italy, 1600–1800* (Cambridge: Cambridge University Press, 1991), 102–47;

[41] D. Garrioch, *The Formation of the Parisian Bourgeoisie, 1690–1830* (Cambridge, MA: Harvard University Press, 1996), 105–22.

Table 2.6 *Occupations of apprentices' representatives, Madrid 1700–99*

| | Apprentices' representative | | | | | |
	Father	Stepfather	Brother	Other relatives	Guarantor	Tutor
	%	%	%	%	%	%
	Trade apprentice placed in:					
Same as rep.	18.2	42.8	41.6	21.4	24.5	15.3
Different to rep.	81.8	57.2	58.4	78.6	75.5	84.7
	Types of different trade:					
Other artisanal	26.2	21.5	33.7	42.8	30.2	15.3
Related trade	7.0	0	4.2	2.4	3.7	0
Servants	7.0	7.1	0	0	0	0
Bricklayers	8.0	0	4.2	4.8	3.7	0
Soldiers	5.0	14.3	0	4.8	3.7	0
Other	27.8	14.3	16.6	23.8	34.0	69.4
N	99	14	24	42	53	13

fathers remains uncertain. But when an artisan's son was to be apprenticed elsewhere, indentures became a preferable – though still voluntary – option. Most of the surviving contracts involving artisans' sons were written for youths entering a different trade to their fathers. In our seventeenth-century sample, only 42 indentures report the occupations of the apprentice's parents. Only 8 apprentices were following their father's trade. Among the other 34, many were entering a different sector entirely. Similarly, in the eighteenth-century sample, only 18 out of nearly 100 contracts mentioning the parents' occupation involved apprentices entering their father's trade. Often parents preferred their sons to follow a higher status trade than their own. But this does not seem to have been the case when the apprentice's representative was not a parent. Stepfathers and brothers were more prone to allocate boys to their own trades, unlike other relatives and guarantors, who were usually artisans.

A substantial number of apprentices had lost their father, mother or both parents. In the sixteenth century this group were among the poorest youths indentured. Some were newly arrived immigrants who usually lacked social connections in the city and resorted to legal tutors to arrange a contract with a master. They tended to be older than the average (they supplied 40% of apprentices older than 15), and received lower pay than other apprentices. Our seventeenth-century sample includes 714 apprentices who had

Table 2.7 *Orphaned apprentices, Madrid 1700–99*

| | | | Parent deceased | | | |
| | Orphans | | Father | Mother | Both parents | Orphanage |
	N	%	%	%	%	%
Passementerier	506	35	24	2	9	0
Wig-maker	200	34	25	4	5	0
Shoemaker	99	35	31	1	3	0
Doublet-maker	96	30	18	1	9	2
Carpenter	77	36	31	0	5	0
Tailor	66	38	30	2	6	0
Glove-maker	51	39	31	0	6	2
Silversmith	51	37	29	2	6	0
Stocking-weaver	51	31	25	2	4	0
Saddle-harness	45	36	22	9	0	4
Braid-maker	41	29	27	0	2	0
Hemp-work	40	50	25	13	13	0
Carpet-maker	37	8	8	0	0	0
Printer	36	33	28	3	3	0
Glazier	36	17	8	0	8	0
Cabinetmaker	35	31	29	0	3	0
Silk art	35	37	26	3	9	0
Surgeon	34	29	18	6	6	0
Locksmith	31	52	42	0	10	0
Cutler	31	32	26	0	6	0
Coach-maker	30	23	17	3	3	0
Hatter	29	24	17	0	7	0
Bookseller	27	30	22	0	7	0
Packsaddle-maker	27	33	22	0	11	0
Blacksmith	24	42	21	8	8	4
Coppersmith	23	43	35	0	9	0
Silk manuf.	23	52	30	13	9	0
Esparto-work	22	18	14	0	0	5
Gilder	20	45	45	0	0	0
All	1,823	34	25	2	7	0
N	1,823	622	453	43	119	7

lost a parent, 40.5% of the total; most of them were represented by their widowed mothers. In the eighteenth-century sample, apprentices who had lost a parent account for 34.1% of the total (Table 2.7). By contrast, in London only 25% of apprentices were orphans. This suggests that either Madrid hosted more orphans than the British capital, or that in Madrid orphans' tutors regarded apprenticeship as a more suitable or available means to better the youths' prospects.[42]

These figures must be taken as a minimum since not every contract gives details on the apprentice's family. Nonetheless, if youths who had lost a parent always supplied over 30% of apprentices in early modern Madrid, the majority of whom were poor, then it is fair to claim that the lower classes regarded apprenticeship as a reliable means for their offspring to better their prospects in the context of the hard living conditions of the court city. It is suggestive that in many orphans' indentures the surviving parent or legal guardian declared that they put the lad to apprenticeship 'to spare him from begging'.[43]

We do not know the age of all those who had lost a parent on entering apprenticeship. Of the 315 indentures in the eighteenth century that provide this data, 55.7% were between 13 and 15, and 18% were 18 or older. The apprentices' representatives, in the majority of cases, were their widowed mothers. This is hardly surprising if we consider that Madrid hosted the highest percentage of widows in the kingdom (10% of all women in the capital).

In sum, working families saw apprenticeship as a survival strategy or, in some cases, an opportunity for upward social mobility. Not all apprentices came from impoverished families, but those who did, many of whom were orphans and immigrants, made up a substantial share.

Female Apprenticeship in Madrid

As in some other parts of Europe, early modern Spain witnessed the consolidation of a craft system shaped in the image of the patriarchal family, wherein skills, their transmission and formal recognition became a male prerogative.[44] In seventeenth-century Madrid, even those trades in which women played a major part issued rules that prohibited female apprentices, and obliged masters' widows to hire an examined journeyman or marry a member of the trade, if they wanted to continue the family business. Passementeriers were particularly adamant in this respect, and

---

[42] P. Wallis, Chapter 9 in this book.

[43] The deteriorating living conditions of Madrid's working population are discussed in Soubeyroux, 'Pauperismo y relaciones sociales'; López (ed.), *El impacto de la Corte*, 269–77; E. Llopis and H. García, 'Precios y salarios en Madrid, 1680–1800', *Investigaciones de Historia Económica* 7 (2011), 295–309; J. I. Andrés and R. Lanza, 'Prices and real wages in seventeenth-century Madrid', *Economic History Review* 67 (2014), 607–26.

[44] See M. Wiesner, 'Guilds, male bonding and women's work in early modern Germany', *Gender and History* 1 (1989), 125–37; J. Farr, *Artisans in Europe, 1300–1914* (Cambridge: Cambridge University Press, 2000).

the revised version of their ordinances, published in 1677, devoted the opening four clauses to limiting the presence of women in the guild.[45] However, this restrictive trend had been brewing in other Castilian towns with substantial manufacturing sectors since the previous century. As early as 1554 the ordinances of the silk weavers of Toledo allowed women who had learned the trade in a master's household to practise it, but not to teach it to anyone else.[46] These rules prevented women from entering formal apprenticeship and therefore from reaching the highest echelon of the crafts. The scarcity of female indentures (59 out of 4,579 in our sample) is in itself a significant indicator of the effectiveness of these measures, as is the limited number of mistresses taking apprentices in the seventeenth century sample: only 4 out of 26 contracts.

The four mistresses in the seventeenth-century sample (one took two female apprentices) were a passementerier, a cloak-weaver, a lacemaker and a woman making *guardainfantes*.[47] Only the first trade mentioned was organised into a guild, and the mistress, a widow, was probably a member of it. The cloak-weaver and the *guardainfantes* maker were married women represented by their husbands in the contract. Indeed, the 26 female apprenticeships in the sample belong to a cluster of textile-related crafts: passementerie, silk-weaving and twisting, hosiery, tailoring, old cloths tailoring, lacemaking and espadrille-making. This occupational crowding reflects the restructuring of the gendered division of labour that occurred in textile manufacturing in the early modern period. We know that in the thriving urban industries of the late middle ages, such as the woollens of Cuenca, women worked as carders, spinners, weavers and dyers, and in other roles,[48] while later in the eighteenth century we find them concentrated in either the first stages of the production process (preparing the material and spinning), or finishings (tailoring, lacemaking, braid-making, etc.) as well as weaving in the so-called minor silk art.[49]

Although their contracts were very similar to male apprentices' indentures, female apprentices started at a younger age and served shorter

---

[45] See V. López, *Las trabajadoras en la sociedad madrileña del siglo XVIII* (Madrid: ACCI/ Libros del Taller de Historia, 2016), 78–79.

[46] J. M. Nombela, *Auge y decadencia en la España de los Austrias: La manufactura textil de Toledo en el siglo XVI* (Toledo: Imprenta Torres, 2000), 153.

[47] *Guardainfante* (literally, 'infant-coverer') was a controversial gown that was banned – with little success – in the second half of the seventeenth century on the allegation that it hid pregnancies. The trade was exclusively in women's hands.

[48] P. Iradiel, *Evolución de la industria textil castellana en los siglos XIII–XVI. Factores de desarrollo, organización y costes de la producción manufacturera de Cuenca* (Salamanca: Universidad de Salamanca, 1974).

[49] Devoted to narrow pieces of cloth, passementeries and other trimmings.

terms. In the 17 seventeenth-century indentures that report this data, the average age of new apprentices was 12 years old, much lower than that calculated for males (15.02). One six-and-a half-year-old girl, a widow's daughter, was taken by a master tailor for a period of ten years, the longest in the sample, while a nine-year term was agreed for a seven-year-old girl. Seemingly, their age influenced the length of their service. The oldest apprentice was a 20-year-old freed slave, whose judicial guardian settled her with a master passementerier for three years, during which her master would give her room, food, clothing and footwear, plus 88 *reales* at the end of her service. However, a shorter, two-year term was fixed for an eight-year-old orphaned girl, whose legal guardian agreed to pay her master, a tailor, 200 *reales*. It is possible that in this case a limited budget might have had more importance than the apprentice's age in deciding the duration. The shortest term that shows up in the sample of female apprentices is for one year, but in this case the girl's age is not stated and the deposition of her mistress, a lacemaker, suggests that she had already acquired the groundings of the craft. In general, the average term of these female apprentices was 4.4 years, below the average 5.3 years for males.

The scribe took down the apprentice's birthplace in only three cases, so we cannot examine this variable. References to the representatives' occupations are more abundant. Most were craftsmen. Only two, a master tailor and a master silk-weaver, apprenticed their daughters in the same craft. There is evidence that many masters' daughters learned the family's trade and became skilled artisans, but, as with masters' sons, these periods of training were not usually formalised as apprenticeships. Indentures seem to have been used only when the master entrusted his daughter's training to another.

The conditions specified in female apprentices' contracts were much the same as those found for males. In five cases the apprentice's representative (two fathers, a cabinetmaker and a tanner, two widows and a guardian) agreed to pay for the girls' training and, in two instances, they also promised to cover their maintenance and clothing. The apprentices' wages were largely in kind (bed, food, drinks, laundry, some health assistance and a new outfit or its equivalent in cash). A cash payment, usually around 200 *reales,* is included in eight indentures as a reward on completing the term. As in male's indentures, contracts frequently included the condition that a failed apprenticeship would oblige the master or mistress to keep the apprentice as an *oficiala* (literally, 'journeywoman'), paying her accordingly. Generally, the master agreed to teach the craft to the girl until she was fully prepared to work anywhere as an *oficiala,* and required that she should serve him in the trade as well as in other chores 'in and out of the household'. This clause, which appears very frequently in male apprentices' indentures too, underlines the character of apprenticeship as halfway between occupational training and domestic service.

Most artisan women had been pushed outside (though were not entirely detached from) the areas governed by Madrid's craft guilds. Madrid experienced the growth of an informal garment-production sector involving female artisans, while other textile items were also made and sold by women.[50] Many female artisans probably learned their craft within the family. Others were trained in a different workshop by an unrelated mistress. After the arrival of the court in 1561, Madrid hosted a number of independent women artisans willing to take apprentices, usually girls, whose parents paid for their training. The mistress could thereby increase her income via pupils' fees and gain auxiliary labour in the workshop. There were certainly families that could afford to have their daughters taught by a skilled woman. Although these agreements were mostly made orally, a few were formalised by written indentures, as the notary records reveal. The case of the lacemaker in 1650 is particularly interesting in this regard. It is a craft that seems to have been exercised only by women (as had the shorter-lived *guardainfante* making). The woman that signs the contract, a widow, defines herself as *maestra de niñas* (girls' mistress), a heavily gendered occupational title that anticipates a central concern in the labour policies of the following century. Uniquely, she agrees not only to teach the girl to make lace, but also to read – a commitment that would become part and parcel of an eighteenth-century girls' mistress' curriculum, though one not always realised in practice.

From 1681 to 1781 written female indentures disappear, a century-long gap in the notarial record that seems to indicate the collapse of formal apprenticeship for girls in the crafts. Female apprentices' indentures show up again, albeit in scanty numbers, in the last third of the eighteenth century, this time with new characteristics. This second wave of female indentures emerged against the backdrop of the growing system of pauper training and the liberalisation of women's training and work. In 1779 a royal edict authorised female apprentices in trades which were 'appropriate to female strengths and decorum'. These included all sorts of needlework, silk-weaving on narrow looms, stocking-making, ribbon-making, lacemaking, embroidery, braid-making and all kinds of spinning, precisely the handicrafts that women had long exercised and those being taught in public workshop-schools. In 1784, another royal edict

---

[50] See López, *Las trabajadoras*, 205–25.

permitted women to work freely in the same crafts, a measure which legally recognised a long-standing practice.

In the wake of these measures, some girls did enter indentures in the private sector. Unfortunately, we have been able to identify only ten examples. However, even this small cluster of cases reveals that private female apprentices were not impoverished orphans, but the daughters of better-off working families who were seeking higher status trades for them. Between 1776 and 1788, a French dress-and-coif-maker couple, who worked for the nobility, took six girl apprentices.[51] Their parents were French or Catalonian, and the two which mention the occupation of the girl's father refer to a scribe in the royal chamber and a wig-maker. The contracts lasted around 4–5 years. Several stipulated that during the first half of the term the parents would pay a monthly fee for the girl's maintenance and clothing; others stated that the mistress should provide board and lodging, while her parents provided clothing and footwear. In all indentures, the apprentice only began to receive a wage in the later part of their terms.[52]

However, the three indentures from the early nineteenth century reveal apprentices from a quite different social background, whose parents could not pay the mistress for training or even for maintenance. The turn of the century had brought an agrarian crisis that caused mortality to rocket in 1804. The crisis played havoc with the living conditions of the working population of Madrid and elsewhere, no less than the subsequent Napoleonic invasion of 1808. The two indentures signed by the queen's lacemaker in 1802 stipulated that the girls would receive training, full board, clothing and healthcare for a six-year term, on the condition that they obeyed whatever was ordered 'be it decent'. Some wages, left unspecified, would be granted, but only when the mistress considered they had made enough progress in their learning. Some years later, in 1818, another mistress, a lacemaker, agreed to take a girl whom she 'would train and look after properly, not to my own interest but to the benefit of the girl and her parents', on the sole condition that they did not break the four years of service.

Neither private nor public apprenticeships prepared girls for a future as a master, unlike the boys apprenticed in the male-dominated guild system. Instead, female apprentices were trained to work as journey-women (*oficialas*) or as self-employed artisans subcontracted to a guild master,

---

[51] Dress-and-coif-maker is the translation of *modista y escofietera,* two closely related trades linked to that of *batera* (gown-maker). These were clearly the same as the 'merchandes de modes', milliners and mantua-makers in France and England.

[52] Unfortunately, none of these indentures state the age of the apprentices.

a merchant-manufacturer or the state. The highest status a craftswoman could achieve was that of *maestra de niñas* (girls' mistress), a title which did not formally recognise her skills in the art, but rather her capacity to transmit it to other women.

Conclusions

In early modern Madrid, the prototypical apprentice was a 15-year-old male, born in the capital or elsewhere in Castile, who served a 4–5-year term on conditions not much influenced by guild ordinances, but rather by the customs of the individual trade. Apprentices older than 18 years of age were mostly looking to complete or improve their training. Most apprenticeships were completed, as the limited number of broken contracts suggests, while most apprentices never achieved mastership but rather remained journeymen. This should not be interpreted as failure, however, since we still do not know the circumstances and opportunity costs which might have led so many to stay at this level. Although the real number of apprentices and their distribution in workshops are hard to figure out, the evidence suggests that apprentices were not the mainstay of the reproduction of guild and non-guild trades. Rather, in Madrid, the ranks of masters were filled by journeymen who came to the capital to obtain their mastership licences and then decided to stay for good, which accounts for the characteristic adult-male predominance in the population of the city throughout the greater part of the period studied.

The apprenticeship system in Madrid does not fit into any of the three European models we have singled out as comparative references: neither the English, nor the Continental models of France and Germany and the Low Countries. In early modern Madrid there was no unifying apprenticeship law. The master and the apprentice's representative – sometimes the apprentice himself – agreed the conditions of the transaction freely and directly, without further constraints other than those imposed by the highest tribunal of the city (the Hall of Mayors of House and Court). Guilds, thus, had little influence on the basis of labour recruitment. This is the reason why indenture contracts and the conditions stipulated in them were so diverse. Nevertheless, guild and non-guild trades display some common features and trends. Masters of all kinds were interested in keeping the apprentice in the workshop until the end of their agreed term, in order to make up for the expenses incurred in the apprentice's training and maintenance. This explains the numerous clauses aimed to stop apprentices from absconding, and the incentives in the form of wage increases or bonuses on productivity that masters often offered to apprentices on reaching the latter half of their terms. Moreover, in both guild and non-guild trades, a failed apprenticeship meant that the master was obliged to keep the apprentice at his own expense until the youth was fully skilled, paying him a journeyman's wages. This caused frictions between masters and journeymen.

Apprenticeship in early modern Madrid experienced some changes over time that broadly followed the evolution of the city itself. Although the city authorities showed no reluctance in incorporating apprentices coming from elsewhere, it is evident that the seventeenth-century crisis diminished migration. Only during the later part of the eighteenth century was the flow of migrants into apprenticeship renewed. It is true that their numbers did not equal those of Madrid-born apprentices, but the city was clearly open to outsiders.

Changes also occurred in other dimensions. The share of payments in cash within apprentices' remunerations became increasingly important. The exam at the conclusion of the apprentice's term, which was customary in some trades during the sixteenth and second half of the seventeenth centuries, was later abandoned only to reappear at the end of the eighteenth century under the influence of state-sponsored apprenticeship reforms.

Also during the second half of the eighteenth century, and especially after the popular uprising of 1766, political and economic reforms were implemented in order to liberalise the labour market, enlarge the manufacturing labour force and channel working class youths to a new form of apprenticeship directly controlled by state agencies. Certain textile crafts (needlework, silk-weaving, lacemaking, embroidering, spinning), which were of paramount concern in the government agenda, were seen as more suitable to the 'strengths and decency of women', not least because this allowed the lowering of wages. Thus, female apprenticeships, which had for a long time been squeezed out by the guilds, became institutionalised in a new form of public workshop-schools in neighbourhoods and poor relief institutions. In the last third of the eighteenth century, women could once more be legally apprenticed and employed as 'journey-women' in workshops or factories, although they only worked within a few textile handicrafts. In contrast to male artisans, this newly legal form of female training did not entitle women to mastership, but to the category of 'girls' mistress'. Gender divisions in apprenticeship reflect those prevailing in the social organisation of labour, which relegated women and youths, especially the impoverished, to dependent and exploited positions.

In sum, in early modern Madrid, apprenticeship was not restricted to corporative trades. It was a long-living phenomenon that was already in place before the guild system developed in Castile, and outlived the legal extinction of trade guilds in 1836. This might have been the result of the relative autonomy that traditional apprenticeship kept from guild regulation, and the success of a mode of know-how transmission based on practice and experience.

3 A Large 'Umbrella': Patterns of Apprenticeship in Eighteenth-Century Turin

Beatrice Zucca Micheletto

This chapter focuses on apprenticeship in pre-industrial Turin: it investigates the actors and institutions involved in training and how it was organised. I show that in eighteenth-century Turin, apprenticeship encompassed a broad range of training modalities and labour relationships. As I argue, the apprenticeship contract provided a large nominal and juridical umbrella covering many different types of relationship. 'Traditional' apprenticeship contracts, in which the training and work of young people were combined in varying proportions under the supervision of a master, were at one end of a spectrum of situations; at the other end were people hired under a contract of apprenticeship who actually worked as underpaid labourers.

Apprenticeship was further complicated by the fact that at least three main actors, all with a different social status, were involved in training: guilds, charity institutions and family/kinship networks. While the literature has always emphasised the role of guilds, in Turin their political and economic weakness was reflected in their superficial regulation of apprenticeship, when measured against the range of issues settled privately between masters and apprentices' families. Turin's guilds lacked their own court: disputes over apprenticeship were heard by the *Consolato di Commercio*, an institution founded by the duke that supervised the city's economic life. Moreover, numerous masters performed trades and economic activities which were not organised in guilds. Charity institutions in turn provided training for many young people, often bypassing or ignoring guild regulations, with the aim of contributing to workhouse budgets and preparing boys and girls to earn their livelihoods once they left. Finally, youths were trained within their family or kinship network. All used 'apprenticeship' to describe the relationship, even though the content of agreements could vary depending on the purpose or policy pursued. In addition, the category of apprentice did not encompass all those who might be gaining skills in a household, just as apprentices' contribution was embedded in a household where they might perform a wide variety of tasks.

78

The framework in which apprenticeship developed and was regulated in Turin resulted from a specific political context. The city's development depended on Emmanuel Filbert's decision in 1563 to move the capital of the duchy of Savoy from Chambéry to Turin. Within a century, despite disruptions from war and plague, it had become the principal city of Piedmont: it was both the seat of the court and administration and the main economic centre. From the court's arrival onwards, the duke and his entourage tried their utmost to weaken and domesticate the Turinese elites and to influence the economic and social policy of the city and its chief institutions. This affected the guilds and the welfare system, both actively involved in apprenticeship. This process was fully accomplished during the reign of Victor Amadeus II (1684–1730).

During the eighteenth century, Turin was a mid-sized city, containing over 60,000 inhabitants in 1754 and about 70,000 after 1781.[1] Domestic service and craft production were the cornerstones of the economy, employing over half the population: according to the 1802 census, 42% of the female working population (aged 15 and over) and more than 38% of the male working population were employed as servants, waiters and waitresses, cooks, coachmen, grooms, porters, laundresses and ironers, while about 33% of women and 38% of men worked in one of the crafts. A workshop census from 1792 provides information on 60 crafts and, while it certainly underestimates the artisan labour market, it offers a sense of the key sectors. Artisans were mostly employed in silk manufacturing, which extended from spinning to upholstery, or in producing clothing, shoes and accessories. Others were involved in manufacturing and selling metal or wooden items, such as jewellers, goldsmiths, smiths and armourers. Finally, many produced and sold foodstuffs, spirits and wine.[2] As this suggests, besides catering to the needs of a growing population, many artisans produced luxury goods for the city's upper classes, which included aristocrats, the royal court, wealthy merchants, state officials, military men and high-ranking ecclesiastics. In addition, the region was a centre for silk production, an industry which the government had supported since the seventeenth century. Thanks to this, Piedmont became a leading exporter of raw silk thread, while Turin produced silk fabrics, trimmings, clothing

---

[1] P. Castiglioni, *Relazione generale con una introduzione storica sopra i censimenti delle popolazioni italiane dai tempi antichi sino all'anno 1860*, vol. 1: *In Statistica del Regno d'Italia, Popolazione. Censimento degli antichi stati sardi (1 gennaio 1858) e censimenti di Lombardia, di Parma e di Modena (1857–1858)* (Turin: Stamperia Reale, 1862).

[2] The population census of 1802 has been transcribed into a database by a team at the University of Turin under the supervision of M. C. Lamberti. The 1792 workshop census is preserved at Archivio di Stato di Torino (hereafter AST), I. sez., *Magistrato del Consolato*, m. 2, *Volume contente li nomi, cognomi e patria de' mastri e padroni e de' loro rispettivi lavoranti ed apprendizzi delli arti e mestieri*.

and lingerie.[3] Within the city, the royal factories (a glass factory, the royal printing press and a tobacco factory) and a few larger textile enterprises, hosted in charity institutions and employing several journeymen, coexisted with a multitude of artisans who worked in small- and medium-sized family-run workshops, either selling goods independently or operating within putting-out systems coordinated by merchant bankers.

The chapter is organised as follows. The first section discusses the characteristics of apprenticeship in so far as they are revealed by the (problematic) population census of 1802. The second and the third sections cover guild regulations and the range of issues left to private negotiation, including forms of indentured labour. In section four, I focus on disputes between masters and apprentices, and the court, the *Consolato di Commercio*, where these conflicts were heard. Section five analyses apprenticeship by charity institutions. The last section considers training within the family or kinship network.

Apprentices' Trades and Ages

Unlike some other European cities, Turin has no surviving long-running registers of apprentices. This prevents us from estimating the number of apprentices over time. However, some idea can be gained from the 1802 population census, carried out after Piedmont's annexation to Napoleonic France. The census is a problematic source, as we will see, but still tells us something. In the census, 323 boys and 35 girls were described as 'apprentices'. Male apprentices were found in many of the city's crafts: bakers (38), shoemakers and cobblers (37), brandy- and candy-makers (34), tailors (20), bonnet-makers (17), locksmiths and armourers (11), carpenters and barrel-makers (7), weavers (7), silk-sock-makers (7). They were also common in retailing and trade: grocers (10), tool and hardware retailers or wholesalers (5), butchers and foodstuff retailers (3); others were trained as innkeepers (4), servants and cooks (3), and construction workers (3). There was also an apprentice 'clerk at the bank'. Female apprentices were involved in a restricted group of typically female activities, especially textiles: 16 out of 35 were with seamstresses, alongside 5 bonnet-makers and milliners, 3 embroiderers, 2 ribbon-makers and 2 silk-weavers. The census shows that apprenticeship was not a prerogative of the guilds: domestic service, construction, retail and trade, and clerical jobs were not covered by guilds.

[3] G. Chicco, *La seta in Piemonte 1650–1800* (Milan: F. Angeli, 1995); G. Chicco, 'Alla periferia della moda: Mercanti e tessitori nel Settecento', in: G. Recuperati (ed.), *Storia di Torino: La città fra crisi e ripresa (1630–1730)* (Turin: Einaudi, 2002), vol. 4, 911–38.

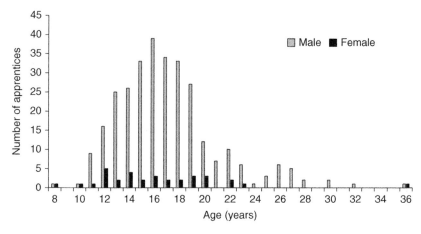

Figure 3.1 Ages of Turin apprentices in the population census of 1802
Note: Data not available for 25 apprentices (23 boys and 2 girls).
Source: see text.

Most apprentices (over 77%) were aged between 11 and 20 (Figure 3.1). Only two boys and two girls were younger (aged eight and ten respectively). In addition, 12% of male apprentices were between 21 and 29 years old, as were three female apprentices (aged 22 and 23). Finally, one man and one woman were 36 years old. All were unmarried, with one exception: the woman aged 36, who was an 'apprentice shopkeeper'. This pattern is analogous to other Italian cities.[4]

The census also tells us where apprentices lived: 38% of male apprentices lived with their parents, while 35% lived with their master. Among girls, fewer (23%) lived with their masters, and 37% still lived at home.[5] We cannot tell if apprentices registered in their own family were living there permanently, or if their presence was coincidental; however, the majority of them were learning a different occupation to their parents and siblings.

This data is very likely biased, however. The number of apprentices is very low when compared to city's size (1 per 200 residents). A survey of the two hundred or so silk-weaving workshops in Turin in 1798, only four years before the census, had found many more apprentices: about one quarter of workshops contained between one and three apprentices (80 were girls and 81 boys). There is no almost trace of this group in the

[4] A. Bellavitis, 'Apprentissages masculins, apprentissages féminins à Venise au XVIe siècle', *Histoire Urbaine* 15 (2006), 56–61.
[5] We possess no data on the remaining boys (27%) and girls (40%).

census, which registered just three male and two female apprentices in silk weaving.

One reason for this discrepancy is the fact that the census was taken soon after a war in which the city had been surrendered to the French army. In the aftermath, Turin shrank sharply, from 76,700 inhabitants in 1792 to 60,000 in 1802. The census was also carried out in a way that engendered inaccuracy: house owners – not family heads – were responsible for listing everyone living in a property.[6] Some landlords approached the heads of the resident families, while others merely relied on their (potentially inaccurate) knowledge of their tenants. Details about children's and women's work were often omitted as being unimportant. In Ancien Régime societies the head of the household – the father and husband – was perceived to be responsible for its economic survival and morality. To the people filling in the census forms, children's and women's work was secondary and could easily be ignored or reported inaccurately.[7]

We can overcome some of the source's inherent bias by comparing apprentices' occupations to the trades of all children and unmarried youths aged between 7 and 20 observed in the census.[8] Working children and youths far outnumbered 'apprentices' and were employed in a broader range of activities, including crafts (44% of girls and 51% of boys), domestic service (31% of girls and 12% of boys), and retail or trade (5% of girls and 7% of boys).[9] These young people were not all apprentices. They include 'garzoni' (journeymen) and 'lavoranti' (wageworkers), who in theory were former apprentices, and numerous children and youths without categorisation. Were they apprentices or salaried journeyman? Had they been trained? Did the tasks of an 'apprentice silk-weaver' differ from those of a child just labelled 'silk-weaver'? It is likely that apprenticeship only partially covered the varied working conditions of children, who were often salaried or low-waged workers. Conversely, as shown below, training and working were not clearly separated: many apprentices were required to work and were paid for this. The line between apprenticeship and salaried work was blurred – and not particularly important – in the eyes of the authorities too: in the 1792 workshop census and the annual population censuses, the city's officials made no distinction between apprentices and journeymen, placing them into one category.

[6] Most families in Turin lived in rented rooms not a whole property.

[7] B. Zucca Micheletto, 'Reconsidering women's labor force participation rates in eighteenth-century Turin', *Feminist Economics* 19 (2013), 200–23.

[8] Apprentices have been excluded.   [9] Percentages of youths registered with a job.

Public and Private Norms: Guilds and Contracts

From as early as the thirteenth century, guilds were an important institution in training skilled labour in Western Europe. The history of Turin's guilds (the *Università*) followed the history of the city. A small number of guilds can be traced to the late Middle Ages, but unlike much of Europe, as Turin consolidated its economic position in the later seventeenth and first half of the eighteenth century its guilds gained renewed vigour: their regulations were revised and reprinted; their privileges were reconfirmed; and they enforced strict controls on the entry and movement of the labour force.[10] Turin's guilds still faced limits on their power. They never covered all parts of the labour market. Moreover, they lacked full autonomy in the political arena, because they remained subject to, and dependent on, ducal favour.

Significantly, guild statutes needed royal approval. The duke considered every article and in some cases imposed changes. When presenting their rules in 1738, for example, the carpenters and cabinetmakers set a five year apprenticeship term, but the duke held them to four years; similarly, in 1737 the apprenticeship term in the silk-button-makers' rules was cut from four to three years. Ducal interference also touched fees, foreigners and so on, and may explain why in Turin mastership and apprenticeship were not connected to citizenship.

The limits of Turin's guilds are also demonstrated by the frequency with which privileges and patents were granted by the duke. From the beginning of his reign, Victor Amadeus's economic strategy involved welcoming to the state 'good' foreigners who could introduce new modes of production, products or techniques (while overriding or ignoring the guild that regulated that field if necessary). By petitioning the duke, foreign entrepreneurs, artisans and merchants, along with their families and specialised workers, could obtain a number of privileges, including exemptions from taxes and the *ubena* law,[11] permission to bear arms and work under the royal insignia, and authorisation to follow their religion (if not Roman Catholics).

In order to retain these benefits, however, patentees were required to train local people. From 1680 to 1799, 440 economic privileges were granted in the duchy. They covered everything from manufacturing textile goods in silk, wool and cotton to making soap and porcelain stoves,

---

[10] S. Cerutti, *La ville et les métiers: Naissance d'un langage corporatif (Turin, 17ᵉ–18ᵉ siècles)* (Paris: Éd. EHESS, 1990); E. De Fort, 'Mastri e lavoranti nelle università di mestiere tra Settecento e Ottocento', in: A. Agosti and G. M. Bravo (eds.), *Storia del movimento operaio, del socialismo e delle lotte sociali in Piemonte* (Bari: De Donato, 1979), 89–142.

[11] According to the *ubena* law, foreigners who had not been naturalised who died in the kingdom were not permitted to transmit real estate to their (foreign) offspring.

and, for Turin, extended over both the city and the surrounding country-side. Almost 9% explicitly required the entrepreneur-artisan to train a local labour force.[12] For example, Claudina Borghese, a silk, gold and silver trimmings maker, born in Lyon, was granted 400 livres, plus 100 livres to rent a shop, provided she maintained and trained 'three or four girls' for three years,[13] while in 1724 Francesco Schwarz obtained a generous privilege for dyeing woollen thread in a workshop on the outskirts of Turin: in exchange for abundant economic support, he pledged to teach three young Piedmontese boys for five years in order to spread his technical knowledge to the countryside.[14]

In Turin, the workshop census of 1792 identified 22 guilds, including a few with more than 100 masters, such as the brandy-makers, the shoe-makers and the silk-weavers with 129, 147 and 245 masters respectively. Some masters held considerable power and influence. The tailors and the artisan-merchants of silk, gold and silver textiles, for example, were part of the urban elite. As well as maintaining large business networks, they held office in the city government or positions at court.

The guilds set a range of restrictions on apprenticeship. With the exception of the tailors, silk-weavers and ribbon-makers, they barred women from becoming apprentices or masters (although, of course, female labour made a crucial contribution in the workshops). Guilds required a written apprenticeship contract: the wig-makers referred to it as a *patto* or *convenzione*, the tailors and bonnet-makers as a *scrittura*, and the locksmiths and ribbon-makers as a *capitolazione*. A written copy of the contract would be presented in court in a lawsuit; it seems that appren-ticeships were rarely made by verbal agreements. The tailors' statutes required apprentices to sign an agreement with their master within the first month of training and to pay *mezzo scudo d'oro* to the guild.[15] Locksmiths' apprentices had to pay 3 *soldi*. In addition, guilds established the length of apprenticeships. Thus, ribbon-makers and silk-sock-makers should be trained for four years, aspiring locksmiths for three years, and upholsterers and clockmakers for five years. The carpenters and cabinet-makers required four years if the child was 12 years or older, but more if

[12] Data on economic privileges was collected for the project 'Economic privileges in Europe, 15th–19th centuries: a quantitative and comparative study', funded by the French Agence Nationale de la Recherche during 2012–15.

[13] AST, I sez., *Materie economiche, Commercio*, II add. m. 17.

[14] F. A. Duboin, *Raccolta per ordine di materie delle leggi ... pubblicate sino all'8 dicembre 1789 sotto il felicissimo dominio della Real Casa di Savoia* (Turin: Marcio Tip., 1818–69), l. IX, 973–78.

[15] AST, I sez., *Materie economiche*, m. 20 bis, II add., *Memoriale a capi con patenti ... all'Università de Sarti ... in data delli 12 e 15 novembre 1737*.

they were younger.[16] However, there is evidence that contracts could be shorter or longer than the guild specified.

Guild regulations did cover the apprentice's behaviour toward his master, but only superficially and mostly by emphasising the apprentice's duties. *Obbligo* (duty) and *servitù* (service) were the words employed by the wig, sock and bonnet-makers. The locksmiths affirmed that 'allegiance and obedience' were expected from 'every subaltern'. The braziers and coppersmiths required apprentices of 'sound morality'; the bonnetmakers declared they would banish apprentices caught stealing. Apprentices were not to leave their master's shop 'without a valid reason'.

Guilds also regulated masters' conduct. Masters had to register new apprentices with the guild's officers. Poaching was, in principle, prohibited. Masters in the brandy-makers', the silk-sock-makers' and the braziers' guilds could only accept young workers who possessed a certificate from their previous master (the *benservito* or the *certificato di fedele servitù*). More explicitly, carpenters and cabinetmakers were forbidden from hiring apprentices who were employed by other masters. Just as apprentices could not leave their masters before their contracts finished, masters could not dismiss apprentices without good cause. Guilds also limited the number of apprentices that masters could keep, usually to two at a time. Of course, these limitations reflected the fact that masters did not hesitate to use apprenticeship contracts to hire skilled labourers at low wages.

Several aspects of apprenticeship were left to private negotiation. Guild regulations lacked details on the content of apprenticeship, or the accommodation and conditions offered: the youth's family privately agreed these with the master. Consequently, the terms specified in contracts were not standardised or homogeneous: their variety reveals that individuals retained bargaining power. Indeed, the quality and quantity of resources that the apprentice's family invested could influence the balance of power and contents of the contract.

We can gain a fuller understanding of the nature of apprenticeship agreements from the records of the *Consolato di Commercio*. We have reviewed the *Consolato*'s work in 1752 and 1753, as well as the few extant eighteenth-century apprenticeship contracts from Turin. This data allows us to examine the aspects of apprenticeship that were decided by families and masters. In particular, they highlight the range of financial agreements used in apprenticeship, and the treatment apprentices received.

---

[16] Guild regulations are recorded in Duboin, *Raccolta*, l. IX.

First, payment: did the apprentice's family pay the master, or did the master pay the apprentice a wage? Moreover, was there a trade-off between work and fees, with apprentices paying fees for shorter training terms, or accepting a longer contract as the price of earning a wage? In Turin, both waged and unwaged apprentices appeared before the *Consolato*, but no simple connection existed between contract duration and wages.

In the majority of cases in which the apprentice's family paid a fee and the apprentice took no wage, the contracts followed guild rules. They were not shorter. The fees families paid varied substantially, even in the same trade. For example, in June 1750 Giacomo Antonio Maurino promised to pay 200 *lire* to Giuseppe Eula, a master silk-stocking-maker, for a four-year apprenticeship. Yet on entering an apprenticeship for the same duration in the same trade in March 1752, Maurizio Bonanate's family specified they would only pay the master for 'food and clothes'.[17] Both youths served the term set by the guild. In fact, when contracts stipulated terms that were shorter than the guild rule, masters tended to receive less. Aspiring cabinetmaker Gio Michele Pichiotino, for example, was indentured for three years (not the required four) for just 160 *lire*.[18]

Waged apprentices' contracts usually included a yearly pay increase, turning the apprenticeship into a genuine work contract. Alongside their wage, apprentices also received lodging and food. However, wages do not seem to have been associated with longer terms: most matched guild regulations and some were shorter. In November 1769, for example, Francesco Miroglio was apprenticed to Giorgio Perdomo, a master and merchant of silk, gold and silver fabrics, for six years. Miroglio started on 6 *soldi* per day rising to 9 *soldi* by his last year.[19] Similarly, in November 1754 Caterina Chayre (an orphan placed by her uncle), was taken by Filippo Graneri, a weaver of silk taffeta fabrics, for three years. He paid 8 *soldi* a day for two years, then 10 *soldi*, 'in addition to a place to sleep and soup'.[20] Both these contracts complied with guild rules. In February 1755, Anna Gerarda was taken by the silk-weavers Antonio and Maria Margherita Aperlo for five years – below the guild rule. They would train Gerarda, 'feed her every day and provide her with decent shelter in their bedroom', and pay her 5 *soldi* a day during the first year, increasing by 1 *soldo* annually.[21]

[17] AST, sez. riun., *Consolato di Commercio, Ordinanze*, vol. 38, ff. 116r–v and f. 358v.
[18] Ibid., vol. 39, ff. 573r–574r.   [19] Ibid., *Bindellaj*, vol. 37, n.f.
[20] Ibid., *Registro dei taffetieri*, vol. 67, f. 1r–2r.   [21] Ibid., n.f.

Contracts mixing training and paid work seem part of a long-lasting Italian pattern. In thirteenth-century Genoa, for example, a significant portion of apprenticeship agreements made before notaries specified that the child would be paid by the master, and their wage would increase over time.[22] In early modern Germany also, wages for apprentices were commonplace.[23]

Wages were only one aspect of apprentices' remuneration. As important, and as often disputed, were food, clothing, lodging and cleaning. These were not covered by guild regulations. Expenses could become a delicate matter during negotiations, as exemplified by the case of Luisa Rousset, a seamstress with two children, who had been abandoned by her husband. In December 1767, Luisa apprenticed her eldest child, aged eight, to a master armourer, Galleani. Luisa's father and two brothers were armourers, and her family connections probably helped in placing the child. Despite her connections, Galleani refused to feed and clothe the child, requiring Luisa to cover these expenses.[24] The document does not specify whether Galleani lodged the boy, or if he only came during the day. As we saw, the 1802 census shows a significant number of apprentices living with their families, but training in different crafts; it is unclear if they returned home daily or were present on census day through chance.

Apprenticeship agreements also specified who would provide care during illness, with conditions varying from case to case. For example, if he fell sick Jean Mathieu Coraglia was entitled to remain with his mistress, the baker Madame Vinardi, and be fed for eight days; medical expenses such as doctors, surgeons or apothecaries' fees, however, were paid by his family.[25] Conversely, the contracts of the orphans Angela

---

[22] F. Franceschi, 'I salariati', in: *Ceti, modelli, comportamenti nella società medievale* (Pistoia: Fondazione Cassa di risparmio di Pistoia e Pescia, 2001), 175–201; D. Bezzina, *Artigiani a Genova nei secoli XII–XIII* (Florence: Firenze University Press, 2015); A. Bellavitis, 'Genres, métiers, apprentissages dans trois villes italiennes à l'époque moderne', *Histoire Urbaine* 15 (2006), 5–12. For France, see: F. Michaud, 'Apprentissage et salariat à Marseille avant la peste noire', *Revue Historique* 278 (1994), 3–36; F. Rivière, 'Salariat et apprentissage à travers la réglementation professionnelle normande: Réflexions à partir des cas de Lisieux et de Gisors (1430–1540)', in: P. Beck, Ph. Bernardi and L. Feller (eds.), *Rémunérer le travail au Moyen Âge: pour une histoire sociale du salariat* (Paris: Picard, 2014), 265–77.

[23] R. Reith, 'Apprentices in the German and Austrian crafts in early modern times: Apprentice as wage earners?', in: B. de Munck, S. L. Kaplan, H. Soly, *Learning on the Shop Floor: Historical Perspectives on Apprenticeship* (New York: Berghahn, 2007), 179–203.

[24] AST, sez. riun., *Notai di Torino*, vol. 5166, ff. 170r–181v. ('che la medema proveda detto suo figlio degli decenti indumenti e le somministri li allimenti *senza del che non volendo Galleani accettarlo*').

[25] Archivio Storico della Città di Torino (hereafter ASCT), *Vicariato*, vol. 250, ff. 12r–13r.

Maria Ferrera and Margherita Cassula, apprentice ribbon-makers, established that they would be sent to the hospital if they failed to recover after three days of illness.[26]

Another crucial point of contracts concerned the content of training: what skills were apprentices to learn? And how? The guilds' regulations ignore these issues, but private agreements shed some light in their explicit use of the language of family: the master or mistress promised to teach the craft 'as a good father/mother of a family' (come un buon padre di famiglia/madre di famiglia). This notion was rooted in Roman law, and referred to a hierarchical household headed by a 'good father' who protected and provided for the subordinate members of his family – his wife, children, apprentices and servants – and enjoyed specific rights over them.[27] Such expressions had a strong symbolic value, reminding those involved that apprenticeship was also a moral engagement.

In Turin, as elsewhere in Italy, no clear-cut distinction can be detected between labour and training. Even waged apprentices were learning 'on the job'. Training was acquired while participating in the workforce. During the first weeks or months, some kind of training may have been given, but it is likely that as soon as the apprentice could perform parts of the job alone, they would be working autonomously.[28] Wallis has questioned the 'two-stage' model in which the apprentice initially received training 'before repaying the master's investment' during the residue of their term. He argues that pre-industrial 'training was less intensive and more fragmented than in the standard account. Instead of preceding useful work, apprentice's training occurred in parallel with their engagement in profitable labor for their master. This made for a closer matching between the timing of the master's expenditure on the training and the apprentice's repayment of these costs.'[29] Yet the case of Margherita Griva, apprenticed to Margherita Peret, a button-maker, in 1733, reveals that masters could not make excessive requests of their charges. Griva

---

[26] AST, sez. riun., Consolato di Commercio, Bindellaj, vol. 37, n.f.

[27] M. Cavina, Il padre spodestato. L'autorità paterna dall'antichità a oggi (Rome: Laterza, 2007).

[28] In some Italian contexts, differences in the content of the training between salaried and non-salaried apprentices could exist. In Piacenza, guild regulations distinguished between 'fanticelli ad discendum' (children to be trained) and 'fanticelli ad mercedibus' (children to be paid). Twelfth-century Florentine guilds discriminated between apprentices who were paid and apprentices who were not paid. Only the latter were to receive full training and obtain the mastery. Waged apprentices were required to work after learning some basic tasks. Franceschi, I salariati; R. Greci, 'L'apprendistato nella Piacenza tardo-comunale tra vincoli corporativi e libertà contrattuali', in: R. Greci, Corporazioni e mondo del lavoro nell'Italia padana medievale (Bologna: CLUEB, 1988), 157–224.

[29] P. Wallis, 'Apprenticeship and training in premodern England', Journal of Economic History 68 (2008), 832–61.

ought to do 'everything that Peret would licitly ask, but [the mistress] must take into account the physical strength of the apprentice'.[30] In addition, Peret was required to teach her the secrets of the trade, and was forbidden from setting her to activities aside from button manufacturing. The contract was for only two years (not the three the guild expected), and surprisingly it mentions no fee, which could perhaps explain these restrictions.

Enforced Contracts?

Apart from the pattern of apprenticeship just discussed, which was clearly based on a strong didactic commitment, a 'second pattern' existed that deserves special attention. It is exemplified by the case of Tommaso Tosco, who agreed a written contract to 'apprentice' himself to Gio Domenico Gotta, a silk-weaver, for one-and-a-half years and 'with a salary of 7 *soldi* a day', in January 1752. Less than six months later, Gotta sued him for leaving his workshop. The judge affirmed that, without a valid reason for leaving, Tosco must honour the contract or reimburse his master. In reply, Tosco – who contrary to custom, appeared before the court alone, without his father or a guarantor – claimed he had the right to abandon his master, and explained that he had only accepted the contract 'because at that time work in the silk trade was scarce', but the 'wage' (*paga*) 'was insufficient to cover the daily expenses for his own sustenance'.[31] Tosco's response suggests that he was a young journeyman in desperate need of employment who accepted a debasing, low-waged apprenticeship contract, probably not including training, in order to make ends meet. Though the extent of this phenomenon cannot be gauged, it shows how apprenticeship could be used to address economic uncertainty, with the contract masking labour relationships devoid of training.

We can ask if Tosco entered a form of indentured labour, similar to that used to fund emigration to seventeenth and eighteenth-century North America. Although not slaves, indentured labourers were not allowed to leave, needed permission to marry and were subject to corporal punishment.[32] As in the case of indentured workers, Tosco was ordered

---

[30] AST, sez. riun., *Consolato di Commercio, Bottonaj*, vol. 6, n.f. ('tutto ciò e quanto verrà da detta signora Peret licitamente comandato, havuto però riguardo alle forze di detta imprendissa').

[31] Ibid. *Ordinanze*, vol. 38, ff. 320v–321r. 'Di aver passata detta scrittura a motivo che in quel tempo vi era nell'arte suddetta poco lavoro e non potere la paga convenuta equivalere al vitto giornaliero'.

[32] On the topic, see e.g. D. W. Galenson, 'The rise and fall of indentured servitude in the Americas: An economic analysis', *Journal of Economic History* 44 (1984), 1–26;

by the court to meet his obligations. However, there were some important differences: like other apprentices, Tosco could choose to compensate his master for his departure – although he probably could not afford to. Secondly, his term was short, compared to the 3–5 years expected of indentured labourers in America.

There is one other significant nuance. Tosco and his master were able to appear in court because the agreement was written (as with colonial indentures); however, this is the only case of this type in our sample. In Turin, suspicious contracts seem often to have been made orally. Masters who used oral agreements avoided guild fees, and were freer to exploit apprentices as *de facto* low-paid labourers. This was a form of 'deregulation from below':[33] without a written contract, actors could reshape the labour relationship at their convenience. Accepting a verbal agreement meant renouncing the right to legal redress: masters could not force apprentices to remain, but equally they were not obliged to keep them when work was scarce.

These dynamics were often denounced by journeymen who had been damaged by both masters and apprentices. In July 1752, for example, Pallavicino, a journeyman printer, and his colleagues complained that their master Gerardo Giuliano had hired 'two children, two alleged pupils' (*due figlioli supposti scholari*) to work as typesetters at a paltry wage (*paga*) in order to 'save the costs of one or more journeymen who were regularly approved by the guild'. 'Because of this kind of abuse', they explained, 'many of them were out of work.' Moreover, one of the children had no written contract and had not been declared before the guild. He was even illiterate.[34] Seemingly, Giuliano was masking a low-skilled worker by labelling him as an apprentice.

The exploitation of apprentices as cheap labour became an increasing issue during the later eighteenth century, when Turin experienced an economic crisis and growing social tensions. The city's silk industry struggled against poor harvests, bad weather and growing competition from other textiles, such as cottons. Violent conflicts broke out between the guilds over the control of the labour force and production, while tensions increased between small craftsmen and merchant-manufacturers: 'journeymen were reduced to the condition of casual workers or day-labourers, masters were employed as wage-earners, and mere apprentices carried out work [that was] previously domain

---

C. Tomlins, 'Reconsidering indentured servitude: European migrations and the American labour force, 1600–1775', *Labour History* 42 (2001), 5–43.

[33] L. Allegra, 'Fra norma e deroga: Il mercato del lavoro a Torino nel Settecento', *Rivista Storica Italiana* 126 (2004), 872–925.

[34] AST, sez. riun., *Consolato di Commercio, Ordinanze*, vol. 38, ff. 410r-v.

of journeymen'.[35] Workers accused their masters of employing apprentices at tasks usually assigned to journeymen, worsening the grievous situation of the unemployed journeymen.

The battle between journeymen and masters over apprentices is visible in the dispute among the silk-stocking-makers that was provoked in September 1748 by a royal decree that limited apprentice numbers: masters with up to three looms could not take apprentices, those with 4–6 looms could keep one, and those with more than six looms could take two simultaneously. The guild did not prescribe any restrictions, and the decree was opposed by the masters, who maintained that the additional labour force was needed to satisfy the growing demand for silk goods. The journeymen retorted that this was a pretext for reducing wages and exploiting cheaper apprentices.[36] These arguments suggest two scenarios: on the one hand, apprentices could acquire useful skills in a relatively short time. They were less competent than experienced workers, but clearly capable of basic tasks. On the other, it is possible that the journeymen were attacking the kind of alleged apprentices – young, untrained workers employed under unfavourable conditions – which I discussed above.

Keeping the Peace: The *Consolato di Commercio*

Turin's guilds did not have their own courts in which their officers acted as judges. This, of course, does not mean that conflicts between apprentices and masters were absent, but rather that they were regulated by an 'external' institution, the *Consolato di Commercio*. This court was established in 1676 by a group of merchants to oversee trade and business. Originally, four merchants acted together as judges, but in 1687 Victor Amadeus replaced two of them with senators to strengthen ducal control. This configuration held during most of the eighteenth and nineteenth centuries (between 1723 and 1733 the judges were all merchants again, while Napoleon suppressed it).[37] Victor Amadeus also transformed the *Consolato* into the key agency of his economic policy, using it to develop regulations for manufacturing and product quality, to prepare guild regulations, and to hear disputes between guilds and artisans, and settle cases

---

[35] S. Cavallo, *Charity and Power in Early Modern Italy: Benefactors and their Motives in Turin, 1541–1789* (Cambridge: Cambridge University Press, 1995), 244.

[36] AST, I sez., *Commercio*, cat. IV, I add., m. 9, *Sentimento del Consolato sovra la supplica dei Mastri Fabricatori di Calzetti e contro-supplica de loro lavoranti.*

[37] S. Cerutti, 'Nature des choses et qualités des personnes: Le Consulat de commerce de Turin au XVIIIᵉ siècle', *Annales HSS* 6/57 (2002), 1491–520; S. Cerutti, *Giustizia sommaria: Pratiche e ideali di giustizia in una società di Ancien Régime (Torino XVIII secolo)* (Milan: Feltrinelli, 2003).

between masters, journeymen and apprentices.[38] The *Consolato* offered only summary judgements (*giustizia sommaria*), so plaintiffs and defendants appeared in person without lawyers. When lawsuits concerned guilds, judges first required guild officers to seek a 'friendly agreement' (*un'amichevole terminazione*). If this failed, the judge would initiate arbitration. As a result, we can only partially reconstruct such cases: proceedings were often lengthy, and in several cases the final result is unknown. The *Consolato* provides further evidence of the weakness of the city's guilds: although their officers were sometimes consulted, their participation in disputes was not systematic. The *Consolato*'s authority and power were higher than those of the guilds.

The registers of the *Consolato* for 1752 and 1753 show that during these two years the court heard 46 disputes involving apprenticeship. Disputes concerned three main issues: the conduct of masters and apprentices, the content of training and the right to terminate the agreement and claim reimbursement. They highlight the main features of apprenticeship under the guilds, and the critical points of agreements. In particular, they bring out in detail the range of financial agreements involved in apprenticeship and the treatment apprentices received.

Among the most frequent sources of dispute were runaway apprentices, as illustrated by the case of Maddalena Sala. In June 1785, Maddalena and her father Felice signed an apprenticeship contract with Anna Rovere, a silk-weaver. Maddalena agreed to a five-year term, in exchange for a salary that increased progressively. However, in July 1786 Anna initiated a lawsuit against Maddelena, claiming that after staying for one year and receiving her salary (*salario*), she had abandoned her to return home. The court accepted Anna's claim that Maddalena had no valid reason for leaving, and that she had been harmed by this since she was 'charged with work' at that time. It ordered Felice to either send back his daughter or pay an indemnity. Unfortunately, the judge's laconic sentence omits the reasons for Maddalena's exit. We are left ignorant of why Maddalena's father paid an indemnity instead of returning his daughter: were the conditions in Rovere's workshop too harsh? Or, since he was also a silk-weaver, did he want his daughter back to work with him?[39]

According to Turin's guilds' statutes and the judgements of the *Consolato*, apprentices and journeymen were not allowed to leave without

---

[38] G. Symcox, 'La reggenza della seconda Madam Reale (1675–1684)', in: G. Ricuperati (ed.), *Storia di Torino*, vol 4: *La città tra crisi e ripresa (1630–1730)* (Turin: Einaudi, 2002), 235–36.

[39] AST, sez. riun., *Consolato di Commercio, Ordinanze*, vol. 106, f. 63*v*–64*r* and 140*r*. A silk-weaver called Felice Sala appears in the 1792 census.

a valid reason. If they did, they could be sued by their master, and obliged to either return to their master or compensate him, as the Sala case shows. If the apprentice's family compensated the master, or the judge recognised a valid reason for departure, the apprentice could terminate his or her agreement and seek training elsewhere. The registers of the *Consolato* reveal that the crucial factors were the timing and the amount of compensation paid to the master, not his power to force the apprentice back to work.

Turin's guilds never had sufficient authority to enforce contracts themselves. Their powers remained limited, as is reflected by the dominant role of the *Consolato* and also by their unsuccessful efforts to control the staggering mobility of workers (including apprentices) sparked by the economic and social crises of the later eighteenth century. At this time, guild regulations on apprentices and journeymen did become stricter: every apprenticeship had to be registered immediately with the guild beadle (*bidello*), an official whose powers were increasingly important. The bakers' revised statutes from 1794 required the *bidello* to act as an intermediary between masters and their apprentices and journeymen, and to supervise workers' conduct. He collected certificates of 'good conduct' and 'achievement' from apprentices and journeymen and kept a register of unemployed workers, who he could send to understaffed workshops.[40] Despite these plans, there is no evidence that they had any effect.

Another common reason for disputes in the *Consolato* was masters' behaviour towards their apprentices, particularly their use of violence. Often agreements included clauses protecting children, suggesting that parents were aware of this risk. The contract for Angela Gerardi specified that her master and mistress were 'to correct and teach her with neither harsh words nor harsh facts'.[41] Several cases concerned children who claimed they had left their master because of abuse or threats. For example, Vincenzo Clapié claimed he had been beaten by his master, a locksmith, 'with an iron blade' because he misbehaved. Alessandro Albertano fled from carpenter Gioannini 'because he did not provide him with sufficient food and he had been threatened because one of his master's knives was missing'.[42] Such 'paternal violence' did not automatically terminate the agreement: Clapié, for example, was urged by the judge to return to his master and 'avoid acts and words that were not

[40] AST, I sez., *Materie economiche*, m. 20, II add., *Capi d'aggiunta al memoriale a favore dell'Università dei panatari*. On the *bidello* in the printers and bookbinders: S. Cerutti, *Étrangers: Étude d'une condition d'incertitude* (Montrouge: Bayard, 2012).

[41] AST, sez. riun., *Consolato di Commercio, Registro dei taffetieri*, vol. 67, ff.nn. ('coregendola ed insegnandole senza severità di parola e molto meno di fatti').

[42] Ibid., *Ordinanze*, vol. 39, ff. 161v–162r and 174r–v.

suitable for apprentices', while his master was admonished 'not to beat, not even mildly, the apprentice'.

The content of training was another frequent cause of dispute. In February 1753, Anna Maria Grosso and her father Pietro sued her master, the silk-weaver Bernardino Brosolo. The contract stated that Brosolo was to teach Anna Maria 'to unwind the silk yarns and weave, by warping and wefting the threads' (*dipanare le sete, torcere ed ordire le medesime*). Nevertheless, after a year, she had not yet learned the trade, since 'Brosolo does not care to teach her'; moreover, he resorted chiefly to external workers. Brosolo replied that he had taught Anna Maria to unwind yarn 'with care', but she was inattentive. As for the external workers, he had to hire them because his wife was ill. Furthermore, Anna Maria's training would take two years, so sufficient time remained for him to teach her.[43] The *Consolato*'s registers only rarely provide details on such matters. The dispute in 1752 between master shoemaker Gio Majna and his apprentice Rocco Baldassarre Droneto merely records that Giuseppe, Rocco's father, had been 'obliged to take his son back home because [Majna] did not teach him the craft as a master should'.[44]

As these cases highlight, apprentices could easily be set to tasks which had not been specified in the contract or which were not pertinent. This was precisely what the shoemaker's apprentice Gio Franceschetti complained about, when he declared that 'often, several times during working hours, even' his master sent him 'to make errands outside the workshop … and take care of his children and perform various other chores inappropriate for learning the craft'.[45]

Finally, some apprentices complained that their masters had violated the guild's prescription and failed to train them personally, instead 'abandoning' them to a salaried journeyman. Thus, the apprentice Gio Batta Bianchi and his mother sued his master because he had been placed under a journeyman, Giorgio Fodrà, who not only received half the fee they paid the master, but also lacked mastery and mistreated Bianchi.[46]

If the master could be sued for negligence, it was also possible for him to be too assiduous. Teaching apprentices a trade quickly could be detrimental to masters, who then risked losing them prematurely and being unable to take full advantage of their work. This is illustrated in the

---

[43] Ibid., ff. 92r–v.
[44] Ibid., vol. 38, ff. 157v–158r. (Giuseppe stated that he was 'astretto di levare dal travaglio sotto detto Majna il figlio a motivo che quello non li insegnava l'arte come si conviene ad un mastro').
[45] Ibid., ff. 630r–v.   [46] Ibid., ff. 606v–607r.

dispute between Stefano Flandinet and his mother Anna, and master sculptor Francesco Bonaveri. Flandinet agreed to serve for four years, but after one year and eight months he was determined to leave, since he 'was sufficiently expert in the craft'. As he had no valid reason to leave, the judge ordered Flandinet to fulfil his contract; nevertheless, it is notable that he attempted to justify his departure by claiming to have received *sufficient* training.[47]

Flandinet's behaviour bears comparison to the dispute between the master apothecary Bressa and his apprentice Ferrari, who decided to leave his master after one year instead of the four fixed in the contract. Bressa explained, and a colleague confirmed, that he taught with such 'care and dedication' that the boy could now work independently. This probably encouraged Ferrari to leave for other opportunities. Bressa was damaged by Ferrari's departure since 'he could no longer count on [his] help and work'.[48] In order to prevent early departure, it is likely that other masters taught 'with prudence', dispensing knowledge over years to prolong training.[49]

Workhouses and Charity Institutions: Exploitation or Opportunity?

In eighteenth-century Turin, many almshouses and charitable institutions offered aid to people of different social standing. Most also organised economic activities for their occupants. Historians have properly highlighted the hard living and working conditions of poor children in workhouses. Yet at the same time, workhouses served as reference point for factory owners and businessmen.[50] While it is certainly true that pre-industrial workhouses exploited their inmates' work, Turin's most important charity institutions reveal the need to nuance this statement by highlighting a more complex situation.

Welfare policy was shaped by the struggle between the municipal elites and ducal power: the duke sought to control the administration of the *Ospedale di Carità* (the chief institution providing relief to large families) and was also active in founding new institutions, such as the *Albergo di Virtù* (established in 1580 to offer training for poor children). In the eighteenth century, some workhouses were established to shelter women whose sexual honour was in danger, while older almshouses,

---

[47] Ibid., f. 357*v*.   [48] Ibid., f. 283 *r-v*.
[49] On this point, see Wallis, 'Apprenticeship and training'.
[50] J. Humphries, *Childhood and Child Labour in the British Industrial Revolution* (Cambridge: Cambridge University Press, 2010).

such as the *Opera della Provvidenza*, were renovated.[51] The majority of these institutions provided work for their inmates and training for young people. These activities developed within a specific ideological context. Welfare was imbued with a mixture of paternalistic and coercive attitudes: inmates' work was intended to establish order and discipline, on the premise that idleness endangered society and the deserving poor should maintain themselves by work. In turn, training was intended to prepare youths for life outside the institution.

At the city's oldest hospital, the *Ospedale di San Giovanni*, which received abandoned babies, children were trained and employed once they were old enough. Girls and (a few) boys were employed in the silk workshop within the hospital, while other boys were placed in external workshops. Both the *Ospedale di Carità* and the *Albergo di Virtù* followed similar policies. At the *Ospedale*, many of the children who were placed in apprenticeships came from large families in dire financial straits, and had been admitted temporarily, aged around seven, to relieve their families. The *Albergo* admitted children aged 11–15, who were sponsored by a guarantor, usually a court member or royal artisan. In 1664–65, the *Ospedale* established a ribbon-making workshop, and in 1767–68 it added workshops producing shoes, bonnets and woollens.

Institutions trained a significant number of children. In 1721, the *Albergo* hosted 31 boys and 45 girls: boys were trained in crafts such as ribbon-making, shoemaking, carpentry and wool or silk weaving. Girls were instructed as silk-veil makers (*fabbricanti di garze*), in sewing linens and gloves, or in less skilled activities such as spinning silk thread.[52] In 1732, two entrepreneurs, Brunetta and Benissone, who produced Bolognese style veils and silk cloths were allowed to employ apprentices from the *Albergo* in their workshop.[53] By 1798, 14 masters and merchants worked in the institution's workshops, with up to 119 looms. External workers and apprentices were also employed there: of the 88 apprentices present, only 75 were patronised by the institution.

Like private apprenticeships, the agreements made for training in charity institution workshops specified that the master must teach the children 'like a good father' and could only make limited use of them for generic chores. In addition, boys and girls received a daily salary. The

---

[51] See Cavallo, *Charity and Power*; S. Cavallo, 'Assistenza femminile e tutela dell'onore nella Torino del XVIII secolo', *Annali della Fondazione L. Einaudi* 16 (1980), 127–55; M. Moody, *The Royal Poorhouse in 18th-Century Turin, Italy: The King and the Paupers* (Lewiston, NY: Edwin Mellen Press, 2001).

[52] AST, sez. riun., *Albergo di Virtù, Fondazione e dotazione dell'opera*, 1700–1750, vol. 5. Girls were present in the *Albergo* only until the early eighteenth century.

[53] *Regio Biglietto ... pel quale dànnosi alcuni giovani dell'Albergo quali apprendisti alla manifattura di lustrini e di veli di Bologna*, in Duboin, *Raccolta*, l. VII, 213.

administration expected the wage to be spent on clothes, although there is evidence that, despite the regulations, salaries were spent on foodstuffs or other goods with the complicity of guards and porters who could access the outside world. Apprentices received 4 or 5 *soldi* per day; they were not paid during holidays, absences or illnesses, or during the initial three-month trial period (*di tolleranza*). Trainee silk and wool sock-makers in the *Ospedale di Carità* received 5 *soldi* per day during their first four years, rising to 6 *soldi* for the next two years, and worked unpaid for just the first 20 days of their contract.[54]

Those charity institutions that did not contain workshops similarly acknowledged the educational function of labour for the destitute. In 1731, for example, the *Opera della Provvidenza*, an almshouse for girls aged between 10 and 25, dispatched five girls to join masters working at the *Ospedale* and sent another six to work with a French entrepreneur, Boullement, 'to learn lacemaking'. Later, around 1760, the *Opera* hired a Parisian mistress to teach girls silk lacemaking.[55]

This training provision relied on a close-knit network of masters, merchants and entrepreneurs whose businesses depended on their relationships with these institutions. They managed workshops inside the institutions' walls, employed external workers and apprentices alongside inmates and children, and supplied commodities to both almshouses and outside customers. Merchant-entrepreneurs were usually experienced and well-connected, with strong relationships at court. For example, Gio Sebastiano Eula, the master silk-sock-maker at the *Ospedale di Carità* between 1756 and 1766, also held two royal patents for the manufacture of woollen socks and caps and white silk laces on the same looms used for making socks. Eula also held some fiscal exemptions and could display the royal insignia outside his shop.[56] Other entrepreneurs held high-ranking positions in guilds: Boullement, a French master silk-weaver who took girls from the *Opera della Provvidenza*, was a guild officer, as was the silk-weaver Brunetta. Both received royal patents, a privilege which reflected their involvement with these institutions.[57]

The guilds were forced to recognise the training given at these institutions, and even to allow youths membership on favourable terms, during the later eighteenth century. Following a request from the *Ospedale di Carità*, and despite guild protests, two royal decrees in 1758 required that

[54] AST, sez. riun., *Insinuazione di Torino*, a. 1757, l. 2, ff. 819r–823r.
[55] *Regio Biglietto . . . col quale si ordina di mandare cinque alunne dell'Opera della Provvidenza ad imparare l'arte dei merletti nella fabbrica Boullement*, in Duboin, *Raccolta*, l. VII, 262; Cavallo, 'Assistenza femminile', 148.
[56] Duboin, *Raccolta*, l. IX, 892 and 363–64.   [57] Ibid., l. IX, 305–10 and 828–33.

children trained as silk-sock-makers in the *Ospedale* be admitted as guild masters after an abbreviated period as journeymen, and without the usual charges (3 *lire* for apprentices and 4 *lire* for journeymen). Similarly, shoe-makers trained at the institution had to work for only three years as journeymen (instead of four) and were exempt from apprentice and journeymen fees (of 2 and 4 *lire*) and the mastership fee.[58] Comparable privileges were granted to children trained in silk weaving at the *Albergo di Virtù*: under the guild's 1738 statutes, former apprentices of the *Albergo*, or men who married girls trained there, were exempt from the 50 *lire* fee charged to new masters. In 1753, *all* former apprentices of the *Albergo*, irrespective of trade, were exempted from guild fees and given the right to enter the guild as journeymen.[59]

The advantages that the crown granted to the city's charitable institutions reveal the guilds' weakness. But above all, they show that, for poor families, entrusting a child to a charitable institution could be advantageous, allowing the child to learn a trade and enter a guild. These institutions trained many youths who later gained mastership. This was the experience of Giacinta Maria Bonelli, who spent eight years at the *Opera delle figlie dei Militari*, an eighteenth-century institution for soldiers' daughters: she was trained in silk weaving and, on leaving the *Opera*, was granted a royal patent allowing her to establish a business.[60] Similarly, Maria Margherita Revella, housed at the *Ospedale* from infancy, learnt the art of weaving silk and taffetas. She left the institution in 1753 to marry (with a charity dowry of 60 *lire*), and the following year she was admitted as a mistress in the taffeta weavers' guild.[61]

The quality of the training provided by these institutions and its recog-nition by the guilds was a distinctive characteristic of Turin. However, some limits existed. Firstly, almost all institutions placed inmates in low-skilled activities. In the woollens workshop at the *Ospedale,* which made clothing for the army, most inmates – except the weavers – performed repetitive, low-skilled tasks such as combing, spinning and processing thread. From their first day they received a fixed salary and had to reach a minimum daily output. Excessive exploitation was prevented by

---

[58] ASCT, *Ospedale di Carità*, cat. XI, fasc. 3 ; *Regie patenti . . . a favore de' giovani ricoverati nell'Ospedale di Carità di Torino che apprendono ivi l'arte di calzettajo*, in Duboin, *Raccolta*, l. IX, 893.

[59] *Memoriale a capi dell'Università de' mastri mercanti fabbricatori di stoffe d'oro, d'argento, e seta*, in Duboin, *Raccolta*, l. IX, 322–26; *Regie patenti . . . a favore de' giovani che ne fanno il tirocinio nell'Albergo di Virtù di Torino*, in Duboin, *Raccolta*, l. VII, 215–16.

[60] AST, sez. I, *Materie economiche, Commercio*, II add., m. 20bis.

[61] Ibid., sez. riun., *Insinuazione di Torino*, a 1758, l. 2, f. 85r–86v; ibid., *Consolato di Commercio, Registro dei taffetieri*, vol. 66, n.f.

a ceiling on daily production.[62] The weavers, who needed training, worked for free for their first three months. During the subsequent two years they earned the same as external journeymen (plus a premium of 1 *lira* for every cloth, 'to encourage them to work'). Finally, they had to donate their last three months' wages to the *Ospedale* as reimbursement.[63] Secondly, not all institutions emphasised training; some merely put children to work. The *Opera di San Giovanni di Dio*, founded in 1755 by Rosa Govona, admitted young, poor girls between the ages of 13 and 25, and was essentially a coercive workhouse. Girls were employed without significant training in low-skilled textile activities (wool spinning and weaving) and in manufacturing textiles, gloves, socks and silk ribbons. The commodities they produced were sold at low prices – inciting guild hostility – while the institution's harsh conditions were notorious throughout the city.[64] In sum, the panorama of training and work within Turin's charity institutions was multifarious and riddled with ambiguities.

The fate of poor children depended on which institution they entered. Once an inmate, their treatment and training was defined by a gendered 'double standard'. While boys might be sent daily to one of the city's workshops, this was more problematic for girls, whose sexual honour and conduct had to be constantly monitored: therefore, girls were customarily trained internally. While boys' training aimed to give them the means to survive independently, even to the extent of gaining guild membership, this was not the case for girls, who were trained in a limited set of trades or domestic activities considered suitable for a future as a wife and mother. Female apprentices who finished their training were not automatically allowed to leave: if they lacked a suitable place to live (i.e. in a family of sound morality or with a relative) or were not betrothed, they could spend their lives in the institution.

We cannot establish exactly how many youths were trained in charity institutions. The workshop census of 1792 contains traces of them, but only a prosopographical reconstruction would reveal their full careers.[65] Yet, as in the guilds, the apprentices these institutions trained demonstrated the high rates of mobility and exit typical of the urban labour

---

[62] The *Opera della Provvidenza* trained girls to prepare them for professional careers later: Cavallo, 'Assistenza femminile', 148–51.

[63] ASCT, *Ospedale di Carità*, cat. XIX, *Atti* vol. 17, anno 1753; Ibid., vol. 29, a. 1776; Ibid., cat. XI, fasc. 5, a. 1793; AST, sez. riun., *Insinuazione di Torino*, a. 1763, l. 3, f. 582r–588r; Ibid., a. 1784, l. 9, f. 961r–969r.

[64] Cavallo, *Charity and Power*, 229.

[65] The 1792 census includes 5 apprentices from the *Ospedale di San Giovanni* ('figli dell'Ospedale') with shoemakers, 3 in bakeries, and 1 with a silk-weaver, while 26 'apprentices of the *Albergo di Virtù*' were with silk-weavers and 8 with silk-stocking-makers.

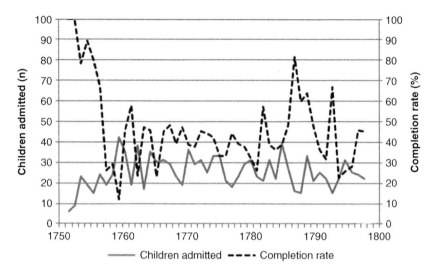

Figure 3.2 Admissions and completion rate of apprentices at the *Albergo di Virtù*, Turin 1751–1800

market. From the seventeenth century, the *Albergo di Virtù* forbade youths from leaving before their apprenticeships ended, and prohibited masters from hiring former apprentices from the *Albergo* who lacked their *benservito* certificate.[66] Yet the register of apprentices at the *Albergo* shows that a significant number of boys never completed their training (this seems true also for the *Ospedale di Carità*). It lists for 1751–1838 all the children who were admitted (with age and place of birth), their guarantors, and the master who took them. The final column was to record the date they completed their apprenticeship and received permission to leave the *Albergo*, or else to register an early departure.[67]

As Figure 3.2 shows, the *Albergo* received a substantial number of children each year, but only around half completed their training. Youths left for a range of reasons: illness, fleeing the *Albergo*, expulsion for bad conduct, rudeness, theft or laziness. Some of them died. Those who left early include a fair number who had served more than half of

---

[66] *Ricorso … e relativo decreto del consiglio dell'Albergo col quale si vieta ai giovani ivi ricoverati d'uscirne prima del tempo prefisso ed a qualunque persona d'accettarli se non riportino il ben servito del Consiglio; Ordine del Consiglio dell'Albergo col quale si proibisce ai mastri tessitori, filatori e fabbricanti di seta di ricevere nelle loro botteghe lavoranti dell'Albergo stesso, che non abbiano ottenuto la loro licenza*, in Duboin, *Raccolta*, l. VII, 209.

[67] AST, I sez., *Albergo di Virtù, Ruolo degli allievi*, vol. 203, 1757–1813. (Contrary to what is written on the cover, the register starts in 1751.)

their terms: like many private apprentices, they had probably acquired some skills and preferred to take their chances in the urban labour market. In thinking about this high exit rate, we should not underestimate the harsh conditions that children faced – rigid discipline, strict religious education and long working hours probably encouraged many children to flee, despite the prospects on offer.[68]

Training within the Kinship Network

In Turin, family ties played a crucial role in training offspring. Cerutti and Cavallo have shown how kinship ties permeated society and intersected with economic and political organisations. Cavallo's work on those Turinese artisans – surgeon-barbers, tailors, wig-makers and upholsterers – that she dubs 'artisans of the body' argues that they constituted a 'culturally defined milieu' with common values and professional interests and a shared environment in which kinship shaped training. Her biographical reconstructions show extensive networks comprising blood relatives (siblings), diagonal relations (e.g. uncles and nephews) and godparents.[69]

Unfortunately, we cannot evaluate the share of training supplied within kinship networks, since connections were not always documented. But by using a range of archival sources, we can gain a sense of this phenomenon. First, the 1792 workshop census reports some kinship ties between masters and their subordinates, although it does not distinguish journeymen from apprentices. Table 3.1 summarises the nature and the frequency of ties in the most common crafts. Since this information was not required for the census, the actual rates are underestimated.

Workshops containing the sons, sons-in-law, brothers and nephews of the master were recorded in most crafts. For example, the workshop of Gio Batta Boretto, master shoemaker, incorporated his son, Giuseppe, and three journeymen or apprentices. Other ties also mattered, mostly nephews and sons-in-law. Francesco Dionisio, spirit-maker, trained Pietro Antonio, his nephew, while Carlo Germano, master wig-maker, worked with his son-in-law. Kinship ties played a crucial role in training and structuring employment. This was reinforced by guild rules giving

---

[68] B. Zucca Micheletto, 'Temps pour travailler, temps pour éduquer: Le travail des pauvres dans les institutions de charité (Turin, XVIIIe siècle)', in: C. Maitte and D. Terrier (eds.), *Les temps du travail : Normes, pratiques, évolutions (XIVe–XIXe siècle)* (Rennes: Presses Universitaires de Rennes, 2014), 81–99.

[69] S. Cavallo, *Artisans of the Body in Early Modern Italy: Identities, Families and Masculinities* (Manchester: Manchester University Press, 2007).

Table 3.1 *Workshops and kinship ties, Turin 1792*

	Workshops	Widow plus:			Master only	Master plus:				All with kin
		Widow only	child	child & grandchild		1 child	2+ children	brothers	brothers & nephews	
	N	N	N	N	N	N	N	N	N	%
Silk-weavers	227	2	11	0	178	19	12	5	0	21
Shoemakers	219	9	0	0	200	9	1	0	0	5
Carpenters, cabinetmakers, wainwrights	113	1	0	0	95	9	2	6	0	15
Wig-makers	92	0	0	0	79	6	5	1	1	14
Bakers	86	10	6	2	46	7	13	2	0	35
Ribbon-makers	81	0	0	0	76	3	1	1	0	6
Locksmiths	63	1	0	0	57	0	2	2	1	8
Jewellers	46	2	1	0	37	2	1	3	0	15
Saddle-makers	31	0	1	0	23	6	1	0	0	26
Turners	31	0	0	0	24	6	1	0	0	23
Silk-sock-makers	33	0	0	0	24	4	3	2	0	27
Mattress-makers	28	0	0	0	26	2	0	0	0	7
Leather goods	21	1	0	0	17	0	2	1	0	14
Total	1071	26	19	2	882	73	44	23	2	15

Source: AST, Magistrato del Consolato, mazzo 2, *Volume contenente li nomi, cognomi e patria.*

masters' children advantageous access to membership, often including avoiding a formal apprenticeship.

The importance of kinship to training is also visible in the petitions artisans presented to the duke throughout the eighteenth century. Many sought guild membership or permission to work, despite lacking all the necessary requirements. Others requested a reduction in fees or an exemption from presenting a costly masterpiece. In their petitions, artisans retraced their careers and training, revealing the role of kinship. Pietro Todino, for example, was a tinker, who before leaving Turin to improve his skills in France, spent four years apprenticed to his father.[70] Bartolomeo Rissetto, a shoemaker, was apprentice and journeyman to his father, and after a period in France, requested an exemption from mastership examination and fees. In some cases, professional and kinship ties overlapped. Maurizio Roero served the tinker Gian Battista Bono, who later became his father-in-law, as an apprentice for four years, a journeyman for three and a partner for two.[71]

Kinship was particularly important for women's training. The activities of widows and wives in family businesses demonstrate that marriage was a watershed in women's lives: joining their husband's shop meant improving – or learning – a job. The 1792 census lists 76 widows heading craft workshops. Widows ran a fifth of bakeries, and around 5% of silk weaving, jewellery and leatherworking shops. Wives, sisters and daughters likely worked in workshops in a more informal and less visible way, and only a few were recorded in the census. Among silk-weavers, in the workshop of Giuliano Mariano, 13 journeymen and apprentices worked alongside Orsola Mariano, his wife. Similarly, the tripery of Francesco Lanza employed his wife Giacinta and two children – a boy and a girl – with a servant, while Gioanna Carbonina ran her husband's smithy, declaring that she worked 'on behalf of her husband, who was absent from the kingdom'.[72]

The few guilds that admitted female members provide further evidence of the importance of kinship in female training. In 1754, an edict from Charles Emmanuel allowed women to join the taffeta weavers' guild, a branch of the powerful silk-weavers guild. Two registers of female masters from 1754 to 1795 survive. Of the 82 women admitted, one quarter had trained within their family: most others just declared their master's name, leaving kinship ties unclear. Sixteen were daughters of master silk-weavers, five learned from their mothers, one from an aunt,

---

[70] AST, sez. riun, *Consolato di Commercio, Registro dei Mastri stagninari della presente città*, vol. 40 n.f.
[71] Ibid., vol. 9 and vol. 40, n.f.   [72] All examples are from the 1792 workshop census.

one from a paternal uncle and one from her stepfather. Most had abundant experience. Maddalena Formica was trained for ten years by her father Maurizio, a master silk-weaver,[73] while Francesca Torsengo spent 20 years working alongside her mother Caterina.[74] The register of the silk, gold and silver button-makers for 1737–79 records 33 female masters, 3 trained by their fathers and 2 by their mothers, such as Maria Massa, who entered in 1740 after training with her mother Teresa.[75] Kinship could be particularly important when the parent training a girl died. Irene Teresa Giró, for example, trained as a silk-weaver with her father from the age of 17. When he died, she continued her instruction with her maternal uncle, spending eight years with him, three as an apprentice and five as a worker, before becoming a master in 1771.[76]

The fact that the training of girls and women was influenced by several factors, not least their marital status, makes it difficult to say when training started. It is likely that, for many, their father's shop provided the first step on an educational path that continued after marriage in their husband's shop. In this situation, as Cavallo describes, different kinship bonds overlapped, as exemplified by Giacinta Grassi, an orphaned daughter of a master silk-weaver, who trained in an uncle's shop before working in her husband's atelier.[77]

Girls and boys who were trained by their parents formed a crucial resource for the family business, making a concrete contribution long after their training. Beyond this, however, several questions about their training and the conditions they faced remain unanswered: were children learning and working within their families paid or not? If so, how much? Did they have a formal agreement, and how did this impact on family relationships?[78] Among the lower classes, wills were occasions to thank and reward wives and other family members for their domestic work, care for household members and contribution to the family business. But they lack information about the timing and context of training.[79] Again,

---

[73] AST, sez. riun., *Consolato di Commercio, Registro dei taffetieri*, vol. 66, n.f.

[74] Ibid., vol. 67, f. 199r–204v.   [75] Ibid., *Bottonaj*, vol. 6, n.f.

[76] Ibid., *Registro dei taffetieri*, vol. 66, n.f.   [77] Ibid., vol. 67, f. 356r–361v.

[78] On these points, see M. Martini and A. Bellavitis's special issue on 'Households, family workshop and unpaid market work in Europe from the 16th century to the present', *History of the Family* 19/3 (2014), and A. Bellavitis, M. Martini and R. Sarti's special issue 'Familles laborieuses: Rémunération, transmission et apprentissage dans les ateliers familiaux dans la fin du Moyen Age à l'époque contemporaine en Europe', *Mélanges de l'Ecole Française de Rome, Italie-Mediterranée, MEFRIM*, 128/1, 2016, online at https://journals.openedition.org/mefrim/2366. Also, Cavallo, *Artisans of the Body*.

[79] G. Lumia, 'Mariti e mogli nei testamenti senesi di età moderna', in: G. Calvi and I. Chabot (eds.), *Le ricchezze delle donne: Diritti patrimoniali e poteri familiari in Italia (XIII–XIX secc.)* (Turin: Rosenberg & Sellier, 1998), 43–63; A. Bellavitis, *Famille, genre, transmission à Venise au XVIᵉ siècle* (Rome: École Française de Rome, 2008).

apprenticeship appears to have been intertwined with work, and the boundary between them was not clear.

Conclusion

In pre-industrial Turin, apprenticeship provided a large nominal and legal umbrella which masters, children and their families could use to cover and legitimise a wide range of (at times ambiguous) training and working relationships. Two main findings justify this conclusion. Firstly, apprenticeship involved a wide range of actors: some of them, including guilds and charity institutions, were pursuing specific goals and followed a consciously developed policy. However, apprenticeship was also used in trades which were not institutionally organised. Moreover, the task of training a child could be achieved through the broader kinship network or simply achieved within the immediate family. Secondly, an analysis of the state's economic policy and its efforts to control the guilds shows that Turin's guilds had limited control over apprenticeship. Indeed, with the exception of a few specific points such as their duration, guild regulations on training and contracts were limited to general clauses and statements and lacked concrete details. A wide range of issues, therefore, were settled privately within contracts, and resulted from negotiations between apprentices, their sponsors and families, and the master. As a consequence, enforcement of contracts was not carried out. In the same way, disputes between masters and pupils were not regulated by guild officers, but settled by a city court, the *Consolato di Commercio*, whose authority on economic matters went beyond the power of the guilds.

4 Apprenticeship in Early Modern Venice

Giovanni Colavizza, Riccardo Cella and Anna Bellavitis

The desire of the Venetian state to regulate the production and sale of food led to the establishment, during the twelfth century, of the *Giustizia Vecchia*, a court that later developed an authority over the majority of the city's guilds. The further decision to create a public register of contracts of apprenticeship reflects the ambition of Venetian authorities to regulate and control both vocational training and access to the urban job market, acting as a guarantor between masters and young apprentices. This chapter presents a historical overview of apprenticeship in early modern Venice, examining the development of the city's legislation on the matter, and analysing a new sample of contracts recorded in the city's apprenticeship registers during the sixteenth and seventeenth centuries to investigate the implementation of these rules. In particular, we discuss the complex relationship between the general legal framework established by Venetian public authorities and the particular set of norms detailed in guilds' statutes.[1]

Our analysis reveals that apprenticeship contracts were used to accommodate a variety of situations, while following the general framework provided by state and guild regulations. We then present an in-depth study of apprenticeship contracts from three crafts (goldsmiths, carpenters and printers), chosen for their economic importance, and because they represented different realities in terms of technological specialisation,

---

[1] Previous research on apprenticeship in early modern Venice focuses on institutions: V. Lazzarini, 'Antichi ordinamenti veneziani a tutela del lavoro dei garzoni', *Atti del Regio Istituto di Scienze, Lettere ed Arti* 88 (1929), 873–94; M. Costantini, *L'albero della libertà economica: Il processo di scioglimento delle corporazioni veneziane* (Venice: Arsenale, 1987); M. Costantini, 'La formazione professionale dal tramonto delle corporazioni al sorgere del sistema di fabbrica', *Studi storici Luigi Simeoni* 41 (1990), 129–35; specific crafts: A. Vianello, *L'arte dei calegheri e zavateri di Venezia tra XVII e XVIII secolo* (Venice: Istituto Veneto di Scienze, Lettere ed Arti, 1993); F. Trivellato, *Fondamenta dei vetrai: Lavoro, tecnologia e mercato a Venezia tra Sei e Settecento* (Rome: Donzelli, 2000); M. della Valentina, 'The silk industry in Venice: guilds and labour relations in the seventeenth and eighteenth centuries', in: P. Lanaro (ed.), *At the Centre of the Old World: Trade and Manufacturing in Venice and the Venetian Mainland (1400–1800)* (Toronto: Centre for Reformation and Renaissace Studies, 2006), 109–42; or its relationship to the economic decline of Venice during the seventeenth century.

capital (or labour) intensity and market typology. Our results highlight yet another aspect of apprenticeship in Venice: the influence of guilds. Some guilds such as the goldsmiths, were more closed to foreigners, favouring Venetians instead. Apprenticeship in early modern Venice was an institution which, despite appearing to be highly regulated and formalised, accommodated a variety of realities with remarkable flexibility.[2]

The Institutional and Historical Framework

Apprenticeship in Italian cities was diverse in its structure and functions, and its edges were blurred. The variety of lengths, salaries and clauses found in apprenticeship contracts reflected the craft, the age and gender of the apprentice, and also the diverse relationships between the master and the apprentice or their family. The registration of a contract was not necessarily the beginning of a work relationship between two actors without any previous social or economic relationship. It was sometimes the conclusion of a probationary period, during which masters tested the apprentices.[3] As an apprentice, the boy or girl was involved in several activities: learning the trade, working, taking part in the general family life of the master. Domestic tasks were commonly expected of apprentices, especially girls, but other activities, ranging from selling in the shop to helping with the harvest, were also mentioned in contracts.[4]

---

[2] The chapter is the result of collaborative work, and is part of the research project GAWS (*Garzoni*: Apprenticeship, Work, Society), funded by the *Agence Nationale de la recherche* (France) and the *Fonds National Suisse de la Recherche*, in collaboration with the universities of Lille 3 (Valentina Sapienza), Rouen Normandie (Anna Bellavitis) and the École Polytechnique Fédérale de Lausanne (Frédéric Kaplan). We would also like to acknowledge the support of the State Archive of Venice and thank all the *Garzoni* team for their contribution. For more information see: http://garzoni.hypotheses.org.

[3] P. Curatolo, 'Apprendistato e organizzazione del lavoro nell'industria auroserica milanese (XVI–XVII secolo)', in: E. Brambilla and G. Muto (eds.), *La Lombardia spagnola: Nuovi indirizzi di ricerca* (Milan: Unicopli, 1997), 91–109; A. Caracausi, 'The price of an apprentice: Contracts and trials in the woollen industry in sixteenth century Italy', *Mélanges de l'École française de Rome – Italie et Méditerranée modernes et contemporaines*, 128 (2016), https://journals.openedition.org/mefrim/2476; C. Maitte, '"Garzonetti" et "garzoni" dans les arts du verre italiens, XVIe–XVIIIe siècle', in: A. Bellavitis, M. Frank and V. Sapienza (eds.), *Garzoni: Apprendistato e formazione tra Venezia e l'Europa in età moderna secolo* (Mantova: Universitas Studiorum, 2017), 191–216.

[4] S. Sciarrotta, 'Artigiani nella Salerno Settecentesca', *Annali Storici di Principato Citra* 8 (2010), 97–117; C. Klapisch-Zuber, 'Disciples, fils, travailleurs. Les apprentis peintres et sculpteurs italiens au XVe et XVIe siècle', *Mélanges de l'École française de Rome – Italie et Méditerranée modernes et contemporaines*, 128 (2016), https://journals.openedition.org/mefrim/2469.

A recent study has shown that fewer than half of Italian guilds, in all kind of crafts, had specific rules on apprenticeship.[5] The guilds' rules and apprenticeship contracts give very little information about what was actually taught to an apprentice or what they needed to know in order to become a member of a guild. This has certainly a lot to do with the 'mysteries' and the secrets of the crafts, but also with the continuous evolution of standards and quality requirements that was necessary in order to deal with competition. As pointed out by Mocarelli, in several Italian cities 'apprenticeships were not officially recognized. However, that does not necessarily mean they were non-existent. In various cases, in fact, it has been possible to discover that increasingly a private contract between the parties was adopted.'[6] Nevertheless, apprenticeship regulations did exist in the most important Italian manufacturing centres, resulting in a variety of different legal frameworks.

The variety of contract terms also affected the methods of payment. Sometimes apprenticeship contracts were used to provide similar conditions to those given to journeymen. Even when they came closest, as in the textile industries of the great industrial cities of the Italian Renaissance – Florence, Milan and Venice – where apprentices did not commonly pay a premium to their master and received instead a *salario* (literally 'salary', but in most cases a one-off payment) at the end of their terms, the use of an apprenticeship contract entailed an institutional distinction with journeymen. In most cases, when compared to journeymen's salaries, 'apprenticeship salaries' look almost symbolic: for example, in the wool industry of Florence, apprentices were paid up to 15 *lire* per year, while the average annual salary of a journeyman was about 500 *lire*.[7] On the one hand, this payment can be considered an incentive to complete the contract, but on the other it sometimes resulted in sums that support the idea that apprentices could constitute a cheap labour force or compensate for a scarcity of waged workers.

Another difficulty in interpreting rules is the endpoint and language of apprenticeship, which are often vaguer than we might expect. Not only should the career trajectory from apprentice to journeyman to master not be taken for granted, but the meaning of the words used to designate those

---

[5] L. Mocarelli, 'Guilds reappraised: Italy in the early modern period', in: J. Lucassen, T. De Moor and J. L. van Zanden (eds.), *The Return of the Guilds*, supplement 16, *International Review of Social History* 53 (Cambridge: Cambridge University Press, 2008), 159–78.

[6] Ibid., 175–76.

[7] L. Marcello, 'Andare a bottega: Adolescenza e apprendistato nelle arti (sec. XVI–XVII)', in: O. Niccoli (ed.), *Infanzie. Funzioni di un gruppo liminale dal Mondo classico all'età moderna* (Florence: Ponte alle Grazie, 1993), 231–51.

stages is debated by historians.[8] Masters could head a workshop, with journeymen and apprentices under their authority, but they could also work under someone else's authority. In some crafts, this distinction was captured by different titles: 'chief-masters' (*capo maestro*) headed the workshop while 'masters' (*maestro*) had passed the masters' examination but lacked a workshop of their own.[9] A crucial ambiguity sometimes existed in the language used for apprentices and waged workers: *garzoni* could either be apprentices or junior salaried workers.[10] But this was not always the case. In the Venetian glass industry two words, *garzonetto* and *garzone*, designated separate stages in apprenticeship, with the first used for younger apprentices who were not yet trained in glass-blowing.[11]

We focus here on apprenticeships between individual masters and apprentices. However, apprenticeship within charity institutions was also widespread across Europe. In early modern Italy, institutions that provided an education and a dowry to poor girls were particularly important.[12] The likelihood that girls would leave their family home to become apprentices or servants is debated among historians and has even been offered as an explanation for the so-called 'little divergence' between Northern and Southern Europe.[13] We shall not enter that debate here but will merely emphasise some simple facts. As part of the guild system, apprenticeship was much more accessible for boys, while domestic service was one of the most widespread activities for young women. Yet, the boundaries between domestic service and apprenticeship were often blurred.[14]

The Institutions of Apprenticeship in Venice

The existence in Venice of a specific court charged with recording apprenticeship contracts for the majority of guilds, albeit not all, is an exceptional opportunity for historians. The *Giustizia Vecchia* supervised all guilds, except those in wool, silk and Murano glass, which fell under the *Provveditori di*

[8] M. Martinat, 'L'apprendistato', in: R. Ago (ed.), *Storia del lavoro in Italia: L'età moderna Trasformazioni e risorse del lavoro tra associazioni di mestiere e pratiche individuali* (Rome: Castelvecchi, 2018), 79–102.

[9] L. Molà, *The Silk Industry of Renaissance Venice* (Baltimore: Johns Hopkins University Press, 2000); della Valentina, 'Silk industry in Venice'.

[10] A. Caracausi, *Dentro la bottega: Culture del lavoro in una città d'età moderna* (Venice: Marsilio, 2008).

[11] Maitte, '"Garzonetti" et "Garzoni"'.

[12] A. Groppi, 'Dots et institutions: La conquête d'un "patrimoine" (Rome, XVIIIᵉ–XIXᵉ siècle)', *Clio: Femmes, Genre, Histoire* 7 (1998), https://journals.openedition.org/clio/349.

[13] T. De Moor and J. L. van Zanden, 'Girl power: The European marriage pattern and labour markets in the North Sea region in the late medieval and early modern period', *Economic History Review* 63 (2010), 1–33.

[14] A. Bellavitis, *Women's work and rights in early modern urban Europe* (London: Palgrave, 2018).

Comun, Consoli dei Mercanti and the *Podestà di Murano* respectively. After 1291, Venetian craftsmen had to inform the *Giustizia Vecchia* about any apprentices in their workshops. This rule aimed to protect apprentices from abuse by their masters, and to safeguard masters from misbehaviour by their apprentices. The master was obliged to record the *accordo* (agreement) with the apprentice in a register at the *Giustizia Vecchia*; sometimes this agreement could be preceded by a written contract (*cum carta*) made before a notary. The court's main task was to check whether the length of the agreement respected guild statutes; it could also change the salary and sometimes impose a tax on the agreement.[15]

Formally, guild statutes also had to be approved by the *Giustizia Vecchia*. Guild laws passed by the assembly of their members needed confirmation from the *Giustizieri* to obtain the force of state laws. Therefore, in disputes between artisans – including apprenticeships the *Giustizia Vecchia* was the relevant court.

In 1396, the *Giustizia Vecchia* passed a new law about the registration of apprenticeship contracts. The main difference from the earlier system was an explicit prohibition against using a notary for contracts. The reason given was that apprentices were being forced to sign less favourable contracts in front of a public notary or the *Capi di Sestiere*, the magistrates that supervised domestic service.[16] In 1444, the law became even stricter, with a fine of 100 *lire* for offenders. Masters were now obliged to hire only apprentices who were over a certain age (set by the guild) and to ensure they had adequate living and working conditions. Forty years later, the *Giustizieri* passed another law requiring the recording of both 'apprentices hired for a long time' (*garzoni ... accordati per lungo tempo*) and those hired yearly. At the end of the fifteenth century, Venetian craftsmen were required to register any apprentices hired for a period longer than one month.[17]

The surviving records of the *Giustizia Vecchia* cover the years 1575–1772, with some gaps.[18] The number of apprenticeship contracts exceeds

---

[15] State Archive of Venice (ASVe), *Compilazione Leggi* (*CL*), b. 49, 10 March 1396; Lazzarini, 'Antichi ordinamenti', 885.

[16] ASVe, *CL*, b. 49, 10 March 1396; Lazzarini, 'Antichi ordinamenti', 885–86.

[17] Lazzarini, 'Antichi ordinamenti', 889.

[18] ASVe, *Giustizia Vecchia* (*GV*), b. 112, r. 151 (1575–76), 152 (1582–83); b. 113, r. 153.1 (1583–84), 153.2 (1584–85), 154 (1591–92); b. 114, r. 155 (1592–93), 156 (1594–95); b. 115, r. 157 (1596–97), 158 (1597–98); b. 116, r. 159 (1598–99), 160 (1606–07); b. 117, r. 161 (1609–10), 162 (1620–21); b. 118, r. 163 (1621–22), 164 (1625–27); b. 119, r. 165 (1632–33), 166 (1642–44); b. 120, r. 167 (1644–46), 168 (1646–48); b. 121, r. 169 (1653–54), 170 (1656–58); b. 122, r. 171 (1658–60), 172 (1662–64); b. 123, r. 173 (1664–65), 174 (1669–71); b. 124, r. 175 (1681–82), 176 (1703–07), 177 (1707–10); b. 125, r. 178 (1710–13), 179 (1713–18), 180 (1724–36); b. 126, r. 181 (1736–51), 182 (1766–72).

53,000. The *Giustizia Vecchia* did not register journeymen, although some guilds kept their own registers. As mentioned, three of the most prominent guilds, the silk-weavers, the wool producers and the Murano glassmakers, were not included, nor was the most important state industry, the Arsenal. From 1586 to 1624 the population of Venice declined from 148,637 to 141,625.[19] Given that during the 1590s approximately one thousand contracts a year were recorded by the *Giustizia Vecchia*, apprentices in the guilds it covered represented less than 3.5% of the population.[20] This is just a rough approximation, but it indicates that apprenticeship was not as widespread as it was in London, for example. Instead, in Venice apprenticeship was, at least from an institutional point of view, strictly linked to the crafts and regulated by the guilds and the state. This contrast was noted in 1498 by the Venetian ambassador in London, who wrote that English parents did not love their children, because at the age of seven or eight they sent them as servants into someone else's house for seven or nine years, calling them *aprendizi*.[21]

Interestingly, the expression used in the *Giustizia Vecchia* registers is not contract (*contratto*), but *accordo*, literally 'agreement'. According to an eighteenth-century handbook of Venetian legislation, a contract is a 'pact made between two or more people, with which one of the parties or each of them is obliged to give or do something, or agrees to give or do something for a third party', while an agreement is a 'consensus ... between two parties, who are contending' and generally is an out-of-court settlement whose main purpose is to solve a conflict.[22]

According to the formula set out in the law, the contracting parties were the apprentice, most of the time underage, and the master. Contracts were, typically, brief, for example:[23]

Baldissera de Zuanantonio boatman, now about 8 y.o., registers to work as *depentor da casse* and to stay with messer Francesco de Philippo painter in San Biagio for eight years, starting from next 1 June and if he loses any day, he is

---

[19] D. Beltrami, *Storia della popolazione di Venezia dalla fine del secolo XVI alla caduta della Repubblica* (Padova: Cedam, 1954), 38.

[20] In 1592, 984 contracts were registered with an average length of five years. Other contracts have been recorded in a less systematic way by other magistrates or by notaries; research on these sources is still in progress.

[21] A. Bellavitis, 'Maestre e apprendiste a Venezia tra Cinque e Seicento', *Archivio Veneto* 3 (2012), 127–44

[22] M. Ferro, *Dizionario del diritto comune e veneto* (Venice: Andrea Santini, 1845–47).

[23] 'Baldissera de Zuanantonio Barcharol [al] presente de età de annj 8 jn circa se scrive a star et lavorare al arte de depentor da casse con messer Francesco Philippo pittor a San Biagio per anni otto principianti adi primo Zugno infrascritto et sel falara alcun zorno sii obligato reffar, qual patron si offrisse insegnarli l'arte sua, li da per suo salario ducati vintj a spese e vestir di Baldissera', ASVe, *GV*, b. 112, r. 151, 23 June 1575.

obliged to recover it, and the master will teach him his trade, and he gives him a salary of 20 ducats and the apprentice has to buy his clothes.

The name of a guarantor, usually the apprentice's father or widowed mother, was not always registered. The *accordo* established two sets of mutual obligations: the master committed to teach his trade and to provide adequate living conditions (and sometimes a salary); the apprentice committed to remain with and work for their master for the full term of the contract. Sometimes other obligations were also mentioned, such as providing clothing. From a legal perspective, these agreements were not exactly contracts in their own right, because contracts needed to be undertaken by adults, who were fully accountable for their acts, in the presence of witnesses.

Apprenticeship contracts had to respect the law as well as each guild's rules. Compared to many Italian cities, the statutes of Venetian guilds are quite detailed on apprenticeship. The majority of guild statutes were first established in the thirteenth or fourteenth centuries and were modified over time. In 1519, the Council of Ten instituted a special magistracy, the *Cinque Savi sopra le Mariegole*, tasked with revising all guild statutes 'for the good of our Venetians and of our city'.[24] The senate passed numerous laws, often at the request of individual guilds, to regulate apprenticeship in particular crafts.

The rules of the Venetian crafts were complex and changeable. They mainly concerned contract duration, apprentices' starting ages, the number of apprentices that masters could take, and exams for journeymen to become masters. For example, the silk and gold weavers set the minimum length of apprenticeship at four years, while the mirror makers required five years. The statutes of the glassmakers did not mention duration but set a minimum age for apprenticeship at 14 years. The statutes of the mirror makers specified two exams and 'masterpieces', one to become a journeyman and another for mastership, while the silk and gold weavers only examined new masters. The mattress-makers demanded apprenticeships of two years. The fustian makers expected six years, yet reduced this to two at the end of the sixteenth century.[25] The goldsmiths did not specify a length for apprenticeship, but required that seven years pass between starting one and taking the master's exam: after his apprenticeship, a young man could work in a goldsmith's shop before sitting the mastership exam.[26] At the beginning of the sixteenth century, the cap

---

[24] ASVe, *Provveditori di Comun*, b. 1, *Capitolare*, f. 235, 13 October 1519, in the Council of Ten.

[25] ASVe, *CL*, b. 50, 23 January 1512.

[26] E. Fiorucci, 'L'apprentissage dans les statuts des corps de métiers vénitiens', in: Bellavitis, Frank and Sapienza (eds.), *Garzoni*, 29–48.

makers required a new master to have served as an apprentice for four years and as a journeyman for two, to be older than 20, to pay taxes and entry fees, and to pass the exam.[27] In 1623 the dyers' guild forbade contracts with apprentices older than 18; the limit imposed by the brick-layers' guild was 20, and 25 in the boatmen's guild.[28]

The openness of Venetian guilds varied according to economic circum-stances. In the fifteenth and sixteenth centuries, some guilds, such as the silk weavers and wool weavers, excluded foreigners, or required them to attain Venetian citizenship to become members and, especially, officers of the guild. However, it seems that it was only the goldsmiths that always had different rules for Venetians and foreigners.[29] Guilds became increas-ingly closed to foreigners during the eighteenth century, as a consequence of the crisis of the Venetian economy. Laws passed at the start of the century were relatively permissive. For example, a 1719 law established that in guilds that 'have already been opened admitting subjects and foreigners', someone who had trained in another city, in the Venetian state or abroad, and who lacked the capital to open a workshop as a 'chief master', could just pay the admission tax for workers. However, by the 1760s, the focus had changed. A law in 1767 restricted access to appren-ticeship in many guilds. Apprentices in many food-retailing guilds, and also, ironically, in the German goldbeaters' guild, now had to be from the city of Venice. In other guilds, for example the shoemakers and the carpenters, apprentices had to be Venetian natives or subjects; guild officers now inspected apprentices' baptismal certificates.[30] Other regu-lations passed in 1767 and 1768 also tried to protect the Venetian labour force. The guilds were divided into three groups: guilds for those born in Venice; guilds for those born in Venice or the Venetian mainland; and guilds open to Venetians and foreigners.[31]

Venice's formal regulations on apprenticeship were not always fully enforced. According to a report by the *Inquisitorato alle Arti*, at the end of the eighteenth century more than 300 apprentices in 35 guilds were not registered; some had been with their master for more than three years.[32]

---

[27] ASVe, *CL*, b. 50, 16 July 1506.   [28] Lazzarini, 'Antichi ordinamenti'.

[29] A. Mozzato, *La mariegola dell'Arte della lana di Venezia, 1244–1595*, 2 vols (Venice: Il Comitato per la pubblicazione delle fonti relative alla storia di Venezia, 2000); S. Rauch, *Le mariegole delle arti dei tessitori di seta. I Veluderi (1347–1474) e i Samitari (1370–1475)* (Venice: Il Comitato per la pubblicazione delle fonti relative alla storia di Venezia, 2009); C. Perez, 'Apprentissage, transmission des connaissances et insertion professionnelle chez les orfèvres de Venise au XVIIe siècle', in: Bellavitis, Frank and Sapienza (eds.), *Garzoni*, 97–124.

[30] ASVe, *CL*, b. 59, f. 833, 19 April 1721; f. 1009, 12 September 1767.

[31] ASVe, *Inquisitori alle Arti (IA)*, b. 2, after 1771.

[32] ASVe, *IA*, b. 2, no date but end of the eighteenth century.

The degree to which apprenticeship rules were enforced is still debated; it is clear that several regulations were widely ignored, especially in the eighteenth century. Guilds monitored apprenticeship, yet they needed the support of the *Giustizia Vecchia* to enforce their regulations. The apprenticeship system became less and less effective during the last century of the Republic, as Venetian manufacturing, with a few exceptions, shrank, and new industries outside the guilds grew on the mainland.

Apprentices in Venice

We consider here a sample of apprenticeships registered at the *Giustizia Vecchia*. Our data set includes 5,962 contracts,[33] selected to represent specific trades from three periods: the late sixteenth century (2,474 contracts, from 1582 to 1598), which was a period of renewed prosperity and demographic growth after the 1576–77 plague; the early seventeenth century, when Venice was struck again by a major epidemic (1,099 contracts, from 1621 to 1633); and the middle of the seventeenth century (2,389 contracts, from 1640 to 1665, plus a few later contracts), when the decline of the Venetian economy had commenced; see Figure 4.1. Our sample covers trades in several sectors: luxury and fashion (jewellers, goldbeaters, tailors, shoemakers, mercers); art, architecture and furniture (painters, stonecutters, carpenters, glassmakers); and printing. Unfortunately, partly as a consequence of this selection, it contains only 11 female apprentices and 59 female masters: women were mostly apprenticed in textile trades.[34]

By including three periods in our sample, we can examine the stability of the terms of contracts. It has been suggested that during periods of crisis, even though many masters were unemployed, the number of apprentices did not collapse. Apprentices were instead used as an unskilled labour force and were rarely trained properly. As a consequence, during such periods, apprenticeship contracts were a means to control and exploit the workforce.[35]

---

[33] Our full sample includes 6,117 contracts, but we exclude contracts without a registration date (18) or which use foreign currency for payments, instead of Venetian ducats (137). The contracts are from: ASVe, *GV, Accordi dei Garzoni*, b. 112, r. 152; b. 113, r. 153–54; b. 114, r. 155–56; b. 115, r. 157–58; b. 118, r. 163–64; b. 119, r. 165–66; b. 120, r. 167–68; b. 121, r. 169–70; b. 123, r. 173.

[34] A. Bellavitis, 'Apprentissages masculins, apprentissages féminins à Venise au XVIe siècle', *Histoire Urbaine* 15 (2006), 49–73.

[35] R. T. Rapp, *Industry and Economic Decline in Seventeenth-Century Venice* (Cambridge, MA: Harvard University Press, 1976); L. Pezzolo, *Il fisco dei veneziani* (Verona: Cierre, 2003).

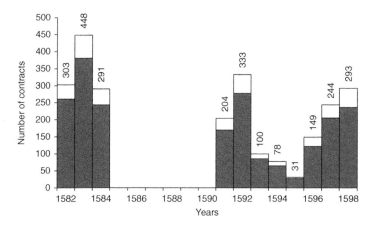

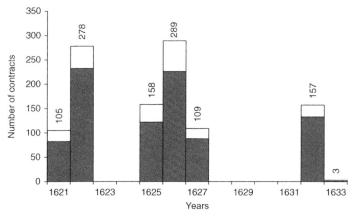

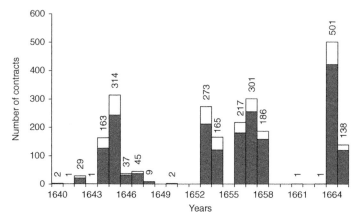

Figure 4.1 The distribution of apprenticeship contracts per year, for three periods (1582–98, 1621–33, 1640–65)

Note: The shaded section of each bar records contracts that included a salary for the apprentice; the unshaded sections are contracts without a salary. The total number of contracts is given above each bar.

To ease comparison, we have grouped the occupations in our sample into a hierarchy. An *activity sector* contains occupations which relate to the production or sale of similar goods or services and/or use similar materials. An *occupation* or trade is a recognised activity within a sector. A *specialisation* is an identifiable sub-group within an occupation. A guild in Venice usually contained the masters of a single occupation or specialisation, as in many textile guilds, but could sometimes cover more activity sectors. For example, the guild of printers and booksellers included all aspects of the production and distribution of books. It was organised in this way to sustain censorship as well as to control the market. Its registers usually state both the master's occupation and their apprentice's specialisation: a master printer might register apprentices in specific specialisations, for example as workers at the press. Occasionally contracts mention multiple specialisations, and for simplicity we have excluded these relatively rare cases in our analysis. The most important guilds and activity sectors in our sample are relatively stable across the sixteenth and seventeenth centuries, with two notable exceptions: printers virtually disappeared during the seventeenth century, while mirror making was a new occupation which quickly became the most common craft in our sample.

Who Became an Apprentice?

Several cities in the Venetian dominions, such as Padua, Vicenza, Verona, Bergamo and Brescia, possessed thriving economies with their own guilds and apprenticeship systems. Yet Venice was always in need of workers, even if this also depended on economic circumstances. The crisis of the seventeenth century may have reduced the importance of the capital compared to the mainland.[36]

Signs of this change are apparent in the increase from 34% to 44% in the share of Venetians among the city's apprentices (Table 4.1), even though the city encouraged foreign immigration after the plague of 1630–31. Nonetheless, Venetians never exceeded half of registered apprentices, showing how important immigration continued to be for the city. Figure 4.2a illustrates the origins of Venetian apprentices at the European level. Despite Venice attracting new apprentices from Spain, German Europe, France and Italy, the bulk came from Venice's own mainland. In general, all the main areas of the Venetian mainland were well represented:

---

[36] P. Lanaro, 'Corporations et confréries: Les étrangers et le marché du travail à Venise (XVᵉ–XVIIIᵉ siècles)', *Histoire Urbaine* 21 (2008), 32.

Table 4.1 *The characteristics of new apprentices in Venice, 1582–1665*

	1582–98	1621–33	1640–65	All
Age (years)	14.4	14.7	14.4	14.4
Term (years)	5.2	5.1	5.0	5.1
Male (%)	99.6	100.0	99.9	99.8
Female guarantor (%)	6.8	4.9	3.3	5.1
Father deceased (%)	38.2	42.9	31.4	36.3
Geographical origins (%):				
Venice	34.6	44.7	44.9	40.6
Venetians (father deceased)	35.1	34.8	28.3	32
Foreign (father deceased)	39.8	49.3	34.0	39.3
Share of contracts giving master responsibility for:				
Accommodation	72.6	70.9	80.1	75.3
Personal care	72.5	67.8	67.6	69.7
Expenses	72.3	71.8	80.1	75.5
Clothes	20.4	12.0	15.4	16.9
N	2,474	1,099	2,389	5,962

Source: see text.

Bergamo, Brescia, Verona, Vicenza and Padua, Treviso, the Bellunese area and Friuli. Also noteworthy are the Grisons and Milan.

The pattern of migration into apprenticeships in Venice changed between the late sixteenth and mid-seventeenth centuries, as can be seen in Figures 4.2b–d. In the late sixteenth century, Venice was still the main hub of the state, a position it gradually lost during the seventeenth century. The importance of Venice had dropped sharply by the 1620s and 1630s. By the 1640s to 1660s, Venice was attracting immigrants from nearby surrounding cities and countryside, and from the more underdeveloped areas of its territory, such as the Friuli, rather than the metropolitan centres in the western parts of the mainland.

Previous studies show that apprenticeships in Venice on average started at around age 14. The majority of contracts lasted 4–6 years, meaning apprentices finished their contract at around 18–20 years old. There were some, exceptional, younger apprentices, but few older ones, whose occasional presence can be explained by the need to meet the minimum requirements for mastership.[37] Our data supports these

---

[37] Lazzarini, 'Antichi ordinamenti', 877–78.

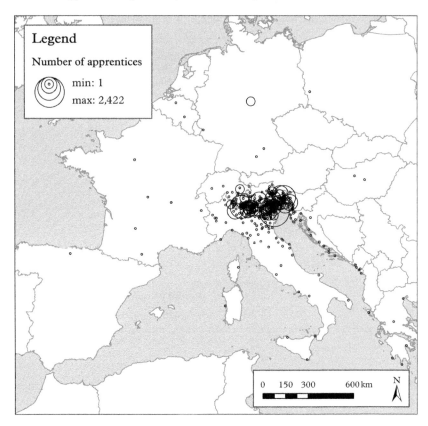

Figure 4.2a The origins of Venetian apprentices, 1582–1665
(GIStorical Antwerp)
Note: The size of the circles is proportional to the logarithm of the
number of apprentices from that place.

previous findings. Both the age of apprentices and the length of their contracts were stable over time, and normally distributed. In general, apprentices' age affected the length of their contract. Older apprentices tended to
have shorter contracts and younger apprentices had longer contracts.[38] For
example, the 1,884 apprentices who were over 15 years old entered contracts
that on average lasted for four years; the 240 apprentices who were over 25
years old had just over three years on average; while the 1,574 apprentices
below 13 years old were apprenticed for six years, on average.

Although apprenticeships for older apprentices were usually shorter,
they were not below the minimum duration set by guild rules. In general,

[38] Bellavitis, 'Apprentissages masculins, apprentissages féminins'.

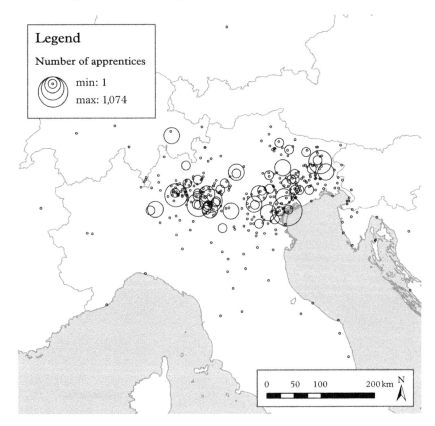

Figure 4.2b The origins of Venetian apprentices, 1582–98
(GIStorical Antwerp)
Note: The size of the circles is proportional to the logarithm of the
number of apprentices from that place.

most contracts were designed to finish when the apprentice was around
19. However, a considerable number of contracts did not meet the guilds'
minimum terms. While perhaps not surprising in itself, as internal regulations could easily be overlooked, this disregard for guild requirements
indicates that not all apprenticeships were expected to lead to becoming a
journeyman or master.

Masters in different occupations had specific preferences for apprentices who shared certain common characteristics, or *occupational profiles*,
including their age at entry.[39] This preference was stable over time. Some

[39] G. Colavizza, 'A view on Venetian apprenticeship from the *Garzoni* database', in:
Bellavitis, Frank and Sapienza (eds.), *Garzoni*, 235–60.

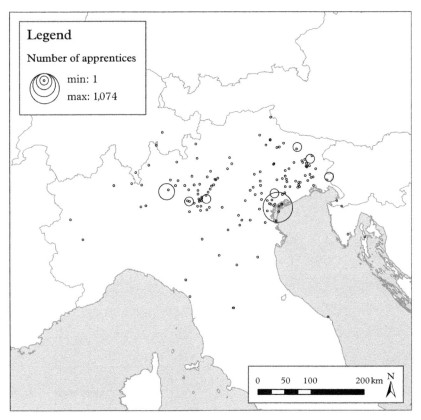

Figure 4.2c The origins of Venetian apprentices, 1621–33
(GIStorical Antwerp)
Note: The size of the circles is proportional to the logarithm of the
number of apprentices from that place.

occupations recruited older apprentices, for example mirror makers or
press workers in a print shop, while others usually recruited younger
apprentices, such as goldsmiths or stonecutters. It is difficult at this
stage to explain this, as these occupations had no obvious commonalities
in terms of the strength required, the geographical origins of the apprentices or the degrees of specialisation involved.

Apprenticeship was also part of the system for welfare and poor relief. A
substantial proportion of apprentices had deceased fathers, as Table 4.1
shows, although it is difficult to know if the share was higher than in the
wider population, particularly at times of plague. The drop in the proportion
of orphans during the mid-seventeenth century might be due to the recovery
through immigration after the plague.

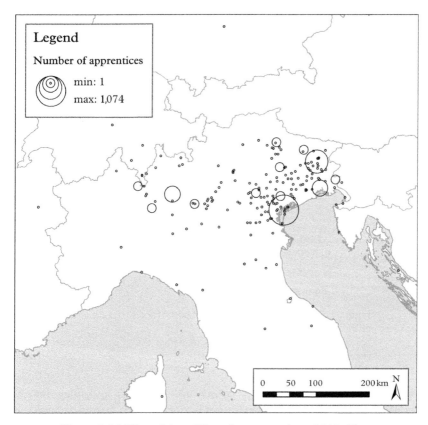

Figure 4.2d The origins of Venetian apprentices, 1640–65
(GIStorical Antwerp)
Note: The size of the circles is proportional to the logarithm of the
number of apprentices from that place. Longitude and latitude
coordinates have been approximated to second digit precision.
Source: see text.

Our data only contains a very limited number of female apprentices.
However, the powerful way gender affected apprenticeship has been
recently explored through a random sample of 1,000 contracts from the
end of the sixteenth century. Only 7% of apprentices were girls, mostly in
textile crafts, retail and domestic service. The length of their contracts was
extremely variable: apprenticeships in wool weaving could last from two
to seven years; in silk weaving from six to eight; in sewing from two to
eight. In some cases, these differences depended on the age of the
apprentice, but this was not always so. While boys were mostly apprenticed at the age of 14, girls started at a wider range of ages. Some, mostly

Figure 4.3 Histograms of the age of entry (a) and length of contracts (b) in Venice
Note: We exclude 246 contracts in which the apprentice was over 24 years old.

in knitting or sewing, were very young, only 4–6 years old; they did not lodge with their masters or mistresses but returned home every night. A wage was usually paid at the end of these contracts, mostly in money, but sometimes in goods.[40]

A crucial issue for our understanding of apprenticeships is the rate of completion. The practice of switching masters or interrupting a contract and registering a new one at a subsequent time seems to have been relatively uncommon in Venice.[41] When a contract was terminated with the mutual consent of both parties, the master and the apprentice asked the *Giustizia Vecchia* to cancel the agreement in the register, and cancellation entries usually concluded with the statement 'they declare themselves satisfied and pleased'. The proportion of contracts that ended by mutual agreement has been estimated at under 10%.[42] Similarly, the

---

[40] Bellavitis, 'Apprentissages masculins, apprentissages féminins'; Bellavitis, 'Maestre e apprendiste a Venezia'.

[41] Colavizza, 'A view on Venetian apprenticeship'.

[42] R. MacKenney, 'The guilds of Venice: State and society in the longue durée', *Studi Veneziani* 34 (1997), 37–38.

Table 4.2 *The proportion of early terminations because the apprentice ran away, Venice 1585–1665*

	1582–98	1621–33	1640–65	All
Apprentice (%)	14.0	12.6	7.0	10.8
Venetians (%)	12.6	8.0	5.2	8.4
Foreigners (%)	14.8	16.4	7.9	12.5

Source: see text.

number that ended by a court decision was likely negligible due to the costs involved.

In Table 4.2, we report the proportions of apprentices who were declared to have run away in the registers of the *Giustizia Vecchia*. We distinguish between Venetian and foreign apprentices. On this evidence, only a small proportion of apprentices, around 11%, ran away. The share decreased over time among both Venetians and foreigners, although locals were consistently less likely to run away. Possibly, some foreign apprentices went to Venice for training and then returned to their homeland to work, giving them little interest in official recognition by the city's guilds.

These figures are based on the registers of the *Giustizia Vecchia*, where an interruption of any kind could be recorded in the margins beside a contract. Interruptions were likely to be systematically recorded only when the apprentice was declared as a 'runaway': this kind of evidence was the only proof a master could offer to support his wish to register a new apprentice, and at the same time respect guild caps on apprentice numbers.

Paying for Opportunity

One important aspect of apprenticeship in Venice was the degree of freedom to negotiate payments between parties. Compensation was given to either the apprentice or the master (no contract mentions both receiving payments), during or upon completion of the apprenticeship. There is no evidence that premiums were paid in advance to the master, although this practice existed in several other Italian cities. Colavizza suggests that, as a result, apprenticeship in Venice followed a *double-track* system.[43] On the one hand, large numbers of contracts stated that the apprentice would receive a regular wage or end-of-term payment. In

[43] Colavizza, 'A view on Venetian apprenticeship'.

Table 4.3 *The distribution and size of payments in apprenticeship contracts,*
Venice 1582–1665

	1582–98	1621–33	1640–65	All
Master to apprentice	2,074 (84%)	884 (80%)	1,935 (81%)	4,893 (82%)
At end of contract (% relative to row above)	1,867 (91%)	771 (87%)	1,755 (92%)	4,393 (90%)
Average amount	4.4 (3.3)	5.1 (4)	5.9 (5)	5.1 (4)
Regular wage	83 (4%)	94 (11%)	143 (7%)	320 (7%)
Average amount	13 (6)	8 (6)	9.7 (6)	10 (6)
Incremental wage	105 (5%)	17 (2%)	17 (1%)	139 (3%)
Average amount	7.8 (6)	6.1 (6)	10.9 (8)	8 (6.3)
No payment	333 (13%)	169 (15%)	371 (15%)	873 (15%)
Apprentice to master	67 (3%)	46 (4%)	83 (3%)	196 (3%)
Average amount	15 (10)	17.7 (14.5)	21.5 (20)	18.4 (15)

Note: Payments are normalised by the duration of the contract and given as amounts per year in ducats. The average size of payments is presented as the arithmetic mean with the median in parentheses.

these, the amount of (skilled and unskilled) work required of the apprentice likely surpassed the time spent on training. This was a *slow track* into the occupation, in which apprentices accepted less intense training and extra work in exchange for higher wages. On the other hand, another, smaller group of contracts included no wage or payoff for the apprentice, or even required payments to the master during or after the apprenticeship. These contracts emphasised training, and perhaps the apprentice's good positioning to later enter the craft, offering a *fast track* into the occupation.

The most common practice in Venice was for an apprentice to be rewarded at the end of their contract, usually with a sum of money, or goods of an equivalent value. Most end-of-term payments were relatively small, but not negligible. As Table 4.3 shows, 74% of apprentices in our sample received an end-of-term payment. On average, they received 5 Venetian ducats for each year they served: 25 ducats in total, given the average length of contracts of five years. As in Florence, these were almost token payments, if compared to the wages received by other workers. Yet most apprentices also received food and shelter.[44] The size of end-of-term

[44] For comparison, see A. Zannini, 'L'economia veneta nel Seicento: Oltre il paradigma della "crisi generale"', in: Società Italiana di Demografia Storica (ed.), *La popolazione*

payments was relatively stable over time, even if perceptible differences existed that depended on the craft, the apprentice's age and the length of the contract. These final payments provided both an incentive to complete the contract, and compensation for the work supplied by the apprentice.

Three other regimes can be distinguished. Sixteen per cent of apprentices received no payment of any kind, and nor did their masters. This type of agreement became increasingly common over time. The other two regimes are more distinctive, representing two extremes: in one, apprentices received a regular wage, with contracts that equated to regular employment (very slow track); in the other, a payment was given to the master (fastest track).

In the first case, apprentices' average wages were substantially higher than most end-of-term payments. Wages which rose over time – usually increases occurred every one or two years – were common during the late sixteenth century but were later mostly replaced with fixed wages. We consider these later payments to be akin to salaries because, despite being lower than the wages paid to living-in journeymen, they were paid in yearly, half-yearly, monthly or sometimes even weekly instalments, and the lack of an increase over time implied that the apprentice was not being compensated for their improved capacity due to training. Regular wages of this kind could perhaps also be the result of unregistered, pre-contract training, occurring during the period of assessment of the apprentice prior to formal registration. This might have led to a better deal being given to apprentices who were in fact already partly trained.

In the second case, when payments were made to the master, it is striking that the amounts paid were substantially higher, on average 16 ducats for each year. These payments were made by the apprentice's parents or close relatives. Several times, contracts specify that the payment was a contribution to the cost of lodging and training the apprentice; at times, they even detail how the training was to unfold. For example, Colavizza discusses an apprentice apothecary whose family paid decreasing amounts of money to his master to guarantee his training, and who was to be sent to school to learn how to read and write during his first year.[45]

The distribution of payments, given in Figure 4.4, highlights the variety of tracks taken by Venetian apprentices. Negative payments are sums given by the master to the apprentice; positive are payments from

---

italiana nel Seicento: Atti del convegno di studi, Firenze, 28–30 novembre 1996 (Bologna: Clueb, 1996), 473–502.

[45] Colavizza, 'A view on Venetian apprenticeship'.

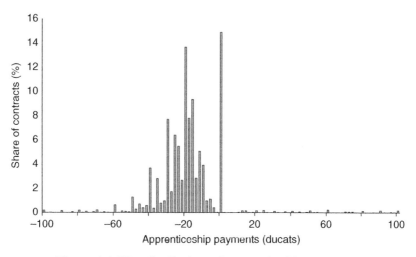

Figure 4.4 The distribution of apprenticeship payments, from the master's perspective, Venice 1585–1665
Note: The plot is trimmed at plus and minus 100 ducats.

apprentices to their master. The long tails visible on both sides reflect the very slow and fast tracks, while the bulk of contracts involved a small payment or no payment being given to the apprentice.

Payments between masters and apprentices have to be considered alongside the other elements of apprenticeship. These included accommodation, clothes and other expenses, and care provided to the apprentice, as in the case of illness. A small number of contracts also involved securities, given in kind or money to the master. Masters were usually expected to house and feed their apprentices, who typically lived with them, and supply other basic needs. Apprentices mostly provided their own clothes (see Table 4.1). More complex arrangements do appear, for example when special and costly tools were needed, but were uncommon.

The impact of other contextual factors on the size and direction of payments is clear from our data. Younger apprentices were less likely to receive a payment, implying they were less useful, or needed less incentive and perhaps more training: whereas 88% of apprentices aged over 15 received a payment, only 78% of apprentices under 13 did. The shorter contracts entered into by older apprentices were also associated with higher wages, further hinting at the use of apprentices as workers. Both trends are visible in Figure 4.5. Furthermore, conditions differed between Venetians and foreigners. Table 4.4 reports the proportion of each group whose contracts involved a payment to the apprentice. This was lower

Table 4.4 *The share of apprentices receiving payments from their masters, by origin, Venice 1585–1665*

	1582–98	1621–33	1640–65	All
All (%)	83.8	80.4	81.0	82.0
Venetians (%)	79.6	79.2	77.2	78.5
Foreigners (%)	86.0	81.4	84.1	84.5

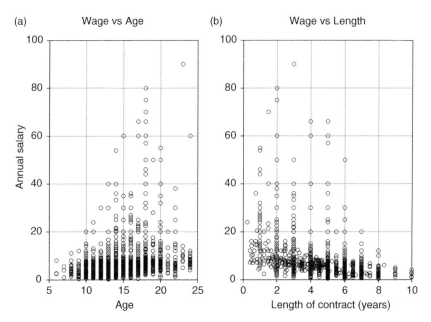

Figure 4.5 The relationship of apprentice wages to their age of entry (a) and length of contract (b), Venice 1585–1665
Note: The figures only include wages paid to apprentices. We exclude apprentices older than 24 years to reduce the effect of older, trained workers using apprenticeship contracts to circumvent guild rules.

among Venetian apprentices, which may reflect their preferential access to guild occupations, or their lower propensity to run away, which reduced the need for masters to provide them with an incentive to finish their term. Differences are also visible between apprentices who had lost their fathers and those who had not. Only 45% of orphans received a payment, compared to 55% of non-orphans, suggesting they had less bargaining power. The lower wages received by apprentices whose guarantor was female is a further indicator of this effect.

Various trade-offs emerge as partial explanations for the mechanics of the contracts of apprenticeship in Venice: (a) higher wages to the apprentice likely signify less intense training, while payments to the master reflect more intense training; (b) shorter contracts, especially below guild regulations, entailed higher wages as compensation; (c) younger apprentices received lower wages, probably because they were less fit and lacked previous training; (d) less-well-represented apprentices received lower wages (father deceased, woman as guarantor); (e) apprentices who were less likely to quit received lower wages; (f) other contractual conditions could impact on wages, for example wages fell if the apprentice lodged with their master.

Points (a) and (b) are particularly relevant for the double-track system, and the possible use of apprenticeships to secure workers, or anyway balance work and training intensity. The rest are part of a relatively standard model of apprenticeship.[46] We provide the results of an ordinary least squares regression in Table 4.5, where the average annual wage is regressed upon a set of predictor variables, including a control on the master's guild modelled as fixed effect. Both models (with and without outliers) provide similar results. This analysis only considers payments to the apprentice, thus point (a) can only be discussed indirectly. That said, the results support the trade-offs just discussed. The length of the contract was negatively correlated and the age of the apprentice was positively correlated to the wage: older apprentices serving shorter contracts, a correlation previously observed by Hamilton in Montreal,[47] were also paid more in Venice, implying that their main interest lay in the wage. Contract length had a greater effect than the apprentice's age in this respect. Wages were also lower when apprentices received accommodation and expenses from their master. In some cases, when regular salaries were paid, the wage was higher: these contracts may represent a rare win–win situation where initial training and subsequent compensation were given in order to retain the skilled apprentice until completion. Incremental salaries do show a minor effect, further balanced by their rarity (see Table 4.3). We cannot see conclusively that less-well-represented apprentices were discriminated against, at least with respect to

---

[46] C. Minns and P. Wallis, 'The price of human capital in a pre-industrial economy: Premiums and apprenticeship contracts in 18th-century England', *Explorations in Economic History* 50 (2013), 335–50.

[47] G. Hamilton, 'The market for Montreal apprentices: Contract length and information', *Explorations in Economic History* 33 (1996), 496–523.

Table 4.5 *OLS regressions on the determinants of the payments given to Venetian apprentices*

	Dependent variable	
	Average annual wage	
	(1)	(2)
Venetian (yes = 1)	−0.004	0.015
	(0.017)	(0.014)
Year	0.004***	0.003***
	(0.0002)	(0.0002)
Length of contract	−0.193***	−0.118***
	(0.005)	(0.005)
Age of apprentice	0.027***	0.023***
	(0.003)	(0.003)
Orphan by father (yes = 1)	0.003	0.011
	(0.016)	(0.014)
Apprentice fled (yes = 1)	0.003	0.012
	(0.019)	(0.016)
Accommodation (paid by master = 1)	−0.203***	−0.269***
	(0.047)	(0.040)
Personal care (paid by master = 1)	−0.043	0.023
	(0.029)	(0.024)
Clothes (paid by master = 1)	−0.014	−0.014
	(0.017)	(0.014)
Generic expenses (paid by master = 1)	−0.122***	−0.141***
	(0.042)	(0.036)
Female guarantor (present = 1)	−0.023	0.006
	(0.030)	(0.024)
Gender of apprentice (male = 1)	0.060	−0.019
	(0.126)	(0.104)
Gender of master (male = 1)	0.013	0.029
	(0.067)	(0.059)
Periodisation of salary (one final instalment = 1)	−0.335***	−0.147***
	(0.026)	(0.024)
Incremental salary (yes = 1)	−0.087*	−0.019
	(0.048)	(0.042)
Venetian orphan by father (yes = 1)	0.018	0.006
	(0.026)	(0.022)

Table 4.5 (*cont.*)

	Dependent variable	
	Average annual wage	
	(1)	(2)
Observations	4,533	4,010
R^2	0.527	0.511
Adjusted R^2	0.521	0.504
Residual std error	0.406 (df = 4475)	0.319 (df = 3952)

*p<0.1; **p<0.05; ***p<0.01

Note: The dependent variable is the total payment to the apprentice divided by contract duration. The model includes a control for guilds as fixed effects, see the text for details. Robust standard errors are given in parentheses; * = significant at the 1% level; ** = significant at the 5% level; *** = significant at the 1% level. Model 1 includes all data; model 2 has outliers trimmed. Outliers were detected using Cook's distance. This excluded all contracts with an annual salary above 10 ducats per annum; apprentices below 5 or over 20 years old; contracts below 1 and above 10 years long. Model 2 passed all standard diagnostics for OLS. In model 1 both the dependent average annual salary and the length of contracts are skewed. We maintained the original values for comparison with model 2, where transformations are not warranted (by Box-Tidwell tests).

orphans. Female apprentices and guarantors were so rare that any result in this respect is essentially inconclusive. Venetians were neither disadvantaged nor favoured if they received a wage or payment, yet we know they were less likely to be in this category in the first place (see Table 4.4). There existed a correlation between some guilds and the chance for the apprentice to be paid, and the amount of the wage. In particular, in a set of mostly luxury professions (drawers, painters, diamond cutters and jewellers, carvers, miniaturists, gilders, goldsmiths and turners), masters usually paid lower than average salaries, while in other professions (especially carpenters, colours and wax makers, bricklayers, stonecutters, glassmakers and sand dealers) there was both a higher chance of getting a payment,[48] and a higher one at that. It is worth noting that the former group of guilds showed a higher than average proportion of Venetians taken as apprentices, despite the general lack of influence of the apprentice's origins on the wage.

---

[48] This results from a probit model considering contracts with a wage to apprentices or not, which we omit for brevity. The model can be found in the accompanying code (https://doi.org/10.5281/zenodo.2652855).

In conclusion, Venetian apprenticeships mostly followed guild regulations and fitted well with standard models of apprenticeship in terms of the trade-off between the youth's need for training and the master's need for compensation for the risks and effort involved. There were exceptions. Masters sometimes used apprenticeships to hire skilled or semi-skilled workers, in order to secure a cheap workforce in times of need. On the other hand, some apprentices were able to pay for speedier training and privileged conditions.

Case Studies: Goldsmiths, Carpenters and Printers

In order to delve deeper into the practical use of apprenticeship, we now compare five trades, spanning three activity sectors and their respective guilds: goldsmiths, a luxury, high-value trade; carpenters, both general carpenters and furniture builders; and printers, including typesetters and press workers. The characteristics of apprentices in these three sectors can be found in Table 4.6.

These trades were among the largest in the sample. Mirror makers and mercers, two other guilds with numerous apprentices, were not considered because of the former's relative novelty and growth during this period, and the overly varied composition of the latter. Moreover, the three trades each had different markets, systems of production, amounts of training and capital, and workshop organisation. Carpenters produced a variety of goods of both high and low value and assisted in other manufacturing activities as well. Goldsmiths specialised in luxury objects, such as jewellery, where the market was smaller, but valuable, and workers' skills were likely higher. Lastly, print shops produced very specific goods through a well-defined division of labour between typesetters and press workers (plus more episodic activities such as proof reading).

Goldsmiths

The guild of goldsmiths was established in 1233. According to their statutes, in order to become a full member, an artisan from Venice had to work for a master for seven years and pay a fee of 3 ducats, while artisans from the mainland and foreigners paid 15 ducats.[49]

Apprentices were 13 on average when they started, younger than the norm, and served five years, around the median for the city. Combined with the period spent afterwards as journeymen, youths normally met the guild's regulations. An unusually high proportion of contracts were

---

[49] Biblioteca del Museo Correr, *Manoscritti, Classe IV*, n. 139.

Table 4.6 The characteristics of Venetian apprentice carpenters (C), goldsmiths (G) and printing-press workers (P)

Period	1582–98			1621–33			1640–65			All		
Sector	C	G	P	C	G	P	C	G	P	C	G	P
Age (years)	14.6	13.6	15	15	13.2	12.6	14.2	13.6	13	14.5	13.5	14.5
Term (years)	6	5	5	6	5	6	6	5	5	6	5	5
(range)	(1–8)	(1–9)	(1–10)	(2–8)	(1–8)	(3–8)	(1–8)	(1–10)	(2–7)	(1–8)	(1–10)	(1–10)
Male (%)	100	100	99.1	100	100	100	100	100	97	100	100	98.9
Female guarantor (%)	3.5	8	2.3	5	7	15	1	5	6	2.7	7	3.4
Father deceased (%)	43	24	44	53	25	0	30	27	41	39	25	41
Venetians (%)	20	58	22	24	81	46	32	81	68	26	73	29
Contract terms												
Payment from master	96	66	98	88	77	77	91	66	91	93	69	96
Amount paid (A/M)	3.4/3	6/2.6	4.8/4	3.2/3	4/3	3.7/3	4/3.3	7.4/4	5.7/5	3.6/3	6/3	4.9/4
Venetians, payment from master (%)	94	69	100	90	81	83	92	69	87	92	73	95
Payment to master (%)	0.3	8.5	0	0.8	6.3	15	0.6	7	0	0.5	7.4	0.8
No payment (%)	3.2	25	2	11	16	8	8.1	27	9	6.5	24	3
Outcome												
Ran away (%)	19	7	18	17	5	15	9	2	15	15	4	17
N	311	224	214	119	159	13	307	255	34	736	634	261

Note: Payments are mean ducats per year of contract. Legend: A/M = mean/median.

without payments to the apprentice (31%), and relatively few apprentices had lost their fathers (25%). Furthermore, Venice supplied an overwhelming majority of apprentices: 73% on average, increasing to 81% by the 1640s to 1660s. Probably as a consequence of this, relatively few runaways were recorded. If quitting reflected a disregard for a working future in the city, then this also suggests that the goldsmiths' guild was relatively closed, with a higher barrier to foreigners. As such, the high proportion of 'fast track' contracts, without any payment to the apprentice, may have been motivated either by the desire to guarantee training or simply the reduced need to incentivise completion.

Carpenters

The guild of carpenters was founded in the fourteenth century.[50] The guild included four groups (*colonelli*) by the sixteenth century, defined by their products (furniture, frames, building, etc.). The contracts, however, reference several different specialisations. The two we consider here, generic 'carpenters' and furniture makers, a more focused specialisation, were numerous. After a minimum five-year training period, an apprentice could become a *lavorante* ('worker', or journeyman) by enrolling in the guild within six months; there was no exam. An exception was provided for the sons of masters, who simply had to register themselves as masters and pay an entry fee once they reached the age of 18. Most *lavoranti* specialised as generic carpenters, for which the mastership exam was likely easier; once they passed, they could use any specialisation within the craft. Perhaps the most dangerous consequence was that some masters reached only low skill levels.[51] The exam required the construction of a square and a round door and a framework. The relative high share of apprentices who ran away (15%) was linked to one of the major problems for the guild: these unfinished ex-apprentices worked for other masters in an informal labour market outside guild control. Similarly, in the eighteenth century, according to the *Inquisitori alle Arti*,[52] many apprentices quit after two years of training; this suggests that the time needed to acquire the basic skills of the craft was shorter than the period required by the guild and the continued importance of the parallel 'black' labour market and opportunities outside Venice for youths.

The variety of specialisations pursued by apprentices in carpentry increased over time. During the last period, among 167 apprentices, 49

---

[50] Biblioteca del Museo Correr, *Manoscritti, Classe IV*, n. 152.
[51] G. Caniato and M. Dal Borgo, *Le arti edili a Venezia* (Rome: Edilstampa, 1990).
[52] ASVe, *IA*, b. 58, Scrittura 3, September 1752 and Scrittura 5, May 1753.

specialised in mirror frames, 37 in veneering, 28 in wooden chests, 10 in walnut-wood furniture, and 7 in construction, as well as a few other specialisations. General 'carpenters' accounted for only half of contracts, compared to nearly four-fifths during the late sixteenth century. Apprentices in carpentry were slightly older (14.5 years) than the overall average, and usually served longer terms than the guild required. Most masters offered a modest payment to their apprentice on completion. One apprentice in four was from Venice, and there was no obvious difference between the treatment of locals and foreigners. The proportion of locals varied between specialisations, but contractual terms were similar. Finally, the ratio of apprentices recorded as running away was just above average (15%).

In the carpenters' guild, apprentices possibly had a greater importance as a source of skilled and unskilled labour. The wage or final payment offered to the apprentice in the large majority of contracts suggests the need for an incentive to encourage completion and implies that youths contributed significantly to the productivity of workshops while they were training.

Printers

The guild of booksellers and printers, the *Università de librai e stampatori*, was officially established by the Council of Ten in 1548–49, as part of an effort to control the sector through censorship and workshop regulation. In 1572, the guild revised its admission procedures, requiring new masters to serve a five-year apprenticeship, properly registered at the *Giustizia Vecchia*, followed by three years as a journeyman: 'he shall then be examined by experts named by the prior and officers of the guild, and, if found able, he shall, on the payment of 5 ducats, receive matriculation'. Foreigners needed to work for five years in the city before taking the exam; their fee was 10 ducats. Sons of masters paid nothing.[53] No further regulations were introduced until the later eighteenth century, when several attempts at reform and regulation occurred. For example, in 1767, the *Riformatori allo Studio di Padova*, responsible for regulating the sector, imposed a limit of one apprentice per master and banned any workshop from taking new apprentices for the next 15 years, in an attempt to recover the long-gone quality in the activity.

Printers' apprentices fell into one of three groups: press workers (*torcoleri*), typesetters (*compositori*) and general printers (*stampatori*). In general,

---

[53] H. F. Brown, *The Venetian Printing Press* (London: J. C. Nimmo, 1891), 88.

they were slightly older (14.5 years) than average, entered contracts of around five years, as specified by guild regulations, and nearly all (96%) received a wage or final payment from their master – above the sample average. Both the share with deceased fathers, and the share who absconded were around average. The distribution of locals across the three specialisations was uneven: press workers included few from the city (14%), typesetters fell in the middle (25%), while most general printers were Venetians (55%). The explanation for this is uncertain. However, we do know that the press workers incorporated two specialisations: the *battitore* inked and changed sheets, and the *tiratore* operated the press. Their work was repetitive and fatiguing. The two roles required different levels of skill, and *tiratori* were usually paid more than *battitori*, sometimes even more than typesetters.[54] In our sample *tiratori* were on average older, served shorter contracts and were paid more; typesetters were younger and had longer contracts and less pay; while generic *stampatori* fell in the middle. It is not clear whether the *torcoleri* apprentices registered in the *Giustizia Vecchia* included both *battitori* and *tiratori*: it is possible, though, that some apprentices to the better paid *tiratori* specialisation were following a slow track, which would explain their contractual terms and fit with their origins abroad.

In sum, we find many similarities and few specificities between apprenticeship in these three trades. Apprenticeship contracts generally remained within the bounds of guild regulations, with most contracts lasting long enough to qualify the youth for entry to the guild. However, some specific guild and trade characteristics do emerge. Goldsmiths stand out as a strongly local, Venetian guild, with a larger share of apprentices who did not need the incentive provided by a payment to complete their contracts, and who were more likely to follow a fast track. By contrast, carpenters and printing-press workers provided a basic payment to the large majority of apprentices, and very rarely used fast-track contracts. Compositors and workers at the press further highlight how even within the same guild different trades adapted contracts to match the profile of the apprentices they needed.

Conclusions

Apprenticeship in Venice was only one of the ways in which vocational training could be provided. Hospitals and charitable institutions offered opportunities for training to orphans or poor children. At the same time,

---

[54] B. Richardson, *Stampatori, autori e lettori nell'Italia del Rinascimento* (Milan: Sylvestre Bonnard, 2004), 34–35.

official apprenticeship rarely accounted for training within the family: from father to son, mother to daughter or husband to wife. These alternative paths to training remain obscure due to the lack of formal records. In other cases, often oral or notarial apprenticeship contracts were simply never registered officially, as witnessed by the frequent, futile reminders of masters' obligations issued by the authorities. Nevertheless, both the state and the guilds put much effort into regulating apprenticeship. Both were interested in apprenticeship for a variety of reasons, including responding to the specific needs of a craft, assuring the reproduction of a skilled workforce while limiting exploitation during training, and regulating the city's labour markets, whether by opening them to foreigners after major epidemics or closing them during periods of economic crisis. As the cases of goldsmiths, carpenters and printers show, trades attracted different types of apprentices, varied the incentives they provided and differed in their openness to foreign workers. For example, goldsmiths hired a substantially higher proportion of Venetians and in general paid lower wages, while printers adjusted their preferences and contractual conditions to different tasks (printing-press worker or compositor). The provenance of apprentices also changed over time, as Venice's role in its subject territories shifted and the city drew immigrants from an increasingly smaller area on the mainland.

Apprenticeship in early modern Venice possessed some strong common features, in terms of the age of entry (14 years), the length of contracts (five years) and the adjustments used to accommodate a variety of situations, especially the payments to masters or apprentices. Most contracts entailed a payment to the apprentice from the master (82%), which depended on the apprentice's trade and age, the contract's length and the form of the payment. Importantly, contracts for locals and foreigners specified similarly sized payments to apprentices when these were included in the agreement, and the proportion of contracts including a payment did not differ significantly. Nevertheless, payments from apprentices and their families to masters were more common among local apprentices.

Our data therefore suggests the possible existence of a double-track system of apprenticeship in Venice, reflecting different balances between training and working. At one end, the amount of work expected from an apprentice receiving an end-of-term payment or wage, even if it was still inferior to that of a journeyman, was likely greater, and their training less intense, than that expected from an apprentice who received no payment or who paid their master. Such a system, largely identified in previous studies during periods of economic crisis, may have been a regular feature of apprenticeship in Venice. Indeed, despite its changes and adaptations, the main feature of Venetian apprenticeship was its high degree of flexibility, to be sure a characteristic that is shared by other cities in the Italian peninsula.

Data and Code Availability

All the data and code supporting this chapter are openly available: https://doi.org/10.5281/zenodo.2652855.

5   Actors and Practices of German Apprenticeship, Fifteenth–Nineteenth Centuries

Georg Stöger and Reinhold Reith

During the early modern period the craft system in the German-speaking territories[1] was shaped by institutions, especially guilds that could operate with a degree of self-government, by formalised rules and by a differentiation between apprentices, journeymen and masters.[2] Pre-modern crafts have been a subject of historiographical research since the second half of the nineteenth century; a large number of studies have dealt with various aspects of the crafts and the guild system. Traditionally, research on the pre-modern period focused on legislative sources, or on specific crafts in local settings. During the 1980s, the engagement of social historians in this field led to a broader perspective: serial sources, court proceedings and ego-documents were (re)considered, as well as such topics as migration, conflicts or the everyday life of specific social groups (especially journeymen). However, since this revival, fewer studies have continued in this direction, and those that did mostly still focus on specific crafts, or particular towns or regions. Even though there has been a renewed interest in the history of pre-modern crafts and guilds in several parts of Western Europe since the 1990s, our knowledge about apprenticeship in the German-speaking areas remains limited. Apprentices and apprenticeship have been investigated in several studies, but we lack broader – and systematic – knowledge. There is especially a lack of comprehensive and comparative studies; the larger crafts, such as tailoring and shoemaking, and early modern commercial centres have also been neglected.[3] The educational sciences, however,

---

[1] That is, the German-speaking parts of the 'Holy Roman Empire' and the Swiss regions.
[2] See as recent surveys: K. Schulz, *Handwerk, Zünfte und Gewerbe: Mittelalter und Renaissance* (Darmstadt: Wissenschaftliche Buchgesellschaft, 2010); A. Kluge, *Die Zünfte* (Stuttgart: Steiner, 2007); R. Reith, 'Handwerk', in: *Enzyklopädie der Neuzeit*, vol. 5 (Stuttgart and Weimar: Metzler, 2007), 148–73.
[3] E.g. A. von Dirke, 'Die Rechtsverhältnisse der Handwerkslehrlinge und Gesellen nach den deutschen Stadtrechten und Zunftstatuten des Mittelalters', PhD thesis,

have formulated a thesis, interpreting pre-modern guild-based training as maintaining static traditions and norms, and providing poor quality instruction. Some newer studies challenge this view, highlighting the historical embeddedness and efficiency of vocational training.[4]

Despite these limitations, it is still possible to paint a picture of the German apprenticeship system. For our discussion of various aspects we supplement the literature with data from the proceedings of the Augsburg trade court, which have been preserved for the period 1722–1806.[5] This chapter traces the actors and practices of apprenticeship for the German-speaking regions of Europe from the fifteenth century through to the changes of the nineteenth century. We argue that the apprenticeship system in the German-speaking regions derived from practical needs and it evolved into an institution during the early modern period. Largely, it was an efficient solution for the actors involved: for the apprentices (and their families), for the masters and for the journeymen as well. The apprenticeship system was the basis for the transregional labour market of the journeymen and it still maintained a certain importance during the unfolding of the industrial system.

Apprenticeship as Formal Institution

In many German-speaking areas we find the first documents referring to formal apprenticeship in the fourteenth century.[6] Its emergence was an urban phenomenon and was closely connected to the differentiation between apprentices and journeymen. Some apprenticeship contracts

University of Berlin, 1914; A. Knoll, *Handwerksgesellen und Lehrlinge im Mittelalter* (Berlin: Verlags-gesellschaft des Allgemeinen Deutschen Gewerkschaftsbundes, 1931); P. Hollnsteiner, 'Das Lehrlings- und Gesellenwesen Österreichs im 15. Jahrhundert', PhD thesis, University of Vienna, 1937; A. Bruns, 'Die Arbeitsverhältnisse der Lehrlinge und Gesellen im städtischen Handwerk in Westdeutschland bis 1800', PhD thesis, University of Cologne, 1938; K. Landolt, 'Das Recht der Handwerkslehrlinge vor 1798 im Gebiet der heutigen Schweiz', PhD thesis, University of Freiburg, Switzerland, 1977; K. Wesoly, *Lehrlinge und Handwerksgesellen am Mittelrhein: Ihre soziale Lage und ihre Organisation vom 14. bis ins 17. Jahrhundert* (Frankfurt am Main: Kramer, 1985); E. Schlenkrich, *Der Alltag der Lehrlinge im sächsischen Zunfthandwerk des 15. bis 18. Jahrhunderts* (Krems: Medium Aevum Quotidianum, 1995); cf. R. Reith and G. Stöger, 'Lehrzeit', *Enzyklopädie der Neuzeit*, vol. 7 (Stuttgart and Weimar: Metzler, 2008), 798–803.

[4] Cf. N. Hammerstein and C. Berg (eds.), *Handbuch der deutschen Bildungsgeschichte* (Munich: Beck, 1996); N. Hammerstein and U. Herrmann (eds.), *Handbuch der deutschen Bildungsgeschichte* (Munich: Beck, 2005); R. Hasfeld, *Berufsausbildung im Großherzogtum Baden: Zur Geschichte des 'dualen Systems' im Handwerk* (Cologne: Böhlau, 1996).

[5] City Archive Augsburg, Protokolle des Kunst-, Gewerbs- und Handwerksgerichts Augsburg (hereafter: KGH).

[6] *Lehre* or *Lehrzeit* – which can be translated as 'teaching' and 'time of teaching'.

from the late fourteenth century did not make this distinction,[7] but by the mid-fifteenth century apprenticeship seems to have become both common and compulsory in many crafts. Other professions – like merchants – developed similar frameworks for training. From that period formal apprenticeship became a central element within German crafts – despite the diverse structures of the crafts, and the fragmented political situation of the German-speaking territories.

What were the main reasons for the relevance of formal apprenticeship? Following S. R. Epstein, this might be explained by the question of skills and by the interests of masters as well as journeymen. Formal apprenticeship helped to achieve – more or less – comparable skills at the end of the learning phase. On the one hand these skills allowed masters to recruit qualified workers (journeymen), and on the other trained apprentices could expect to find suitable work within their craft more easily.[8] This was a prerequisite for the functioning of a transregional labour market and the tramping system of the journeymen.[9] As a rule journeymen did not take over their fathers' workshops and many journeymen did not return to either the place of their birth or their apprenticeship. Thus, unlike in peasant families, craftsmen relied heavily on a non-familial labour force, which often consisted of short and long-distance migrants.[10]

With the establishment of guilds in urban areas and the exchange of labour between towns, apprenticeship spread and was transformed into formalised rules, which tended to converge in large parts of the German-speaking regions to a uniform system. As guilds were able to gain privileges from the towns, or from territorial authorities, the apprenticeship

---

[7] Cf. e.g. H. Gutzwiller, 'Das Handwerks-Lehrlingswesen in Freiburg i. Ue. im Ausgang des 14. und zu Beginn des 15. Jahrhunderts', *Freiburger Geschichtsblätter* 47 (1955/56), 14–34; H. Ammann, *Mittelalterliche Wirtschaft im Alltag: Quellen zur Geschichte von Gewerbe, Industrie und Handel des 14. und 15. Jahrhunderts aus den Notariatsregistern von Freiburg*, 3 vols. (Aarau: Sauerländer, 1942–54).

[8] S. R. Epstein, 'Craft guilds, apprenticeship, and technological change in preindustrial Europe', *Journal of Economic History* 58 (1998), 684–713.

[9] R. Reith, 'Circulation of skilled labour in late medieval and early modern Central Europe', in: S. R. Epstein and M. Prak (eds.), *Guilds, Innovation, and the European Economy 1500–1800* (Cambridge: Cambridge University Press, 2008), 114–42; J. Ehmer, 'Rural guilds and urban–rural guild relations in early modern Central Europe', *International Review of Social History* 53 (2008), supplement, 143–58; J. Ehmer and R. Reith, 'Die mitteleuropäische Stadt als frühneuzeitlicher Arbeitsmarkt', in: P. Feldbauer, M. Mitterauer and W. Schwentker (eds.), *Die vormoderne Stadt: Asien und Europa im Vergleich* (Munich: Oldenbourg, 2002), 232–58.

[10] M. Mitterauer, 'Zur familienbetrieblichen Struktur im zünftischen Handwerk', in: H. Knittler (ed.), *Wirtschafts- und sozialhistorische Beiträge: Festschrift für Alfred Hoffmann zum 75. Geburtstag* (Munich: Oldenbourg, 1979), 190–219.

system expanded.[11] Most of the work by craftsmen outside guilds was limited to specific products or services and to rural areas. In the German-speaking areas, rural craftsmen often formed guilds as well, or were forced to join such institutions, even if these were mostly bound to urban guilds or maintained close contacts with them.[12]

Like guild masters, journeymen were important for the establishment of formalised apprenticeship, but have been overlooked in this context. Establishing rules for apprenticeship enabled journeymen to influence and even control parts of the craft system. They were especially interested in controlling the number of apprentices, because apprentices could – to a certain extent – substitute for the labour of journeymen and a higher number of apprentices inevitably resulted in a higher number of skilled workers. Vocational training was similarly relevant for merchants, but it wasn't institutionalised in a formal way. Even for members of mercantile families, training outside the family firm – and beyond territorial boundaries – helped them to acquire language skills and build up new contacts.[13]

Female apprentices were active during the late Middle Ages (mainly in textile production), but – as in other parts of Europe – females were excluded from formal training from the sixteenth and seventeenth century onwards.[14] In Nuremberg, for example, there were no female apprentices after the Thirty Years War.[15] Only a few branches – usually within textile production – remained 'free trades' (*freies Gewerbe*), in which females could be trained and work.[16] The production of silk textiles is one example. In Vienna, silk production was a mercantile project, promoted by the Habsburg state during the eighteenth century.

---

[11] Kluge, *Die Zünfte*; Schulz, *Handwerk, Zünfte und Gewerbe*.

[12] Ehmer, 'Rural guilds', 143–58; R. Kießling, 'Ländliches Gewerbe im Sog der Proto-Industrialisierung? Ostschwaben als Textillandschaft zwischen Spätmittelalter und Moderne', *Jahrbuch für Wirtschaftsgeschichte* (1998), vol. 2, 62–65; H.-G. Haupt (ed.), *Das Ende der Zünfte: Ein europäischer Vergleich* (Göttingen: Vandenhoeck, 2002).

[13] M. Beer, 'Migration, Kommunikation und Jugend: Studenten und Kaufmannslehrlinge der Frühen Neuzeit in ihren Briefen', *Archiv für Kulturgeschichte* 88 (2006), 355–87.

[14] C. Crowston, 'Women, gender, and guilds in early modern Europe: An overview of recent research', *International Review of Social History*, 53 (2008), supplement, 1944; Ch. Werkstetter, *Frauen im Augsburger Zunfthandwerk: Arbeit, Arbeitsbeziehungen und Geschlechterverhältnisse im 18. Jahrhundert* (Berlin: Akademie Verlag, 2001); A. Hanschmidt and H.-U. Musolff, *Elementarbildung und Berufsausbildung 1450–1750* (Cologne: Böhlau, 2005), 209–24; N. Z. Davis, 'Women in the crafts in sixteenth-century Lyon', *Feminist Studies* 8 (1982), 47–80.

[15] W. Riedl, 'Die rechtliche Stellung der Lehrjungen und Gesellen des Nürnberger Handwerks in der Zeit vom Ende des Dreissigjährigen Krieges bis zur Einverleibung der freien Reichsstadt in das Königreich Bayern im Jahre 1806', PhD thesis, University of Erlangen, 1948, 21.

[16] E. Höfinghoff, *Die bremischen Textilgewerbe vom 16. bis zur Mitte des 19. Jahrhunderts* (Bremen: Staatarchiv, 1933); cf. on Eastern Swabia, Kießling, 'Ländliches Gewerbe', 66f.

One strategy involved the education of female apprentices: during the 1830s nearly half (730) of the 1,677 apprentices in this craft were female.[17] As a whole, however, the crafts excluded female apprentices into the twentieth century.[18] Nonetheless, we find skilled female workers even in crafts that did not allow girls to enter apprenticeship, as examples from Augsburg show. They must have received informal training, probably as family members or as labourers labelled *Mägde* ('girls', meaning servants). Some urban institutions also actively sought to put females into apprenticeship: the Augsburg orphanages, for example, provided outdoor and indoor training by seamstresses.[19] Even if they had been properly trained, females were limited to certain parts of the labour market, lacking as they did formal proof of their qualification and institutional support (such as guilds or journeymen organisations).

Eighteenth and nineteenth-century manufactories employed adolescent workers, whom they labelled 'apprentices'. They usually operated outside the guild system, but they imitated the guilds' apprenticeship model, obviously hoping to generate skilled labourers. Sometimes the establishment of manufactories was connected to orphanages and poorhouses, sometimes they recruited workers from such institutions, a practice promoted by central administrations as in the case of the Viennese and Berlin silk industries.[20]

We have only limited data for estimating the number of apprentices in the various crafts, and this mostly concerns the late eighteenth and nineteenth centuries. Unsurprisingly we find more journeymen than apprentices. In 1770, for example, 1,162 journeymen and 257 apprentices were counted for all the crafts in the city of Mainz.[21] In Munich, 6,118 journeymen and 1,126 apprentices worked in crafts during the late 1840s.[22] Bigger cities,

---

[17] A. Steidl, *Auf nach Wien! Die Mobilität des mitteleuropäischen Handwerks im 18. und 19. Jahrhundert am Beispiel der Haupt- und Residenzstadt* (Vienna/Munich: Böhlau/ Oldenbourg, 2003).

[18] A. Schlüter, *Neue Hüte – alte Hüte? Gewerbliche Berufsbildung für Mädchen zu Beginn des 20. Jahrhunderts. Zur Geschichte ihrer Institutionalisierung* (Düsseldorf: Schwann, 1987).

[19] Werkstetter, *Frauen im Augsburger Zunfthandwerk*; Th. M. Safley, *Kinder, Karitas und Kapital: Studien zur Wirtschafts- und Sozialgeschichte des frühmodernen Augsburg* (Augsburg: Wißner, 2009/10), vol. 1, 234–38, and vol. 2, 290; cf. Crowston, 'Women, gender, and guilds', 22–34.

[20] E. Herzfeld, *Preußische Manufakturen: Großgewerbliche Fertigung von Porzellan, Seide, Gobelins, Uhren, Tapeten, Waffen, Papier u.a. im 17. und 18. Jahrhundert in und um Berlin* (Berlin: Verlag der Nationen, 1994); M. Zelfel, *Geschichte der Seidenfabrikanten Wiens im 18. Jahrhundert (1710–1792). Eine wirtschafts-kulturhistorische als auch soziologische Untersuchung* (Vienna: Verb. d. Wissenschaftl. Gesellschaften Österreichs, 1974).

[21] R. Reith, *Lohn und Leistung: Lohnformen im Gewerbe 1450–1900* (Stuttgart: Steiner, 1999), 79 and 400ff.; the city had c. 30,000 inhabitants at the time.

[22] K.-J. Hummel, *München in der Revolution von 1848/49* (Göttingen: Vandenhoeck, 1987), 314; the city had c. 96,000 inhabitants at the time.

Table 5.1 *Apprentices and journeymen per master, in selected German crafts, 1761–1801*

		Brunswick		Nuremberg	Berlin		
		1761	1771	1785	1776	1795	1801
Shoemakers	A	0.3	0.2	0.3	0.1	0.2	n/a
	J	0.9	0.7	1.0	0.7	0.8	n/a
Tailors	A	0.4	0.3	n/a	0.1	0.3	n/a
	J	1.3	0.4	n/a	0.7	0.8	n/a
Joiners	A	0.6	0.6	n/a	0.3	0.6	n/a
	J	1.3	0.7	n/a	0.8	1.6	n/a
Masons	A	3.0	2.0	n/a	2.4	2.7	5.7
	J	6.3	16.7	n/a	20.7	24.9	23.7
Carpenters	A	2.0	1.8	1.8	3.4	3.4	4.0
	J	9.8	13.6	8.0	17.9	25.2	19.5

A = apprentices, J = journeymen
Source: Grießinger and Reith, 'Lehrlinge im deutschen Handwerk' (n. 24), 158–60.

especially, hosted an impressive number of apprentices. In 1855, for example, 1,450 apprentices worked in 3,003 Viennese tailoring workshops.[23]

Many masters did not have any apprentices, as examples from the German cities of Brunswick, Nuremberg and Berlin show (Table 5.1). In particular, the larger crafts, such as tailoring and shoemaking, had few apprentices and journeymen compared to the number of master craftsmen. Usually, these crafts were executed in small businesses; masters worked by themselves and could not afford or had little use for coworkers. The number of apprentices and journeymen per master was much higher in construction, as they needed a larger workforce.

Usually, master craftsmen demanded premiums (*Lehrgeld*) for the training they offered. The level of the premium was not fixed by regulations; premiums were negotiated in individual and private agreements by the parents or legal guardians of the apprentices and they could vary significantly, even within the same craft. For crafts that demanded high and specific skills, such as for clockmakers, goldsmiths and printers, relatively high sums had to be paid. Premiums also reflected the social stratification of crafts and the reputation of their masters; they might thus have functioned as a means of social gatekeeping.[24] The premium could

[23] Steidl, *Auf nach Wien*, 152f.
[24] K. Schulz, *Handwerksgesellen und Lohnarbeiter: Untersuchungen zur oberrheinischen und oberdeutschen Stadtgeschichte des 14. bis 17. Jahrhunderts* (Sigmaringen: Thorbecke, 1985), 258, 260; Wesoly, *Lehrlinge und Handwerksgesellen*, 64; A. Grießinger and

Table 5.2 *Premiums and terms in Augsburg, 1590s–1790s*

Date	Craft	Term (years)	Premium (fl.)	(days work)	Source
1572–1670	Tailor		8–30 (mean 18)	n/a	AO
1728	Tailor		30	64	KGH
1789	Tailor	6	0	0	KGH
1572–1670	Shoemaker		6–30 (mean 19)	n/a	AO
1730s–50s	Shoemaker		26–50 (mean 38)	81 (mean)	KGH
1572–1670	Locksmith		6–30 (mean 19)	n/a	AO
1791	Locksmith	4	0	0	KGH
1720s–90s	Clockmaker	6	100–200 (mean 157)	334 (mean)	KGH
1730s–50s	Case maker		25–42 (mean 34)	72 (mean)	KGH
1752	Case maker	3	36	77	KGH
1751 and 1763	Goldbeater	7 and 8	n/a	n/a	KGH

Note: The days of work calculation assumes a daily wage of 28 Kreuzer, paid for carpenter or mason journeymen during the eighteenth century: R. Reith, *Arbeits- und Lebensweise im städtischen Handwerk. Zur Sozialgeschichte Augsburger Handwerksgesellen im 18. Jahrhundert (1700–1806)* (Göttingen: Schwartz, 1988), 219–21.

Sources: KGH = noted by the Augsburg trade court; AO = apprentices from the Augsburg orphanages, see Safley, *Kinder, Karitas und Kapital*, vol 1, 238f. and vol. 2, 280–82.

be lower if the future learner already had some work experience.[25] In eighteenth-century Augsburg, premiums mostly varied between 10 and 50 *Gulden* (florins, hereafter fl.), which is equal to 20–106 days' wages for a carpenter or mason journeyman at that time (see Table 5.2). In 1780, Augsburg's orphanages set the maximum premium they paid for outdoor apprentices at 30 fl.; nevertheless, the orphanages occasionally paid higher premiums (e.g. 180 fl. in the case of an engraver).[26] Premiums below 50 fl. would only partially cover the master's expenses for the apprentice's room and board during the early stages of their training.[27] After this, the apprentice 'paid' with his work.

Some masters demanded further payments or services. For example, apprentices could be required to bring their own tools (especially common for shoemakers), bedclothes or a certain amount of a foodstuff, such as grain. This was more common in the sixteenth

---

R. Reith, 'Lehrlinge im deutschen Handwerk des ausgehenden 18. Jahrhunderts: Arbeitsorganisation, Sozialbeziehungen und alltägliche Konflikte', *Zeitschrift für historische Forschung* 13 (1986), 161; R. Reith, 'Apprentices in the Central European crafts in early modern times: Apprentices as wage-earners?', in: H. Soly, B. De Munck and S. L. Kaplan (eds.), *Learning on the Shop Floor: Historical Perspectives on Apprenticeship* (New York: Berghahn, 2007), 179–99.

[25] KGH 1722, fol. 8ff. (15 April).   [26] Safley, *Kinder, Karitas und Kapital*, vol. 1, 242.
[27] Cf. ibid., 239; KGH 1791, fol. 105f. (23 February).

century and in rural areas.[28] Payment of a higher fee could result in a shorter apprenticeship: this was labelled 'buying an apprenticeship' (*Abkaufen der Lehre*). Smaller fees, or learning 'freely' (*frey lernen*) without paying fees, led to longer terms. This was common in the larger crafts such as tailoring or shoemaking: in the South German city of Regensburg, 57% of the shoemaker apprentices and 71% of the tailor apprentices were trained under this regime at the end of the eighteenth century.[29] Until the 1860s, fees tended to increase, as they were bound to the cost of living. In the second half of the nineteenth century they decreased, and also lost their importance in many crafts due to competition from the industrial sector.[30] In addition to the premiums, the apprentices usually had to pay fees to the guild, probably set at 10% of the premium, as is suggested by examples from the Augsburg trade court.[31]

Until the mid-fifteenth century a term of 2–3 years seems to have been usual for apprentices, although several contracts mention durations ranging from six months to 12 years.[32] During the fifteenth and sixteenth century, the duration of apprenticeship increased in many crafts. In Saxony a 2–5-year apprenticeship was common from the second half of the sixteenth century, and some crafts – such the goldsmiths in Leipzig – demanded up to eight years.[33] Until the eighteenth century, a three or four year apprenticeship became the norm. As a result of the journeymen tramping system and transregional labour markets, terms did not differ much within individual crafts, but there were significant variations between crafts. While construction crafts demanded 2–3 years, other occupations could go up – in exceptional cases – to seven or even eight years. Crafts that required high skill levels, such as goldsmiths, goldbeaters and clockmakers, tended to have comparatively long terms (see

[28] Schlenkrich, *Der Alltag der Lehrlinge*, 33f.; F. Göttmann, *Handwerk und Bündnispolitik: Die Handwerkerbünde am Mittelrhein vom 14. bis zum 17. Jahrhundert* (Wiesbaden: Steiner, 1977), 76; Schulz, *Handwerksgesellen und Lohnarbeiter*, 258; Wesoly, *Lehrlinge und Handwerksgesellen*, 77; J. Schwarzlmüller, *Die Berufslaufbahn Lehrling – Geselle – Meister in den Handwerkszünften Oberösterreichs* (Vienna: Verband der wiss. Gesellschaften Österreichs, 1979), 32; KGH 1733, fol. 107 (15 April).

[29] Grießinger and Reith, 'Lehrlinge im deutschen Handwerk', 161.

[30] Ibid., 153; R. Reith, 'Zur beruflichen Sozialisation im Handwerk vom 18. bis ins frühe 20. Jahrhundert: Umrisse einer Sozialgeschichte der deutschen Lehrlinge', *Vierteljahrschrift für Sozial- und Wirtschaftsgeschichte* 76 (1989), 6; B. Jauch, *Das gewerbliche Lehrlingswesen in Deutschland seit dem Inkrafttreten des Handwerkergesetzes vom 26. Juli 1897 mit besonderer Berücksichtigung Badens* (Freiburg: Herder, 1911), 39f.

[31] KGH 1741, fol. 69 (30 January) and 615 (18 December); KGH 1796, fol. 189 (2 May).

[32] Gutzwiller, 'Das Handwerks-Lehrlingswesen'.

[33] Schlenkrich, *Der Alltag der Lehrlinge*.

Table 5.2).[34] For merchants, apprenticeship lasted for five or more years.[35]

This extension of apprenticeship terms during the early modern period might be interpreted as a consequence of, and a reaction to, evolving and more specialised qualifications, as the 'world of goods' was changing equally.[36] However, we have to remember that the length of the term was usually not determined by the guild, which only set a minimum, but was negotiated by the parties involved. Guild registers provide testimony to their flexibility. Older studies were misled by legislative sources. By law the Viennese silk-weavers were obliged to educate (male) apprentices for six years. In practice, the duration of apprenticeship ranged between one and eight years during the eighteenth and early nineteenth centuries. Apprentices who paid fees served a shorter term, as did apprentices with previous knowledge, such as masters' sons or job changers.[37] Usually, shorter terms were not challenged by the masters, as they were able to replace the journeymen if they did not meet their expectations. Journeymen were more likely to oppose shorter terms, as some examples from the Augsburg trade courts indicate. The engagement of – mostly non-local or rural – journeymen who had not finished their term properly, or who had learned outside the guild system, was often met with protest from other journeymen, who might threaten to 'withdraw from work'.[38]

During the second half of the nineteenth century, the duration of apprenticeship started to decrease. This was a reaction to the growing importance of the industrial labour market and it happened especially in crafts that did not offer bright prospects or competed directly with the factory system. In 1904 hardly any crafts still demanded more than a four-year term of apprenticeship, and a three-year apprenticeship seems to have become the norm by then. The general adoption of similar durations and the introduction of compulsory education therefore led to a homogenisation and standardisation of careers, and to age segmentation of the labour market.[39]

Despite important continuities, industrialisation changed the craft system and with it apprenticeship. During the second half of the eighteenth

[34] Grießinger and Reith, 'Lehrlinge im deutschen Handwerk', 149–99.
[35] H.-P. Bruchhäuser, *Quellen und Dokumente zur kaufmännischen Berufsbildung im 18. Jahrhundert* (Cologne: Böhlau, 1999), 161–70, and E. Dauenhauer, 'Kaufmännische Erwachsenenbildung in Deutschland im 18. Jahrhundert', PhD thesis, University of Erlangen-Nuremberg, 1964, 28.
[36] Schulz, *Handwerksgesellen und Lohnarbeiter*; C.-P. Clasen, *Die Augsburger Weber: Leistungen und Krisen des Textilgewerbes um 1600* (Augsburg: Mühlberger, 1981).
[37] Steidl, *Auf nach Wien*, 249.
[38] E.g. KGH 1725, fol. 68 (19 February); KGH 1723, fol. 362f. (13 September).
[39] Reith, 'Zur beruflichen Sozialisation'.

century there were already enlightened discussions that referred to a 'crisis' of the crafts – following mercantilist criticism – and interpreted guilds as inefficient monopolists, pointing to the deficiencies of vocational training. Likewise, contemporaries criticised the education of merchants and promoted the idea of trade schools, which were established from the 1740s.[40] Subsequently, many territorial authorities and larger cities initiated trade schools and these became more important for the crafts, when – following the French example – guilds were abolished in the Austrian and German territories during the 1860s. Yet this new approach did not aim at a complete replacement of apprenticeship: rather, it combined schooling and craft apprenticeship, and was later labelled the 'dual system' of vocational training. Formal apprenticeship survived, as both political actors and craftsmen – albeit from different motives – agreed on its relevance. When trade liberalisation was followed by an anti-liberal movement, compulsory associations for certain crafts were reinstalled and apprenticeship became regulated once more. Training on the shop floor remained a *conditio sine qua non* for skilled workers within the craft system well into the twentieth century.[41] Even though industrial apprenticeship evolved from 1900 onwards, in 1907 two-thirds of German apprentices were still trained within the craft system.[42]

Actors and Policies

Most adolescents started their apprenticeship between the ages of 13 and 15.[43] In some occupations, such as construction workers, brewers

---

[40] Bruchhäuser, *Quellen und Dokumente zur kaufmännischen Berufsbildung*; cf. Haupt, *Das Ende der Zünfte*.

[41] C. Zimmermann, 'Blinde Anschauung soll sich zum klaren Begriffe und zu fertiger Übung erheben: Die Wertheimer Gewerbeschule 1836 bis 1862', *Wertheimer Jahrbuch* (1996), 195–226; I. Andruchowitz, 'Die Entwicklung des berufsbegleitenden Unterrichts für Lehrlinge des Gewerbes in Österreich von 1848 bis 1882, dargestellt insbesondere am Beispiel Wien', PhD thesis, University of Vienna 1985; K. Thelen, *How Institutions Evolve: The Political Economy of Skills in Germany, Britain, the United States, and Japan* (Cambridge: Cambridge University Press, 2004), 43f. and 53f.; Hasfeld, *Berufsausbildung*.

[42] G. Adelmann, 'Die berufliche Aus- und Weiterbildung in der deutschen Wirtschaft 1871–1918', in: H. Pohl (ed.), *Berufliche Aus- und Weiterbildung in der deutschen Wirtschaft seit dem 19. Jahrhundert* (Wiesbaden: Steiner, 1979), 19; M. von Behr, *Die Entstehung der industriellen Lehrwerkstatt. Materialien und Analysen zur beruflichen Bildung im 19. Jahrhundert* (Frankfurt: Campus, 1981).

[43] M. Mitterauer, 'Gesindedienst und Jugendphase im europäischen Vergleich', *Geschichte und Gesellschaft* 11 (1985), 177–204; U. Ludwig, 'Die soziale Lage und soziale Organisation des Kleingewerbes in der ersten Hälfte des 19. Jahrhunderts', PhD thesis, University of Göttingen, 1982, 14; Steidl, *Auf nach Wien*, 96; this might also have been the case for merchant apprentices: cf. Beer, 'Migration, Kommunikation und Jugend', 355–87; and Dauenhauer, 'Kaufmännische Erwachsenenbildung'.

and butchers, older and even married apprentices could be found, as they required more physical strength than teenagers could supply. During the late eighteenth century the mean age of carpenter apprentices in Hamburg was 18–19 years. Some of these older apprentices had been working for master craftsmen as labourers beforehand. The higher age of apprentices could also be due to a change of occupation: in Vienna many former weavers entered apprenticeships in silk production from the 1840s, when their own occupation was losing ground. In many crafts the age at entry increased slightly during the nineteenth century.[44]

Apprentices came from a wide variety of social backgrounds. Some, sometimes many, came from the crafts themselves, as masters' or journeymen's sons. In the Nuremberg construction crafts, three-quarters of all apprentices enrolled between 1771 and 1807 had family links to this particular craft, confirming, it seems, suspicions about the closed-shop practised by the guilds.[45] There is only limited information available on this issue, but the picture was surely different for other occupations, places and times. Neolocality determined the possibility of advancement within the guild system. Direct succession from father to son was relatively rare, because of compulsory tramping by journeymen. As tramping systems began to lose their importance, the family transfer of master positions increased. Even then, father to son successions were less important in crafts that were not bound to specific buildings or workplaces.[46] Privileges given to masters' sons, such as reduced premiums or terms, might increase the likelihood of family succession, especially when they had already had been taught by their fathers. Cases brought before the Augsburg trade court frequently refer to the training of masters' sons or

[44] Steidl, *Auf nach Wien*, 124f.; Reith, 'Zur beruflichen Sozialisation', 7; R. Reith, *Arbeits- und Lebensweise im städtischen Handwerk. Zur Sozialgeschichte Augsburger Handwerksgesellen im 18. Jahrhundert (1700–1806)* (Göttingen: Schwartz, 1988), 201ff.; W. Gerber, *Die Bauzünfte im alten Hamburg. Entwicklung und Wesen des vaterstädtischen Maurer- und Zimmerergewerbes während der Zunftzeit* (Hamburg: Bauhütte, 1933), 40; K. Schwarz, *Die Lage der Handwerksgesellen in Bremen während des 18. Jahrhunderts* (Bremen: Stadtarchiv, 1975), 185; Th. Kreuzkam, 'Das Baugewerbe mit bes. Rücksicht auf Leipzig' in: Verein für Socialpolitik (ed.), *Untersuchungen über die Lage des Handwerks in Deutschland mit besonderer Rücksicht auf seine Konkurrenzfähigkeit gegenüber der Großindustrie* (Leipzig: Duncker & Humblot, 1897), vol. 9, 543–628, here p. 618; K. H. Kaufhold, *Das Handwerk der Stadt Hildesheim im 18. Jahrhundert: Eine wirtschaftsgeschichtliche Studie*, 2nd edition (Göttingen: Schwartz, 1980), 112; R. Gömmel, *Vorindustrielle Bauwirtschaft in der Reichsstadt Nürnberg und ihrem Umland, 16.–18. Jahrhundert* (Stuttgart: Steiner, 1985), 210.

[45] P. Fleischmann, *Das Bauhandwerk in Nürnberg vom 14. bis zum 18. Jahrhundert* (Nuremberg: Stadtarchiv, 1985), 258f.

[46] Mitterauer, 'Zur familienbetrieblichen Struktur im zünftischen Handwerk'.

other relatives.[47] When asked in 1758, the pewterers' guild stated that six of the seven apprentices working in 18 workshops were masters' sons.[48]

Some data for the city of Göttingen indicates that big differences existed between occupations. Among nearly three thousand apprentices enrolled in local guilds between the 1810s and 1870, only 8.5% were masters' sons. Only in some occupations – usually smaller ones – was the percentage above 25.[49] The Augsburg trade court proceedings suggest that the majority of apprentices were 'outsiders', the sons of urban labourers or urban or rural craftsmen.[50]

Inevitably, many apprentices came from lower social strata. A first indication of this is the widespread practice of learning without paying fees mentioned earlier. Charitable institutions also put poor adolescents and orphans into apprenticeship, for example the Augsburg orphanages that sent boys (29 during the 1650s and 40 during the 1760s) to be trained as shoemakers or tailors, but also as braiders, weavers or goldsmiths.[51] Formal apprenticeship also gave journeymen and masters the ability to control access to their craft and to exclude members of certain social, ethnic or religious groups. This generally affected females and non-Christians, especially Jews, who were excluded from the German apprenticeship system into the nineteenth century.[52] However, it could also hit individuals from 'disreputable' backgrounds, such as illegitimate children or those descended from hangmen or knackers. This view of honour (*Ehre*) was prominently discussed in the older historiography and it was heavily criticised in contemporary mercantilist and enlightened discussions.[53] The evidence from the Augsburg trade courts suggests a more complex picture. Some cases fit the stereotypical picture of the rigid exclusion of 'others', but there are also examples that point up differentiated perceptions, diverging practices or negotiated consents. Payments might facilitate the acceptance of such a learner, as in 1761, when a master printer was said to have received a significant

---

[47] E.g. KGH 1722, fol. 12f. (20 April); KGH 1736, fol. 163 (5 March) or KGH 1742, fol. 58–60 (31 January).

[48] KGH 1758, fol. 25 (16 January).

[49] Ludwig, 'Die soziale Lage und soziale Organisation des Kleingewerbes', 129.

[50] E.g. KGH 1723, fol. 341f. (30 August); KGH 1736, fol. 148f. (27 February) or KGH 1771, fol. 33f. (25 February).

[51] Safley, *Kinder, Karitas und Kapital*, vol. 1, 231–67, and vol. 2, 268–94; R. Reith, *Der Aprilaufstand von 1848 in Konstanz. Zur biographischen Dimension von 'Hochverrath und Aufruhr'. Versuch einer historischen Protestanalyse* (Sigmaringen: Thorbecke, 1982), 118f.

[52] D. Diner, *Enzyklopädie jüdischer Geschichte und Kultur* (Stuttgart: Metzler, 2012), vol. 2, 534–37.

[53] This is reflected in laws against 'inappropriate customs' (*Missbräuche*) within the crafts – cf. e.g. *Reichsordnung zur Abstellung von Handwerks-Mißbräuchen vom 16.8.1731* (s.l., 1732).

premium while knowing of the illegitimate birth of his apprentice.[54] Journeymen opposed such decisions: in 1735, when a master had accepted another apprentice born out of wedlock, the guild masters expected the journeymen not to let him 'pass' and therefore asked the city council to decide on the issue.[55] When another master started training a hangman's son in 1738, the trade court asked the master to stop his education, as the masters should 'not expose themselves publicly'.[56] Other cases also shared this concern for the trade's honour vis-à-vis the outside world. The same concerns remained in the nineteenth century, but were limited to the more prestigious crafts.

Many apprentices were migrants. For Western and Central Europe Prak et al. have pointed out that family members were, with some exceptions, a minority among guild members and apprentices.[57] In late eighteenth-century Regensburg, apprentices born locally formed a minority: 41% of masons' apprentices, 31% of brewers' apprentices and only 26% of carpenters' apprentices were natives.[58] In 1848, 61% of Munich apprentices were migrants, among them 4% were from 'foreign territories', i.e. from outside Bavaria.[59] Although we lack comprehensive studies, it seems that many apprentices came from the urban hinterland or from smaller towns nearby.[60] This pattern is reflected in the proceedings of the Augsburg trade court: when places of origin were mentioned for apprentices – which was not done very often – it was mainly Augsburg, followed by smaller cities in Swabia or neighbouring rural areas. Only a few apprentices came from remoter destinations, such as Switzerland, Hesse or Vienna.

The spatial dimension of labour recruitment displayed major variations between occupations, as the example of Vienna demonstrates (see Table 5.3). Bigger cities and centres of trade could attract middle and long-distance migrants.[61] Many Viennese apprentices came from the various territories of the Habsburg Empire, and from the mid-nineteenth century onwards Bohemia and Moravia became an important region of origin. At the start of the twentieth century, 6,000 apprentices came to Vienna from these regions annually. As early as the mid-nineteenth century, 87% of urban craftsmen had not been born in Vienna. Usually the percentage of

[54] KGH 1761, fol. 145 (27 April).   [55] KGH 1735, fol. 401f. (12 October).
[56] KGH 1738, fol. 705 (5 November).
[57] M. Prak et al., 'Access to the trade: Monopoly and mobility in European craft guilds, 17th and 18th centuries', *Journal of Social History* 53 (2020).
[58] Reith, *Lohn und Leistung*, 79.
[59] Hummel, *München in der Revolution von 1848/49*, 314.
[60] Grießinger and Reith, 'Lehrlinge im deutschen Handwerk', 156.
[61] Cf. the survey by Prak et al., 'Access to the trade'.

Table 5.3 *Geographical origin of Viennese apprentices in selected trades, 1790–1862*

Origin	Chimney sweeps 1790–1856		Silk-weavers 1790–1862		Butchers 1790–1819 and 1844–58	
	n	%	n	%	n	%
Vienna	68	14.3	4,335	69.1	1,227	67.5
Lower Austria	91	19.2	664	10.6	353	18.7
Rest of Austria	16	3.4	242	3.9	37	2.0
Bohemia, Moravia	65	13.7	771	12.3	136	7.2
Galicia, Bucovina	5	1.1	3	0	2	0.1
Hungary	14	3.0	86	1.4	55	2.9
Rest of Habsburg Monarchy	23	4.9	41	0.7	–	–
Bavaria	8	1.7	42	0.7	21	1.1
Rest of German territories	2	0.4	70	1.1	11	0.6
Switzerland	163	34.4	8	0.1	–	–
Rest	19	4	16	0.3	–	–
Sum	474	100	6,278	100	1,842	100

Source: Steidl, *Auf nach Wien*, 158.

migrants was higher in crafts with fewer job opportunities, poor reputations or hard labour conditions. Mobility could, however, also be a consequence of occupational specialisation.[62] For merchant apprentices mobility was a must. During the sixteenth century, sons from wealthy Nuremberg families were trained in Antwerp, Lyon and Silesia, and from Southern Germany and the Austrian territories apprentices often went to the Northern Italian urban centres of trade, such as Venice. With the colonial expansion of the early modern period, apprentices were also sent to destinations outside Europe.[63]

Norms and policies affected apprenticeship to a different extent. General 'trade laws', such as the *Reichsordnung* issued in the early

[62] J. Ehmer, 'Die Herkunft der Handwerker in überregionalen städtischen Zentren: Zürich, Wien und Zagreb zur Mitte des 19. Jahrhunderts', in: K. Roth (ed.), *Handwerk in Mittel- und Südosteuropa. Mobilität, Vermittlung und Wandel im Handwerk des 18. bis 20. Jahrhunderts* (Munich: Südosteuropa-Gesellschaft, 1987), 47–67; Steidl, *Auf nach Wien*, 156–84; Reith, 'Zur beruflichen Sozialisation', 7–9.

[63] Beer, 'Migration, Kommunikation und Jugend', 355–87; Bruchhäuser, *Quellen und Dokumente zur kaufmännischen Berufsbildung*, 163–5; Hanschmidt and Musolff (eds.), *Elementarbildung und Berufsausbildung*, 95–107.

1730s, contained little detail about apprenticeship.[64] Similarly, the trade courts which were established in several bigger German cities during the early modern period as an extension of urban self-government did not usually aim at regulating apprenticeship.[65]

Regulations, even though they emanated from local authorities and the crafts themselves, tended to be fairly uniform across the German lands. Clearly, artisan mobility contributed to their diffusion. Perhaps this also indicates that craftsmen or local authorities were trying to solve problems that were not specific to one craft or town, but applied more generally. One common regulation concerns the maximum number of apprentices within a single workshop. Early regulations from the fourteenth century limited their number to two, and in some crafts only one apprentice could be educated by a master at any one time. It is unclear if this rule was initiated by the masters themselves, or resulted from demands by journeymen or the local authorities. While journeymen were anxious about competition for work, the authorities might have aimed for a certain 'balance' within the guilds. However, this limitation has also been linked to the quality of training. Several studies have emphasised that the journeymen were relatively powerful actors in the German guild system.[66] Another related regulation imposed a pause on the admission of apprentices. This is known to have occurred in the late fifteenth century: in the 1470s the master hatters in the Middle Rhine area agreed to wait six years before accepting another apprentice. These norms, called *Interim* or *Stillstand*, were debated and adopted on a supra-regional scale during the sixteenth century, but were limited to bigger towns and commercial centres.[67]

In eighteenth-century Augsburg many crafts had fixed the number of apprentices that a master could take. Usually, this was set at two at a time,

---

[64] Cf. *Reichsordnung zur Abstellung von Handwerks-Mißbräuchen.*

[65] On the German trade courts cf. R. Reith, A. Grießinger and P. Eggers, *Streikbewegungen deutscher Handwerksgesellen im 18. Jahrhundert. Materialien zur Sozial- und Wirtschaftsgeschichte des städtischen Handwerks 1700–1806* (Göttingen: Schwartz, 1992), 25–36.

[66] E.g. W. Reininghaus, *Die Entstehung der Gesellengilden im Spätmittelalter* (Wiesbaden: Steiner, 1981); A. Grießinger, *Das symbolische Kapital der Ehre. Streikbewegungen und kollektives Bewußtsein deutscher Handwerksgesellen im 18. Jahrhundert* (Berlin: Ullstein, 1981); Schulz, *Handwerksgesellen und Lohnarbeiter*; Reith, Grießinger and Eggers, *Streikbewegungen deutscher Handwerksgesellen.*

[67] Schulz, *Handwerksgesellen und Lohnarbeiter*, 253–6; Reith, *Arbeits- und Lebensweise*, 103; Wesoly, *Lehrlinge und Handwerksgesellen*, 70 and 89; B. Rajkay, 'Lehrlinge in Oettinger Handwerksbetrieben nach dem Ende des Dreißigjährigen Krieges', in: G. Hetzer and A. Löffelmeier (eds.), *Wanderstab und Meisterbrief. Rieser Handwerk im Wandel der Zeit 1700–1850* (Nördlingen: Steinmeier, 1986), 90–96; Reith, 'Zur beruflichen Sozialisation', 16f.; Reith, Grießinger and Eggers, *Streikbewegungen deutscher Handwerksgesellen.*

as was the case for the carpenters, shoemakers and goldbeaters. Some crafts had a fixed ratio between apprentices and journeymen. Master tanners, for example, were not allowed more than two journeymen or one journeyman and one apprentice each.[68] In addition, guilds also barred particular masters from training apprentices. In the 1720s, one carpenter who had passed his examination for the master's certificate 'very poorly' was not allowed to train apprentices for the first seven years of his mastership.[69] Like their journeymen, Augsburg masters also opposed allowing 'too many' apprentices and frequently denounced those with more apprentices than was permitted.[70] Some masters explicitly stated that they did not want to educate potential competitors, who could establish businesses outside the guild-controlled city.[71]

Numerical limits on apprentices were debated intensely by urban and central governments at the end of the eighteenth century. These discussions, typically coming from the political centre, preceded the trade liberalisations of the early nineteenth century. When the Brunswick authorities feared a 'breeding of apprentices' in 1791, they called in guild officials and asked them about their experience of numerical constraints. It turned out that most of the masters actually had only one apprentice. Some saw limitation as beneficial, because poorer masters could avoid employing journeymen, while others feared that master craftsmen might lose their reputation by offering inferior goods or work produced by apprentices.[72] The 'breeding of apprentices' was discussed again during the second half of the nineteenth century, when the number of apprentices in many workshops had increased significantly – especially in printing shops and bakeries. Once again journeymen stood against these developments and managed to get numerical constraints implemented for some crafts.[73]

Apprenticeship contracts can be seen as a tool to mediate between the interests of apprentices and masters and to avoid conflicts.[74] The older German craft historiography interpreted these arrangements primarily as the outcome of patriarchal structures. Many studies – following Otto Brunner – suggested the 'whole house' (*ganzes Haus*) as a dominant feature of pre-modern society, which was organised around a male-

---

[68] KGH 1735, fol. 153f. (9 May); KGH 1744, fol. 243 (10 June); KGH 1772, fol. 336 (6 May); KGH 1777, fol. 70 (14 April).
[69] KGH 1727, fol. 67 (29 January).
[70] E.g. KGH 1731, fol. 130 (14 March) or KGH 1734, fol. 84 and 87 (17 March).
[71] KGH 1739, fol. 375–77 (10 June).
[72] City Archive Brunswick, Polizei Departement, C VII G1 vol. 28 (1791).
[73] H. Reichel, 'Über Lehrlingszüchtung im Handwerk', PhD thesis, University of Greifswald, 1907; Reith, 'Zur beruflichen Sozialisation', 18.
[74] Following Epstein, 'Craft guilds, apprenticeship, and technological change'.

dominated 'relationship of protection and fidelity'. Benefits, for example, were seen as gestures of paternalism or care, not of exchange. When early craft historians, such as Rudolf Wissell, came across apprenticeship contracts, they portrayed them as makeshift solutions without much importance.[75] However, contracts are frequently mentioned in local studies that cover different parts of the German territories, for example the Upper Rhine area, Saxony, Austria and the southwestern parts of Germany. Sometimes they were made as verbal agreements, but written ones seem to have been more common and they were more or less compulsory when local poor relief agencies or legal guardians were involved.[76] It is difficult to gauge the overall relevance of contracts, but the mutual obligations of apprentices (or their parents) and masters and a broad variety of different sources (from trade courts and contemporary literature) suggest that written contracts were a common feature of the apprenticeship system. Although no rule required that contracts were recorded by notaries or local institutions, such as trade courts or city councils, they do sometimes seem to have certified or at least documented them. Usually, however, these institutions did not enforce contracts, because they were considered to be private arrangements.

If apprenticeship contracts were intended to prevent conflicts or cover areas of tension, they allow insights into the economic and social dimensions of the apprenticeship. Contracts from the fourteenth and fifteenth century are short and diverse. Nevertheless, some basic features appear in several of these contracts. The contracts specified the duration of the apprenticeship, sanctions to enforce it, terms of resignation and – if applicable – the payment of a premium. In addition, the master's obligations were declared, which mostly concerned board and lodging, or the provision of clothing for the apprentice, sometimes even supplies of wine or fixed payments for the purchase of bread.[77] In a contract issued in Basel in 1486, a master weaver promised to train the apprentice for three years and to provide him with a well-defined amount of clothing. If the youth ran away, the contract only allowed compensation for the master if he was not to blame.[78] Contracts could also define specific training objectives that should be reached at the end of the apprenticeship: two contracts from early fifteenth-century Freiburg obliged the master to train his apprentice in weaving broad cloth and other special types. In 1579 in

[75] R. Wissell, *Des alten Handwerks Recht und Gewohnheit*, 2 vols. (Berlin, 1929), vol. 1, 275.
[76] Kluge, *Die Zünfte*, 154–6; Schulz, *Handwerk, Zünfte und Gewerbe*, 250–62; Gutzwiller, 'Das Handwerks-Lehrlingswesen in Freiburg'; Schlenkrich, *Der Alltag der Lehrlinge*, 97ff. and 198; Reith, *Der Aprilaufstand von 1848 in Konstanz*, 118f.
[77] Gutzwiller, 'Das Handwerks-Lehrlingswesen in Freiburg'.
[78] Schulz, *Handwerksgesellen und Lohnarbeiter*, 262.

Frankfurt, master rope-maker Engelhart Zahn made a contract with the father of his future apprentice in which he agreed to train the adolescent for three years, during which the boy's family would provide his clothing. The boy should behave 'faithfully' and 'diligently', but if the master caused any 'problems or hindrances' (*irrung oder hinderung*), he would be responsible for organising and funding the boy's training in another workshop. If Zahn died, his widow would have to see to the boy's training in her or another workshop. The contract (*Zedel*) was duplicated and kept by both parties.[79] Templates in guild record books and contemporary literature indicate that most pre-modern contracts were composed in a comparable way.[80]

Due to a lack of studies it is difficult to gauge how contracts evolved during industrialisation, when the guild system faced profound changes. Templates for contracts were still included in publications from the second half of the nineteenth century, and eventually German laws, such as the amendment to trade regulation in 1878 and the *Handwerkergesetz* (artisan law) in 1897, even insisted on written contracts.[81]

Practice

The practice of apprenticeship has attracted far less scholarly attention than its normative or quantitative aspects. Some researchers have followed the thesis of a decline of the craft system during the early modern period, an idea voiced since the late eighteenth century by critics of the guild system. This view also questions the quality of occupational training.[82] This negative view seems to be corroborated by sources, but we should remember that such evidence usually stems from conflicts and it hardly allows a direct view of 'normal' situations. If the training was so poor, how could journeymen subsequently work in often highly specialised settings and produce ever more differentiated consumer goods?

The training would be determined by the masters – guild norms and regulations did not clearly specify the learning process and its targets.[83] Both masters and apprentices had an interest in the quality of training, and this is documented in the proceedings of the Augsburg trade court. In

---

[79] Wesoly, *Lehrlinge und Handwerksgesellen*, 402.
[80] E.g. W. Brauser, *Der ganz Neue [. . .] Briefsteller [. . .]* (Nuremberg: Martin Endter, 1701), 1187–91 or P. J. Marperger, *Getreuer und Geschickter Handels-Diener* (Nuremberg: Monath, 1715), 31–94.
[81] Hasfeld, *Berufsausbildung*, 301 and 378.
[82] Grießinger and Reith, 'Lehrlinge im deutschen Handwerk', 163.
[83] Cf. e.g. *Reichsordnung zur Abstellung von Handwerks-Mißbräuchen*.

1725, for example, a mason's apprentice asked for permission to work with another master, as he had 'only worked for three weeks' during the whole summer.[84] There are also several cases when masters complained about inept apprentices.[85] The fact that many masters paid wages to apprentices during the final phase of their training suggests the overall effectiveness of the learning-by-doing system.

Wage payments to apprentices were obviously bound to their abilities and they were affected by the labour market: in the 1540s, the Augsburg weavers, for example, agreed on paying a piece-rate to apprentices if they could produce a cloth in the same amount of time that would be expected of a journeyman. In 1610, the rate was increased, but it was reduced during the mid-eighteenth century as demand had diminished while a large workforce was still available. Examples from the metal-working crafts show a differentiated system of payments. In sixteenth-century Nuremberg, the weekly wage for apprentices was bound to the production of a certain number of knives. During his term the apprentice's wage – and the number of knives he had to produce – increased, and during the last year the apprentice received a piece-rate wage. Wages were also common in construction; there is evidence of carpenters', roofers', stonemasons' and bricklayers' apprentices receiving wages from the late Middle Ages onwards. This was also necessary because these crafts had high physical requirements and the apprentices were usually older; they might already have experience of work and often lived outside the master's home and were even married. Payments for apprentices were also more common in export-oriented occupations, which had achieved a measure of standardisation for their goods and therefore might have integrated the apprentice more effectively into the production process than other crafts.[86] During the second half of the nineteenth century regular wage payments became more common, when the craft system began to compete with the industrial labour market.[87]

Apart from in the construction crafts, apprentices usually lived in the masters' households. This aspect of apprenticeship remained important into the nineteenth and, in some branches, even the twentieth century. The Viennese censuses from the 1850s and 1860s reveal that

---

[84] KGH 1725, fol. 277–80 (2 July); cf. KGH 1751, fol. 147 (15 September).

[85] E.g. for the 1720s: KGH 1722, fol. 63 (2 September); KGH 1724, fol. 80 (9 February); KGH 1726, fol. 11f (7 January).

[86] Reith, 'Apprentices in the Central European crafts', 179–99.

[87] Schulz, *Handwerksgesellen und Lohnarbeiter*, 261f.; Reith, 'Zur beruflichen Sozialisation im Handwerk', 24f.; Grießinger and Reith, 'Lehrlinge im deutschen Handwerk', 155f.; Reith, *Lohn und Leistung*, 315; K. Thiess, *Die Lohnverhältnisse in Berlin seit 1882* (Berlin: Schuhr, 1894).

three-quarters of apprentices lived in the masters' households.[88] The portrayal of apprentices' everyday life as determined by subordination under their masters and journeymen might be a consequence of the patriarchal view developed by Brunner in his 'whole house' concept.[89] But were apprentices really the 'most vulnerable parties in their master's household'?[90] The numerous conflicts documented by the trade courts can be read as consequences of vulnerability, but also as manifestations of agency.[91]

Among the proceedings from the Augsburg trade court in the eighteenth century are many conflicts concerning apprenticeship. Per year or per craft, their number is small; in some crafts many years and even decades passed without conflicts that reached the court. Nevertheless, the proceedings gives us a sense of the nature of conflicts between masters, journeymen and apprentices. Most frequently – at least once a year – the trade court dealt with violent behaviour by a master. When apprentices were treated 'very harshly' 'without a sufficient reason', such as laziness or improper behaviour, they were usually given the chance to join another master.[92] In that case, their former master would lose part of the premium, a penalty that was also used as a threat by the trade court and the guilds.[93] Less common, but still a regular feature, were complaints about deficient training. Again, after hearing from the two parties, the trade court often gave masters a warning or allowed apprentices to change master, and sometimes it ordered the partial refunding of the premium.[94] Likewise, masters complained about disobedient, idle or disorderly apprentices, as did one master goldbeater, who stated in 1726 that his apprentice 'won't learn'.[95] In this case, as in others, the master was allowed to dismiss the apprentice.

Persistent conflicts – especially when the apprenticeship lasted for a longer period – could result in the apprentice running away (*Entlaufen*). Leaving an apprenticeship without the master's consent

[88] J. Ehmer, 'Räumliche Mobilität im mitteleuropäischen Handwerk', in: J. Ehmer, *Soziale Traditionen in Zeiten des Wandels: Arbeiter und Handwerker im 19. Jahrhundert* (Frankfurt/M.: Campus, 1994), 101–29.
[89] Grießinger and Reith, 'Lehrlinge im deutschen Handwerk', 149f.
[90] B. De Munck and H. Soly, 'Learning on the shop floor in historical perspective', in: De Munck, Kaplan and Soly (eds.), *Learning on the Shop Floor*, 21.
[91] Grießinger and Reith, 'Lehrlinge im deutschen Handwerk', 150f., 159 and 164.
[92] E.g. KGH 1723, fol. 173f. (26 May), KGH 1729, fol. 192f. (22 June), KGH 1738, fol. 596f. (22 September), KGH 1740, fol. 320f. (22 June) KGH 1751, fol. 147 (15 September).
[93] E.g. KGH 1747, fol. 512f. (11 October) or KGH 1767, fol. 198 (19 October).
[94] E.g. KGH 1726, fol. 11f. (7 January); KGH 1738, fol. 669–72 (20 October); KGH 1791, fol. 149–51 (14 March).
[95] KGH 1726, fol. 485 (16 December).

was a problem frequently addressed in regulations. One instrument used to prevent this was the provision of a deposit or a guarantor: if an apprentice left without his master being at fault and later returned, he might be obliged to pay him money or work for longer to compensate for his master's loss.[96] The rules also covered the possibility of the master being at fault, which might result in a temporary ban on taking other apprentices.[97] At the beginning of the seventeenth century, the Nuremberg city council identified the reasons that could justify running away: insufficient food or lodging, physical violence, unsuitable work or poor education.[98] Some crafts required the masters to pay a deposit to the guild, to prevent such problems.[99] The documents on runaways show different patterns: apprentices tended to run away during an early or a late stage of their training. During the early phase the main issue was their adaption to a new trade and environment with hard labour or long working hours, which might be intensified by individual problems. But there are also several cases of apprentices wanting to expose problems or conflicts concerning violence, board and lodging or training by leaving work. Running away can also be interpreted as a means of exerting pressure on the masters.[100] Unsurprisingly, running away during a late phase happened mainly in apprenticeships with longer terms, as indicated by the register books of the Augsburg goldbeaters.[101]

Sometimes masters tried to get rid of their apprentices through hostile behaviour. This might happen when a shortage of work occurred. If the master had employed an apprentice during a period of high demand, he would still have to pay for his lodging and board during a period of weakening demand or rising food prices. Fees usually lagged behind the cost of food.[102] Like their apprentices, the contract bound the masters for years on end. When, in 1722, the guild of the Augsburg coppersmiths

---

[96] F. Hähnsen, *Geschichte der Kieler Handwerksämter* (Kiel: Lipsius & Tischer, 1920), 178; Schlenkrich, *Der Alltag der Lehrlinge*, 38–41 and 112; Grießinger and Reith, 'Lehrlinge im deutschen Handwerk', 177f.

[97] Schulz, *Handwerksgesellen und Lohnarbeiter*, 256; Wesoly, *Lehrlinge und Handwerksgesellen*, 79; cf. e.g. KGH 1737, fol. 296 (19 June).

[98] Wissell, *Des alten Handwerks Recht und Gewohnheit*, vol. 1; Wesoly, *Lehrlinge und Handwerksgesellen*, 80; Riedl, 'Die rechtliche Stellung', 37.

[99] F. Frisius, *Der vornehmsten Künstler und Handwerker Ceremonial-Politica* (Leipzig: Groschuff, 1708/16).

[100] Grießinger and Reith, 'Lehrlinge im deutschen Handwerk', 177–80; P. Eggers, 'Das Konfliktverhalten Hamburger Handwerker von 1700 bis 1860', PhD thesis, University of Constance, 1988, 228.

[101] Grießinger and Reith, 'Lehrlinge im deutschen Handwerk', 154; Reith, *Arbeits- und Lebensweise*, 188; e.g. KGH 1805, fol. 53 (4 March).

[102] Wesoly, *Lehrlinge und Handwerksgesellen*, 69.

discussed accepting new apprentices, the masters refused to do this because of their poverty. As one master argued, he could dismiss his journeyman 'any time', but this would not be possible with an apprentice.[103]

Can we estimate the number of runaways or apprentices not finishing the term? When we look at the number of apprentices who finished their training, it seems remarkably high at first sight, particularly given that the Augsburg trade court documented cases of apprentices who ran away no less than seven times.[104] Some studies have compared the number of apprentices registered to those that finished their terms. In Mainz, only 2 out of 190 carpenters' and barbers' apprentices registered between 1575 and 1618 did not finish their term properly. In Leipzig, from the sixteenth to the eighteenth century the percentage was 5.2% for the goldsmiths and 10.5% for the cloth makers. Among Augsburg locksmiths' apprentices from 1700 to 1799, 12% of apprentices failed to finish their term, as did 6.4% of Augsburg goldbeaters' apprentices between 1690 and 1800. Times of crisis – such as the Thirty Years War – seem to have pushed up the number of dropouts, with some apprentices leaving to join the armed forces.[105] Between 1660 and 1800, the records of the rural Nuremberg shoemakers document 566 apprentices who took up training: 24 moved to new masters inside the craft, while 19 (i.e. 3%) left the guild. Another 7% did not complete their training for other reasons: 'misfortune' (e.g. accidents) (3), 'poor eyesight' (1), other health issues (3), change of craft (1) or moving into the urban craft (2), military service (8), marriage (2), 'lack of motivation' (*Unlust*) (1) and 'genuine runaway' (*regelrecht entlaufen*) (3).[106] For nineteenth-century Göttingen there is some data suggesting that the nature of the trade might influence the decision to stay or leave and hence completion rates (see Table 5.4).

Where the labour market offered alternatives – as in larger cities and with the evolution of the factory system – the share of dropouts seems to have increased significantly.[107] In Vienna, 20% of apprentice bookbinders (1750–1804), 35.5% of cabinetmakers (1814–40), 41.9% of silkweavers (1810–1903) and 57% of locksmiths (1785–1803) did not finish their training.[108] A survey from 1875 noted an overall increase of

---

[103] KGH 1722, fol. 13 (20 April).

[104] E.g. KGH 1725, fol. 266f. (20 June); KGH 1728, fol. 19 (14 January); KGH 1792, fol. 367f. (16 July).

[105] Wesoly, *Lehrlinge und Handwerksgesellen*, 79; Schlenkrich, *Der Alltag der Lehrlinge*, 112–19; Reith, *Arbeits- und Lebensweise*, 188; cf. e.g. KGH 1758, fol. 84 and 279; KGH 1759, fol. 110 and 116.

[106] O. Puchner, *Die Lehrjungen des Nürnberger Schuhmacherhandwerks auf dem Land, 1660–1808* (Neustadt/Aisch: Degener, 1960), 24–26.

[107] Reith, 'Zur beruflichen Sozialisation', 22–24.   [108] Steidl, *Auf nach Wien*, 252f.

Table 5.4 *Completion rates in selected trades, Göttingen 1814–70*

Trade	Number	Completion rate (%)	Term range (years)	Term mean (years)
Cabinetmaker	302	98.0	3 to 5	3.6
Carpenter	328	96.3	3 to 4	3.0
Thatcher	320	94.4	3 to 4	3.2
Mason	471	91.5	3	3.0
Baker	223	86.5	3 to 4	3.1
Bookbinder	33	81.8	3 to 4	3.1
Rope-maker	44	77.3	2.5 to 4	3.5
Shoemaker	442	75.8	2 to 4	3.5
Tailor	830	73.6	3 to 4.5	3.6

Source: Ludwig, 'Die soziale Lage und soziale Organisation des Kleingewerbes', 125f., 143f.

runaways, especially during the latter part of the apprenticeship. Apprentices were prone to leave if they had reached a certain level of skill and thus employability.[109] In Leipzig, the percentage of shoemaker apprentices who completed their training dropped from 91% for the period 1835–59, to 81% between 1865 and 1879.[110]

These changes during the nineteenth century were a major contrast with the preceding centuries, when a large proportion of apprentices finished their training. There were several reasons for this. Premiums and the guild-related fees formed an investment for apprentices' parents or guardians that could equal a significant amount of money, which was lost if the apprentice left without the master giving consent or being at fault. However, the crucial factor determining the completion of terms was the labour market. Before the Industrial Revolution only the formal completion of training offered the chance of working as a skilled labourer and, eventually, of self-employment.[111] In general, apprenticeship was ended by the 'release' (*Freisprechen*), which was sometimes – especially in smaller crafts – bound to an elaborate *rite de passage* and usually also

---

[109] *Ergebnisse der über die Verhältnisse der Lehrlinge, Gesellen und Fabrikarbeiter auf Beschluß des Bundesraths angestellten Erhebungen, zusammengestellt im Reichskanzleramt* (Berlin: 1877), 97ff.

[110] N. Geissenberger, 'Die Schuhmacherei in Leipzig und Umgebung', in: Verein für Socialpolitik (ed.), *Untersuchungen über die Lage des Handwerks*, vol. 2, 191f.

[111] De Munck and Soly, 'Learning on the shop floor', 9f.; Ehmer and Reith, 'Die mitteleuropäische Stadt als frühneuzeitlicher Arbeitsmarkt', 232–58.

included the guild's journeymen.[112] A formal examination was unusual (there are only a few references for some textile crafts and for goldsmiths), but often a certificate (*Lehrbrief*) was issued by the guild, which was both a requirement for entering the labour market and an attempt by the guild and territorial authorities to assert their authority.[113] These certificates were, like the contracts, quite short and followed a standard form.[114] Documents from the Augsburg trade court suggest that the acquisition of a certificate was important for journeymen. The lack of a certificate did not result immediately in a ban from working, but when conflicts arose, the court would ask for the document, often pushed by other journeymen keen to identify 'illicit' competiton.[115]

Conclusion

German apprenticeship developed from the late Middle Ages and remained crucial for skilled craft work until the end of the nineteenth century. This long continuity suggests that apprenticeship formed a viable solution for the crafts and for the learners. The acquisition of skills was primarily exchanged for labour (and secondarily for money), while masters and journeymen were able to influence the reproduction of the craft and the skilled labour market to a certain extent. Furthermore, it allowed the supra-regional circulation of skilled labour, which unfolded from the late medieval period.

Apprenticeship was developed and maintained by the urban guilds and it was adopted by many rural crafts as well. There was skilled labour outside the guilds,[116] but apprenticeship was a necessity for working as a journeyman and for becoming a master within the guilds. The framework of the apprenticeship was shaped by the guilds, but the practice was determined by individual masters, with urban and central authorities only interfering at the margins before the nineteenth century.

The conditions of each apprenticeship were negotiated directly between the masters and the apprentices (or their parents or guardians)

---

[112] Cf. KGH 1740, fol. 267f. (12 October).

[113] Wesoly, *Lehrlinge und Handwerksgesellen*, 82; H. Sakuma, *Die Nürnberger Tuchmacher, Weber, Färber und Bereiter vom 14. bis 17. Jahrhundert* (Nuremberg: Stadtarchiv, 1993), 284; A. Kutschbach, *Geschichte der Tuchscherer-Innung in Leipzig* (Leipzig: Bielefeld, 1931), 37; Schlenkrich, *Der Alltag der Lehrlinge*, 83; cf. KGH 1748, fol. 204f. (6 May) and *Reichsordnung zur Abstellung von Handwerks-Mißbräuchen*, 3.

[114] Cf. the templates from the early eighteenth century in Brauser, *Der ganz Neue [. . .] Briefsteller*, 1194–2000.

[115] This happened frequently in the case of masons: cf. KGH 1726, fol. 15–17 (7 January); KGH 1731, fol. 301f. (23 July); KGH 1762, fol. 167 (20 August); KGH 1766, fol. 161 (1 October); KGH 1800, fol. 154f. (11 August).

[116] R. Reith, 'Zünfte im Süden des Alten Reiches', in: Haupt, *Das Ende der Zünfte*, 51–54.

and they were often documented in contracts. The interests in these contracts were mutual. Risks needed to be reduced and the investment should pay off for both sides. Conflicts were an inevitable side effect of the social and economic situation within the workshop, but violence and exploitation were not the regular experience of the apprentices. This is indicated by the overall tendency to complete the terms as they were agreed. Likewise, complaints about inferior training – which were also voiced by contemporaries outside the craft – are not confirmed in sources such as the proceedings from trade courts.

The persistence of craft apprenticeship during industrialisation is another sign of the effectiveness and flexibility of the crafts' learning-by-doing system. During the nineteenth century, the apprenticeship system went through significant changes, but it was not replaced. Rather, it was enhanced by schooling, creating the so-called dual system. Labourers trained in the crafts were relevant for industry into the twentieth century. Until the end of the nineteenth century, journeymen, who worked as industrial wage labourers, still had the ambition and opportunity to become independent master craftsmen, as is indicated by the occupational censuses (*Berufs- und Gewerbezählungen*) of that time.[117]

---

[117] Cf. J. Ehmer, 'Lohnarbeit und Lebenszyklus im Kaiserreich', *Geschichte und Gesellschaft* 14 (1988), 448–71.

6 Rural Artisans' Apprenticeship Practices in Early Modern Finland (1700–1850)

Merja Uotila

In 1775 Gustaf Haqvin, a tailor, recommended to his local district court that a young man called Johan Carlsson Tirberg should be appointed as a parish tailor for Hollola district.[1] Haqvin testified that Tirberg had begun his apprenticeship with Haqvin's late father 18 years earlier and had continued with Haqvin before being released from his service. He affirmed in writing that Tirberg had already worked for parishioners, and, more importantly, was sufficiently skilled to be a parish tailor.

In this chapter, I shall outline how rural artisans in Finland organised their apprenticeships from the beginning of the eighteenth century to the 1840s. Apprenticeship and the three-stage career pattern of artisans (apprentice–journeyman–master) have traditionally been associated with craft guilds in urban environments,[2] but that is not the whole picture. There were also artisans like Haqvin working in rural areas, who legitimately kept apprentices and trained younger artisans such as Tirberg. In fact, when one looks more closely at the specific training practices of rural artisans one sees more clearly how craft knowledge and skills were transferred from one generation to the next. Rural apprenticeships can thus help us to distinguish guild-based particularities from the more universal features of craft apprenticeship. We can also analyse the extent to which rural artisans emulated their urban counterparts and demonstrate when they relied on their own local training customs.

In line with mercantilist principles, the authorities in Finland (and Sweden, of which Finland was a part until 1809) regarded craftwork as an urban occupation and expected trade and manufacturing to be centred in towns. Nevertheless, in an agrarian state where the few towns that existed were small and the distances between them considerable, rural craftsmen were tolerated as a necessity. In the kingdom of Sweden,

---

[1] National Archives (NA), archives of Hollola District Court, autumn 1775, §12. Language editing: Murray Pearson.
[2] B. De Munck and H. Soly, '"Learning on the shop floor" in historical perspective', in: B. De Munck, S. L. Kaplan and H. Soly (eds.), *Learning on the Shop Floor: Historical Perspectives on Apprenticeship* (New York: Berghahn, 2007), 10–11.

ordinances passed in 1680 and 1686 formally integrated rural crafts into a parish artisan[3] system. Rural artisans had to be licensed and paid special taxes to the crown.[4]

The general attitude of urban guilds towards rural crafts was restrictive and controlling. For instance, town artisans (and their guilds) were protected by the so-called 'ban mile', an area extending for several miles around towns within which rural artisan were barred from working without guild approval.[5] However, aside from this, town guilds only controlled urban crafts and not rural manufacturing, as they did in some other parts of Europe.[6] It was local and provincial authorities who supervised rural crafts. The artisans' clients, mainly peasant folk living by agriculture, also had a voice in deciding on the number of artisans allowed in a locality.

The prestige and skills of rural and urban artisans differed, with urban artisans enjoying greater esteem. Apart from the restrictions imposed by the parish artisan system, there were differences in training: the craft skills one acquired by serving a rural master were not as advanced as those learned in an urban apprenticeship.[7] If a rural apprentice wanted to achieve the status of master artisan he would have to continue his training under an urban guild master for an additional period. (By definition, new guild masters had to have been taught by a guild master.[8]) These restrictions also served to limit guild membership. Rural artisans were only permitted to work in rural areas, as they were only meant to satisfy the basic needs of rural clients. Indeed, guild standards occasionally dwelled explicitly on the difference between town and countryside. For instance,

[3] *Sockne hantverkare.* Titles are given in Swedish as in the original texts.
[4] I define rural artisans as persons who made handicraft goods for local markets. Cottage industry and proto-industry are excluded from this definition because their production was aimed at distant markets.
[5] U. Heino, *Käsityö ja sen tekijät 1600-luvun Satakunnassa* (Helsinki: Finnish Literature Society, 1984), 67–68; C.-J. Gadd, *Själrvhushåll eller arbetsdelning? Svenskt lant- och stadshantverk ca 1400–1860* (Gotenborg: Göteborgs universitet, 1991), 244.
[6] See for instance J. Ehmer, 'Rural guilds and urban–rural guild relations in early modern Central Europe', *International Review of Social History* 53 (2008), supplement, 148–50.
[7] K. J. Kaukovalta, *Hämeen läänin Historia I* (Hämeenlinna: Arvi A. Karisto Osakeyhtiö, 1931), 440; S. Möller, 'Ammattikuntien kukoistuskaudelta Helsingissä', *Entisaikain Helsinki* 1 (1936), 52; A. Halila, *Iitin historia vahaisimmista ajoista 1860-luvulle* (Iitti, 1939), 598; E. Jutikkala, 'Maan omistus ja väestöryhmät', in: V. Voionmaa et al. (eds.), *Längelmäveden Seudun historia I. Kangasalan historia 1* (Forssa, 1949), 299; R. Papinsaari, 'Turun räätälien ammattikunta vuosina 1721–1809', *Turun Historiallinen Arkisto* 20 (1967), 259; K. Vainio-Korhonen, *Käsin tehty – miehelle ammatti, naiselle ansioiden lähde. Käsityötuotannon rakenteet ja strategiat esiteollisessa Turussa Ruotsin ajan lopulla* (Helsinki: Finnish Literature Society, 1998), 130–31.
[8] E. Söderlund, *Hantverkarna. Andra Delen. Stormaktstiden, frihetstiden och gustavianska tiden* (Stockholm: Tidens Förlag, 1949), 102, 114.

in Turku, the main town in Finland, the tailors' guild masterpiece was a man's outfit matching the town dwellers' fashion in style and fabric.[9] Rural apprentices were not unusual; their training was a legitimate practice that aimed to transfer craft skills. There were many similarities between the conventions of rural apprenticeship and urban guild-based apprenticeship: urban guild rules set the norms for several aspects of apprenticeship, such as the proper starting age, that rural craftsmen adopted. In order to understand some of the details of rural training, therefore, we also have to know about urban practices. However, rural artisans also generated their own customs, and these practices differed between trades.

To overcome the limitations imposed by the paucity of surviving sources, I examine rural apprenticeship in detail in one area, through a prosopographical study of Hollola, a large parish in southern Finland.[10] Hollola was in most respects a typical rural parish, located outside the 'ban mile' and so free from urban craft regulations. It was well known and prosperous, attracting artisans from neighbouring parishes as well as journeymen from the towns. From 1700 to 1850, Hollola's population increased from 5,000 to nearly 8,000 inhabitants, who were mostly free-holding farmers or members of farming households.[11] By 1840, the parish contained over 50 settlements of different sizes, from large villages with over 200 residents and more than 30 farms to small settlements of one or two farms.[12] Hollola spread over a width of 20 kilometres, but enjoyed a good road network.

As with most of Europe, our current understanding of rural apprenticeship in Finland is fragmentary.[13] There have been no studies of rural apprenticeship as such, although the topic is touched upon in many local histories and historical studies, especially of the eighteenth century.

---

[9] Papinsaari, 'Turun räätälien ammattikunta', 304.

[10] On prosopography, see: K. S. B. Keats-Rohan (ed.), *Prosopography Approaches and Applications: A Handbook* (Oxford: Prosposgraphica et Genealogica, 2007); D. Broady, 'French prosopography: Definition and suggested readings', *Poetics* 30 (2002), 381–85; M. Uotila, 'Tavallisuuden tavoittelua: Prospografia elämäkerrallisen tutkimuksen välineenä', in: H. Hakosalo, S. Jalagin, M. Junila and H. Kurvinen (eds.), *Historiallinen elämä: Biografia ja historiantutkimus* (Helsinki: Finnish Literature Society, 2014); M. Uotila, *Käsityöläinen kyläyhteisönsä jäsenenä. Prosopografinen analyysi Hollolan käsityöläisistä 1810–1840* (Jyväskylä: University of Jyväskylä, 2014), 31–43.

[11] E. Jutikkala, *Suomen talonpojan historia* (Helsinki: Finnish Literature Society, 1958).

[12] Uotila, *Käsityöläinen kyläyhteisönsä jäsenenä*, 103; S. Kuusi, *Hollolan pitäjän Historia. Muinaisuuden hämärästä kunnallisen elämän alkuun 1860-luvulle. Toinen osa* (Porvoo: WSOY, 1937), 75–95.

[13] H. Schultz, *Landhandwerk im Übergang vom Feudalismus zum Kapitalismus* (Berlin: Akademie-Verlag, 1984), 242; H. Schultz, *Handwerker, Kaufleute, Bankiers. Wirtschaftsgeschichte Europas 1500–1800*, 2nd edition (Frankfurt am Main: Fischer, 2002), 99.

A long-standing research project at Turku University on early modern artisans offers some insights, while Veikko Laakso's studies provide a useful reference point on rural apprentices, as does Raimo Ranta's examination of the parish artisan system.[14] Because Finland and Sweden share a common history, it is also important to take Swedish research into account. Ernst Söderlund's generic description of the history of Swedish crafts gives an overall picture of urban guilds, complemented by Lars Edgren's examination of one Swedish town's guilds.[15] What we mainly lack are studies on the decline of apprenticeship.

Studying rural apprentices' careers and backgrounds is not straightforward; there are no records of the kind maintained by urban guilds. Crucially, there were no registers of apprentices (*inskrivningsbok*)[16] and because in rural areas there were no guilds to produce such records, there was no recorded proof that artisans were fully qualified. Rural artisans were only weakly connected; they were not organised collectively. As we saw earlier, individual rural masters occasionally wrote letters attesting to a completed apprenticeship, but few such have survived.[17] Instead, information about rural apprentices must be gleaned from other sources: annual church records of communions, in which all household dependents were listed;[18] annual census lists kept by the state, which enumerate all members of households between 15 and 62 years old for whom poll tax was paid; and local court records of artisan and apprenticeship licences, permits and disputes. These allow us to compile short biographies of apprentices, including data on boys' dates and places of birth, their parents' social status, masters' names and domiciles, the duration of apprenticeships, and activities thereafter. Unfortunately, these sources

---

[14] V. Laakso, 'Loimaan ja Huittisten suurpitäjien käsityöläiset vuosina 1721–1809', unpublished MA thesis, University of Turku, 1974; Heino, *Käsityö ja sen tekijät*; R. Ranta, *Pohjanmaan maaseudun käsityöläiset vuosina 1721–1809 I. Käsityöläiseksi pääsy ja käsityöläisten lukumäärä* (Helsinki: Finnish Literature Society, 1978); Vainio-Korhonen, *Käsin tehty*.

[15] Söderlund, *Hantverkarna*; L. Edgren, *Lärling, gesäll, mästare: Hantverk och hantverkare i Malmö 1750–1847* (Lund: Dialogos, 1987); Gadd, *Själrvhushåll eller arbetsdelning*.

[16] Möller, 'Ammattikuntien kukoistuskaudelta Helsingissä', 50; Söderlund, *Hantverkarna*, 238, 392; Papinsaari, 'Turun räätälien ammattikunta', 249; Vainio-Korhonen, *Käsin tehty*, 127–28; K. Vainio-Korhonen, 'Kaupan ja käsityön ammattikasvatus' in: J. Hanska and K. Vainio-Korhonen (eds.), *Huoneentaulun maailma. Kasvatus ja koulutus Suomessa keskiajalta 1860-luvulle* (Helsinki: Finnish Literature Society, 2010), 232–33.

[17] These letters were sometimes copied or mentioned in court records.

[18] Apprentices' membership of artisans households was a necessary legal protection. Everybody in the kingdom of Sweden had to be registered as belonging somewhere and have this kind of protected status, otherwise they were deemed unprotected vagrants. Parish artisans' had independent status that meant they could provide legal protection to their own households, just as a peasant could for his family, servants and lodgers. Edgren, *Lärling, gesäll, mästare*, 134.

do not always give precise dates, and church records only survive from the later eighteenth century.[19] All in all, the careers of 300 apprentices in Hollola between 1749 and 1840 have been extracted.

Rural apprentices can only be recognised in the sources when they are identified as such; inevitably, if a person in training was not thus referred to, his apprenticeship remained hidden. Official records are in Swedish, because that was the language of administration up to the second half of the nineteenth century. Apprentices and artisans' assistants were described as *lärling, lärodräng, läropojke/lärögosse* – or appropriate abbreviations.[20] These titles had Finnish equivalents: *oppilas, oppirenki, oppipoika*. The key elements in these titles are the verbs *lära* (Swedish) and *oppia* (Finnish): to learn. Naturally, language and terms developed over the time, an issue that I shall return to later.

Artisans in Rural Parishes

Rural apprenticeship in Finland was fundamentally shaped by the parish artisan system, through which artisans obtained their licence to work (*gärningsbrev*) and paid special handicraft taxes (*gärningsöre*). Although licences were granted by provincial governors, in the eighteenth century applicants first needed a written testimonial from their local court (which consisted of landowning peasant members of the local community). This allowed the number of local craftsmen to be regulated by their clients.[21] (Naturally, the local elite, priests and administrators, such as bailiffs, also had a say.[22]) Applications were made in the name of the whole community, who first publicly complained about the need for a craftsman, then subsequently announced that they had a good candidate. In the nineteenth century, artisans usually applied independently. Parish artisans also needed official permission to leave a parish or their position – at least in principle; in practice, they often simply stopped work or moved without permission. These procedural customs would suggest that rural artisans were the servants of their clients. This was often mentioned in legal texts (as a duty to serve their clients faithfully) and in court rulings, but one may assume that it was also the case in reality.[23]

---

[19] The vicarage of Hollola was burnt down in 1750 and 1770 with the loss of earlier records. Kuusi, *Hollolan pitäjän Historia*, 213.

[20] See e.g. Svenska Akademiens ordbok (SAOB), word lära, http://g3.spraakdata.gu.se/saob.

[21] See Ranta, *Pohjanmaan maaseudun käsityöläiset*, 104.

[22] The gentry had a right to employ their own manor artisans (*gårds hantverkare*), but they did not usually have apprentices: Heino, *Käsityö ja sen tekijät*, 193–201.

[23] Uotila, *Käsityöläinen kyläyhteisönsä jäsenenä*, 140–41.

Up to the early eighteenth century only a few occupations were recognised by parish artisan law: blacksmiths, shoemakers and tailors. For brief periods in the mid-eighteenth century a few other crafts (masons, glaziers and bricklayers) were included in this provision,[24] while other craftsmen were only permitted to work in towns under the supervision of the appropriate guild. However, provincial governors could grant permits to most craftsmen (except goldsmiths) using a 1604 statute which stated that rural peasants could keep the artisans they needed. As a result, weavers and tanners did sometimes gain licences as parish artisans.[25] Much depended on the individual governor. This situation changed in 1824 when several more crafts, including tanners, glaziers and hatmakers, gained the right to become parish artisans. Finally, in 1859 all rural residents were granted the right to follow any craft for their livelihood. The ban mile, the distinction between rural and urban crafts, and the parish artisan system remained intact, but were much weakened.[26] In Finland, the practice of crafts remained restricted until the 1879 freedom of trade act.

One peculiar characteristic of rural artisans, apart from smiths and tanners, is that they did not necessarily have their own workshops. Instead, tailors and shoemakers (and their apprentices) moved from one client to another, receiving board and lodging for a week or two while working for them.[27] These artisans did have their own houses, where their families remained while the master was away. Smiths, on the other hand, were tied to the smithy, which was often jointly owned by the villagers. Rural masters usually sold only their labour. The raw materials came from the client and everything was bespoke, not ready-made. Shoemakers and tailors received a payment for each piece, while smiths had yearly contracts with the village, including annual payments.

---

[24] Masons (from 1756), bricklayers (1762) and glaziers (1766) were allowed to work in rural areas until 1789. Masons and glaziers were permitted to do so again in 1802: Söderlund, *Hantverkarna*, 230; Ranta, *Pohjanmaan maaseudun käsityöläiset*, 90; Gadd, *Själrvhushåll eller arbetsdelning*, 299–300.

[25] Ranta, *Pohjanmaan maaseudun käsityöläiset*, 90–94.

[26] *Samling af placater, förordningar, manifester och påbud, samt andre allmänna handlingar, hwilka i stor-furstendömet Finland sedan 1808 års början ifrån trycket utkommit. Fjerde Delen 1821–1824* (Åbo: J. Frenckell & Son, 1826), 311; *Samling af placater, förordningar, manifester och påbud, samt andre allmänna handlingar, hwilka i stor-furstendömet Finland sedan 1808 års början ifrån trycket utkommit. Sjuttonde Delen 1858–1859*, (Kejserliga Senatens för Finland tryckeri, 1862), 725–30.

[27] NA, archives of Hollola District Court, autumn 1832, §251; R. Ranta, 'Talouselämä, asutus ja väestö Etelä-Pohjanmaalla 1809–1917', in: H. Ylikangas (ed.), *Etelä-Pohjanmaan historia V. Autonomian kausi 1809–1917* (Seinäjoki: Eteläpohjanmaan maakuntaliitto, 1988), 731.

Only a few parish artisans worked in each parish in the seventeenth and early eighteenth centuries. The institution evolved gradually, and general social and economic developments also served to keep numbers low. In particular, the war years of the first half of the eighteenth century severely curtailed demand for artisans' services.[28] From 1750, however, the number of artisans began to increase rapidly. Most parishes took their first parish artisan around this time. This so-called first-generation of artisans also took on more apprentices, raising the volume and availability of craft goods. In Finland, industrialisation did not affect artisans' livelihoods until the later nineteenth century. During the first half of the nineteenth century, the number of rural artisans still exceeded that of their urban counterparts.[29] With the decline of self-sufficiency, the growth of material wealth and changing consumption patterns, there was more scope for rural artisans. The result was that town artisans and craft guilds had to deal with increasing competition from rural craftsmen.[30]

Despite the parish artisan system, there were also unlicensed artisans working in rural parishes.[31] Most of the time, these unlicensed artisans worked without legal difficulty, as the parish artisan system was sometimes ignored. Unlicensed artisans did not pay craft taxes and do not appear in the census records as artisans.[32] Unlike the situation in towns, official and unofficial rural artisans usually coexisted peacefully, even though there were considerable numbers of unofficial artisans. Unlicensed craftsmen were only taken to court when a parish artisan felt that his position and livelihood were threatened. In the nineteenth century, those rural artisans who were brought to court were usually former apprentices who had not yet been licensed by the governor.[33] A major difference between licensed and unlicensed artisans is that the latter did not usually have apprentices. The main issue was not that the

---

[28] The great wrath (1712–21) in particular had a dire effect on local economies and living conditions: T. J. Paloposki, 'Kauppa, käsityö ja teollisuus', in: J. Tuominen, E. Jutikkala, O. Vuorinen, V. Heikkilä and Y. S. Koskimies (eds.), *Hämeen historia III:2. Vuodesta 1721 noin vuoteen 1870* (Hämeenlinna: Hämeen heimoliitto, 1976), 368.

[29] P. Schybergson, *Hantverk och fabriker III. Finlands konsumtionsvaruindustri 1815–1870: Tabellbilagor* (Helsinki: Finska Vetenskaps-societeten, 1974).

[30] R. Hjerppe, 'Käsityöläiset uuden yhteiskunnan murroksessa', in: Y. Kaukiainen (ed.), *När samhället förändras. Kun yhteiskunta muuttuu* (Helsinki: Finnish Literature Society, 1981).

[31] Ranta, *Pohjanmaan maaseudun käsityöläiset*, 90–94; Uotila, *Käsityöläinen kyläyhteisönsä jäsenenä*, 79–81.

[32] In tax registers, unofficial artisans were listed as farmhands (*dräng*), tenant farmers (*landbonde* or *torpare*) or landless agrarian workers (such as *inhysning, spannmålstorpare, backstugusittare*), not as artisans. Church records, on the other hand, usually revealed craft occupations.

[33] For instance, NA, archives of Hollola District Court, winter 1830, §192; winter 1832, §27; Uotila, *Käsityöläinen kyläyhteisönsä jäsenenä*, 86–91.

Table 6.1 *Number of parish artisans per year, Hollola 1751–1840*

	1751	1761	1771	1780	1790	1800	1810	1820	1830	1840
Smiths	1	4	6	11	14	14	17	20	22	15
Tailors	2	4	3	10	7	11	10	10	12	20
Shoemakers	0	0	1	3	5	6	6	13	17	26
Weavers	2	1	1	5	5	2	1	0	1	1
Carpenters*	0	1	0	2	1	4	3	2	3	3
Tanners	0	0	0	1	2	0	0	0	2	2
Total	5	10	11	32	34	37	37	45	57	67

Note: The table gives the number of artisans observed in a single year in the census; *carpenters and masons are combined, as these trades were often practised together.
Source: Census records, see text.

parish artisans had superior skills – there is no proof of that. It was rather a question of status. Young boys were expected to train with a proper, licensed master, whose position and reputation were commonly acknowledged.[34] Because unofficial artisans often had other sources of income besides their craft, such as farming, they had little time to train others.

Although rural artisans often had to be jacks of all trades, far fewer trades were followed in rural areas than in towns. Most parish artisans were blacksmiths, tailors or shoemakers. Smiths were especially important in rural areas as they made and repaired farm tools, whereas in towns they usually represented only a small percentage of artisans.[35] The second and third largest groups in the countryside were usually tailors and shoemakers. The common people of the countryside could make everyday clothing and shoes, but tailors made men's clothes and fine attire for women. Similarly, shoemakers made finer shoes. Tailors and shoemakers were particularly affected by the rise of consumption in the nineteenth century. Together, these three occupations constituted the majority of the official parish artisans working in rural parishes (Table 6.1).[36]

---

[34] The fate of free masters in towns supports this claim. Free masters were artisans working outside the guilds, under royal licences. As guilds did not approve free masters or their apprentices, parents were reluctant to place their children with them: Söderlund, *Hantverkarna*, 193, 200.

[35] I. Talve, *Suomen Kansankulttuuri* (Helsinki: Finnish Literature Society, 1990), 105.

[36] The distribution of the three trades varied by time and place; see: V. Laakso, *Suur-Loimaan historia II. Isonvihan päättymisestä 1900-luvun alkuun* (Alastaro, 1994), 76. See also Ranta, *Pohjanmaan maaseudun käsityöläiset*, 206–11; Gadd, *Själrvhushåll eller arbetsdelning*, 115, 144.

The numbers of other artisans in rural areas, such as weavers or carpenters, fluctuated. For instance, weaving was an important male occupation from the 1750s up to the end of century, but this trade gradually lost its position when it became economically unviable due to the rising costs of materials and to competition from domestic weaving by women. Male weavers and their apprentices almost disappeared from towns and countryside in the early nineteenth century. Weaving continued, but because only males were accorded the status of artisan female weavers were not labelled as artisans[37] and their work therefore remain unrecorded. We cannot therefore take female artisans into account. This also meant that there were no female apprentices – at least not officially.[38] Rural artisans in other trades had few apprentices. Most had served apprenticeships under urban artisans. For instance, none of Hollola's tanners took apprentices, although carpenters and masons provide a few rare exceptions.

The Law of Apprenticeship

In the sixteenth and seventeenth centuries, Sweden aimed to keep its apprenticeship practices consistent with general European conventions, maintaining a tripartite occupational structure and granting written documents that conformed to general, mainly German, standards. Guild-trained Swedish and Finnish journeymen travelled and worked in other parts of Europe, especially in German countries. Later this connection loosened and occasionally there were attempts to prevent journeymen travelling abroad.[39] The legal framework under which urban artisans and apprentices worked was set by the state in its general guild orders (*skråordning* from 1669 to 1720), which stipulated the limits of guild activities. Swedish and Finnish craft guilds were under crown supervision and needed government approval for their regulations. Although the guild orders were designed for urban craft guilds, they also set the norms for rural artisans and apprenticeship. For instance, they stipulated for apprentices a minimum enrolment age of 14 years old and a maximum trial period of two months. They also specified master craftsmen's rights and responsibilities towards their apprentices. For instance, artisans could expect apprentices who lived with them to carry out ordinary

---

[37] Söderlund, *Hantverkarna*, 75; K. Vainio-Korhonen, 'Handicrafts as professions and source of income in late eighteenth and early nineteenth-century Turku (Åbo)', *Scandinavian Economic History Review* 48 (2000), 48–49.

[38] Vainio-Korhonen, *Käsin tehty*, 16–18.

[39] Söderlund, *Hantverkarna*, 141, 152, 214, 243–44; Edgren, *Lärling, gesäll, mästare*, 249; L. Edgren, 'What did guilds do? Swedish guilds in the eighteenth and early nineteenth century', in: I. A. Gadd and P. Wallis (eds.), *Guilds and Association in Europe, 900–1900* (London: University of London, 2006), 52–51.

household chores. They could not dismiss apprentices before their term was competed.[40] The number of apprentices they took was not restricted by law, although some guilds capped the number per master to ease competition.[41]

Guild ordinances and urban craft culture provided an important model for rural artisans since the formal rules for apprenticeships outside towns were few and non-specific. Under the 1686 parish artisan ordinance, shoemakers and tailors were allowed to take apprentice boys (*läropojke*) and one assistant (*lärodräng*) – the latter with permission from the county administration. In 1727, this entitlement was repeated, with the clarification that the *lärodräng* had to have already served an apprenticeship.[42] In Swedish and Finnish, *dräng* meant a hired helper, implying that they received wages. In short, artisans needed a licence to employ paid assistants, whereas training apprentices was free from licensing.[43] Assistants and apprentices were thus clearly distinct, although the difference is not always evident as the usage of these terms varies from one source to another.[44] Unlike town-trained craftsmen, rural apprentices could apply to be a parish artisan immediately after their apprenticeship, without working as journeymen for a period, although it was more common for them to practise a trade on their own or as an assistant for a while before acquiring this formal status. Guild-trained journeymen (Swedish: *gesäll*), were, as their different title suggests, a case apart.[45] A guild-trained apprentice was awarded a *gesällbref* – a certificate of completed training – by the guild. Hence, in the eighteenth century a rural *lärodräng* was not quite the same as a *gesäll*. For clarity, I have translated the first as *assistant* and the latter as *journeyman*.

In the nineteenth century, the distinction between apprentices and assistants became blurred. A new term, *lärling* (or the equivalent abbreviation), became commonplace, eventually replacing the older, more

[40] R. G. Modée, *Utdrag utur alle ifrån den 7. decemb. 1718. /1791 utkomne publique handlingar, Del I.* (Stockholm, 1742), 211 (General guild orders, Art. IX:2, 4.); Söderlund, *Hantverkarna*, 169, 405–20; Edgren, *Lärling, gesäll, mästare*, 65.

[41] Söderlund, *Hantverkarna*, 112; Papinsaari, 'Turun räätälien ammattikunta', 246, 314; Edgren, *Lärling, gesäll, mästare*, 154.

[42] A. A. von Stiermann, *Alla riksdagars och mötens beslut 1521–1731, del III.* (Stockholm, 1733), 2006–07; Modée, *Utdrag*, 673. See also Heino, *Käsityö ja sen tekijät*, 73–77; Gadd, *Självhushåll eller arbetsdelning*, 248.

[43] Apprentices were more often styled *lärogåsse*: Laakso, 'Loimaan ja Huittisten', 65.

[44] For instance, eighteenth-century census lists described all apprentices and assistants with one term, *lärodräng*, while communion records use more varied terms.

[45] The title *lärodräng* is also found in towns, where it referred to new journeymen who were expected to stay with their master for one year after the end of their apprenticeship: Papinsaari, 'Turun räätälien ammattikunta', 273.

exact titles.[46] Clearly, artisans did also employ paid assistants, but it is often impossible to distinguish them from apprentices. A statute of 1859, however, confirmed the distinction between apprentices and assistants, and stated that artisans needed permission to hire more than one waged assistant.[47] Court rulings were mixed: sometimes courts required artisans to obtain a licence to take apprentices.[48] However, applications for permission to take apprentices or assistants are scarce after 1800.[49] In Hollola, only one master applied to the district court for permission between 1810 and 1840. Yet in that period there were more than one hundred apprentices in Hollola. Obviously, artisans did not feel the need to ask for official permission, indicating that the licensing system was in decline.

The distinction between assistant and apprentice has not been widely noticed in studies of rural crafts. It is often suggested that rural artisans did not employ journeymen, and there is little discussion of assistants.[50] The reason that parish artisans were required to obtain court permission to hire skilled servants was mainly economic. They did not need approval to train apprentices, but when it came to employing workers, local clients needed to decide whether there was sufficient demand – the same criterion that held for licensing a parish artisan.[51] Accordingly, when artisans applied for permission to take on an assistant, they usually referred to their heavy workload in their petition, implying that they needed an experienced, capable assistant – effectively a journeyman – rather than an unseasoned apprentice. In the nineteenth century, in the county of

---

[46] Laakso, 'Loimaan ja Huittisten', 129 also notes the inconsistent use of these terms.

[47] *Samling af placater*, statute 12 December 1859, §12.

[48] E.g. Uotila, *Käsityöläinen kyläyhteisönsä jäsenenä*, 219. Some historians have suggested that apprentices needed permissions: Kaukovalta, *Hämeen läänin Historia*, 440; Jutikkala, 'Maan omistus ja väestöryhmät', 298; N. Berndtson, *Laukaan historia II. 1776–1868* (Laukaa, 1986), 171; M. Kuisma, *Helsingin pitäjän historia III. Isostavihasta maalaiskunnan syntyy 1713–1865* (Vantaa, 1991), 260–61.

[49] Uotila, *Käsityöläinen kyläyhteisönsä jäsenenä*, 135 (fig. II:9), 218–19. Laakso also notes the small number of applications, which he links to the problem of monitoring the rules, and the difficulty of separating apprentices and assistants: Laakso, 'Loimaan ja Huittisten', 65

[50] E. Jutikkala, *Sääksmäen pitäjän historia* (Sääksmäki, 1934), 470; S. Suvanto, *Akaan historia: Toijala-Kylmäkoski-Viiala. Ensimmäinen osa* (Vammala, 1954), 190; J. Saarenheimo, *Vanhan Pirkkalan historia* (Nokia, 1974), 416; S. Suvanto, *Kalvolan historia I. Esihistoria ja Ruotsin vallan aika* (Kalvola, 1992), 232.

[51] Söderlund, *Hantverkarna*, 345. See also Jutikkala, 'Maan omistus ja väestöryhmät', 300; A. Rosenberg, 'Väestö Suomen sodasta itsenäisyyden alkuun', in: A. Rosenberg, J. Lomu and K. Manninen (eds.), *Mäntsälän Historia II* (Mäntsälä, 1993), 128; A. Rosenberg, 'Väestö ja elinkeinot', in: A. Rosenberg and R. Selin (eds.), *Suur-Tuusulan historia. Tuusula – Kerava – Järvenpää. 3, Suomen sodasta 1808–1809 itsenäisyyden ajan alkuun* (Tuusula, 1995), 131.

Uusimaa and Häme, several artisans applied to take assistants at the same time as they applied for their own licence.[52] Perhaps this was for practical reasons, because of court fees. In towns, in contrast, taking apprentices was more strictly regulated. Usually artisans had to work independently for a period before recruiting one.[53]

Apprenticeship Practices

Official artisans had a monopoly on apprenticeships. In towns each new generation was taught by guild masters, while in rural areas it was licensed parish artisans who trained their successors.[54] Some craftsmen were self-taught, it is true, especially in earlier times when there were fewer artisans,[55] but to be accepted into a guild or licensed as a parish artisan without the evidence of having completed an apprenticeship, they would usually have to demonstrate their skills by producing a masterpiece.[56] Completion of a rural apprenticeship, however, did not entail any formal test of skill. This was a clear difference from the demands of urban guilds, where journeymen had to produce a masterpiece before admission as a master artisan.[57] For a rural apprentice, serving their time with a master sufficed. Sometimes courts asked for written proof of the apprenticeship, as in the case of Johan Tirberg, but this was not usually necessary. But then, people applying to become parish artisans were usually well known, having often already worked for a number of years (effectively a trial period) in the area.[58]

[52] NA, Province of Uusimaa and Häme, Governors' Secretariat, Records of applications 1790–1830; Uotila, *Käsityöläinen kyläyhteisönsä jäsenenä*, 135.

[53] Papinsaari, 'Turun räätälien ammattikunta', 246; Edgren, *Lärling, gesäll, mästare*, 231.

[54] Unofficial artisans or free masters in urban areas (artisans operating outside guilds) rarely had apprentices. Söderlund, *Hantverkarna*, 193, 200; Uotila, *Käsityöläinen kyläyhteisönsä jäsenenä*, 276–78.

[55] In Swedish towns, Söderlund calls these self-taught men amateurs. In addition, some parish artisans cannot be linked to any master, so may have been self-taught: Söderlund, *Hantverkarna*, 269; Uotila, *Käsityöläinen kyläyhteisönsä jäsenenä*, 230–31.

[56] Ranta, *Pohjanmaan maaseudun käsityöläiset*, 103–04.

[57] Masterpieces were universal in Finnish and Swedish guilds and sometimes apprentices were tested before becoming a journeyman. Söderlund, *Hantverkarna*, 169, 259; Vainio-Korhonen, 'Kaupan ja käsityön ammattikasvatus', 230; E. Aaltonen, 'Väestö ja yhteiskunta', in: E. Aaltonen, E. Matinolli, H. Helminen-Nordberg and Y. Blomstedt, *Suur-Jämsän historia III* (Jämsä, 1963), 42; P. Tommila, *Nurmijärven pitäjän historia. II osa. Itsenäisen Nurmijärven pitäjän vaiheet* (Nurmijärvi, 1959), 203; O. K. Kyöstiö, *Suomen ammattikasvatuksen kehitys käsityön ja teollisuuden aloilla 1. Ammattikasvatuksen esivaihe vuoteen 1842* (Jyväskylä, 1955), 61.

[58] Uotila, *Käsityöläinen kyläyhteisönsä jäsenenä*, 126.

When a boy entered an apprenticeship, the terms of the contract were arranged between the master and the youngster or his guardians; no guarantors were needed.[59] This was the same in both town and countryside. In general, guilds set a minimum term of three years and a maximum of five, but apprenticeships could be shorter if the youth learned quickly.[60] Written contracts were not compulsory; in the countryside, in particular, agreements were often oral.[61] Only a few written contracts survive (see Figure 6.1).[62]

Evidence of disputes between apprentices and masters is rare. Disputes, when they did occur, were usually settled in local courts. Common issues include masters complaining about apprentices leaving their household without permission, and apprentices complaining about trivial assignments or a lack of instruction.[63] For instance, the tailor Mats Siljander's two runaway apprentices complained that he did not give them enough to eat and lacked work, so that they were not doing anything useful.[64] In another case, the shoemaker Henrik Willberg's apprentice, Johan Påhlsson, complained that he was set to farming and forestry; the local villagers thought he was a farmhand, not an apprentice. When his master admitted that he lacked work and had not obtained permission to take apprentices, the court cancelled Påhlsson's contract.[65] Sometimes the county administration and governor became involved: governors, for instance, occasionally issued warrants to apprehend runaway apprentices.[66]

Occasionally, apprentices paid masters for their training. It is difficult to establish the size of payments and how common they were.[67] Only a handful of examples survive, usually in court records from disputes

[59] Möller, 'Ammattikuntien kukoistuskaudelta Helsingissä', 50; Papinsaari, 'Turun räätälien ammattikunta', 261; Heino, *Käsityö ja sen tekijät*, 223; Edgren, *Lärling, gesäll, mästare*, 145.

[60] Modée, *Utdrag*, 210–11 (General guild orders, Art. IV:3).

[61] There were no public notaries. Cf. C. Crowston, 'From school to workshop: Pre-training and apprenticeship in old regime France', in: De Munck, Kaplan and Soly (eds.), *Learning on the Shop Floor*, 46.

[62] Heino, *Käsityö ja sen tekijät*, 222; Edgren, *Lärling, gesäll, mästare*, 145.

[63] Söderlund, *Hantverkarna*, 393; Papinsaari, 'Turun räätälien ammattikunta', 265–66; Edgren, *Lärling, gesäll, mästare*, 155.

[64] NA, archives of Hollola District Court, autumn 1833, §63; winter 1834, §27. Cf. G. Hamilton, 'Enforcement in apprenticeship contracts: Were runaways a serious problem? Evidence from Montreal', *Journal of Economic History* 55 (1995), 551–74; P. Wallis, 'Apprenticeship and training in premodern England', *Journal of Economic History* 68 (2008), 843–44.

[65] NA, archives of Hollola District Court, winter 1823, §113.

[66] NA, Province of Uusimaa and Häme, Governors' Secretariat, Records of applications 1790–1830; Papinsaari, 'Turun räätälien ammattikunta', 266–67; Edgren, *Lärling, gesäll, mästare*, 155.

[67] Even from towns the evidence of payments is scarce. Söderlund, *Hantverkarna*, 391–92.

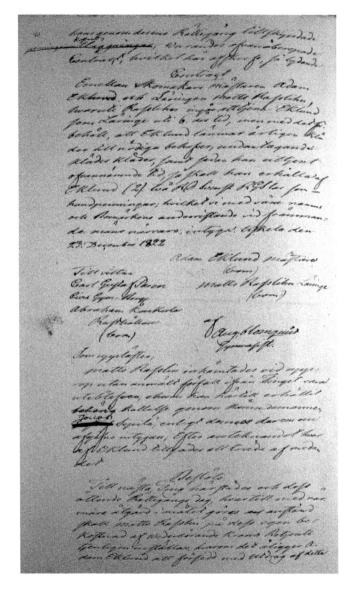

Figure 6.1 A written contract from Finland
Source: National Archives of Finland, archives of Hollola District Court, winter 1826.

about the price or quality of instruction.[68] In one rare example from Messukylä parish in 1759 a smith had promised to train a boy for three years, taking a fee of 10 daler in the first two years, but in the final year, he would receive no fee if his apprentice had learned something and could help him work.[69] For nineteenth-century Hollola, there are no references to payments in the court books or anywhere else.

In Finnish towns, apprenticeships began with enrolment in a guild's apprenticeship records or the general minutes. Guilds recorded the boy and his father's names, the father's occupation and the training period. Without guild records, one has to seek separate evidence of residence and work to gain a picture of the conditions of apprenticeship. Rural masters reported their apprentices to the parish priest as new members of their households, and they were registered in church lists of households that were kept to ensure attendance at communion. In a dispute between the tailor Siljander and his runaway apprentices, the local priest testified that the boys were listed in the communion records as members of his household. Customers then also gave evidence that the boys had worked with Siljander when he was fulfilling their orders.[70] With guild records, this kind of approach would have been unnecessary.

Masters were obliged to teach their apprentices everything they knew of their trade without holding anything back. How this knowledge transfer was effected, however, is unknown. Training was probably a trial and error process in which apprentices started on easier assignments, to gain hands-on familiarity with the material, style and working culture of the craft, before later assuming more complicated tasks. Technical knowledge and the acquisition of skills were only part of the training; an apprenticeship also initiated youths into the culture of artisans.[71] This was evident in rural areas. One sign was artisans' and their apprentices' surnames. In western Finland, there were no traditional family names, but along with the patronym the name of the farm was used. Artisans did not have farms, so they often used typical Swedish family names or names derived from their occupation, such as *Stålhammar* (steel hammer) or *Sax*

---

[68] K. Arajärvi, *Lempäälän historia* (Lempäälä, 1959), 297; Tommila, *Nurmijärven pitäjän historia*, 202; Laakso, 'Loimaan ja Huittisten', 136; Berndtson, *Laukaan historia II*, 171–72

[69] K. Arajärvi, *Messukylän historia I. Messukylän – Teiskon – Aitolahden historia* (Tampere, 1954), 413.

[70] NA, archives of Hollola District Court, autumn 1833, §63; winter 1834, §27.

[71] De Munck and Soly, 'Learning on the shop floor', 13–16; Wallis, 'Apprenticeship and training', 847–50; S. R. Epstein, 'Transferring technical knowledge and innovating in Europe, c. 1200–c. 1800', in: M. Prak and J. L. van Zanden (eds.), *Technology, Skills and the Pre-Modern Economy in the East and the West: Essays dedicated to the memory of S. R. Epstein* (Leiden: Brill, 2013), 29.

(scissors). For apprentices, it was a rite of passage at a certain point in their career to change their name to one suitable for an artisan. Usually this occurred shortly before they began their own independent career.[72]

As members of an artisan household, apprentices were under their master's authority and had to obey his directions; this was a universal feature of early modern patriarchal societies. Likewise it was generally accepted that apprentices must perform household duties and chores – as long as this did not interfere with their training.[73] What was not acceptable, however, was excessive discipline. The use of violence, for instance hitting an apprentice without good reason, or out of drunkenness or spite, was forbidden.[74]

The Growing Number of Apprentices

The number of apprentices and journeymen in Hollola fluctuated widely. There were several reasons for this. Most obviously, the number of parish artisans affected the number of apprentices. When there were only a few artisans, inevitably there were fewer apprentices.[75] The economic situation, demographic trends and general social developments could also lead to substantial variations between decades. When demand was low, a single artisan could meet the needs of several parishes. Apprentices and assistants rarely appear in the census lists of the early eighteenth century. The first in Hollola parish was recorded in 1747, when the tailor Anders Haqvin had an assistant named Anders Matsson.[76] From the 1750s, apprentices and assistants become more common, as Table 6.2 shows. By and large, the number of apprentices was small compared to the number of boys in the same age group: only a few youngsters were apprenticed.

The number of apprentices and journeymen depended on the particular craft. For instance, tailors and shoemakers usually had more

---

[72] Möller, 'Ammattikuntien kukoistuskaudelta Helsingissä', 52; Söderlund, *Hantverkarna*, 264; B. Hanssen, *Österlen: En studie över social-antropologiska sammanhang under 1600- och 1700-talen i sydöstra Skåne* (Stockholm: LTs Förlag, 1952), 506; Arajärvi, *Messukylän historia*, 414; Berndtson, *Laukaan historia II*, 170; Gadd, *Självhushåll eller arbetsdelning*, 155–56.

[73] Söderlund, *Hantverkarna*, 393–94; Papinsaari, 'Turun räätälien ammattikunta', 265–66; Edgren, *Lärling, gesäll, mästare*, 155.

[74] Modée, *Utdrag*, 211 (General guild orders, Art. IX:3).

[75] Rural youths could still be apprenticed, but not locally; presumably, boys were often sent to towns.

[76] Anders Matsson was registered as a *lärödräng*. He probably was first apprenticed and later received wages. He lived with Haqvin for ten years, during which he married. NA, Hollola parish census records 1747–57.

Table 6.2 *Number of apprentices in Hollola parish, 1750–1839*

	1750s	1760s	1770s	1780s	1790s	1800s	1810s	1820s	1830s	Total
Smiths	4	11	15	11	8	4	9	8	17	87
Tailors	7	20	28	9	6	6	3	13	18	110
Shoemakers	2	3	6	2	5	2	7	20	19	66
Carpenters*	2	0	3	8	3	1	0	0	0	17
Weavers	2	2	8	3	1	0	0	0	0	16
Total	17	36	60	33	23	12	19	41	54	296

Note: Observed from the starting point of the apprenticeship career; *carpenters and masons are combined, as these trades were often practised together.
Source: Apprentice biographies from Hollola, 1700–1840.

apprentices than blacksmiths.[77] In Hollola, tailors had a lot of apprentices compared to other trades, one reason for this being that tailoring was deemed suitable for peasants' younger sons who would not inherit the farm: the trade's status was high enough and it was thought to offer lucrative prospects.[78] Smiths, on the other hand, tried with some success to keep the trade within their own families; in several families, only sons were trained and no outsiders were employed.[79] One result was that smiths had fewer apprentices than the tailors, despite this being the most common craft (see Table 6.1). For the few who did obtain an apprenticeship with a smith, career prospects were bright, and many went on to become parish or village smiths.

In the eighteenth and early nineteenth centuries, there were few parish shoemakers, making it hard to become an apprentice in Hollola.[80] In the 1820s, however, the demand for finer shoes began to grow and shoemakers responded by taking on more assistants, with the trade becoming a more attractive prospect for poorer boys – although this may be a peculiarity of the parish.[81] The lack of local masters meant that many of the shoemakers working in the parish in

---

[77] Laakso, 'Loimaan ja Huittisten', 68–69; Gadd, *Själrvhushåll eller arbetsdelning*, 164.
[78] Laakso, 'Loimaan ja Huittisten', 120, 138.
[79] Ibid.; Uotila, *Käsityöläinen kyläyhteisönsä jäsenenä*, 265.
[80] Making shoes was a common trade among ex-soldiers, who reduced demand for parish shoemakers. Söderlund, *Hantverkarna*, 226; J. Niemelä, *Tuntematon ruotusotilas. Ruotsinajan lopun ruotuarmeijan miehistön sosiaalinen ja taloudellinen asema Satakunnassa* (Helsinki: Finnish Literature Society, 1991), 127–28. See also Laakso, 'Loimaan ja Huittisten', 121–22.
[81] In 1810 there were only six parish shoemakers and over 600 peasants' households. Uotila, *Käsityöläinen kyläyhteisönsä jäsenenä*, 117.

the 1820s and 1830s were guild-trained journeymen who had returned to the countryside.[82]

The weavers and carpenters present a different picture. In these trades, apprentices were more common in the eighteenth century than subsequently. Weaving was a declining occupation, increasingly limited to women and performed as a cottage industry. When the weaver Mats Cajander took on two assistants in the 1750s, the craft was presumably still viable. By the nineteenth century, however, there were no parish weavers left. The carpenters' reasons for having no apprentices was different. With improvements in housing, the prospects for carpenters were good: houses began to be built with chimneys and glass windows, which attracted more masons and carpenters to the countryside. Three carpenters active in Hollola between 1750 and 1805 had taken 17 apprentices. Their successors did not, however, keep assistants, but instead relied on their families to supply labour. For example, Mats Häggsted worked with his son Jacob for many years, and was eventually succeeded by him as a parish artisan. Jacob was not recorded as his apprentice, however, but as his son. Boys who were taught by their own father were rarely listed as apprentices; they were simply raised as artisans.[83]

Not every artisan had apprentices or assistants. Only artisans who were skilful and had sufficient work could train or find uses for a skilled helper. Taking on a large number of apprentices can be seen as an indicator of a master's reputation, skill and prosperity.[84] Usually, parish artisans had just one or two apprentices – who then might remain in their service as assistants – over their whole career. But some had several. One could say that this was the focus of their profession. For instance, the tailor Jeremias Uhrman (1730–91), one of the first generation of tailors in Hollola, had as many as 13 apprentices and assistants, mostly in the 1770s. Uhrman took on several at a time; some were young lads, others were already trained. Uhrman was probably guild-trained, and moved to Hollola from the town of Hamina.[85] Many of his apprentices and assistants later launched their own careers in Hollola and its neighbouring parishes, and in turn trained the next generation of tailors.

---

[82] Uotila, *Käsityöläinen kyläyhteisönsä jäsenenä*, 222–23.

[83] Laakso, 'Loimaan ja Huittisten', 132; Uotila, *Käsityöläinen kyläyhteisönsä jäsenenä*, 221. In towns, guild members' sons served shorter apprenticeships and paid reduced mastership fees: Södenlund, *Hantverkarna*, 117; Papinsaari, 'Turun räätälien ammattikunta', 262.

[84] Laakso, 'Loimaan ja Huittisten', 69–70.

[85] He is first mentioned in the 1751 census list working in Pyhäniemi mansion. From there, he moved to Parinpelto village near the vicarage. He had three daughters and two sons. His sons did not become tailors; the elder became a shopkeeper in Porvoo, the younger an officer.

Among the few smiths who had apprentices, the blacksmith Fredrik Rosenström (1724–84), who had eight apprentices in his 20-year career in Hollola, stands out.[86] Rosenström, who like Uhrman had been recruited from a town, was responsible for producing a new generation of smiths.[87] He was occasionally described as *klensmed*, meaning he could execute especially fine work. This higher level of skill presumably explains why he attracted numerous apprentices.

Apprentices' Age, Duration of Training and Social Background

We can sketch out the general characteristics of apprentices in rural Finland, at least at the local level. Some figures are inevitably estimates, although the accuracy of these estimates increases with time. Unfortunately some questions, such as apprentices' ages, can only be answered from the 1760s and 1770s onwards.

If we start with the ages of apprentices, we see little variation over this period. There were, however, differences between trades. Smiths' apprentices were usually slightly older: the average age on entering the smithy was over 20 years old – an obvious reason being the strength required in the trade.[88] It was common for smiths' apprentices to have worked elsewhere previously, for example as common farmhands. In contrast, tailors' apprentices were usually well under 20 years old. Indeed, they were often quite young when they started: tailors' apprentices are often listed in the church's children's books, indicating that they had not yet been confirmed, which usually occurred at around 15 years old.[89] Some were probably younger than 14, the official minimum age for apprenticeship.[90] Given their youth, they often came directly from their fathers' households and lacked much work experience. Shoemakers' apprentices generally fell between tailors' and smiths' apprentices in age.[91] Eighteenth-century weavers' and carpenters' apprentices were

---

[86] Rosenström was an ex-soldier who had worked in Lovisa garrison. He moved to Hollola around 1761 and remained for 20 years. His son become a provincial doctor; his daughter married a town smith.

[87] A few shoemakers can also be seen as similarly establishing the trade, but their apprentices did not usually follow in their footsteps.

[88] Papinsaari, 'Turun räätälien ammattikunta', 262; Laakso, 'Loimaan ja Huittisten', 132–33.

[89] The age of confirmation depended on how well they learned the catechism. NA, pre-confirmation registers of Hollola c. 1750–1840.

[90] We cannot be more exact because the children's books do not include the time of removal.

[91] In the nineteenth century, the average starting age was 21 for smiths' apprentices, 16 for tailors and 18 for shoemakers: Uotila, *Käsityöläinen kyläyhteisönsä jäsenenä*, 237. See also

often slightly older than shoemakers' apprentices, and had had time to work as farmhands before starting training.

The length of apprenticeships varied between trades and depended on the trade and the apprentice's age and prior experience, as well as on whether the apprentice was compensating his master for the cost of training by working for longer.[92] In general, apprenticeships lasted for 3–5 years.[93] In rural Hollola, between 1810 and 1840 the average term for smiths' apprentices was four years, while tailors and shoemakers served around five years.[94] Laakso estimated slightly lower figures of 3–4 years in eighteenth-century Loimaa, a lower figure than for urban apprenticeships.[95] The evidence that younger boys served for longer is weak, although this has been found sometimes in the nineteenth century.[96] Overall, the length of apprenticeship varied more between individuals than between trades.

In general, apprentices and assistants rarely stayed with a master for more than six years, although apprenticeships tended to last longer in the nineteenth century. At the same time, and especially from the 1830s, an increasing share of apprentices never set up their own businesses, but instead worked permanently for wages, often moving between different masters' households over a number of years.[97] For example, Carl Evasson Hellman started his apprenticeship with parish tailor Johan Ingelin in 1833 when he was about 14 years old. He trained with Ingelin for three years, then moved to the tailor Adolf Hellman's household. After a short while, he changed master again, moving to serve a tailor in a neighboring parish. After a year he returned to Hellman, and, although he was still labelled as an apprentice, he presumably received wages because during his seven years of service he married a housemaid and started his own family. He then worked for a period as a farmhand before returning to Hellman again. He never secured an independent career.

Short apprenticeships, on the other hand, tell us different things. They were sometimes a sign that training had been interrupted. It is difficult to

Söderlund, *Hantverkarna*, 397; Edgren, *Lärling, gesäll, mästare*, 146; Vainio-Korhonen, 'Kaupan ja käsityön ammattikasvatus', 233.

[92] S. R. Epstein, 'Craft guilds, apprenticeship and technological change in pre-modern Europe', *Journal of Economic History* 53 (1998), 60–61; De Munck and Soly, 'Learning on the shop floor', 9, 12–14; Epstein, 'Transferring technical knowledge', 29–31.

[93] Kaukovalta, *Hämeen läänin Historia*, 445; Söderlund, *Hantverkarna*, 397; Edgren, *Lärling, gesäll, mästare*, 147–48; Vainio-Korhonen, *Käsin tehty*, 130.

[94] These are estimations based on parish register entries: Uotila, *Käsityöläinen kyläyhteisönsä jäsenenä*, 236, 240.

[95] Laakso, 'Loimaan ja Huittisten', 131–32.

[96] Uotila, *Käsityöläinen kyläyhteisönsä jäsenenä*, 233; cf. Söderlund, *Hantverkarna*, 398.

[97] The same phenomenon is apparent in Swedish towns: Söderlund, *Hantverkarna*, 387–89; Edgren, *Lärling, gesäll, mästare*, 29.

ascertain whether rural apprentices faced a different trial period from the two months used in towns; the only indirect evidence comes from the very short periods that some apprentices spent with masters. These suggest that occasionally apprenticeships were terminated early. Presumably, this was usually separation by mutual consent; there are only a handful of court cases.

Occasionally, short apprenticeships were arranged to fine-tune skills, building on basic skills acquired with one master (or the father) by spending an additional year with another artisan. For example, the apprentice smith Abraham Andersson moved to Hollola from a nearby parish, Padasjoki, where he had been apprenticed for four years. In Hollola, he entered the smith Johan Sarlunds's service to develop his skills for a year, and then returned to his native parish, where he started his own career with the surname Sikström.[98]

In the countryside, apprentices could have several masters (up to three), although one master was the rule. An example of this is Henrik Johan Majasson, who became a smith's apprentice at 18 years old. Majasson first served Michel Martin for a year until Martin left Hollola. He then spent a year with a second master, and then another year with a third master – although there is no obvious reasons for these later changes, and his second master, Johan Sarlund was a busy and experienced smith. This contrasts with guild-based training, where it was hard to change masters and guild approval was needed.[99]

The social backgrounds of Hollola apprentices differed widely. Information from the eighteenth century is limited, because many apprentices came from neighbouring parishes. It was easy to cross parish borders to find a master – with or without the appropriate travel documents from parish priests that permitted permanent or temporary movement between areas.[100] Mostly, the master was not from the boys' own village.[101] In general, apprentices were a highly mobile group; it was not only journeymen who travelled widely.[102]

---

[98] Although Abraham Andersson could have been working as an assistant, there is no evidence of wages or of Sarlund obtaining a licence to employ him, suggesting he was still an apprentice.

[99] Papinsaari, 'Turun räätälien ammattikunta', 266–63; Uotila, *Käsityöläinen kyläyhteisönsä jäsenenä*, 225–26.

[100] Several types of documents existed: P. Einonen, P. Frigren, T. Hemminki and M. Uotila, 'Leipä taivalten takana – liikkuminen 1800-luvun alun Suomessa', *Ennen ja nyt. Historian tietosanomat* 5 (2016), www.ennenjanyt.net/2016/12/leipa-taivalten-takana-liikkuminen-1800-luvun-alun-suomessa.

[101] Uotila, *Käsityöläinen kyläyhteisönsä jäsenenä*, 225–29.

[102] Tommila, *Nurmijärven pitäjän historia*, 203–05; A. Rosenberg, *Muuttoliike Uudenmaan läänissä esi-industrialistisen kauden lopulla (1821–1880)* (Helsinki: Finnish Literature Society, 1966), 55–56.

Most extant studies suggest that apprentices were mainly peasants' younger sons.[103] This certainly holds for eighteenth-century Hollola, especially among smiths' and tailors' apprentices. For instance, one of the smith Rosenström's apprentices was Jacob Stranden, the second son of the peasant who held Marttila farm. Jacob later returned to work in his native village of Jalkaranta. His only son, Anders, followed in his footsteps at the beginning of the nineteenth century.[104] However, the situation changed in the next century, when it became uncommon for the sons of peasants to enter apprenticeships.[105]

Soldiers, tenant farmers and landless agricultural workers also placed their sons in the crafts. Many apprentices came from these backgrounds, while the sons of landless agricultural workers also became increasingly common among apprentices in the nineteenth century. They were not rare in the eighteenth century, but it seems that apprentices were now coming from more modest backgrounds. It is unlikely that agricultural workers could pay much for their sons' training; they often earned so little that it is impossible to imagine them being able to pay anything at all. Often, in fact, the family was so poor that it was a relief to send a child to find food and shelter elsewhere. Finland had no system of pauper apprentices as such, but there are cases where poor orphans were placed with artisans to provide them with some practical skills. For example, the pauper child Erik Eriksson (who later took surname Ekman) was given by the parish first to his uncle, the tailor Gustaf Halin, and subsequently served another tailor.[106] He spent over ten years working in these artisans' households before he set up his own business, a delay which may well be explained by his humble origins. In some cases apprentices placed by the parish or relatives were disabled, suggesting that in such cases teaching craft skills was akin to providing a kind of welfare.[107]

---

[103] Laakso, 'Loimaan ja Huittisten', 112–17.

[104] The smith's family business, however, ended here, because Anders had no sons.

[105] Uotila, *Käsityöläinen kyläyhteisönsä jäsenenä*, 251, 257–61.

[106] Parishes had an obligation to look after the paupers. To do so, some paupers were circulated among peasant families, who formed a cluster (file) responsible for maintaining paupers. NA, Hollola parish meetings register 1817; Uotila, *Käsityöläinen kyläyhteisönsä jäsenenä*, 235. See also Kaukovalta, *Hämeen läänin Historia*, 445; J. J. Laurila, 'Lounais-Hämeen käsityöläisistä vuoteen 1867. Helsingin yliopistossa 1838 laadittu sosiologian laudatur-kirjoitus "käsityöläisoloista Suomessa 1800-luvun alkupuoliskolla etupäässä Lounais-Hämeen oloja silmälläpitäen"', *Lounais-Hämeen kotiseutu- ja museoyhdistys. Vuosikirja* 40 (1971), 52–53.

[107] P. Virrankoski, *Myyntiä varten harjoitettu kotiteollisuus Suomessa autonomian ajan alkupuolella. (1809- noin 1865)* (Helsinki: Finnish Literature Society, 1963), 436; R. O. Peltovuori, *Suur-Tuusulan historia. Tuusula – Kerava – Järvenpää II. Seurakunnan perustamisesta Suomen sotaan 1643–1808* (Tuusula, 1975), 155; Saarenheimo, *Vanhan Pirkkalan historia*, 414; Edgren, Lärling, gesäll, mästare, 159, 189–92; Uotila, *Käsityöläinen kyläyhteisönsä jäsenenä*, 238.

The gradual decline in the social background of apprentices did not, however, signal a clear fall in the social esteem in which artisans were held. An artisan's position still counted for something in a godparental relationship or in the marriage market.[108] Craftsmanship and dexterity were still held in esteem and as a result, apprenticeships were still sought after, even though the chances of establishing an independent business had declined.

One aspect that deserves mention is the question of illegitimacy. As in parts of Germany, guild rules required apprentices to be of respectable origin, in other words born within wedlock. This was stated explicitly in older rules, and was also a common requirement in eighteenth-century rural apprenticeship. In Hollola, only one boy, a tailor's apprentice, was named by the matronymic, indicating illegitimacy. By the nineteenth century, the climate of opinion had shifted, and several boys born outside wedlock became apprentices. Preserving artisan honour had clearly become less important.[109]

Conclusions

Rural artisans' apprentices were inferior in both rank and skills to guild-based apprentices, but they were not a rarity in rural Finland from 1750 onwards. Because there was no comprehensive legislation covering rural crafts, the practice of rural apprenticeship often emulated urban norms, the guild orders providing a common set of standards and customs, albeit with modest, practical adjustments. For instance, instead of apprentice registers, rural artisans relied on church administration to witness their apprenticeship. Although rural artisans were free of the supervision of guilds, they were still subject to the oversight of the state.

Rural artisans also formulated their own training model in which the tripartite system was not always either necessary or clearly visible. The introduction to basic craft skills took place in the same way as in towns, with new apprentices entering contracts for training. The difference between rural and urban agreements – the length of training or concrete training practices – was slight. After their initial training, rural apprentices were fully competent to start they own independent career; there was no compulsory phase spent as a journeyman, as there was in towns. However, before they were granted the status of licensed parish artisan, former apprentices often had to have worked independently in an area, or

---

[108] Uotila, *Käsityöläinen kyläyhteisönsä jäsenenä*, 184–89,198–203.
[109] Edgren, *Lärling, gesäll, mästare*, 66, 152, 213; M. Uotila, 'Aviottomana syntyneen pojan tie käsityöläiseksi 1800-luvun alkupuoliskolla', *Genos* 86 (2015), 194–204.

served as assistants to existing parish artisans. The position of parish artisans' assistants resembled that of urban journeymen, but a distinction was maintained in their titles, a distinction which was closely observed. On the other hand, without the requirement for journeywork, rural masters lacked the chance that guild masters enjoyed to exploit skilled assistants in their work. Rural artisans' customs, however, demonstrate that it was possible to function and train the next generation of artisans without craft guilds' supervision or powers of enforcement.

7 Apprenticeships with and without Guilds: The Northern Netherlands

Ruben Schalk

After the Dutch Revolt, the Northern Netherlands entered a phase of dynamic economic growth that lasted until the middle of the seventeenth century.[1] Although the eighteenth century was marked by protracted stagnation, the Dutch economy remained relatively advanced.[2] It would take until the last quarter of the nineteenth century for industrialisation to take off.[3] These developments make Dutch apprenticeship all the more interesting. Relatively efficient labour markets and a large stock of human capital are often regarded as indispensable for economic development, while closed labour and training markets are supposed to have been detrimental.[4] Apprenticeship took centre stage in both skill formation and labour-market access for adolescents in the Dutch Republic. How difficult was it for a Dutch youngster to become a skilled artisan during the various stages of the country's economic development?

Historians' views on apprenticeship in the Netherlands vary widely. Ogilvie has argued that the early modern Northern Netherlands had relatively weak craft guilds, allowing youngsters easy access to training.[5] Van Zanden, in contrast, suggests that guilds' regulation of apprenticeship

---

[1] O. Gelderblom and J. Jonker, 'Low Countries', in: L. Neal and J. G. Williamson (eds.), *The Cambridge History of Capitalism*, vol. 1: *The Rise of Capitalism: From Ancient Origins to 1848* (Cambridge: Cambridge University Press, 2015), 314–56.

[2] J. de Vries and A. van der Woude, *The First Modern Economy: Success, Failure, and Perseverance of the Dutch Economy, 1500–1815* (Cambridge: Cambridge University Press, 1997).

[3] J. L. van Zanden and A. van Riel, *The Strictures of Inheritance: The Dutch Economy in the Nineteenth Century* (Princeton: Princeton University Press, 2004); J. Mokyr, 'The Industrial Revolution and the Netherlands: Why did it not happen?', *De Economist* 148 (2000), 503–20.

[4] J. Mokyr, *The Enlightened Economy: An Economic History of Britain 1700–1850* (New Haven, CT: Yale University Press, 2012); P. H. Lindert, *Growing Public: Social Spending and Economic Growth since the Eighteenth Century* (Cambridge: Cambridge University Press, 2004); S. Ogilvie, 'The economics of guilds', *Journal of Economic Perspectives* 28 (2014), 169–92.

[5] S. Ogilvie, *State Corporatism and Proto-Industry: The Württemberg Black Forest, 1580–1797* (Cambridge: Cambridge University Press, 1997), 436–37, 449.

instead enabled a relatively cheap supply of skilled workers.[6] De Vries presents a third position, that access to skilled labour markets became more difficult during the eighteenth century because guilds closed their ranks.[7] What happened to apprenticeship *after* the guilds were abolished and industrialisation set in largely remains an open question, although Knotter has suggested that industrialisation caused deskilling and segmentation in the Amsterdam labour market during the nineteenth century.[8]

This chapter provides a systematic study of Dutch apprenticeship between the seventeenth and nineteenth centuries. We begin by examining craft apprenticeship under the guilds in several different cities. Although apprenticeship was not confined to guild-controlled crafts in the Northern Netherlands, evidence for training outside the guilds is scarce.[9] As the vast majority of urban crafts were organised in guilds, these apprenticeships were arguably the most significant form of training. Even within this setting, apprenticeship contracts were private agreements between masters and youths, with little direct guild involvement. This implies that we can capture both the institutional and private dimensions of Dutch apprenticeship – as we show, pre-industrial apprenticeship training was remarkably similar across the Dutch Republic. We then move on to the nineteenth century, to examine what happened to apprenticeship after guilds had been abolished and industrialisation set in.

Apprenticeship in the Dutch Republic

Apprenticeship in the Northern Netherlands grew in tandem with the rise of urbanisation in the sixteenth century, most notably in Holland and

---

[6] J. L. van Zanden, 'The skill premium and the "Great Divergence"', *European Review of Economic History* 13 (2009), 139–40.

[7] J. de Vries, 'How did pre-industrial labour markets function?', in: G. Grantham and M. MacKinnen (eds.), *Labour Market Evolution: The Economic History of Wage Flexibility and the Employment Relations* (London: Routledge, 1994), 39–63.

[8] A. Knotter, *Economische transformatie en stedelijke arbeidsmarkt: Amsterdam in de tweede helft van de negentiende eeuw* (Zwolle: Waanders, 1991).

[9] For apprenticeships outside craft guilds see C. A. Davids, 'Apprenticeship and guild control in the Netherlands, c. 1450–1800', in: B. De Munck, S. L. Kaplan and H. Soly (eds.), *Learning on the Shop Floor: Historical Perspectives on Apprenticeship* (New York: Berghahn Books, 2007), 65–84; N. W. Posthumus, *Geschiedenis van de Leidse lakenindustrie*, 3 vols. (The Hague: Nijhoff, 1908–39). Dutch municipal orphanages registered apprenticeships of their orphans, but they were also regularly apprenticed at guild-controlled crafts; A. E. C. McCants, *Civic Charity in a Golden Age: Orphan Care in Early Modern Amsterdam* (Urbana: University of Illinois Press, 1997); R. Schalk, 'From orphan to artisan: Apprenticeship careers and contract enforcement in the Netherlands before and after the guild abolition', *Economic History Review* 70 (2017), 730–57.

Zeeland.[10] It had probably been used since the late Middle Ages. Since one prerequisite for establishing a craft guild was a certain concentration of artisans, apprenticeship probably coincided with or preceded their establishment.[11] Apprenticeship here was first and foremost a local and urban institution. The decentralised structure of the Dutch Republic was mirrored in the composition of Dutch apprenticeship in the early modern period.[12] Apprenticeship was not regulated at the national or provincial level. At the urban level, craft guilds were often involved, as was true for many cities in early modern Europe.

Guild involvement with apprenticeship usually consisted of four features: registering apprentices, setting the duration, charging fees and sometimes limiting the number of apprentices per master.[13] Guilds also specified the rules for the test and fee that prospective master's faced on entering the guild. Only those who passed a mastership test could become guild members. Journeymen and apprentices were not formally guild members, and to become a journeyman, a completed apprenticeship was required. The apprentice's service was usually attested by their master in person, or else documented in a letter from their master if they had trained in a different town or city.

Dutch guilds appear to have been more concerned with registering this process than actually overseeing it.[14] Most guilds kept records of new apprentices, journeymen and masters, especially for immigrants. They did also make rules for minimum terms, demand fees and sometimes limited the number of apprentices. Fees and terms were far from uniform, however, both between cities and between guilds.[15] Cooper's apprentices in Haarlem had to serve for twice as long as their peers in Rotterdam at the end of the seventeenth century, for example.[16] Guilds' involvement rarely extended beyond these limited procedural issues.

---

[10] B. De Munck, P. Lourens and J. Lucassen, 'The establishment and distribution of craft guilds in the Low Countries, 1000–1800', in: M. Prak, C. Lis, J. Lucassen and H. Soly (eds.), *Craft Guilds in the Early Modern Low Countries: Work, Power, and Representation* (Aldershot: Ashgate, 2006), 32–73.

[11] Fifteenth-century guild ordinances for instance already contained clauses on apprenticeship fees; P. Lourens and J. Lucassen, 'De oprichting en ontwikkeling van ambachtsgilden in Nederland (13de–19de eeuw)', in: C. Lis and H. Soly (eds.), *Werelden van verschil: Ambachtsgilden in de Lage Landen* (Brussels: VUB Press, 1997), 50–51; B. De Munck and K. Davids, 'Beyond exclusivism: Entrance fees for guilds in the early modern Low Countries, c. 1450–1800', in: K. Davids and B. De Munck (eds.), *Innovation and Creativity in Late Medieval and Early Modern European Cities* (Farnham: Ashgate, 2014), 213–14.

[12] O. C. Gelderblom, *Cities of Commerce: The Institutional Foundations of International Trade in the Low Countries, 1250–1650* (Princeton: Princeton University Press, 2013).

[13] Davids, 'Apprenticeship and guild control', 67.   [14] Ibid.

[15] De Munck and Davids, 'Beyond exclusivism'.

[16] J. Tump, 'Ambachtelijk geschoold: Haarlemse en Rotterdamse ambachtslieden en de circulatie van technische kennis, ca. 1400–1720', PhD thesis, VU Amsterdam, 2012, 88.

The vast majority of urban crafts in the Dutch Republic were incorporated into guilds, meaning that apprenticeships in urban crafts were generally registered by guilds as well. Davids has nevertheless demonstrated that another (albeit unknown) share of apprentices worked outside the guild system.[17] Textile manufacturing, watchmaking and millwrights in the Zaanstreek, for instance, were not organised in guilds.[18] Guilds were rare in small towns with fewer than 1,000 inhabitants, so here too apprenticeships were not monitored.[19] Even within towns, some guilds were more involved with apprenticeship than others. Guilds of merchants, shopkeepers and bargemen generally did not regulate apprenticeships.

Historians have struggled to examine apprenticeship outside of guilds because it left so little evidence. Notaries rarely registered apprenticeship contracts in the Dutch Republic. This suggests that most agreements were made either privately or orally.[20] Those that were put in writing may have contained uncommon elements that motivated the production of legal documentation. In short, notarised apprenticeships cannot be taken as typical. Indeed, eighteenth-century Amsterdam cooper apprentices paid a significantly higher premium (about 10 *guilders*) whenever an additional contract was mentioned in the guild record, suggesting that written contracts were associated with riskier agreements.[21]

We are therefore reliant on guild records for much of our evidence on early modern Dutch apprenticeship. Arguably, these should still be regarded as primarily being records of private agreements between a master and an apprentice or his guardians.[22] While contracts had to meet applicable guild regulations, the precise content of the agreement was neither uniform nor prescribed by law. Many aspects were open and could vary significantly, including premiums (fees), terms, board and lodging, details of training, and penalties for early departure. Apprenticeship terms set by guilds were minimum durations. Many apprentices stayed for longer and, more importantly, varying terms, as will be demonstrated. Magistrates were not closely involved in overseeing

---

[17] Davids, 'Apprenticeship and guild control', 69–70.

[18] On the organisation of Dutch textile manufacturing see H. Soly, 'The political economy of European craft guilds: Power relations and economic strategies of merchants and master artisans in the medieval and early modern textile industries', *International Review of Social History* 53 (2008), 64–65.

[19] Lourens and Lucassen, 'Oprichting en ontwikkeling', Appendices ('bijlage') 1.2 and 1.3.

[20] Within the digitised notarial deeds from Utrecht between 1670 and 1774 only a few dozen apprenticeship contracts survive, a tiny number compared to the estimated number of Utrecht apprentices (Table 7.1).

[21] Stadsarchief Amsterdam (SAA), Archief Gilden, inv. 895.

[22] I. H. van Eeghen, *De gilden: Theorie en praktijk* (Bussum: Van Dishoeck, 1974), 20.

apprenticeships either, although they were sometimes engaged in apprenticing poor boys.[23] Even then, direct supervision was generally left to civic orphanages or almshouses, which stood in for the parents.[24]

One other major source exists. Civic orphanage records, while not entirely representative, provide insights into the more common crafts, because they apprenticed male orphans with local masters. These were not pauper children.[25] Civic orphanages, or *burgerweeshuizen*, only admitted youths whose parents had been middle-class citizens.[26] By apprenticing them into a craft, they aimed to ensure a similarly secure and prosperous future for them.

Figures on the age of starting an apprenticeship are scarce. Orphans in eighteenth-century Leiden and Utrecht generally began apprenticeships at around 14 years old. Apprentices with the Leiden surgeons' guild between 1702 and 1729 on average started at 14.5 years (standard deviation 2.26).[27] The vast majority of apprentices in craft guilds were male. Orphanages generally put girls to work as spinners or housemaids. Some crafts were open to females, however – mostly clothing and textile occupations, such as button-making, sewing and weaving.[28]

The local and private character of apprenticeship means that we lack an overview of the number of adolescents entering training across the Dutch Republic. The best measure is the apprenticeship registers of guilds. A considerable number survive for different cities. Table 7.1 reports the existing evidence on the numbers of apprentices in different crafts for several Dutch cities. These figures are, of course, not representative of all craft apprenticeships, but they are the best available guide to the annual flow of apprentices into these urban, guild-controlled crafts. As one would anticipate, the number of apprentices reflects the size of the local craft. Sizeable crafts such as coopering took on relatively more apprentices. It is not surprising that Amsterdam, the country's largest commercial centre, had a large demand for barrels. Haarlem was renowned for its beer manufacturing, resulting in high demand for coopers as well.[29]

---

[23] Davids, 'Apprenticeship and guild control', 71–72.   [24] McCants, *Civic Charity*.

[25] N. Bakker, J. Noordam and M. Rietveld-van Wingerden, *Vijf eeuwen opvoeden in Nederland: idee en praktijk: 1500–2000* (Assen: Koninklijke Van Gorcum, 2006), 398–99, 411–13.

[26] McCants, *Civic Charity*, 22–23.

[27] Regionaal Archief Leiden (RAL), Archief Gilden, inv. 351.

[28] B. Panhuysen, *Maatwerk: Kleermakers, naaisters, oudkleerkopers en de gilden (1500–1800)* (Amsterdam: IISG, 2000); E. van Nederveen Meerkerk and A. Schmidt, 'Between wage labor and vocation: Child labor in Dutch urban industry, 1600–1800', *Journal of Social History* 41 (2008), 717–36.

[29] R. W. Unger, 'Technical change in the brewing industry in Germany, the Low Countries, and England in the late Middle Ages', *Journal of European Economic History* 21 (1992), 289.

Table 7.1 *Number of apprentices for a selection of Dutch crafts and cities, 1588–1799*

City and craft	Period	Registered apprentices	Average per decade
Amsterdam			
Coopers	1722–83	*5,000*	*806*
Pig butchers	1787–99	517	398
Pastry bakers	1748–74	643	238
Surgeons	1597–1665	1,456	211
Masons	1610–62	*700*	*132*
Utrecht			
Blacksmiths	1646–1795	4,980	332
Coopers	1588–1662	1,062	142
Surgeons	1740–99	614	102
Goldsmiths	1598–1783	1,068	57
Art painters	1611–39	105	36
Linen weavers	1611–1710	121	12
Leiden			
Surgeons	1683–1729	394	84
Glassmakers	1740–90	332	65
Haarlem			
Coopers	1650–1720	*1,500*	*211*
Bois-le-Duc			
Goldsmiths	1700–98	170	17

Note: Estimates in italics.
Sources: SAA, Archief Gilden, inv. nos. 254, 591, 895, 1349, 1470; Het Utrechts Archief (HUA), Archieven bewaard bij het stadsbestuur I, inv. nos. 105, 124, 131–1; RAL, Archief Gilden, inv. nos. 351, 524; N. Slokker, *Ruggengraat van de stedelijke samenleving: De rol van de gilden in de stad Utrecht, 1528–1818* (Amsterdam: Aksant, 2010), 55, 95, 259; Tump, 'Ambachtelijk geschoold', 86; Gemeentearchief Den Bosch, Archief Gilden, inv. 311.

Except for Bois-le-Duc, the cities listed in Table 7.1 all had populations of over 25,000 in 1670. They allow a rough estimate of total apprentice numbers. The table suggests that on average around 19 apprentices enrolled annually per guild. The nine Dutch cities with a population of 25,000 or over contained 296 guilds in total.[30] This would imply that around 5,500 adolescents started an apprenticeship every year in the nine largest Dutch cities. Amsterdam and Leiden may be somewhat unrepresentative because the former was the largest commercial city and the latter a large textile manufacturer. If we take just the average number of annual apprentices in Utrecht, Haarlem and Bois-le-Duc, then on average 12 apprentices enrolled annually per guild. Multiplying this by the number

[30] Lourens and Lucassen, 'Oprichting en ontwikkeling', Appendix 1.3.

of Dutch guilds – 1,153 around 1670 – suggests tentatively that approximately 13,800 youths began apprenticeships in the craft guilds of the Dutch Republic each year.[31]

Assuming that apprentices stayed for four years, and that about 60% fulfilled their contract,[32] the stock of apprentices in urban crafts would have been about 33,120. The total urban population in the Dutch Republic was 837,000 in 1795.[33] Apprentices thus made up about 4% of the urban population. If we repeat the estimate for Utrecht alone, it suggests apprentices formed 4% of the city's population around 1670. These estimates are not too far off from the apprentice share of 2%–7% of the urban population calculated for England (see Chapter 9).[34] The actual number of apprentices surely varied between cities, guilds and periods, but it seems reasonable to imagine that 1 in 12 male inhabitants in Dutch cities was an apprentice.[35]

Enrolling in Apprenticeship

Apprentices had to pay a small fee when enrolling in an apprenticeship regulated by a guild. At times apprentices from outside the city had to pay more. There was too much local and temporal variation to discern a pattern, although whenever fees did discriminate, they did so against migrants.[36] For instance, immigrant apprentice surgeons in seventeenth-century Leiden paid 3 *guilders*, while locals paid half that. In the Northern Netherlands, the sons of masters (sometimes only the eldest) were often exempt from fees.[37] The goldsmiths in eighteenth-century Bois-le-Duc charged masters' eldest sons nothing, while other apprentices paid 6–12 *guilders*. Sons of Leiden's master surgeons were exempt from fees. More prestigious guilds do not appear to have charged more.[38] Haarlem silversmiths' apprentices paid about 6 *guilders* in the eighteenth century,

---

[31] The number of craft guilds correlates with urban population estimates: ibid., 57.

[32] R. Schalk, P. Wallis, C. Crowston and C. Lemercier, 'Failure or flexibility? Apprenticeship training in premodern Europe', *Journal of Interdisciplinary History* 48 (2017), 140.

[33] De Vries and van der Woude, *First Modern Economy*, 857–58.

[34] J. Humphries, 'English apprenticeship: A neglected factor in the first Industrial Revolution', in: P. A. David and M. Thomas (eds.), *The Economic Future in Historical Perspective* (Oxford: Oxford University Press, 2003), 79–81.

[35] Figures on urban occupational distributions are not detailed enough to improve this estimate.

[36] Lourens and Lucassen, 'Oprichting en ontwikkeling', 54; J. Tump, 'The coopers' guilds in Holland, c. 1650–1720: A market logic?', in: Davids and De Munck, *Innovation and Creativity*, 230. There is an overview of apprenticeship fees in the Northern Netherlands in De Munck and Davids, 'Beyond exclusivism', table 9.2.

[37] De Munck and Davids, 'Beyond exclusivism', 201.

[38] Tump, 'Ambachtelijk geschoold', 81; De Munck and Davids, 'Beyond exclusivism', 199.

but Amsterdam surgeons' apprentices only paid 1 *guilder* at most.[39] In early modern Utrecht, the fees for all guilds ranged from 1 to 2 *guilders*; only the goldsmiths' charged outsiders more.[40]

Guild fees for apprentices were not usually used to bar outsiders in the Netherlands, as has been suggested for other parts of Europe.[41] In late seventeenth-century Zierikzee, in Zeeland, the bakers' guild did raise apprenticeship fees to discourage adolescents, yet most other Zeeland guilds never used fees to limit the number of apprentices.[42] Apprentices from municipal orphanages or institutions for poor relief were often exempt from fees. In general, the relatively low level of fees that most guilds charged, even for outsiders, meant that they were a limited discouragement to entry.[43] A fee of 6 *guilders* equated to six skilled daily wages, which seems surmountable. For that reason, Tump argues that the falling number of apprentices in early modern Haarlem reflected adverse economic conditions and war, not high fees.[44] In other cases, fees were raised not to deter apprentices but to alleviate a guild's financial problems.[45] Entrance fees for masters, the mastership test and the cost of setting up a shop provided a more challenging hurdle. Mastership fees were much higher than apprenticeship fees.[46]

Another possible barrier to entry were limits on the number of apprentices a master could take. Apprenticeships outside guilds rarely had limitations on apprentices, as Leiden's textile manufacturing demonstrates.[47] Some guilds did limit the number of apprentices a master could have at any one time, but other guilds had no rule. Surgeons in Amsterdam limited the number of apprentices per master, while the silversmiths and painters in Haarlem and Rotterdam did not.[48] Whenever these rules were present, as in Utrecht's

---

[39] Tump, 'Ambachtelijk geschoold', 81; SAA, Archief Gilden, inv. 232, 19.

[40] Slokker, *Ruggengraat*, 76.

[41] S. Ogilvie, 'Guilds, efficiency, and social capital: Evidence from German proto-industry', *Economic History Review* 57 (2004), 308.

[42] L. H. Remmerswaal, *Een duurzame alliantie: Gilden en regenten in Zeeland, 1600–1800* (Middelburg: Koninklijk Zeeuwsch Genootschap der Wetenschappen, 2009), 96–97.

[43] De Munck and Davids, 'Beyond exclusivism', 203. Although there were certainly exceptions to this rule: Panhuysen, *Maatwerk*, Bijlage IX.

[44] Tump, 'Ambachtelijk geschoold', 85–86.   [45] Tump, 'The coopers' guilds'.

[46] De Munck and Davids, 'Beyond exclusivism', table 9.2; Panhuysen, *Maatwerk*, Bijlage IX.

[47] Posthumus, *Geschiedenis*, vol. 3, 355, 613, 701. Only one of six *neringen* set a (relatively high) maximum of four apprentices: N. W. Posthumus, *Bronnen tot de geschiedenis van de Leidsche textielnijverheid 1333–1795*, 6 vols. (The Hague: Nijhoff, 1910–22), vol. 5, 301–02. *Neringen* were corporatist organisations that regulated and oversaw certain branches in the textile industry, usually with the involvement of urban authorities (my interpretation); E. van Nederveen Meerkerk, *De draad in eigen handen: vrouwen en loonarbeid in de Nederlandse textielnijverheid, 1581–1810* (Amsterdam: Aksant, 2007), 160–62.

[48] SAA, Archief Gilden, inv. 232, p. 13. Tump, 'Ambachtelijk geschoold', 82–83.

carpenters' guild, they usually set a limit of one or two apprentices simultaneously. There is no systematic overview of these by-laws. In Utrecht, about half of guilds set limits on apprentice numbers.[49] In Leiden, too, most surviving by-laws also restricted the number of apprentices.

Masters with fewer apprentices could theoretically devote more time to training each individual. However, high levels of attrition together with apprentices' wages suggest that Dutch apprentices mostly learned by doing, with masters investing little time in direct training.[50] In that case, limiting numbers would probably not have increased training quality much.[51] This would imply that these rules may primarily have served to control the size of the craft. Indeed, in 1766 the cloth shearers complained to the Leiden regents that this kind of regulation prevented their trade from expanding.[52] Data on Leiden orphans shows that the number of starting apprenticeships increased after guilds were abolished around 1820, even though the orphanage population was stable, suggesting that guilds had been restricting access.[53] In late eighteenth-century Amsterdam the tailors' guild pursued an active policy of barring outsiders.[54] Guilds appear to have become more restrictive after the period of economic progress; it is likely they had been less concerned with limiting apprenticeship during the seventeenth-century boom.[55]

Apprentices sometimes paid premiums to their masters as well. Guilds never required premiums. Instead, they were the result of negotiations between master and apprentice. Both premiums and apprentice wages were arguably central to the functioning of the agreement as they (partly) mitigated the risks both parties faced. Recent findings suggest that masters were in practice unable to reclaim their training investments *ex post* from the cheap labour of the apprentice, because attrition rates were so high.[56] Under these conditions, it is likely that masters demanded that

---

[49] Slokker, *Ruggengraat*, 76.   [50] Schalk, 'From orphan to artisan'.

[51] Further supporting this argument is the observation that many Dutch art painters trained some apprentices simultaneously without this having noticeably affected training quality: M. J. Bok, '"Nulla dies sine linie": De opleiding van schilders in Utrecht in de eerste helft van de zeventiende eeuw', *De Zeventiende Eeuw* 6 (1990), 58–68.

[52] Posthumus, *Bronnen*, vol. 6, 528.

[53] R. Schalk, *Splitting the Bill: Matching Schooling to Dutch Labour Markets, 1750–1920* (Amsterdam: Boom, 2015), 71–74.

[54] B. Panhuysen, 'De Amsterdamse en Haarlemse kleermakersgilden en hun concurrenten: De in- en uitsluiting van mededingers op de lokale afzetmarkt in de 17de en 18de eeuw', in: Lis and Soly (eds.), *Werelden van verschil*, 135.

[55] J. M. Montias, *Artists and Artisans in Delft: A Socio-Economic Study of the Seventeenth Century* (Princeton: Princeton University Press, 1982), 74 argues that the Delft painters' guild instead tried to protect local painters against the influx of immigrants from the Southern Netherlands.

[56] P. Wallis, 'Apprenticeship and training in premodern England', *Journal of Economic History* 68 (2008), 832–61; C. Minns and P. Wallis, 'Rules and reality: Quantifying the

apprentices paid up front for any training not directly covered by the value of their work. Although there are few studies on Dutch premiums, de Jager's work suggests that these extra costs were covered by premiums, while, vice versa, other apprentices paid premiums to speed up training. Premiums for artists' and gold and silversmiths' apprentices in the seventeenth century reflected the duration of the contract (longer apprenticeships were cheaper), board and lodging, the quality of instruction and materials, and the master's reputation.[57]

The use of premiums to speed up skill formation can be seen elsewhere too. For example, in 1696 Willem van der Kloest paid a premium of 6 *guilders* to Leiden surgeon Johannes Lasar explicitly to 'reduce the term'.[58] Willem did indeed manage to complete his apprenticeship more quickly than usual. Cooper apprentices from Haarlem also shortened their terms by paying higher premiums.[59] This tendency to pay for additional instruction up front can also explain why premiums were more common in prestigious crafts, such as those examined by de Jager. As masters in these trades could not depend on learning-by-doing to transfer skills, they had to invest more time in actual training – time which was paid for by premiums. Conversely, apprentices who already possessed skills paid lower premiums because of their value in the workshop.[60]

The same logic explains why boarding apprentices paid extra: because they had to cover their food and lodging, especially when the value of their labour was not yet sufficient to meet these expenses. A notarial apprenticeship contract made by an Utrecht goldsmith in 1714 specified that the premium funded board and keep only.[61] Non-boarding apprentices thus paid less. Orphanages, for example, only rarely paid a premium to the masters who took their boys, and the youths even received wages from the start of their contract. Why? Because apprenticed orphans returned to the orphanage every evening. And as they became more skilled, their wages increased annually.[62] Similarly, many regular apprentices in cooping and glassmaking received wages from the

practice of apprenticeship in early modern England', *Economic History Review* 65 (2012), 556–79; Schalk, 'From orphan to artisan'.

[57] R. de Jager, 'Meester, leerjongen, leertijd: Een analyse van zeventiende-eeuwse Noord-Nederlandse leerlingcontracten van kunstschilders, goud- en zilversmeden', *Oud-Holland* 104 (1990), 69–110.

[58] RAL, Archief Gilden, inv. 351, fol. 32.   [59] Tump, 'Ambachtelijk geschoold', 89.

[60] Van Eeghen, *De gilden*, 24, 77. Cf. C. Minns and P. Wallis, 'The price of human capital in a pre-industrial economy: Premiums and apprenticeship contracts in 18th century England', *Explorations in Economic History* 50 (2013), 335–50.

[61] HUA, Notarieel Archief, inv. U083b034 deed no. 46

[62] Schalk, 'From orphan to artisan', 740–44.

start, and paid no premium.[63] The difference with their premium-paying counterparts, appearing in the same ledger, was presumably that they were not boarding. As apprentices became more valuable, they covered more of their subsistence. This is illustrated in an Utrecht clothworker's apprenticeship contract from 1706. The apprentice paid 200 *guilders* for board and training the first year, but only 150 the next.[64]

A random sample of 510 Amsterdam coopers' contracts from the eighteenth century (1722–83) sheds further light on the relationship between premiums and apprenticeship terms.[65] Excluding contracts that give no information about wages or premiums (193), about 37% of apprentices paid a premium. This group probably boarded with their masters. Another 52 apprentices did not pay a premium, but also did not receive a wage. The remaining 149 apprentices received a wage during their term, and presumably continued to live at home. For six, the wage started in the second year of their contract. The rest were paid a wage from the start, suggesting that they were already valuable to their master.

The duration of these contracts indicates that premiums could accelerate training. Apprenticeships involving a premium were generally shorter than apprenticeships in which the master paid a wage. Among those with a premium, 48% lasted two years or less. Only 18% of apprenticeships with wages were that brief. Plausibly, apprentices who paid a premium expected to become skilled relatively quickly. Apprentices who were unable or unwilling to pay a premium may have been less likely to live with their master, and repaid their training by performing more labour over longer terms.

Nevertheless, some premium-paying apprentices served comparable terms to waged apprentices. Moreover, the size of the premium was not inversely proportional to the contract term. As Table 7.2 shows, higher premiums did not significantly shorten apprenticeships. There was no significant difference between premiums for apprenticeships lasting two years and those lasting four years. However, the large variation in premiums paid for contracts lasting the same duration suggests the importance of other factors, such as particularly able masters, or better quality training and board and lodging. Unfortunately, the sample is too small to explore these characteristics in more detail.

---

[63] See also R. Reith, 'Apprentices in the German and Austrian crafts in early modern times: Apprentices as wage earners?', in: De Munck, Kaplan and Soly (eds.), *Learning on the Shop Floor*, 179–202.

[64] HUA, Notarieel Archief, U093a050, deed no. 60.

[65] SAA, Archief Gilden, inv. 895. The sample has been constructed by taking every second apprenticeship contract from each page.

Table 7.2 *Premiums (guilders) of a sample of Amsterdam cooper apprentices, 1722–83*

Term (years)	N	Mean	St. dev.	Min.	Max.
1	3	36.67	20.82	20	60
2	53	30.30	11.67	8	60
3	17	25.00	7.52	15	40
4	42	30.19	12.17	8	50
Total	115	29.64	11.65	8	60

Source: SAA, Archief Gilden, inv. 895.

Completing an Apprenticeship

After paying guild fees and any premium the apprenticeship could begin. Unfortunately, what actually happened on the shop floor is difficult to tell. It seems most likely that apprentices carried out relatively simple chores at first and gradually undertook more skilled work. Masters in the crafts probably provided little direct training, perhaps giving somewhat more to apprentices who paid premiums. Apprentices mostly gained skills through imitation and learning-by-doing. As a result, training was prolonged whenever no premium was paid.

The terms set by guilds varied by city and guild, and were at times altered. Guilds rarely demanded terms longer than five years. Usually, their requirements were much shorter. Surgeon's apprentices in Leiden had to serve five years, but the Haarlem coopers' and the Amsterdam pig butchers' only required two years.[66] In seventeenth-century Utrecht, minimum terms were set by 22 of the 27 guilds. Only three guilds exceeded two years (the glassmakers, goldsmiths, and lace workers).[67] In Bois-le-Duc, similarly, 14 guilds required terms of two years, 4 expected three years and only 2 demanded four years.[68] Although some guild rules envisaged a longer term for immigrants, in practice they served the same term as locals.[69]

Most guilds or masters issued a *leerbrief*, a written proof of completion, once apprentices completed these minimum terms. It is likely that apprentices wishing to enter the craft adhered to this requirement, because they were usually required to show their *leerbrief* to work as

[66] RAL, Archief Gilden, inv. 311; Tump, 'Ambachtelijk geschoold', 88; SAA, Archief Gilden, inv. 1470.
[67] Slokker, *Ruggengraat*, 76.
[68] H. B. M. Essink, *Inventaris van de archieven van de ambachts- en schuttersgilden 1327–1874* (n.p, n.d.), 6.
[69] Tump, 'Ambachtelijk geschoold', 89.

a journeyman. In practice, many apprentices probably stayed for terms that were longer than the guild required in order to actually master their craft. Moreover, as the premiums imply, apprentices' actual terms were also affected by the distribution of working and training over their contract. Depending on their contract, apprentices with the same master could serve different terms.

Contracts are only an indirect measure for the actual terms that apprentices served. Early exits were common in Dutch apprenticeships (as will be discussed later). Contracts do nevertheless indicate the length of time agreed between masters and apprentices at the outset. When combined with the information contracts include on wages, we can identify the term that inexperienced, non-boarding apprentices anticipated needing to learn the craft. New apprentices at the Amsterdam coopers' guild between 1722 and 1785 agreed to a term of 3.75 years (median 4) on average.[70] Glassmaking apprentices in eighteenth-century Leiden agreed to an almost identical 3.74 years, on average.[71]

Apprenticeships of orphans provide information about terms that were actually served. Orphans entered relatively common crafts, and were by and large comparable to regular apprentices.[72] They often appeared alongside regular apprentices in guild records, and their terms were not affected by the time they spent at the orphanage. Figure 7.1 gives the distribution of terms served by orphans in eighteenth-century Leiden and Utrecht, grouped by occupation. Note that these are not contracts, but the actual terms they served.

The figure reveals that the terms that apprentices served within a craft could vary substantially. The shorter terms of around one year mostly relate to apprentices who dropped out or changed masters: almost half moved to a different master or craft, and thus did not complete their training with the first master. We do not know if all apprentices were as mobile as these orphans, but other evidence suggests that around 12% moved masters *within* the same guild (for orphans we also count moves to different guilds), while a similar share quit. It is therefore possible that all apprentices behaved similarly.

Figure 7.1 also shows that a significant share of apprentices served terms that were substantially longer than the 2–3 years required by most guilds. Many stayed for five or more years past the point they qualified for a *leerbrief*. Either it took some time to master a craft, or orphans struggled to move on to journeywork. When orphans from Leiden remained in one

---

[70] N = 550. SAA, Archief Gilden, inv. 895. The start of an apprenticeship is identified by a wage of 12 *stuivers* at most.
[71] N = 30. RAL, Archief Gilden, inv. 524.
[72] Schalk, 'From orphan to artisan', 733–36.

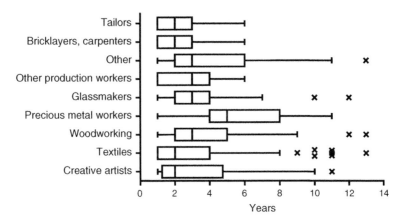

Figure 7.1 Actual terms served by apprenticed orphans from Leiden (1754–82) and Utrecht (1779–93)
Note: N = 428. The boxes represent the middle 50% of individuals, with the vertical line at the median. The whiskers extend for the remaining 25%; where no whisker is included, the distribution is censored or skewed. Xs are outliers.
Sources: RAL, Archief Heilige Geest, inv. 3855, inv. 3390; HUA, Archief Gereformeerd Burgerweeshuis, inv. 769–2, inv. 723–1.

craft throughout their apprenticeship, the average time it took for them to finish was 6.5 years (standard deviation 3.4). In Utrecht, the average time to completion was 4.5 years (standard deviation 2.5). It is difficult to explain this variance, but it surely underlines the diverse experiences of apprentices.

We can also reconstruct the time it took for regular apprentices to become masters in a guild. This was fairly similar between guilds, as Table 7.3 shows. Remarkably, masters' sons took longer to become masters. Possibly, they could only open their shop once their father died. The times taken to make this step seem broadly in line with apprenticeship terms, especially since the standard deviations on the time to master status were around 4–5 years. This meant that the journey from apprentice to master could take anything from 5 to over 20 years, with 8–12 years being fairly commonplace. Leiden surgeons' apprentices were 23.4 years old on average when they became a master between 1700 and 1729 (median 23). Since their apprenticeships started at around 14.5 years old, and were contracted for an average of 3.6 years, this implies that they had worked as journeymen for approximately five years before they set up on their own.

Table 7.3 *Years from beginning an apprenticeship to taking a master's test, Dutch Republic 1588–1799*

City and guild	Period	Apprentices (years)	Masters' sons (years)	Apprentices (N)	Masters' Sons (N)
Amsterdam					
Pig butchers	1787–99	8.3	11.6	25	30
Utrecht					
Coopers	1588–1662	10.6	13.1	84	20
Surgeons	1740–93	10	14.9	42	7
Leiden					
Surgeons	1683–1729	8.2	11.4	55	12
Weighted mean		9.6	12.3		

Note: Sons of masters were identified by matching surnames to existing guild masters, except for Leiden where they are identifiable by apprenticeship fees.
Sources: See Table 7.1.

Becoming a master or even a journeyman was, nevertheless, not the fate of all Dutch apprentices. Guild records allow us to infer how many apprentices completed their terms, and how many later became masters. These were two separate events. Apprenticeship completion meant obtaining the *leerbrief*, certifying that they were qualified to work as a journeyman, which gave access to journeywork in other cities as well.[73] To become a master, a journeyman had to acquire the capital for a shop, pay the guild's entrance fee and pass the master's test. Each aspect could involve substantial costs.

If we compare the number of registered apprentices to the number of registered master's tests, it demonstrates that many apprentices never became a master. The Utrecht goldsmiths' guild registered 1,068 apprentices, but only 431 master's test between 1598 and 1783, a rate of 2.5 apprentices for every test.[74] Some of these new masters may have been journeymen who had been apprentices elsewhere before moving to Utrecht. The Utrecht coopers' guild registered 250 master tests against 1,062 apprentices.[75] Even in prestigious crafts, some apprentices still would not become a master. Of the 29 apprentices taken by the well-known Dutch painter Abraham Bloemaert, renowned for his teaching skills, only 15 became master painters. Of the other 14 apprentices, 4

---

[73] C. Plomp, 'Het leerlingwezen in Den Haag van de 15de tot de 18de eeuw', *Die Haghe Jaarboek* (1936), 16.
[74] HUA, Archieven stadsbestuur I, inv. 130, inv. 131–1.
[75] HUA, Archieven stadsbestuur I, inv. 124.

died, another 4 entered different trades (2 goldsmiths, 1 cloth merchant and 1 in the military) and the remaining 6 apprentices could not be traced.[76] The fates of apprentices who did not take a master's test remain unknown. Perhaps they entered apprenticeships in other crafts or migrated; others surely worked as journeymen and simply never became master.

Lists of *leerbrieven* that allow us to distinguish those apprentices who qualified as journeymen rarely survive. However, we have identified them for three guilds: the Amsterdam pig butchers' (1787–1811), the Amsterdam pastry bakers' (1748–76) and the Leiden surgeons' guilds (1683–1729).[77] In every guild, a considerable share of apprentices did not complete their term. Surgeon apprentices had the highest completion rates, but even in this prestigious craft about 40% of apprentices dropped out. Half of the pastry bakers' apprentices obtained their *leerbrief*. At 32%, this share was even lower among pig butchers' apprentices.[78] These findings are supported by apprenticeship lists from other guilds, which show that attrition was high everywhere. The intervals at which Leiden's glassmakers took new apprentices suggest that at least 16% of regular contracts were terminated early (freeing the master to hire another youth), while at least 22% of the apprenticeships of Leiden orphans were abandoned.

The youth's aptness for the craft played a role in whether they decided to stay. Among Leiden orphans, talented apprentices sometimes moved to crafts related to their previous apprenticeship.[79] For instance, Jan van Kampen switched from chair making to cabinetmaking, earning a higher wage during this second apprenticeship (from 26 to 28 *stuivers* a week). Changing masters within the same craft also helped apprentices to hone their skills, as is evidenced by their pay; orphans who switched master within a craft nearly always received a wage increase.

Conversely, many apprenticed orphans moved to entirely different crafts when they left their first master. This group experienced a cut in wages. In 1770, when Elias Dionet left his candle-making apprenticeship after six years of service to apprentice as a chair maker, his wage dropped from 22 to 10 *stuivers*. Orphans who shifted sector were more likely to drop out of training altogether: 80% of apprentices who moved within

[76] M. Prak, 'Paintings, journeymen painters and painters' guilds during the Dutch Golden Age', in: N. Peeters (ed.), *Invisible hands? The role and status of the painter's journeyman in the Low Countries c. 1450–c. 1650* (Leuven: Peeters, 2007), 133–49. See also Montias, *Artists and Artisans*.

[77] Schalk, Wallis, Crowston and Lemercier, 'Failure or flexibility?', 137.

[78] The pig butchers did not consistently record the fate of all apprentices, but it is likely that unknown observations did not receive their *leerbrief*.

[79] Schalk, 'From orphan to artisan', 741–42.

a sector completed their apprenticeship, compared to 58% of those who moved between sectors. They thus probably moved crafts because they were not suited to their apprenticeships or did not like their craft. This suggests that talented apprentices experienced upward career mobility and higher completion rates, while less talented orphans were gradually filtered out.

The orphanage records are a rare window into these movements. It is much harder to observe regular apprentices. However, guild records show they moved between masters within the guild. Guild regulations allowed masters to transfer apprentices, as long as this was registered – sometimes with a fee. The share of apprentices who moved masters at least once ranged from 8.6% at the Amsterdam pastry bakers' guild to 14.1% at the Amsterdam pig butchers' guild, while the Utrecht coopers and the Leiden surgeons had shares of 11.4% and 11.7% respectively. Interestingly, moving masters did not significantly affect the chance of completion. Dutch apprenticeship was not a rigid system that locked apprentices into their indentures. Instead, they could exit from their agreements or switch masters, just as masters could easily get rid of unsuitable apprentices.

Enforcing Apprenticeship Contracts

Some historians argue that apprenticeship could only operate when guilds, courts or self-enforcing mechanisms (such as a reputational effect) acted as contract enforcers.[80] If these mechanisms were absent, the argument goes, the risks involved would have been too high and the system would have collapsed. Others have argued that working and training in tandem reduced this risk, allowing costs and benefits to be roughly balanced throughout the term.[81] Nevertheless, it is likely that a continuous balance of costs and benefits was not always possible. As a result, mechanisms were needed to resolve conflicts between masters and apprentices resulting from contract frictions. In pre-modern London, for example, the Lord Mayor's Court heard disputes over apprentices' premiums after youths had left their masters. By resolving conflicts, the court lowered the risks of long-term contracts.[82]

---

[80] S. R. Epstein, 'Craft guilds, apprenticeship, and technological change in preindustrial Europe', *Journal of Economic History* 58 (1998), 684–713; Humphries, 'English apprenticeship'.

[81] Wallis, 'Apprenticeship and training'; Schalk, 'From orphan to artisan'.

[82] P. Wallis, 'Labor, law, and training in early modern London: Apprenticeships and the City's institutions', *Journal of British Studies* 51 (2012), 791–819.

Courts of the same scope and magnitude were not present in the Northern Netherlands, possibly because Dutch apprenticeship was more decentralised (London operated as a national training centre). Dutch cities had various institutions for conflict resolution. The most important were the urban civil court, notaries and guilds.[83] The urban civil court was often divided into several benches, each serving a selection of topics ranging from major cases, involving lawyers, to neighbourly conflicts and minor credit disputes.[84] The available literature suggests that civil courts rarely intervened in apprenticeship. In a selection of over 3,000 arbitration cases at the Leiden civil court in 1664, only seven related to labour conflicts.[85] Most of these concerned journeymen, not apprentices.

In pre-modern Utrecht a separate bench of the civil court handled minor cases (*kleine zaken*), much like the Leiden civil court of *Vredemakers* (peacemakers). Many lower to medium-skilled workers appeared here, and suits often related to outstanding payments for goods or wages, house rents, or insults. Almost all cases resulted in financial compensation. It is difficult to be sure whether this court handled all potential apprenticeship conflicts, but several do appear in the list of verdicts. The maximum claim in minor civil courts in the Republic was normally around 50 *guilders*.[86] In the Leiden peacemaker court – which seems more or less comparable to the Utrecht minor court – the majority of claims were settled for less than 20 *guilders*.[87] This court was mostly used by middling to elite groups from Leiden. Other routes of judicial conflict resolution were more expensive and time consuming.[88] It is therefore unlikely that craftsmen or apprentices appeared in large numbers before aldermanic courts.[89]

In Utrecht, the civil court's minor bench heard around 360 cases annually in the mid-seventeenth century, gradually declining to about 200 by 1758. A small share related to apprenticeships. In the sample years (1653, 1655, 1658, 1662, 1663, 1670, 1674, 1689 and 1758), a total of only 32 apprenticeship conflicts could be found.[90] In short, the

---

[83] A. van Meeteren, *Op hoop van akkoord: instrumenteel forumgebruik bij geschilbeslechting in Leiden in de zeventiende eeuw* (Hilversum: Verloren, 2006).

[84] Ibid., ch. 7 and 8.   [85] Ibid., 269–70.

[86] C. M. G. ten Raa, *De oorsprong van de kantonrechter* (Deventer: Kluwer, 1970), 158–76.

[87] G. Vermeesch, 'The social composition of plaintiffs and defendants in the Peacemaker court, Leiden, 1750–54, *Social History* 4 (2015), 217–18, 223–24.

[88] Ibid., 227–28.

[89] Two verdict ledgers of the Utrecht major civil court from 1643 to 1664–74 contained just one apprenticeship dispute. It concerned a merchant apprentice ejected by his master in 1667 because of misbehaviour. He sought to reclaim the 200 *guilders* premium he had already paid (the total premium was fl. 400 in two parts). The court ordered the master to refund the premium because he could not prove the apprentice's misbehaviour. HUA, Gerechtelijk Archief, inv. 2266–17, inv. 2826–7, inv. 2566.

[90] HUA, Gerechtelijk archief Utrecht, inv. 3141–1, inv. 3141–2, inv. 3141–3, 3141–5.

court could settle apprenticeship disputes, but it was rarely used for this purpose.

The cases themselves throw some light on the resolution of apprenticeship conflicts. For instance, in 1689 one master demanded that his runaway apprentice should still pay 20 *guilders* in premiums. The court agreed that compensation was in order, but only required the apprentice to pay 6 *guilders* and 6 *stuivers*.[91] In another case, a mother paid 18 *stuivers* to a button-maker to cancel her son's apprenticeship.[92] In 1670 a father demanded outstanding wages for his apprenticed son. The parties agreed that the master would pay, but only when the apprentice promised to serve the remaining two years of his contract.[93] Several other masters wanted apprentices to return and finish their terms without any wages as leverage. However, these all relate to low-skilled textile occupations, and may suggest that they simply had problems finding workers. Apart from these instances, the court mainly facilitated exits by settling the bill between masters and apprentices. Either masters needed to pay outstanding wages, or guardians coughed up unpaid premiums or settled living costs.

Notarial records suggest that private conflict resolution offered an alternative route. Private settlements were sometimes recorded in notarial deeds, which could then be used in courts if needed; most of the time, this procedure sufficed to settle the issue.[94] Some apprenticeship contracts at Utrecht notaries, for example, contain a clause in which apprentices pay a fine should they leave their master.[95] This could work both ways: in 1691 a Utrecht watchmaker promised a reward of 100 *guilders* if his apprentice served his full term. Should he leave early, however, the apprentice had to pay 100 *guilders* to the master.[96] In 1669, the pharmacist Henricks Junius declared that he was willing to release his apprentice, Petrus Polion, whom he had hired in 1666. In return, Polion's father paid 115 *guilders* as compensation for board and keep.[97] Although a more detailed examination of notarial deeds is required to better understand the role of notaries in contract enforcement, these examples demonstrate that parties could settle contracts in private.

There is little evidence that guilds acted as mediators in apprenticeship conflicts. Guilds in the Dutch Republic were preoccupied with trying to

---

[91] HUA, Gerechtelijk archief Utrecht, inv. 3141–5, 21 January 1689.
[92] HUA, Gerechtelijk archief Utrecht, inv. 3141–1, 24 April 1655.
[93] HUA, Gerechtelijk archief Utrecht, inv. 3141–3, 29 November 1670.
[94] Cf. Van Meeteren, *Op hoop van akkoord*, 172–74.
[95] HUA, Notarieel archief, inv. U138a007 deed no. 165; inv. U083b034, deed no. 46.
[96] HUA, Notarieel archief, inv. U123a001 deed no. 106.
[97] HUA, Notarieel archief, inv. U048a003, deed no. 573. For a comparable resolution see HUA, Notarieel archief, inv. U075c001 deed no. 180.

enforce their monopolies and uphold their regulations. Enforcing apprenticeship was not a priority. Guilds only attended to apprenticeship when masters hired more apprentices than they were allowed, or the acceptance or transfer of youths had not been registered.[98] Although the records of guild meetings have not survived as often as apprenticeship lists, those that do exist are generally silent on contract enforcement. For example, between 1666 and 1782 the Amsterdam blacksmiths' guild dealt with conflicts about payments between guild members and suppliers, and fined members who breached regulations. Yet conflicts about apprentices never appear in the ledger.[99] Guild officials appeared before the Utrecht minor court demanding fines from guild members who had hired too many apprentices or failed to pay their membership dues.[100] That Dutch guilds themselves resorted to external judicial forums further argues against them having a role as contract enforcer.

Take Utrecht: the city contained around 39 guilds around 1670, suggesting that around 468 youths began apprenticeships each year. Around 187 of these apprentices would later drop out.[101] Yet in the three years 1653, 1655 and 1658 only a total of 11 apprenticeship conflicts were heard by the court's minor bench, just a couple of apprentice agreements were notarised, and there is no evidence in the surviving guild records that they enforced contracts. Apparently, only a tiny minority of masters and apprentices resorted to formal conflict resolution. Perhaps they could reach a private understanding. The evidence of the Leiden orphans suggest that many apprenticeships ended without much conflict. Orphans were apprenticed to almost one hundred different masters between 1754 and 1782. Many moved masters or abandoned their contracts. Yet only two masters complained to the orphanage's regents over breach of contract.[102]

Apprentices versus Masters

Since many apprentices dropped out during their apprenticeship, it is not surprising that the share of apprentices becoming masters was low. Ten per cent of apprentices in the Utrecht coopers' guild between 1588 and 1662 took the master's test (see Table 7.4). For the Leiden (1683–1729) and Utrecht (1740–99) surgeons' guilds the shares were 14.4 and 8.7% of

[98] Davids, 'Apprenticeship and guild control', 67–70.
[99] SAA, Archief Gilden, inv. 1435.
[100] HUA, Gerechtelijk archief Utrecht, inv. 3141–3, dated 12 September 1670 and dated 26 September 1670.
[101] Utrecht guild population from Lourens and Lucassen, 'Oprichting en ontwikkeling', 69.
[102] Schalk, 'From orphan to artisan', 746.

Table 7.4 *Number of apprentices taking their master's test with the Utrecht coopers' guild, 1588–1662*

Period	Apprentices	Became master	%
1588–99	111	14	13
1600–09	99	15	15
1610–19	149	21	14
1620–29	134	14	10
1630–39	171	17	10
1640–49	168	12	7
1650–62	230	11	5
1588–1662	1,062	104	10

Source: HUA, Archieven stadsbestuur I, inv. 124.

apprentices, respectively. Among the Amsterdam pig butchers' apprentices, 10.6% took the master's test. These are lower bound estimates: some individual links will have been missed, and some apprentices became masters in another city.[103] In turn, the Utrecht coopers' guild accepted several masters who had joined as immigrant journeymen.

Becoming a master was easier for apprentices who were related to a master in the guild. Although masters' sons took somewhat longer to become a master (Table 7.3), more of them did so than we see among other apprentices. In the Leiden surgeons' guild about 22% of apprentices who were masters' son took the master's test, compared to 16% of local apprentices. Only 4% of apprentices from outside Leiden became masters. Sons of Utrecht master coopers were almost five times more likely to become a master than other apprentices.

Although the share of apprentices who became a master varied by guild, in general the great majority of apprentices would not become a master in the same city, even if they completed their apprenticeship. In the Leiden surgeons' guild, of the 394 boys who started apprenticeships between 1683 and 1729, 237 completed their term; yet only 57 became masters in Leiden. Just one in four locally qualified journeymen took their master's test. Similarly, approximately one in three journeymen in the Amsterdam pig butchers' guild became masters.

If these guilds were typical, they imply that crafts displayed a pyramid-shaped hierarchical distribution, with a broad base of apprentices and a relatively small number of masters. That the number of masters was

---

[103] At both surgeons' guilds full names are spelled in such a standardised manner that mismatching is unlikely.

smaller than the number of journeymen and apprentices seems reasonable. However, it is unlikely that every master employed two to three journeymen, as these estimates could imply. In the Amsterdam blacksmiths' guild only one-quarter of masters had more than one journeyman in 1794.[104] The guild numbered 101 masters and 142 journeymen in that year. These figures indicate that a substantial share of the apprentices who qualified as journeymen but never became masters must have left the trade altogether, or migrated to another city. Unfortunately very little is known about these people.[105]

Many masters did not take on apprentices. Even in guilds that limited the number of apprentices, a large share of masters never provided training.[106] It is difficult to judge whether non-training masters simply did not want apprentices, or whether the supply of training exceeded demand. Masters who provided training nevertheless appear to have done so almost without interruption, taking a new apprentice as soon as one left. This could be interpreted as a market where demand exceeded supply, because training masters could always find new apprentices.

The distribution of apprentices among different masters was skewed in all observed guilds. Although for most guilds we only observe masters who did provide training, Figure 7.2 clearly shows that a small share of masters took most apprentices. When all masters are included, as for the Amsterdam pastry bakers, the distribution becomes even more skewed. In this guild, 30% of masters took no apprentices between 1750 and 1775. In all these guilds, 20% of (training) masters took approximately 50% of apprentices.

Dutch Apprenticeship after the Guilds[107]

After a long political struggle, Dutch guilds were abolished around 1820.[108] How did this affect apprenticeship training? Evidence on orphan apprenticeships indicates that some features remained as before.[109] Apprenticed orphans in Leiden around 1850 and Utrecht around 1860 served similar apprenticeships to orphans who had trained a century earlier when apprenticeships were monitored by guilds. Completion rates in Leiden and Utrecht were much the same in the eighteenth century and

[104] SAA, Archief Gilden, inv. 1494.
[105] J. Lucassen and L. Lucassen, 'The mobility transition revisited, 1500–1900: What the case of Europe can offer to global history', *Journal of Global History* 4 (2009), 363–64.
[106] Bok, 'Nulla dies sine linie'.
[107] This paragraph summarises the results of Schalk, *Splitting the Bill*, chapter 3.
[108] De Munck, Lourens and Lucassen, 'Establishment and distribution of craft guilds', 65–66.
[109] Schalk, 'From orphan to artisan', 748–53.

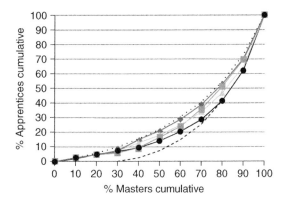

—●— Utrecht coopers 1588–1662, only training masters (n = 1,207)

—■— Utrecht surgeons 1740–99, only training masters (n = 614)

··▲·· Amsterdam butchers 1787–1811, only training masters (n = 607)

—◆— Leiden surgeons 1683–1729, only training masters (n = 623)

···· Amsterdam pastry bakers 1750–75, only training masters (n = 784)

--- Amsterdam pastry bakers 1750–75, all masters (n = 784)

Figure 7.2 Distribution of apprentices among masters for various Dutch guilds, 1588–1811
Notes: The number of observations is in some cases different from Table 7.1 because some apprentices may have had multiple masters.
Sources: See Table 7.1.

the first half of the nineteenth century. Apprenticeship did not become more uncertain after the guilds.

However, nineteenth-century adolescents did have many more craft apprenticeships to choose from. Especially in Leiden, orphans were apprenticed to a broader range of crafts than they had been under the guilds. The number of apprentices per master also changed. Several masters in Leiden and Utrecht now took on more apprentices than had been permitted by guild regulations. Both developments suggest that guilds had in fact limited access to training.

Other than increased access, Dutch masters and apprentices before industrialisation operated in a training market that functioned very much as it had a century before. Both parties had sufficient reasons to partake in training, and as a result enforcement was not a problem. Orphanage records do not show an increase in disputes after the guilds disappeared, and the literature on the abolition of Dutch guilds makes little mention of any effects on apprenticeship.[110] Proponents of the re-establishment of guilds mostly complained about the loss of ways to evaluate product quality.[111] They were also mostly concerned about losing their monopolies. Nor were politicians worried about a decline of apprenticeship without the guilds.[112]

At the dawn of Dutch industrialisation this relatively unregulated and unmonitored vocational training market nevertheless displayed some problems. The incentive structure for both masters and apprentices was altered by, first, the growing demand for unskilled labour and, second, increasing division of labour. The first cut demand for apprentices, while the second reduced masters' interest in providing training. Under the guilds, apprentices perhaps accepted their position in the expectation that it won them access to a privileged labour market with higher wages. With skill certification essentially absent after the guilds' abolition, apprenticeship was no longer the only route to skilled work. The increasing division of labour and associated deskilling in turn would have caused masters to avoid training, using apprentices as cheap labourers instead – further lowering the appeal of apprenticeship.[113] As a result, apprenticeship probably declined when the Dutch economy industrialised around the 1870s.

There is, however, little firm data on apprenticeship during industrialisation. Formal, firm-level apprenticeships seem to have been rare.[114] Only a handful of larger firms, such as the electrical company Philips, the machine factory Stork and some railway companies, offered formal apprenticeships around 1900.[115] Since few third parties monitored or regulated them, these apprenticeships may have been relatively informal

---

[110] C. Wiskerke, *De afschaffing der gilden in Nederland* (Amsterdam: Paris, 1938); Davids, 'Apprenticeship and guild control', 78.

[111] M. Prak, *Republikeinse veelheid, democratisch enkelvoud: sociale verandering in het Revolutietijdvak, 's-Hertogenbosch 1770–1820* (Nijmegen: SUN, 1999), 98–100, 279–84.

[112] A search of digitised Dutch parliamentary debates between 1810 and 1850 using different key words relating to guilds and apprenticeship shows that neither guilds, their proponents nor politicians perceived of a link between the abolition of the guilds and a possible decline of apprenticeship: www.statengeneraaldigitaal.nl.

[113] The relatively open labour market may have caused masters or journeymen to refrain from training because they feared they would 'glut their trade'; K. D. M. Snell, 'The apprenticeship system in British history: The fragmentation of a cultural institution', *History of Education* 25 (1996), 317.

[114] H. P. Meppelink, *Technisch vakonderwijs voor jongens in Nederland in de 19e eeuw* (n.p, 1961), 86–91.

[115] G. J. de Groot, *Fabricage van verschillen: mannenwerk, vrouwenwerk in de Nederlandse industrie (1850–1940)* (Amsterdam: Aksant, 2001); C. Beets, *Tachtig jaar Stork* (n.p, 1948); P. W. N. M. Dehing, *Eene soort van dynastie van spoorwegbeambten: Arbeidsmarkt en spoorwegen in Nederland, 1875–1914* (Hilversum: Verloren, 1989), 49–52.

on-the-job training.[116] The Vocational Training Act regulating apprenticeships was introduced in 1919.[117] However, as late as 1928 only the metal industry had an industry-wide apprenticeship system, with about 2,000 participants.[118]

One party that monitored apprenticeships and on-the-job training before 1919 was, once again, municipal orphanages. As before, orphanages continued to record orphans' training and wages as they sought to ensure that youths learned a trade – and were able to leave the orphanage once grown. The Amsterdam *Diaconieweeshuis der Hervormde Gemeente* (the Reformed Orphanage) kept a register listing the on-the-job training of all male orphans from 1887 to 1902.[119] It includes the employer's name and occupation, the orphans employed, the period of employment and the reason employment ended. The register covers the training of 327 Amsterdam orphans who undertook over 1,400 placements with local employers.

Relations between orphans and their bosses had become more insecure, at least in Amsterdam. Figure 7.3 gives the distribution of the periods that orphans spent with each employer by craft. It captures about 70% of all placements. The majority of all placements were very short. More often than not, the median term was a mere 4–7 months. Only around 20% of placements lasted for longer than one year. Tellingly, 62% lasted between a couple of days and six months. With an overall median duration of five months (and a mode of three months), the periods that Amsterdam orphans spent with employers were now much shorter than those experienced by Leiden and Utrecht orphans in the early nineteenth century.

Figure 7.4 examines the reasons recorded by the orphanage for agreements ending. These short terms were caused by insecurity on both sides: adolescents could lose their job at any moment and bosses were never sure that adolescent workers would return the next day. In 61% of cases, the employer ended the agreement, while orphans initiated the termination of 30%. In the remaining 9%, the regents removed the orphan.[120]

---

[116] K. M. Anderson, 'The long road to collective skill formation in the Netherlands', in: M. R. Busemeyer and C. Trampusch (eds.), *The Political Economy of Collective Skill Formation* (Oxford: Oxford University Press, 2012), 112.

[117] C. Trampusch, 'Co-evolution of skills and welfare in coordinated market economies? A comparative historical analysis of Denmark, the Netherlands and Switzerland', *European Journal of Industrial Relations* 16 (2010), 202.

[118] *De Ingenieur; T. Technische Economie*, Nr. 49 (1928) [Bijlage], 66–69.

[119] SAA, Diaconieweeshuis der Hervormde Gemeente, inv. 1006.

[120] Cf. J. Giele (ed.),*De arbeidsenquête van 1887: Een kwaad leven: heruitgave van de 'Enquête betreffende werking en uitbreiding der wet van 19 September 1874 (Staatsblad n° 130) en naar den toestand van fabrieken en werkplaatsen'* (Nijmegen: Link, 1981), vol. 1, response no. 1334.

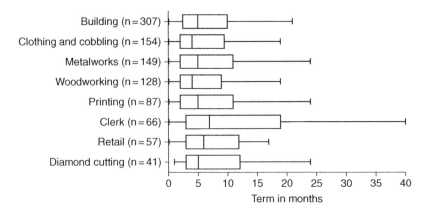

Figure 7.3 Distribution of placements of Amsterdam orphans, 1887–1902
Note: The boxes represent the middle 50% of individuals, with the vertical line at the median. The whiskers extend for the remaining 25%.
Source: Schalk, *Splitting the Bill*, 91.

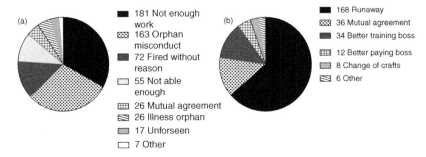

Figure 7.4 Reasons for terminating on-the-job training of Amsterdam orphans, 1887–1902
Note: n = 886; (a) by employers (b) by orphans.
Source: Schalk, *Splitting the Bill*, 92.

Training ended by mutual agreement in only 8% of cases. One orphan, Buckert, for instance, began training with a carpenter in 1890. By the time he left the orphanage in 1895, he had worked for no less than 16 employers. Buckert was never fired because he was unwilling or misbehaving, but simply because the carpenter temporarily had insufficient work. Although he eventually managed to become a carpenter, this was despite and not because of this large number of employers. Employers did also object to the conduct of many orphans,

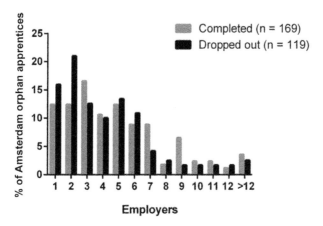

Figure 7.5 Number of employers during on-the-job training of Amsterdam orphans, 1887–1902
Source: Schalk, *Splitting the Bill*, 93.

though we cannot tell if these orphans were troublemakers or if their employers were just finding a reason to fire them. Missing one day's work because of illness was reason enough for some bosses to end a placement. On the other hand, many orphans simply did not turn up for work. Orphans could, and did, leave at any moment. An offer of better training or pay was enough for orphans to quit, but most gave no reason. Generally, these orphans remained at the orphanage, so the regents had to find yet another employer.

Faced with brief and insecure jobs, orphans had to work for multiple firms to become skilled. Orphan Weggelaar was fired by no less than four cabinet-makers because there was too little work.[121] Although in total he spent more than three years as a cabinetmaker's apprentice, because work was slow he had probably learned little. When apprenticed at yet another cabinetmaker in 1892 he was, ironically, fired because of insufficient skills. As Figure 7.5 shows, it was common for orphans to have several employers while living at the orphanage. The number of placements had increased dramatically compared to that experienced by Leiden and Utrecht orphans apprenticed before industrialisation. Because the process of skill formation was erratic, orphans found it harder to leave the orphanage. In December 1897, some complained to the regents that their earnings were too low to support themselves. The regents decided that in future not only age but also weekly earnings should be

---

[121] SAA, Diaconieweeshuis der Hervormde Gemeente, inv. 1006, fol. 30.

considered when deciding to discharge orphans.[122] Apparently, industrial on-the-job training resulted in too little skill formation, and hence in low wages.

Whether the instability of on-the-job training was caused by weaker enforcement remains an open question. As we saw, formal enforcement mechanisms were rarely used in the pre-modern period, making it unlikely that their withdrawal lay behind this. Moreover, courts could still enforce contracts. In 1907, when a father wanted to cancel the diamond-cutting apprenticeship of his daughter due to the master's absence, he took the case to court – which ruled against him, concluding that the master did not have to be present all the time.[123] Whether such cases became more common during industrialisation is unclear, but the legal journal that included this case does not appear to have covered other apprenticeship conflicts in this period. Perhaps apprenticeship had become so informal that few contracts were conducted, rendering them unenforceable in the courts. Apparently, most accepted the increased uncertainty prevalent in on-the-job training.

Thus, by the end of the nineteenth century skill formation in the Dutch craft sector was mostly left to chance and perseverance, even when orphanage regents could have tried to enforce agreements. Only the most adamant and motivated adolescents would become skilled workers. Even after training they had limited ways to signal their skills to other employers. 'These days, boys can no longer learn their craft from bosses', an inspector of secondary education lamented in 1890.[124] A lengthy contribution in the journal of the Dutch Society to Advance Industry in 1891 criticised the condition of Dutch training in detail: 'Nowadays boys leave one boss after the other for the greatest triviality . . .. The boss continuously fears that the boy will leave him to use his acquired skills with another boss. Bosses therefore slow down training by putting boys to work at specialised repetitive tasks, so that they bring in the highest profits.'[125] This caused an abundant supply of mediocre workers to the detriment of skilled workers.[126] Incidental remarks from labour reports underline that these conditions applied more generally.

The decline of apprenticeship was possibly countered by the establishment of vocational evening and daytime schools, which were founded in

---

[122] SAA, Diaconieweeshuis der Hervormde Gemeente, inv. 1006, minutes of 16 December 1897.
[123] *Weekblad van het Recht*, No. 8985 (29–10–1910), 4–5.
[124] *Arbeidsenquete 1890: Tweede afdeeling: Zwolle, Deventer, Kampen*, response no. 1607.
[125] *Orgaan der Nederlandsche Maatschappij ter bevordering van Nijverheid*, vol. 2 (1891), 97.
[126] Ibid., 96.

increasing numbers from the late nineteenth century. Educational and occupational data from Dutch conscripts suggests that these schools did not directly result in higher wages compared to workers trained on-the-job. Nevertheless, vocational degrees did significantly increase the probability of landing a job as a skilled worker, while lowering the chance of becoming an unskilled worker.[127] The absence of skill certification, then, may have been one reason behind the decline in apprenticeship in the later nineteenth century.

Conclusion

During the pre-industrial period, apprenticeships in the crafts looked similar throughout the cities of the Northern Netherlands. Everywhere, contracts settled individual agreements between masters and adolescents. Guild by-laws concerning apprenticeship did vary, but Dutch guilds generally regulated only a few elements: guild fees, (minimum) terms and sometimes the number of apprentices per master. Most other aspects of an apprenticeship were open to negotiation between masters and apprentices. Apprenticeships could be heterogeneous as a result, even within the same craft, or within one master's workshop. Terms, for instance, varied according to the apprentice's skills, his contribution to the workshop and his premium. Nevertheless, in all crafts apprenticeship functioned similarly, with relatively flexible agreements between masters and apprentices.

Apprenticeship contracts were also quite uncertain. In many guilds, a large share of apprentices dropped out during their training; even those who qualified as journeymen often did not become a master. Sons of masters were most likely to complete apprenticeships and to become masters. Sons of masters were also often exempt from guild regulations on apprenticeships. Guilds may sometimes have reduced access to training for youths who were not masters' sons, although this effect varied across guilds. The distribution of apprentices demonstrates that most craft training was supplied by a small number of masters, and this possibly affected access as well.

Apprenticeship survived the abolition of the guilds in the Netherlands, yet it came under pressure during industrialisation in the later nineteenth century. The increasing division of labour coupled with deskilling put further strain on the mix of incentives that had allowed apprenticeship training to work well previously. Together with the loss of skill certification and relatively open labour markets, both youths and masters had

---

[127] Schalk, *Splitting the Bill*, 102–14.

fewer reasons to engage in apprenticeships. At least in Amsterdam, on-the -job training became fraught with insecurity, making it hard to acquire skills. Eventually, vocational schools put skill formation on a more secure footing. Dutch apprenticeship only structurally revived after the Second World War, when apprenticeships and schooling became complements instead of substitutes.[128]

---

[128] P. Slaman, W. Marchand and R. Schalk, *Kansen in het Koninkrijk: studiebeurzen 1815–2015* (Amsterdam: Boom, 2015), 144–57.

8 Apprenticeship in the Southern Netherlands, c. 1400–c. 1800

Bert De Munck, Raoul De Kerf and Annelies De Bie

Introduction

A crucial field of tension in the debates on apprenticeship has been the one between rules and practices, or 'rules and reality'.[1] For the last few decades, the focus has mostly been on the rules and the question of whether they should be understood from the perspective of either their beneficial effects on transaction costs or their detrimental economic role due to rent-seeking.[2] The debate has largely remained inconclusive, because, among other reasons, economic historians tend to focus on effects (including unintended consequences) while social and political historians are interested rather in motivations and intentions. In addition, the approach has been rather ahistorical, with little interest in how the institutional context transformed over time. Partly in response to this, attention is now turning back to practices, which are mostly considered to deviate from the rules because historic actors were often trying to work around them.[3] Here as well, however, the rules themselves are often assumed to be rather immutable and tend to be addressed in a somewhat ahistorical way. The historic context seems to be important for the practices in particular, which would often have deviated from the rules because the latter did not allow for enough flexibility. This is

---

[1] E.g., M. Boone, 'Les métiers dans les villes flamandes au bas moyen âge (XIVe–XVIe siècles): Images normatives, réalités socio-politiques et économiques', in: P. Lambrechts and J.-P. Sosson (eds.), *Les métiers au moyen âge: Aspects économiques et sociaux* (Louvain-La-Neuve: Publications de L'Institut d'Études Médiévales, 1994), 1–22; P. Stabel, 'Guilds in late medieval Flanders: Myths and realities of guild life in an export oriented environment', *Journal of Medieval History* 30 (2004), 187–212.

[2] S. Ogilvie, '"Whatever is, is right?" Economic institutions in pre-industrial Europe', *Economic History Review* 60 (2007), 649–84; S. R. Epstein, 'Craft guilds in the premodern economy: A discussion', *Economic History Review* 61 (2008), 155–74; S. Ogilvie, 'Rehabilitating the guilds: A reply', *Economic History Review* 61 (2008), 175–82.

[3] P. Wallis, 'Apprenticeship and training in premodern England', *Journal of Economic History* 68 (2008), 832–61; C. Minns and P. Wallis, 'Rules and reality: Quantifying the practice of apprenticeship in early modern England', *Economic History Review* 65 (2011), 556–79.

certainly true in some cases, most notably in England, where the Statute of Artificers from 1563 prescribed a minimum term of seven years across trades and cities. However, the rules could alter too, both in reaction to changing economic practices and because of more independent long-term cultural and socio-political transformations.

The Southern Netherlands are an excellent lens through which to look at this. Not only is apprenticeship relatively well studied for this region, historians have worked on both the late medieval and the early modern period, recently also bridging the two periods. Not coincidentally, their focus has often been on guilds.[4] This is because guilds are traditionally considered important in the regulation and institutionalisation of apprenticeship requirements, at least in cities (and with regard to boys). Guilds prescribed minimum terms and the obligation for apprentices to live under a master's roof, which has mostly been seen as proof that they had an impact on practices of learning on the shop floor. Even poor and orphaned children, when boarded out by an orphanage or a municipality's overseers of the poor, were trained in the context of the guilds' regulatory framework. To this can be added the fact that, relative to other regions in Europe, guilds were powerful in the Southern Netherlands. During the urban revolts in the fourteenth and fifteenth centuries, they had gained access to the municipal governments, which were responsible for a major part of economic regulation at the time. In contrast to more absolutist states like France and England, guilds typically obtained seats in the most important municipal councils, where they shared power with the patrician (mercantile) elites.[5] Moreover, within the guilds manufacturing masters often held the reins. Unlike the situation in both the large Italian city-states and the cities in the Northern Netherlands, the guilds' rules reflect the interests of the apprentices' masters rather than those of large merchants. No wonder, then, that historians have often mistaken the guilds' rules for reality.

Proceeding from this observation, our chapter tackles the relationship and tension between, on the one hand, apprenticeship as a practice of learning on the shop floor, and, on the other, apprenticeship as it was defined and regulated by guilds. Our focus will automatically be on the

[4] See in particular B. De Munck, *Technologies of Learning: Apprenticeship in Antwerp from the 15th Century to the End of the Ancien Régime* (Turnhout: Brepols, 2007).

[5] M. Boone, *À la recherche d'une modernité civique: La société urbaine des anciens Pays-Bas au bas Moyen Age* (Brussels: Éditions de l'université de Bruxelles, 2010), ch. 1; J. Dumolyn and J. Haemers, 'Patterns of urban rebellion in medieval Flanders', *Journal of Medieval History* 31 (2005), 369–93; M. Prak, 'Corporate politics in the Low Countries: Guilds as institutions', in: M. Prak, C. Lis, J. Lucassen and H. Soly (eds.), *Craft Guilds in the Early Modern Low Countries: Work, Power and Representation* (Aldershot: Ashgate, 2006), 74–106.

urban context, not only because guilds were almost exclusively an urban phenomenon, but also because cities in the late medieval and early modern period are considered centres of learning and training far more than agricultural or even rural industrial districts are.[6] Of course, even within cities apprenticeship did not only take place with a guild-based master. Vocational training occurred in a wide range of other institutional contexts, with such urban actors as notaries, municipal courts and overseers of the poor being involved too. Nor was the guilds' institutional framework geared towards apprenticeship by necessity, even with regard to the regulations which give that impression on the surface. It is often difficult to tell whether the rules targeted learning on the shop floor and the master–apprenticeship relationship or rather access to the guild as a master and – hence – freeman status. While standardised tests and uniform minimum terms for apprentices suggest the former, it has been shown that apprenticeship requirements often applied only to those apprentices who wanted to become masters.[7] Master trials were mostly not exit tests for apprentices, but rather entry test for masters, and minimum terms were often – perhaps in the majority of the cases – only obligatory for prospective masters.

This chapter will therefore venture beyond a simple version of the rules versus reality dichotomy. First, we will show that the institutional environment of apprenticeship could be variegated. Zeroing in on apprenticeship as a practice, we will pay attention to both apprenticeship contracts and the options for learning a vocation outside a guild context. Second, we will specifically address the relationship and tension between learning on the basis of an apprenticeship contract and the guilds' regulations, arguing that the impact of guilds on apprenticeship contracts was limited, as the duration, fees, payment modalities and even default clauses were agreed upon in the absence of guild representatives and in disregard of the guilds' rules. In our view, the guilds' rules related to apprenticeship – especially the minimum terms and the masterpieces – are better understood from the vantage point of obtaining freeman status. Proceeding from this observation, in the second section we will try to understand exactly why the guilds introduced formal and standardised rules related to apprenticeship in the urban trades and what the impact of the specific economic and demographic context was on their shape.

Our argument will be that they were not introduced with an eye to contract enforcement but rather to guard and define the distinction

---

[6] K. Davids and B. De Munck (eds.), *Innovation and Creativity in Late Medieval and Early Modern European Cities* (Aldershot: Ashgate, 2014).

[7] B. De Munck, 'One counter and your own account: Redefining illicit labour in early modern Antwerp', *Urban History* 37 (2010), 30–31.

between 'free' and 'unfree' work. However, in order to understand their shape, it is nevertheless crucial to appreciate the socio-economic context of the cities in the Southern Netherlands. Specifically, it is important to understand that skills and human capital were extremely important, not only during the run-up to the industrial revolutions, but long before that too. During the so-called 'commercial revolution' in the Middle Ages (c. 1000–1300), the rapid development and expansion of large urban centres in Flanders was primarily related to the production of high-quality textiles. Confronted with competition from cheaper, low-quality products – the so-called 'new draperies' – from the secondary urban centres, during the fourteenth century the larger cities in the urban network started focusing on luxury woollens made of high-quality English wool. Moreover, as the English started producing their own woollens while using the external demand for wool as a political weapon, this resulted in an economic crisis from which the urban network was able to recover only thanks to its capacity to substitute the textile-oriented monoculture with a very diversified production of high-quality and luxury goods – ranging from furniture and tableware to house decoration, clothing accessories and artistic products.[8] As a result, there existed strong incentives for cities and guilds to install and monitor apprenticeship systems.

In this context, the guild authorities introduced apprenticeship requirements but they made sure to avoid exclusionary effects, which from a guild perspective would have been very detrimental due to the patterns of urbanisation in the region. The Southern Netherlands were a densely populated and highly urbanised region, with a broad range of middle-sized cities but without one metropolis dominating. In the county of Flanders alone at least seven cities harboured more than 30,000 inhabitants around the mid-fourteenth century, while another seven counted 5,000–10,000.[9] The duchy of Brabant in the first half of

---

[8] H. Van Der Wee, 'Structural changes and specialization in the industry of the Southern Netherlands', *Economic History Review* 28 (1975), 203–21; H. Van Der Wee, 'Industrial dynamics and the process of urbanization and de-urbanization in the Low Countries from the late Middle Ages to the eighteenth century', in: H. Van Der Wee (ed.), *The Rise and Decline of Urban Industries in Italy and the Low Countries (Late Middle Ages–Early Modern Times)* (Leuven: Leuven University Press, 1988), 307–81; A. K. L. Thijs, 'Antwerp's luxury industries: The pursuit of profit and artistic sensitivity', in: J. Van Der Stock (ed.), *Antwerp: Story of a Metropolis, 16th–17th Century* (Antwerp: Snoeck-Ducaju & Zoon, 1993), 105–13.

[9] A. Derville, 'Le nombre d'habitants des villes de l'Artois et de la Flandre Wallonne (1300–1450)', *Revue du Nord* 65 (1983), 279–93; P. Stabel, 'Stedelijke instellingen (12de eeuw-1795)', in: W. Prevenier and B. Augustyn (eds.), *De gewestelijke en lokale instellingen in Vlaanderen tot 1795* (Brussels: Algemeen Rijksarchief, 1997), 247; Boone, *À la recherche*, 62.

the fifteenth century harboured one city with more than 30,000 inhabitants and another four above 10,000.[10] In other words, these principalities were scattered with small and middle-sized cities, which were moreover surrounded by a relatively densely populated hinterland, favourable for the development of proto-industrial activities. Already in the late medieval period, but increasingly from the sixteenth century on, urban industries faced competition from rural districts, particularly in the textile industry.[11] The economic history of the region can actually be described in terms of cycles in which the field of gravity shifted to and fro between large cities, small cities and rural districts, which suggests that all these entities competed for skills.[12] In this context, introducing such access requirements as minimum terms and trials – not to mention guild fees – must have been a delicate affair. In our view this explains the relatively short apprenticeship terms, which mostly ranged from one to four years. In the same vein, it explains why guilds accommodated the incorporation of skills acquired in other cities, typically by recognising an apprenticeship term completed in another city (with guilds).

The third section will then address the overlap between learning and being officially registered as an apprentice by a guild, pointing to the growing gap between these two processes after the mid-seventeenth century. We will argue that the declining effectiveness of guild-based regulations was part of a long-term trend in which acquiring skills was disconnected from attaining a corporative status – whether as a master or a 'free' journeyman. On the surface, this may resemble a return to the late medieval situation in which apprenticeship was based on contracts in the absence of guild rules related to learning, but this is not necessarily the case. In all likelihood, informal enforcement mechanisms based upon the patriarchal authority of the master had declined over the long term, as a result of which the relationship between master and apprenticeship had become more businesslike. Enforcement mechanisms may thus have shifted from self-enforcement (or enforcement by the municipal authorities in some cases) over enforcement by the guilds to enforcement by the municipal courts. Due to a lack of research, this is still open to debate however.

---

[10] R. Van Uytven, 'De triomf van Antwerpen en de grote steden', in: R. Van Uytven (ed.), *Geschiedenis van Brabant van het hertogdom tot heden* (Leuven: Davidsfonds, n.d.), 242–43.

[11] Van Der Wee, 'Structural changes'; Van Der Wee, 'Industrial dynamics'.

[12] For the importance of small cities, see P. Stabel, *Dwarfs among Giants: The Flemish Urban Network in the Late Middle Ages* (Leuven: Garant, 1997).

Apprenticeship as a Contract and a Practice

Learning on the shop floor was typically based on a contract between a master and the parents or guardians of an apprentice. Information from a limited range of preserved contracts indicates that the contracting parties mostly agreed on the term and the price of the contract, in addition to the learning content. Notarial contracts usually start by listing the names and residences of the contracting parties. Next, the master officially agreed to train the son or pupil of the other party (in case the apprentice is a minor) for a specific period of time and in a specific trade. Both parties then also agreed on the boarding arrangements and how much the father or guardian had to pay in exchange for training and upbringing. On this account, the contracting parties also discussed and bargained about food and lodging, the boy's or girl's clothing and laundry, and clauses related to eventualities such as the apprentice becoming sick or the master passing away.[13] The latter issues raise the question as to what extent learning on the shop floor took place in a patriarchal context, in which learning was entangled with upbringing and socialisation. From a small sample of 272 apprenticeship contracts registered with a notary, at least two-thirds of the apprentices in Antwerp boarded in the seventeenth and eighteenth centuries – although this proportion differed greatly according to trade and declined over time.[14] As has also been argued for other European regions, the masters were thereby held to act as surrogate fathers of sorts.[15] But, as we will see in the last section, this too may have transformed drastically over time.

Before the guilds entered the scene in the fourteenth and fifteenth centuries, the terms of the contracts were probably based on custom and informal practices and bargaining. Apprenticing was embedded in an oral culture, which explains why contracts were seldom registered before a notary or even written down at all. In contrast to other

---

[13] De Munck, *Technologies*, 41–49.

[14] B. De Munck, 'From brotherhood community to civil society? Apprentices between guild, household and the freedom of contract in early modern Antwerp', *Social History* 35 (2010), 10–11.

[15] See, e.g., S. R. Smith, 'The ideal and the reality. Apprenticeship–master relationships in seventeenth-century London', *History of Education Quarterly* 21 (1981), 449–60; A. Grießinger and R. Reith, 'Lehrlinge im deutschen Handwerk des ausgehenden 18. Jahrhunderts: Arbeitsorganisation, Sozialbeziehungen und alltägliche Konflikte', *Zeitschrift für Historische Forschung* 13 (1986), 149–99; N. Pellegrin, 'L'apprentissage ou l'écriture de l'oralité: Quelques remarques introductives', *Revue d'histoire moderne et contemporaine* 40 (1993), 356–86; M. Prak, 'Moral order in the world of work: Social control and the guilds in Europe', in: H. Roodenburg and P. Spierenburg (eds.), *Social Control in Europe*, vol. 1: *1500–1800* (Columbus: Ohio State University Press, 2004), 176–99; De Munck, 'From brotherhood community'.

European regions it was not obligatory in the Southern Netherlands to register a contract even in a guild context.[16] Nevertheless, dozens of contracts have been preserved from the thirteenth and fourteenth centuries, namely for Ypres and Tournai.[17] These contracts were found in the registers of the aldermen and, hence, sanctioned by the urban authorities. In these contracts, terms were customised. The terms for 11 weaver apprentices ranged from two to five years, while in the six contracts for silversmith apprentices this was three to six. Unfortunately, we cannot pinpoint when and why exactly contracts were registered or not. What is clear is that by the end of the sixteenth century, apprenticeship contracts were registered – if at all – with a public notary, which as an institution had taken over a great deal of the private law activities from the urban authorities. The notaries were certified by the central authorities and by this token could legally authenticate contracts. In luxury sectors such as diamond polishing and silversmithing up to about 30% of the contracts were registered with a notary in the seventeenth and eighteenth century, but in most crafts this was far less.[18]

The notarial contracts did not differ fundamentally from the earlier ones registered by the bench of aldermen, although the notaries could not enforce the contracts themselves. While notaries intervened in disputes by registering testimonies, bringing parties together and admonishing others, it was eventually up to either a guild board or the municipal court to pronounce sentence.[19] Unfortunately, current research does not permit us to establish to what extent guilds intervened but their impact would seem to have been limited, at least by the mid-seventeenth century. By then their role resembled that of an arbiter rather

---

[16] De Munck, *Technologies*, 41–49; compare with S. L. Kaplan, 'L'apprentissage au XVIIIe siècle: Le cas de Paris', *Revue d'Histoire Moderne et Contemporaine* 40 (1993), 459–66, and Pellegrin, 'L'apprentissage'.

[17] G. Des Marez, 'L'apprentissage à Ypres à la fin du XIIIe siècle: Contribution à l'étude des origines corporatives en Flandre', *Revue du Nord* 2 (1911), 1–48; L. Verriest, *Les luttes sociales et le contrat d'apprentissage à Tournai jusqu'en 1424*, vol. 9 (Brussels, 1911).

[18] Our estimates are based on a sample of apprenticeship contracts reaped from notarial archives in Antwerp, crossed with fragments of lists of apprentices registered in guild books. See A. De Bie, 'The paradox of the Antwerp rose: Symbol of decline or token of craftsmanship?', in: Davids and De Munck (eds.), *Innovation and Creativity*, 282, fn.91; R. De Kerf, 'De circulatie van technische kennis in het vroegmoderne Antwerpse ambachtswezen, 1500–1800 (casus kuipers en edelsmeden)', PhD thesis, University of Antwerp, 2014, 25.

[19] On judicial procedures and practices, see H. Deceulaer, 'Guilds and litigation: Conflict settlement in Antwerp (1585–1796)', in: M. Boone and M. Prak (eds.), *Statuts individuels, statuts corporatifs et statuts judiciaires dans les villes européennes (moyen âge et temps modernes). Individual, Corporate and Judicial Status in European Cities (Middle Ages and Early Modern Period)* (Leuven/Apeldoorn: Garant, 1996), 171–208.

than a judge.[20] Unlike in France, the guilds' deans were not present when a contract was concluded, and most of the preserved case files about breach of contract found to date originate from the (Antwerp) municipal bench of aldermen.[21]

From the registered contracts and the few written contracts preserved in case files, we can infer some of the logic behind the terms in the contracts. The most important mechanism from an economic and social perspective is the trade-off between learning and working. Cheaper contracts were longer on average, suggesting that apprentices often provided a return for the master's investment by working below market wage rates in the final years of the term.[22] Among the tinsmiths and plumbers in Antwerp, the average premium paid to the master declined from 58 guilders a year for a two-year contract to less than 15 guilders for a six-year contract.[23] In all likelihood, the large majority of the contracts were free, with training, board and lodging being offset by work during and after the actual training. Recent research shows that the revenues from a youth's work were mostly calculated to cover both their maintenance and training. As this was the case in both the lace industry and diamond polishing (considered to be a cheap and an expensive trade respectively), this seems to have applied to a broad range of sectors.[24] One five-year contract from 1770 explicitly stipulates that 'the first four years are to be considered years of apprenticeship, while the fifth and final year, which

---

[20] R. De Kerf, 'The early modern Antwerp coopers' guild: From a contract-enforcing organization to an empty box?', in: Davids and De Munck (eds.), *Innovation and Creativity*, 245–67.

[21] B. De Munck, 'In loco parentis? De disciplinering van leerlingen onder het dak van Antwerpse ambachtsmeesters (1579–1680)', *Tijdschrift voor sociale en economische geschiedenis* 1 (2004), 3–30; compare with Kaplan, 'L'apprentissage', 437–38, 455–56; Pellegrin, 'L'apprentissage'.

[22] De Munck, *Technologies*, 44 n.19; B. De Munck, 'Gilding golden ages: Perspectives from early modern Antwerp on the guild-debate, c. 1450–c. 1650', *European Review of Economic History* 15 (2011), 227. Also: W. Smits and Th. Stromback, *The Economics of the Apprenticeship System* (Cheltenham: Edward Elgar, 2001).

[23] De Munck, *Technologies*, 43. Similar arguments are in Grießinger and Reith, 'Lehrlinghe', 153. In the Southern Netherlands this trade-off has also been found in other sectors, including confection (H. Deceulaer, *Pluriforme patronen en een verschillende snit: Sociaal-economische, institutionele en culturele transformaties in de kledingsector in Antwerpen, Brussel en Gent, 1585–1800* (Amsterdam: IISG, 2001), 281–82), lace production (M. Coppens, 'Réglementation de l'apprentissage du métier de dentellière sous l'Ancien Régime: Quelques exemples', *Revue belge d'archéologie et d'histoire de l'art* 67 (1998), 103) and textiles (A. K. L. Thijs, *Van 'werkwinkel' tot 'fabriek': De textielnijverheid te Antwerpen (einde 15de-begin 19de eeuw)* (Brussels: Gemeentekrediet, 1987), 281). A calculation per annum is in our view justified by the fact that a large part of the premium can be considered to be for room and board.

[24] A. De Bie, 'Education in crisis? Human capital investments from a household perspective in early modern Antwerp', PhD thesis, University of Antwerp, 2017.

said apprentice will perform free of charge, will be a consideration for the first four years'.[25]

Nevertheless, while learning (and being fed and lodged) in exchange for work may often have been the default option, paying for skills was not uncommon either. In the contracts registered with a notary (in which the luxury trades are over-represented) about three-quarters of the apprentices paid a premium to the master (not to be confused with a registration fee payable to the guild).[26] The price often depended on the precise range of skills to be learned. For the Antwerp gold and silversmiths, for instance, some well-known masters were far more expensive than others, depending on the skills and technical expertise available on the shop floor. While most contracts simply record 'learning the craft of' or 'learning the art of', others mention specialised skills or stipulate that the apprentice would 'perfect' their skills or be 'advanced' further in the trade. The contract could, for instance, specifically mention wire drawing or gilding, while a contract with a diamond cutter could refer to a specific cut.[27] One contract even distinguished between learning the craft of gold and silversmithing and learning 'the art of the master'.[28] Juridical litigations confirm that what concerned the apprentices and their parents or guardians most, was the ability to learn, which was itself dependent on the work and skills available on the shop floor.[29]

The customised character of the contracts suggests that they enabled balancing offer and demand – at least for apprentices who were prepared to work in exchange for the acquisition of skills. Instead of receiving intensive training, they started work as servants in the household of the master where they performed household tasks, while also regularly being put to work in the workshop to perform mainly simple tasks; in the meantime, they were thus enabled to steal knowledge with their eyes, as one historian has put it.[30] Subsequently, more complex tasks could

---

[25] 'les quatres premières années seront tenues pour années d'apprentissage, et que le cinquième et dernière année, par ledit apprentif se fera gratis, en consideration des quatres premieres années.' City Archives Antwerp, notarial archives, 1255, nr. 64 (1770); quoted in De Munck, *Technologies*, 43–44 n.17.

[26] This is based on a sample of 244 contracts in the trade of gold and silversmiths (seventeenth and eighteenth century). See B. De Munck and R. De Kerf, 'Wandering about the learning market: Early modern apprenticeship in Antwerp gold- and silversmith ateliers', in: P. Brandon, S. Go and W. Verstegen (eds.), *Navigating History: Economy, Society, Science and Nature – Essays in Honor of Prof. Dr. C. A. Davids*, (Leiden: Brill, 2018), 36–63.

[27] De Munck, *Technologies*, 41–58; De Munck and De Kerf, 'Wandering'.

[28] City Archives Antwerp, notarial archive, 4641, f.21.

[29] De Munck, 'In loco parentis'; De Munck, 'From brotherhood community', 15–16.

[30] S. Steffens, 'Le métier volé: Transmission des savoir-faire et socialisation dans les métiers qualifiés au XIXe siècle (Belgique-Allemagne)', *Revue du Nord* 15 (2001) (supplement:

gradually be performed, depending on the work available. Nor did this apprenticeship system based on private and oral contracting prevent women from being involved. In the Southern Netherlands, women were very active in artisanal shops, where they could serve clients and run the business next to their husbands. Moreover, women were usually prominent in the often lucrative commercial guilds.[31] And they were of course extremely important in the low-skill and labour-intensive jobs related to preparing yarn, as well as in other jobs related to food and textiles outside the regulated guild system. Women could even act as mistresses themselves. While this was often forbidden by the guilds even for widows, female mistresses were the rule in the non-incorporated lace trade, which was extremely important in Antwerp and other cities from the second half of the seventeenth century onwards. In Antwerp in the first decades of the eighteenth century, more than 10,000 women and children were active in this sector – including as apprentices.[32] The number of work mistresses amounted to about 115 in the 1730s.[33] Poor girls in particular were trained by these mistresses, although it could just as well be labelled child labour, given the often young age of the girls involved and the need to quickly recompensate the training with labour.[34]

Some trades were taught in orphanages and schools for the poor, such as the Antwerp girls' orphanage (*Maagdenhuis*), although this too applied to girls in particular.[35] More important in numerical terms was the system in which, not unlike the English system of parish apprenticeship, orphans or poor children were placed as apprentices with a master by the overseers

Les ouvriers qualifiés de l'industrie, XVIe–XXe siècle: Formation, emploi, migrations, edited by B. Gayot and Ph. Minard), 121–35.

[31] See among others P. Stabel, 'Working women and guildsmen in an era of economic change: Discourses on labour and gender identity (Flanders, 13th and 14th century)', unpublished paper, N. W. Posthumus Conference, University of Antwerp (2011); P. Stabel, 'Women at the market: Gender and retail in the towns in late medieval Flanders', in: W. Blockmans, M. Boone and Th. de Hemptinne (eds.), *Secretum scriptorum: Liber alumnorum Walter Prevenier* (Leuven: Garant, 1999), 259–76; L. Van Aert, 'Trade and gender emancipation: Retailing women in sixteenth-century Antwerp', in: B. Blondé, P. Stabel, J. Stobart and I. Van Damme (eds.), *Buyers and Sellers: Retail Circuits and Practices in Medieval and Early Modern Europe* (Turnhout: Brepols, 2006), 297–313.

[32] M. Coppens, *Kant uit België van de zestiende eeuw tot heden: Een keuze uit de verzameling van de koninklijke musea voor kunst en geschiedenis te Brussel* (Antwerpen: Volkskundemuseum, 1981), 28; Thijs, *Van 'werkwinkel'*, 113.

[33] V. Eyckmans, 'Kantonderwijs te Antwerpen (1585–1794): de Antwerpse werkmeesteressen', unpublished MA thesis, KULeuven, 1988, 42; Thijs, *Van 'werkwinkel'*, 112.

[34] De Bie, *Education*, 156–69. See also M. Coppens, 'Lois et usages réglant les rapports des différents acteurs de l'industrie dentellière dans les Pays-Bas autrichiens au XVIIIe siècle', *Belgisch tijdschrift voor oudheidkunde en kunstgeschiedenis* 65 (1996), 157–70.

[35] M. De Vroede, *Meesters en meesteressen: een sociale geschiedenis van de leerkrachten lager onderwijs in België deel I Het Ancien Régime* (Leuven: Universitaire Pers, 1999), 33–42.

of the poor.[36] These apprentices often received preferential treatment within the guilds at the request of the orphanage or the municipality. It was not unusual for craft guilds to accept poor apprentices or orphans for lower registration and entrance fees (typically half the fee) or even for free.[37] The overseers of the poor monitored the system by drafting contracts in which it was stipulated exactly what the poor boy or girl would learn and even the wages. As to the trades involved, young boys often ended up in less prestigious trades, such as tailoring.[38] Poor girls often learned how to make lace, often in combination with lessons in basic reading and writing and the principles of the Catholic faith. In addition to individual work mistresses, several charitable institutions such as the Terninck Foundation and the schools of the *Apostolinnen* offered this kind of apprenticeship. The girls there were taught how to make lace in exchange for the revenues of their labour (and, in some cases, an additional fee).[39]

Schools for vocational training were scarce and mostly limited to supplementary skills. Especially for boys, learning a trade took place mainly on the spot and while doing, instead of in an artificial environment created for educational purposes such as a school. For prospective merchants it could even imply having to travel along with merchants or to a subsidiary of the firm abroad, where languages were learned in addition to the rules of thumb of the trade. As a complement to this, counting, bookkeeping and languages could also be learned in private schools, the teachers of which were sometimes organised in a guild. Given its status as a commercial metropolis, it comes as no surprise that sixteenth-century Antwerp was particularly renowned for this type of school.[40] These schools were of course not restricted to apprentices, and welcomed youngsters in different stages of their careers. The same applies to colleges and academies for the acquisition of more technical skills, which show up

---

[36] E.g., A. Schouteet, *Een beschrijving van de bogardenschool te Brugge omstreeks 1555 door Zeger van Male* (Brugge: Stadsarchief, 1960), 11–12.

[37] E.g., K. Van Quathem, 'Sociale mobiliteit en machtsverdeling in het Brugse schoenmakersambacht (1570–1790)', in: C. Lis and H. Soly (eds.), *Werken volgens de regels: Ambachten in Brabant en Vlaanderen, 1500–1800* (Brussels: VUB-Press, 1994), 112–13; De Munck, *Technologies*, 144–69. Also: K. Davids, 'Apprenticeship and guild control in the Netherlands, c. 1450-1800', in: B. De Munck, S. L. Kaplan and H. Soly (eds.), *Learning on the Shop Floor: Historical Perspectives on Apprenticeship* (London: Berghahn Books, 2007), 65–84.

[38] Deceulaer, *Pluriforme patronen*, ch. 8, esp. 279–80.

[39] De Bie, *Education*, 52–63, and chs. 3 and 4.

[40] Cf. De Vroede, *Meesters*; B. De Munck and H. De Ridder-Symoens, 'Education and knowledge: Theory and practice in an urban context', in: B. Blondé, A. L. Van Bruaene and M. Boone (eds.), *City and Society in the Low Countries (1100–1600)* (Cambridge: Cambridge University Press, 2018), 220–54.

from the seventeenth century onwards. While they were originally limited to mainly surgery, engineering and drawing, apprentices could attend them alongside to journeymen, masters and also amateurs. After the Antwerp art academy was founded in 1663, a number of cabinetmakers, carpenters, masons and silversmiths took courses there in geometry, drawing and/or architecture, but even then they still had to learn the major part of their craft by doing, i.e. in the workshop of a master, in a process of trial and error while handling raw materials.[41]

Books did not matter a great deal for apprentices either. Except for merchants who wanted to learn how to count and keep books, as well as, perhaps, for those collecting special recipes in for example textile dying, handbooks and recipes do not seem to have played a major part in the transmission and circulation of technical knowledge.[42] Nor was reading and writing typically part of an apprenticeship, which suggests that the high literacy rates for which the Low Countries were renowned, cannot be ascribed to apprenticeship as an institution.[43] While most apprenticeship contracts fail to mention these skills at all, reading, writing and some basis arithmetic were often learned in so-called 'Sunday' schools, at least as far as poorer children are concerned – others could learn in private schools too.[44] These schools mostly accepted younger children, which confirms the idea that such basic skills were often acquired before the apprenticeship. While they were often learned between, roughly, six and twelve, an apprenticeship term was more likely to be undertaken between the age of 12 and 18. In the Antwerp apprentice contracts (which are biased towards luxury trades) the average age mentioned is 15.6 years, but while the youngest apprentice was 12, apprentices of 20 years and older were not an exception (the oldest was 25).[45] In the case of girls, learning basic skills

---

[41] B. De Munck, 'Corpses, live models, and nature: Assessing skills and knowledge before the Industrial Revolution (case: Antwerp)', *Technology and Culture* 51 (2010), 332–56; De Munck, *Technologies*, 57; D. Van de Vijver, *Ingenieurs en architecten op de drempel van een nieuwe tijd, 1750–1830* (Leuven: Universitaire Pers, 2003).

[42] For the Northern Netherlands: J. Tump, 'Ambachtelijk geschoold: Haarlemse en Rotterdamse ambachtslieden en de circulatie van technische kennis, ca. 1400–1720', PhD thesis, Vrije Universiteit van Amsterdam, 2012, ch. 7; the Southern Netherlands: De Kerf, 'De circulatie', 157–63; for merchant handbooks, see e.g. M. Kool, *Die conste vanden getale: Een studie over Nederlandstalige rekenboeken uit de vijftiende en zestiende eeuw, met een glossarium van rekenkundige termen* (Hilversum: Verloren, 1999).

[43] De Munck and De Ridder-Symoens, 'Education and knowledge'.

[44] E. Put, 'Schoolboeken in de Nieuwe Tijd: Status quaestionis en perspectieven voor verder onderzoek', in: M. Cloet and F. Daelemans (eds.), *Godsdienst, mentaliteit en dagelijks leven: Religieuze geschiedenis in België sinds 1970* (Brussels: Archief- en bibliotheekwezen in België, 1988), 119–22; E. Put, *De cleijne scholen: Het volksonderwijs in het hertogdom Brabant tussen Katholieke Reformatie en Verlichting (eind 16de eeuw – 1795)* (Leuven: Universitaire Pers, 1990), 267–9.

[45] De Munck, *Technologies*, 178.

may have overlapped more with learning a trade such as lacemaking, as they were often younger.[46]

This raises the question of the extent to which the apprentice was integrated in the master's household and how the socio-cultural context of learning was related to the acquisition of skills. While earlier research had already shown that apprentices often targeted large ateliers in particular,[47] recent research among the Antwerp gold and silversmiths has revealed that genuine 'learning ateliers' materialised from at least the late seventeenth century on.[48] This is at odds with the idea that apprentices learned in a profoundly patriarchal context (with one apprentice at a time learning with a substitute father of sorts) as well as the idea that apprenticeship declined due to deskilling, with the latter in turn resulting from either subcontracting or industrialisation.[49] While some historians have recently suggested that skills were increasingly dispersed over a range of specialised ateliers due to the expansion of subcontracting networks in the eighteenth and nineteenth century,[50] these learning ateliers had a range of both general and specific skills on offer – thus attracting a substantial part of the wandering journeymen who were in search of additional or advanced skills.[51]

This urges us to consider transformations in the master–apprenticeship relationship, which in turn requires a look at the role of guilds. As elsewhere, especially with regard to the late medieval period, the powerful guilds in the Southern Netherlands are seen as profoundly patriarchal organisations that granted the master status and authority. However, either the masters' or the guilds' authority, or both, may have waned in the long run. Although historians disagree about the period when a 'patriarchal moment' materialised, i.e. during the Middle Ages or in the sixteenth century, they seem to agree on the fact that women were

---

[46] De Bie, *Education*, 235–36.

[47] Deceulaer, *Pluriforme patronen*, 268–72; De Munck, *Technologies*, 46–47.

[48] De Kerf, 'De circulatie', 81–90, 215–24; De Munck and De Kerf, 'Wandering'.

[49] K. D. M. Snell, *Annals of the Labouring Poor: Social Change and Agrarian England, 1660–1900* (Cambridge: Cambridge University Press, 1985); Kaplan, 'L'apprentissage'; Grießinger and Reith, 'Lehrlinge'; G. Riello, *A Foot in the Past: Consumers, Producers and Footwear in the Long Eighteenth Century* (Oxford: Oxford University Press, 2006), 161–89.

[50] A. Cottereau, 'The fate of collective manufactures in the industrial world: The silk industries of Lyon and London, 1800–1850', in: C. F. Sabel and J. Zeitlin (eds.), *World of Possibilities: Flexibilities and Mass Production in Western Industrialization* (Cambridge: Cambridge University Press, 1997), 86–87; Riello, *A Foot in the Past*, 184ff.

[51] De Munck and De Kerf, 'Wandering'. For subcontracting networks in the Southern Netherlands, see C. Lis and H. Soly, 'Subcontracting in guild-based export trades, thirteenth–eighteenth centuries', in: S. R. Epstein and M. Prak (eds.), *Guilds, Innovation, and the European Economy, 1400–1800* (Cambridge: Cambridge University Press, 2008), 81–113.

gradually excluded from skill-intensive and high–status jobs in particular.[52] According to Martha Howell, women were progressively denied access to the labour market when specialisation, quality control and formal rules related to apprenticeship became more important.[53] However, in the early modern period, guilds often lost control over the entrance of women into the labour market, including in guild-based trades such as tailoring.[54] Moreover, cracks in the guilds' power and credibility were in the long run reflected in the changing outlook of apprenticeship contracts, which gradually included more default clauses with increasing premiums, in addition to more specific stipulations about payment modalities, wages (or pocket money) and eventualities such as sickness.[55] The resulting question is what the impact of guilds was on apprentices and their way of acquiring skills.

The Slim Institutionalisation of Apprenticeship by Guilds

Guilds, which in this region existed in virtually all urban industries until at least the mid-seventeenth century, could impact upon learning and training in myriad ways. At the apex of their power between roughly the mid-fifteenth and the mid-seventeenth century they typically had minimum terms for apprentices, masterpiece requirements, maximum numbers of apprentices per master, the obligation for apprentices to live on their master's premises and so on. In addition, guild boards could act as courts to enforce these rules and as either a judge or an arbiter at the occasion of disputes between a master and an apprentice or when another master had poached and hired a runaway apprentice. However, it is often difficult to make out whether these regulations targeted practices of skill acquisition and learning on the shop floor or, rather, revolved around regulating access to the trade as a master. While guilds typically registered new apprentices as well as new masters, registration as an apprentice was often only obligatory if an apprentice

---

[52] M. C. Howell, 'Women, the family economy, and the structures of market production', in: B. A. Hanawalt (ed.), *Women and Work in Preindustrial Europe* (Bloomington: Indiana University Press, 1986), 198–222; M. E. Wiesner, 'Women's work in the changing city economy, 1500–1650', in: M. J. Boxer and J. H. Quataert (eds.), *Connecting Spheres: Women in the Western World, 1500 to the Present* (New York: Oxford University Press, 1987), 64–74.

[53] M. C. Howell, *Women, Production and Patriarchy in Late Medieval Cities* (Chicago: University of Chicago Press, 1986).

[54] Deceulaer, *Pluriforme patronen*, ch. 6; also H. Deceulaer, 'Entrepreneurs in the guilds: Ready-to-wear clothing and subcontracting in late sixteenth and early seventeenth-century Antwerp', *Textile History* 31 (2000), 133–49.

[55] Early modern apprenticeship contracts Antwerp. Database by B. De Munck, A. De Bie and R. De Kerf.

wanted to become a master.[56] This implies that one could learn as an apprentice with a guild-based master (and pay a fee to this master, based on a contract), while not being registered by a guild (and, hence, not paying the registration fee to the guild). At least some rules must therefore have been geared towards access to the trade, rather than learning per se.

However, given the demographic context of high-population density and a high density of competing cities sketched above, restricting access by such regulations as minimum terms, trials and maximum numbers of apprentices must have often been counterintuitive too. It is actually more likely that guild boards tried to attract and include unskilled and semi-skilled youths as much as possible – as well as trying to prevent skills produced in the city from being used elsewhere. With regard to the important guild of the cloth dressers in sixteenth-century Antwerp, it has been shown that at least the dominant masters in the guild set up and maintained chain migration networks so as to actively recruit apprentices and journeymen in periods of economic expansion.[57] Previous research on regulations related to migration has, moreover, suggested that municipalities and guild boards alike devised mechanisms to attract and incorporate skilled artisans as much as possible.[58] Only 24% of the new masters entering the Bruges coopers' guild between 1375 and 1500 had learned their craft locally.[59] How to design a formal guild-based apprenticeship system in this context, and why?

One way to shed light on this is to focus on the rules which concern both the acquisition of skills and access to the guild as a master and to connect these to the long-term evolutions in the cultural and socio-political context. Access to guilds was conditional upon either birth or finishing an apprenticeship term in the Southern Netherlands. Masters' sons were considered born into the guild, at least in the late Middle Ages. While they sometimes had to register as an apprentice in order to be able to become master, they were often exempt from registration fees, minimum terms and trial pieces. While in Leuven they were exempt from both

---

[56] De Munck, 'One counter', 30–31.

[57] J. De Meester, 'Gastvrij Antwerpen? Arbeidsmigratie naar het zestiende-eeuwse Antwerpen', PhD thesis, University of Antwerp, 2011, 206–11.

[58] B. De Munck and A. Winter, 'Regulating migration in early modern cities: An introduction', in: B. De Munck and A. Winter (eds.), *Gated Communities? Regulating Migration in Early Modern Cities* (Aldershot: Ashgate, 2012), 6–10, 12–14.

[59] P. Stabel, 'Social mobility and apprenticeship in late medieval Flanders', in: De Munck, Kaplan and Soly (eds.), *Learning on the Shop Floor*, 169–70. There is a recent long-term overview in Maarten Prak et al., 'Access to the trade: Monopoly and mobility in European craft guilds, 17th and 18th centuries', *Journal of Social History* 53 (2020).

apprenticeship years and master trials, in fifteenth-century Brussels they were often not required to pay registration fees, sometimes being obligated to offer an amount of wine only.[60] Up to and including the fourteenth century, this was not too different for outsiders, who could enter the guild by living with a master as an apprentice for a certain time – and hence turn into a master's son of sorts. However, outsiders were progressively confronted with more formal rules. By the sixteenth century, most prospective masters had to serve for a minimum period. In addition, they had to pay an entrance fee, which could be wax or wine, thus referring to practices of religious sociability, but in the fourteenth and fifteenth century strict financial fees were already due as well. A trial piece was usually required from the late fifteenth or sixteenth century on; this is at least when they first emerge in the guilds' ordinances.[61]

Both minimum terms and trial pieces may have had an impact on the acquisition of skills in a way that is similar to what has been suggested by economic historians. The guilds' regulations related to apprenticeship may have lowered the transaction costs involved in apprenticeship contracts. While the trial piece may have objectified training content to the benefit of apprentices, the requirement to serve a specific term may have guaranteed to the master that the apprentice would not abscond before having fulfilled the agreed period of working for free or below the market rate.[62] However, for the Southern Netherlands, it is not at all clear whether the apprenticeship system of the guilds was designed with such mechanisms in mind. In theory, guilds could help enforce apprentices' compliance in fulfilling the agreed term.[63] The Antwerp coopers, for instance, stipulated that an apprentice who had left his master without the latter's approval had to pay the complete tuition nevertheless. A sixteenth-century ordinance even prescribed that the first half of the tuition had to be paid at the start of the first year, and the second half at

---

[60] J. Verhavert, *Het ambachtswezen te Leuven* (Leuven: Universiteitsbibliotheek, 1940), 84; G. Des Marez, *L'organisation du travail à Bruxelles au XV* siècle* (Brussels: Henri Lamertin, 1904), 50.

[61] Des Marez, *L'organisation*, 95; J. Laenen, *Geschiedenis van Mechelen tot op 't einde der Middeleeuwen* (Mechelen: W. Godenne, 1926), 281; Verhavert, *Het ambachtswezen*, 82; J. Dambruyne, *Corporatieve middengroepen: Aspiraties, relaties en transformaties in de 16de-eeuwse Gentse ambachtswereld* Verhandelingen der Maatschappij voor Geschiedenis en Oudheidkunde te Gent (Ghent: Academia Press, 2002), 190, 194–98; De Munck, 'Gilding', 223–24 n.8; De Munck, 'One counter', 33 n.32.

[62] J. Humphries, 'English apprenticeship: A neglected factor in the first Industrial Revolution', in: P. David and M. Thomas (eds.), *The Economic Future in Historical Perspective* (Oxford: Oxford University Press, 2003), 73–102; S. R. Epstein, 'Craft guilds, apprenticeship, and technological change in pre-industrial Europe', *Journal of Economic History* 58 (1998), 684–713.

[63] Epstein, 'Craft guilds, apprenticeship'.

the beginning of the second year.[64] Most guilds, moreover, prescribed heavy fines for masters who hired a runaway apprentice, thus discouraging masters from luring away each other's apprentices and apprentices from breaking their contract.

Yet, guild regulations were clearly not necessary for that. Masters in Montreal had other means to enforce contracts, for instance social pressure in the community and juridical action. English masters protected themselves by asking premiums.[65] Moreover, most of these problems could be anticipated in a contract to be enforced by a municipal court, rather than a guild. In the Southern Netherlands, the contracts often include default clauses, stipulating fines or different kinds of compensations for the masters in case of breach of contract.[66] In theory, guilds could thereby serve as a third party to enforce such clauses and sanction offenders, but based on current research their role appears to have been rather limited. Most guild boards were competent to resolve conflicts between their members, for which they had a special court.[67] Yet, while it is unclear to what extent these courts really enforced contracts, written and preserved apprenticeship contracts from the seventeenth and eighteenth century only seldom mention the guild as an arbiter or judge in cases of breach of contract by the apprentice. It would seem that the guilds typically stepped in only if their privileges were at stake, for instance, when a prospective master had not served a full apprenticeship term (or was exposed as a fictive apprentice). Disputes about the content of learning or the treatment of apprentices were usually handled by the municipal court, the bench of aldermen (*Vierschaar*).[68]

The minimum terms, at least, were in all likelihood not introduced with contract enforcement in mind. According to legal historians, 'the engagement of an apprentice by a master results in a contract the stipulations of which are largely imposed by the trade'.[69] Yet this is not what emerges

---

[64] De Kerf, 'The early modern Antwerp coopers' guild'.

[65] G. Hamilton, 'Enforcement of apprenticeship contracts: Were runaways a serious problem? Evidence from Montreal', *Journal of Economic History* 55 (1995), 551–74; C. Minns and P. Wallis, 'The price of human capital in a pre-industrial economy: Premiums and apprenticeship in 18th-century England', *Explorations in Economic History* 50 (2013), 335–50.

[66] De Kerf, 'De circulatie', 168–72, 209, 213–44; De Kerf, 'The early modern Antwerp coopers' guild', 246–52.

[67] Deceulaer, 'Guilds', esp. 175–82.   [68] Cf. De Munck, 'In loco parentis'.

[69] 'l'engagement d'un apprenti par un maître donne lieu à un contrat dont les stipulations sont en majeure partie imposées par le métier': Ph. Godding, *Le droit privé dans les Pays-Bas méridionaux du 12e au 18e siècle* (Brussels: Palais des Académies, 1987), 470. Also quoted in A. De Bie and B. De Munck, 'Learning on the shop floor in the Spanish Netherlands', in: S. Dupré, B. De Munck, W. Thomas and G. Vanpaemel (eds.), *Embattled Territory: The Circulation of Knowledge in the Spanish Netherlands* (Ghent: Academia Press, 2015), fn.60.

from the contracts in reality. On the whole, the minimum terms were rather short in the Southern Netherlands, usually ranging from two to four years. The average term agreed upon in apprenticeship contracts actually often exceeded the prescribed term. And wherever the average term converged towards the term prescribed – as was the case with the Antwerp gold and silversmiths, who on average trained for 4.3 years – the average conceals a very varied reality in which the length of the terms ranged from one to eight years, the exceptions outnumbering the rule.[70] As shorter contracts often concerned apprentices who had already learned basic skills elsewhere while longer contracts were needed to accommodate poorer or younger apprentices,[71] a uniform term potentially reduced the flexibility of learning based on customised contracts. This was probably the situation for the Antwerp diamond cutters in the seventeenth century, where more than half of the apprenticeship contracts were shorter than the guild's requirement (five years, temporarily raised to nine in 1690).[72]

The introduction of uniform terms may have happened with an eye to product quality and the need for high-level skills. The importance of high-quality, luxury products must have created strong incentives for local cities and guilds to install and monitor apprenticeship systems in order to guarantee product quality, especially when confronted with growing immigration figures. However, the guilds for basic trades in which skills were less sophisticated, such as bakers and shoemakers, also introduced minimum terms to serve and trial pieces. The only exception were guilds in which hands-on skills were altogether unimportant, such as retailers and old-cloth sellers.[73] Moreover, the terms corresponded to the difficulty of the trade only to a degree. As Table 8.1 shows, gold and silversmiths typically learned longer, but the difference between cities could just as well outcompete the difference between trades, as the relatively long terms in Bruges illustrate. Nor were the terms adapted to the difficulty of the trade in a regular way. It happened with the Antwerp cabinetmakers in 1497,[74] but this was the exception rather than the rule – which was that once introduced the term tended not to change at all.[75]

---

[70] De Munck, 'Gilding', 230–32; De Munck and De Kerf, 'Wandering'.
[71] De Munck and De Kerf, 'Wandering'.   [72] De Bie, 'The paradox', 282–91.
[73] Some mercers did require a short apprenticeship term, as was the case in Ghent in the second half of the seventeenth century: Deceulaer, *Pluriforme patronen*, 75.
[74] B. De Munck, 'Construction and reproduction: The training and skills of Antwerp cabinetmakers in the 16th and 17th centuries', in: De Munck, Kaplan and Soly (eds.), *Learning on the Shop Floor*, 89.
[75] Another exception is the Guild of Four Crowned which prescribed a four-year apprenticeship term (instead of three) from 1674 on: De Munck, 'Gilding', fn.27 (with additional references).

Table 8.1 *Selection of apprenticeship terms in Antwerp, Bruges, Ghent and Leuven guilds in 1784*

Trades	Antwerp	Bruges	Ghent	Leuven
Bakers	2	3	2	2
Gold and silversmiths	4 + 2*	6	4	/
Tanners (and/or leather dressers)	2	6	2	2
Tailors	2	3	2	2
Shoemakers	2	2 to 5	2	2
Cabinetmakers and carpenters	3	4	2	2
Pewterers and plumbers	2	2 or 3	3	2

* Four years apprenticeship plus two years' work as a journeyman before mastership could be attained.
Source: See De Munck, *Technologies*, 61.

Nor were the terms lengthened with the objective of excluding outsiders, as would have happened in Germany.[76] In our view, this is because the minimum terms resulted not from a wish to exclude outsiders or to keep apprentices longer on the shop floor, but from the need to monitor access to the trade while avoiding exclusionary effects. One of the problems faced by guilds wanting to introduce a uniform minimum term was that a great number of apprentices arrived in Antwerp with skills they had acquired elsewhere and entered into short-term contracts in order to acquire additional specialised skills or to 'perfect' themselves, as it was often referred to in contracts of gold and silversmiths.[77] Setting the minimum terms too long would have resulted in excluding both unskilled youngsters and semi-skilled journeymen interested in coming to the city or entering an apprenticeship. Given the competition for skills between cities and between guilds, the guilds' officials and masters must have been cautious to prevent this. This explains why the minimum terms were kept short in most trades notwithstanding the high level of skills required.

A similar compromise between the need for an entrance mechanism based on skill acquisition and fear of the exclusionary effects of a uniform system emerges when analysing the introduction of standardised trial pieces. As a rule, the assignment for trial pieces prescribed in the guilds' ordinances was given in very general terms. Very often it amounted to stating that a prospective shoemaker, for instance, had to 'cut and make

[76] R. Reith, 'Zur beruflichen Sozialisation im Handwerk vom 18. bis ins frühe 20. Jahrhundert: Umrisse einer Sozialgeschichte der deutschen Lehrlinge', *Vierteljahrschrift für Sozial- und Wirtschaftsgeschichte* 76 (1989), 3.
[77] De Munck, 'Gilding', 230–2; De Munck and De Kerf, 'Wandering'.

a pair of thick leather shoes, a pair of boots, and a pair of slippers'. Sometimes, the instruction was more accurate and elaborate, as with the Antwerp cabinetmakers at the end of the fifteenth century, who stipulated not only that three items of furniture were to be made, namely two different cabinets and a table, but also specified the cabinets meticulously. Sometimes a drawing was available to serve as a design and plan, as was the case with the cabinetmakers in Antwerp and Mechelen and the carpenters in Ghent.[78] Last but not least, the introduction of the obligation to make a masterpiece was sometimes accompanied by a rule which stated that one had to complete an additional year of training if one failed to make it properly.[79]

All this suggests that the level of skills was at stake for the guilds, but shortly after standardised trial pieces were introduced it was often stipulated in the ordinances that the deans could decide between different options, such as between a round and a square table in the case of the cabinetmakers. Or they could even prescribe a specific trial ad hoc – thus catering to apprentices who had learned only specific skills.[80] An ordinance of 1524 from the Antwerp gold and silversmiths stated that the masterpiece should be either a major work (e.g. a platter) or a gold ring set with a diamond, continuing that the prospective masters concerned might also produce 'what they were used to making'.[81] So, here as well a balance was sought between, on the one hand, the need to monitor the acquisition of skills and the related entrance to the guild, and, on the other, the exclusionary effects in the context of highly specialised trades and the high geographic mobility of the semi-skilled and skilled workforce.[82]

Why, then, were these regulations needed at all? Their genealogy suggests that they were introduced in order to clearly distinguish between regular masters and 'false' or illegitimate masters. While many of the guilds in the Southern Netherlands were founded before the end of the fifteenth century,[83] the first ordinances did not usually prescribe apprenticeship terms or master trials. While the guilds required new masters and (to a lesser extent) apprentices to pay registration and entrance fees (or at least to provide wine or wax), the local authorities only wanted the guilds to inform them about the identity of new masters. Trials were presumably

[78] De Munck, *Technologies*, 70, 74, 76–77, 80.
[79] See e.g., De Munck, *Technologies*, 77.
[80] De Munck, *Technologies*, 68–74 (quotes on p. 70); De Munck, 'Gilding', 232–35.
[81] City Archives Antwerp, Guilds and Trades, 4488, Ordinance 24 November 1524, art. 9, f.115v-11; also referred to in De Munck, *Technologies*, 76.
[82] De Munck, 'Gilding'.
[83] B. De Munck, P. Lourens and J. Lucassen, 'The establishment and distribution of craft guilds in the Low Countries, 1000–1800', in: Prak, Lis, Lucassen and Soly (eds.), *Craft Guilds in the Early Modern Low Countries*, esp. 38–42.

only for immigrants unknown to the local masters. Uniform rules were introduced at times in which it became increasingly difficult to distinguish between prospective masters familiar to the local guild and outsiders entering the trade illegitimately. Specifically, they were, for instance, introduced in the (second half of) the fifteenth century (uniform apprenticeship terms) and the sixteenth century (standardised masterpieces), a period of demographic expansion in which merchants and alien entrepreneurs often tried to circumvent the local masters' monopolies and labour market monopsonies.

Established masters sought to prevent merchants or alien entrepreneurs from bypassing their guilds' monopoly by hiring journeymen (or impoverished masters) themselves rather than buying finished products from regular masters.[84] In 1515, the cabinetmakers adapted their trial piece because artisans who were not really cabinetmakers had managed to enter the trade, and had succeeded in becoming masters nevertheless.[85] In this context, the formal (guild-based) apprenticeship system was designed to make sure that an alleged master had been trained at all. This is why apprentices were typically registered in the guild books. This registration served to track apprentices in case a dispute arose. But this was of course a very limited instrument. Guild officials were particularly anxious about fictitious apprenticeships, in which a fake 'apprentice' (not seldom a merchant) would be registered in the guild's books without really being present on the shop floor in order to learn the trade. Both uniform terms and standardised masterpieces were introduced to prevent exactly that. Accompanying measures included a prohibition against working in company (which enabled 'false masters' to be 'freed' by using the trademark of a regular master or a master's widow) and even the obligation for apprentices to live under their master's roof, which in some ordinances was explicitly attributed to the need to prevent fictitious apprenticeship contracts.[86]

This explains why hereditary guilds such as butchers and fishmongers did not bother about apprenticeship terms and trials at all. It also explains why, as a rule, only prospective masters had to finish the apprenticeship term and make a masterpiece. More often than not, journeymen could freely work in a trade, at least as long as they worked for a regular master.

---

[84] B. De Munck, 'Skills, trust and changing consumer preferences: The decline of Antwerp's craft guilds from the perspective of the product market, ca. 1500–ca. 1800', *International Review of Social History* 53 (2008), 197–233; De Munck, 'One counter'; De Munck, 'Gilding'.

[85] De Munck, *Technologies*, 75–76; De Munck, 'Construction', 90–92.

[86] B. De Munck, 'La qualité du corporatisme: Stratégies économiques et symboliques des corporations anversoises du XVe siècle à leur abolition', *Revue d'histoire moderne et contemporaine* 54 (2007), 116–44; De Munck, 'Skills'; De Munck, 'Gilding'.

In Antwerp this was true for trades ranging from shoemakers to gold and silversmiths and diamond polishers.[87] In a limited number of trades only working as a journeyman was also conditional upon finishing an apprenticeship term and, occasionally, making a 'journeyman piece'. This was typically the case in trades in which journeymen could wield more power thanks to their large numbers, such as the textile and construction sector. In these cases, the journeymen succeeded in creating a privileged position for themselves, claiming preferential access to the labour market at a negotiated minimum wage. So-called unfree journeymen (who had not finished the term) could then only be hired if no free journeymen were able or willing to do the job – at the agreed upon minimum wage.[88]

In addition to guarding and defining privileges, social concerns may have been involved as well. A frequent and related regulation set a maximum number of apprentices per master. Typically, a master was allowed to hire only one apprentice at the time, with two or three per master being exceptional.[89] This regulation could also be connected to the need to monitor the quality of training and to produce proper skills and human capital. After all, the quality of training would be likely to decline if masters hired more apprentices and exploited them as a cheap workforce. However, as this regulation was mostly accompanied by a maximum number of journeymen per master, it rather served to prevent a limited number of masters from cornering the market and employing apprentices at the expense of others. Some guild rules actually stated explicitly that they intended to preserve a minimum of equality among masters.[90]

In short, at least the rules which touched upon training and access to the guilds simultaneously were not introduced with an eye to better training or lowering the related transaction costs. Rules on minimum terms, standardised masterpieces and a maximum number of apprentices were introduced out of social and political concerns, with the aim of distinguishing regular from 'false' masters and distributing the available apprentices over a broad range of masters. The specific shape of the rules

---

[87] De Munck, 'One counter', 30–31.

[88] Thijs, *Van 'werkwinkel'*, 398–99; Deceulaer, *Pluriforme patronen*, 294; C. Lis and H. Soly, 'De macht van "vrije arbeiders": Collectieve acties van hoedenmakersgezellen in de Zuidelijke Nederlanden (zestiende-negentiende eeuw)', in: Lis and Soly (eds.), *Werken volgens de regels*, 15–50; B. De Munck, 'Meritocraten aan het werk: Deregulering van de arbeidsmarkt bij de Antwerpse timmerlieden in de 18de eeuw', in: B. Blondé, B. De Munck and F. Vermeylen (eds.) *Doodgewoon: Mensen en hun dagelijks leven in de geschiedenis. Liber Amicorum Alfons K. L. Thijs* (Antwerp: Centrum voor Stadsgeschiedenis, Themanummer *Bijdragen tot de geschiedenis*, 87 [2004]), 87–106; De Munck, 'One counter', 29–31.

[89] De Munck, 'Gilding', 237–39 (with additional references).   [90] Ibid., 238.

nevertheless betrays the nature of the regional learning market. The context of cities and countryside districts competing for (migrant) skills and journeymen required a fine-tuning of the rules, resulting in short minimum terms and the possibility of assigning masterpieces ad hoc. Nor was the connection between learning with a guild-based master and the acquisition of master status immutable in the long run. In the next section, it will become clear that the two processes gradually drifted apart.

The Decline of Apprenticeship (in Guilds)

Looking at the guild regulations in a long-term perspective, it appears that a great number of the regulations most historians of the early modern period are familiar with were actually introduced only from the mid-fifteenth century and during the sixteenth century. In a way, many of these regulations can perhaps be seen as the first symptoms of the guilds' declining power and authority – or at least as the first signs that the pressures they faced were increasing.[91] More often than not the guilds' zeal to guard their boundaries met its own limits – and increasingly so as the early modern period progressed. Simultaneously, the patriarchal authority of the master may have waned, necessitating other, more formal enforcement mechanisms. Both issues merge in rules related to apprentices, which concerned both the master–apprentice relationship (and contract enforcement) and the acquisition of master status. Significantly, the maximum number of apprentices per master was under pressure in the early modern period. By the sixteenth century, masters must have often neglected the limits, as the rules were gradually relaxed. In 1606, the Antwerp cabinetmakers, for instance, replaced the maximum of one apprentice per master with the rule that a second apprentice could be engaged as soon as the first had completed one year and nine months of his term. Given that the term was two years at the time, this increased the possible turnover of apprentices – if only very slightly.[92]

In the seventeenth and eighteenth centuries, the problem increased. At first sight, this appears to be due to masters in the Southern Netherlands starting to exploit apprentices as a cheap workforce, but this would be jumping to conclusions. While in late-seventeenth-century France the so-called *alloués* emerged (apprentices not entitled to become master later on),[93] masters with large workshops in the Southern Netherlands clashed with the guild boards over the definition of an apprentice. Instead of

[91] De Munck, 'One counter'; De Munck 'Gilding'.   [92] De Munck, 'Gilding', 238.
[93] Cf. Kaplan, 'L'apprentissage'.

hiring too many (registered) apprentices, these masters hired – in addition to the permitted number of apprentices – journeymen who were often partly trained elsewhere but wanted to specialise by working some additional years with a master for free or at a partial wage. From the point of view of these masters, such workers were simply journeymen, but the guilds' deans considered them illegal apprentices and started taking legal action. They set out to fine masters, while the apprentice also would be denied access to the guild if he did not change masters. Related to this, the guild deans prevented masters from hiring apprentices without registering them, occasionally visiting the workshops of their members to check.[94]

The journeymen entering into apprentice contracts in order to simultaneously work and acquire additional skills were often immigrants. This was not something the guilds were opposed to, to be sure. Although no formal tramping system for journeymen similar to the ones in the German lands, France and England existed in the Southern Netherlands, tramping was important as a practice nevertheless.[95] The relatively small distances between the many cities may even have ensured that both information and people circulated at higher speed in this large urban network. Moreover, the guilds in the Southern Netherlands facilitated the tramping of artisans in their own way – by reciprocally recognising an apprenticeship term finished (in a similar guild) in another town. For instance, the cities and guilds of Brabant agreed to mutually 'liberate' each other's apprentices and masters, meaning that a prospective master who had accomplished his apprenticeship term in one city had to be accepted for the master trial in another town.[96] Thus, the guilds again responded to the geographical mobility of skilled artisans in an inclusive way. The fact that they guarded the boundaries or their privileges in no way implies that outsiders had to be excluded – the idea was rather to incorporate them. More than on producing skills locally, they seem to have been focused on the accommodation and inclusion of skills produced elsewhere.

Up to the late seventeenth century, the guilds thus succeeded in reconciling mobility in the labour market and guarding freeman status based upon apprenticeship requirements. But the guilds' loss of credibility and authority became ever more apparent. Up to and including the sixteenth century, the corporative framework would seem to have been self-evident

---

[94] De Kerf, 'De circulatie', 66–69, 217–225.

[95] For the sixteenth century, see e.g., De Meester, 'Gastvrij Antwerpen'.

[96] M. Jacobs, 'De ambachten in Brabant en Mechelen (12de eeuw-1795)', in: *De gewestelijke en lokale overheidsinstellingen in Brabant en Mechelen tot 1795* (Brussels: Algemeen rijksarchief, 2000), 591.

for apprentices and masters, as is exemplified by the fact that masters sometimes had all their sons registered as apprentices – apparently regardless of their chances of becoming masters themselves. By the turn of the eighteenth century, however, apprentices were only registered in the guild books if there was a specific juridical reason for it. In guilds without a right of preference of free journeymen, apprentices were often only registered when they decided to become masters – which is one of the reasons why the number of official apprentices was limited. In Antwerp, Brussels and Ghent respectively only 1.3%, 0.8% and 4.8% of the total population consisted of registered apprentices in 1738 – compared to 10% in sixteenth-century London.[97] In guilds with a right of preference, the incentive to register as an apprentice was stronger theoretically (because it yielded privileged access to the labour market once the term was finished), but the larger masters in these trades by then systematically tried to bypass the free journeymen's rights by hiring unfree journeymen at below the free journeymen's wages. Around the mid-eighteenth century, this culminated in fierce juridical struggles between masters and free journeymen, in which the masters gradually drew the longest straw. In the early eighteenth century, many had already succeeded in having unfree journeymen accepted as a legitimate workforce by the guild authorities – allowing masters, for instance, to hire the latter upon paying a tax.[98]

Put differently, the gap widened between, on the one hand, the reality of learning on the shop floor, and, on the other, the registration of apprentices with the intention of tracking who had a right to either free-man status or privileged access to the labour market as a 'free journey-man'. To be sure, this differs from the decline of apprenticeship thesis as it is traditionally sketched based on the English case.[99] British historians have depicted a decrease in the number of apprentices as well as in the average length of terms (and sometimes also a decline in the rate of apprentices boarding).[100] Yet in our case it may be more an issue of registration. What we perceive in the Southern Netherlands is a double movement in which economic reality increasingly escapes the guilds' grip, with masters circumventing the guild rules about apprenticeship (and workshop size).[101]

The existence of learning ateliers confirms the findings in other research that apprentices in the eighteenth century tended to concentrate

[97] See De Munck, *Technologies*, 22, 162.

[98] De Munck, 'Meritocraten'; De Munck, 'One counter', 32.

[99] Snell, *Annals*, ch. 5 ('The decline of apprenticeship'); also Kaplan, 'L'apprentissage'; S. L. Kaplan, *La fin des corporations* (Paris: Fayard, 2001).

[100] Recent views in Minns and Wallis, 'Rules and reality'.

[101] Des Marez, *L'organisation*, 222.

in a limited number of ateliers.[102] Before attention shifted to the institutional context in the 1990s and 2000s, historians often addressed this through the prism of specialisation and deskilling. Both concentration trends and subcontracting were considered to have led to deskilling, as apprentices would increasingly have either learned only part of the trade with a specialised subcontractor or been exploited as cheap labour in a large atelier.[103] Yet, as recent research has shown, large ateliers welcomed wandering journeymen in search of specialised and advanced skills who were prepared to work and learn simultaneously – thus blurring the distinction not (only) between apprentice and child labourer but between apprentice and journeyman.[104] In response, the more conservative guild boards often tightened their rules and set out to sanction trespassing masters. They did so out of fear that some of these learning journeymen, who were not registered as apprentices locally, would apply for mastership afterwards. This fear was justified given that the central authorities by then easily granted dispensation of apprenticeship. By the early eighteenth century, a practice had developed in which immigrant prospective entrepreneurs turned to the central authorities to request the right to make a masterpiece without first having to finish an apprenticeship term in the city of arrival. They had often already fulfilled a term in another city, which by then was no longer accepted by the local guilds. The central authorities disregarded this and almost systematically granted dispensation.[105]

This practice was the first fundamental crack in the guilds' privileges, and it heralded a flood of attacks after the mid-eighteenth century. Not only was workshop size increasingly deregulated during the eighteenth century – up to the point that the central authorities in 1784 ruled that every master could hire as many workers as he thought convenient, whether or not they had finished an apprenticeship term – masters were increasingly exempt from an apprenticeship term too. From 20 March 1773 on, artists such as painters and sculptors were no longer required to register in the St Luke's guilds and become a master.[106] Other

---

[102] See Deceulaer, *Pluriforme patronen*, 268–72; De Munck, *Technologies*, 46–47.

[103] Cottereau, 'Fate of collective manufactures', 86–87; Riello, *A Foot in the Past*, 184ff; Grießinger and Reith, 'Lehrlinghe'.

[104] De Munck and De Kerf, 'Wandering'.

[105] De Kerf, 'De circulatie', ch. 4, esp. 264–76.

[106] H. Van Houtte, *Histoire économique de la Belgique à la fin de l'Ancien Régime* (Ghent: van Rysselberghe-Rombaut, 1920), 77; J. Dambruyne, 'De Gentse bouwvakambachten in sociaal-economisch perspectief (1540–1795)', in: Lis and Soly (eds.), *Werken volgens de regels*, 56; B. De Munck, 'Le produit du talent ou la production de talent? La formation des artistes à l'Académie des beaux-arts à Anvers aux XVIIe et XVIIIe siècles', *Paedagogica Historica* 37 (2001), 594.

manufacturing guilds were often encroached upon by mercers' guilds, which increasingly bypassed their privileges on production. The Brussels' cloth merchants in 1703 obtained the right to have their cloth dyed by whatever dyer they thought convenient, guild-based or not.[107] In all likelihood, it was partly in response to this that local guilds and urban governments abandoned the system of reciprocal liberation as it had existed for centuries – thus adding to the conflict with the central authorities, who would finally abolish the guilds altogether in 1795 (under French rule, by introducing the French D'Allarde and Le Chapelier laws).[108]

The growing separation between learning and access to freeman status was also reflected in the practice of registering apprentices. In-depth research on Antwerp has shown that while in the fifteenth and sixteenth centuries it had been common for an artisan to have all his sons registered as apprentices in his guild, this was mostly limited to one son by the eighteenth century. This suggests that sons were to an increasing degree only registered as they wanted to take over the family firm (except in trades where journeymen had a 'right of preference'), as is also suggested by the fact that they registered as a master exactly the length of the term afterwards – the relatively short terms notwithstanding.[109] Thus, whether for masters' sons or others, registering as an apprentice by the eighteenth century corresponded to a juridical-bureaucratic logic which was largely separate from quotidian practices and learning on the shop floor. Related to this, masters inexorably lost their status as representatives of a guild and a corporative culture. Recent research on the Antwerp guilds has suggested that master status stopped being heritable. As argued above, masters' sons were often not subject to such requirements as apprenticeship and the related fees up to the late medieval period, as they were considered as being born into the guild. Gradually, however, they had to meet the same or similar conditions, at least in Antwerp, which suggests that the importance of this birthright had declined.[110] This process must have already started in the sixteenth century, when inheritable mastership was abolished in Ghent, where it was then decreed (in 1540 and again in 1585) that mastership could be purchased for one generation only and would no longer be automatically passed from father to son.

Significantly, the practice of boarding too declined in the long run. Boarding was not something which the guilds had introduced. And whenever they made it obligatory, they did so out of fear of fictitious apprenticeship rather than to protect patriarchy. However, it may

---

[107] Van Houtte, *Histoire*, 77–8.   [108] Ibid., Part I; De Kerf, 'De circulatie', ch. 4.
[109] De Munck, *Technologies*, 144–69.   [110] De Munck, 'From brotherhood community'.

nevertheless be significant that – from the contracts reaped from notarial archives – boarding declined between the mid-seventeenth and the end of the eighteenth century from more than 95% to 75% among the Antwerp barbers and surgeons, and from 71% to 25% among the Antwerp tinsmiths and plumbers. While this is based on a small number of, in all likelihood, atypical contracts, it suggests that the master–apprentice relationship grew more businesslike.[111] Thus, from a member of a political body who could pass on membership through either patrimony or apprenticeship, a master incrementally turned into an entrepreneur who could sell knowledge.

Conclusion

Our long-term view of apprenticeship through the framework of guilds in the Southern Netherlands suggests that the focus on the tension between 'rules and reality' might better be replaced with an analysis of a long-term shift 'from status to contract', as it was once summarised. Nevertheless, it would equally be misplaced to tell a linear story in which contractual relationships inexorably became substituted for a situation in which guild rules simply ensured the reproduction and certification of freeman status through apprenticeship requirements. Our overview of the literature pertaining to the Southern Netherlands reveals a more complex history in which the rules themselves emerged and developed first in response to changing practices.

While it is clear that apprenticeship contracts existed before the guilds introduced regulations related to apprenticeship, training was in all likelihood based on custom and informal practices then. The guilds' regulations may partly have been introduced because these customs and practices were under pressure from demographic and economic transformations, especially processes of urbanisation (undermining face-to-face mechanisms for regulating access), the shift towards high-value-added products (necessitating the production of human capital and the guarding of skill levels) and merchant capital venturing into production (hollowing out the manufacturing artisans' labour market monopsony). In this context, learning on the shop floor practices and entry to a privileged status as either a freeman or a privileged journeyman may have gradually converged. This is suggested by the fact that the high point of the guilds' desire to enforce contracts is to be found in the sixteenth century. Another indication is the relative absence of registered apprenticeship contracts in the fifteenth and sixteenth century. Although further research is needed to

---

[111] Ibid., 11.

confirm whether there really was an inverse relationship between the institutional power of the guilds and the presence of registered contracts, the fact that the number of contracts in the Antwerp database peaks for periods in which the guilds' authority declined (especially the second half of the seventeenth century) justifies at least the hypothesis that notarial contracts emerged when guilds lost credibility.[112] So, possibly, training and fulfilling the requirements for attaining privileges – serving a minimum term – largely overlapped in roughly the fifteenth and sixteenth centuries.

This is not to say that the rules were introduced with an eye to regulating practices of learning on the shop floor. In the Southern Netherlands, such typical rules as uniform minimum terms and the obligation to make a standardised masterpiece were introduced to regulate access to the guilds rather than as a complement to contract-enforcing mechanisms. Even so, the shape of these rules bore the imprint of the specificities of the local and regional labour markets and need for skills. While they were introduced in periods of increasing mobility and economic tendencies of concentration and vertical integration, they were clearly tailored to fit urban competition for skills resulting from the relatively high urban density in the region. While uniform terms were needed to guard the manufacturing masters' privileges and the distinction between licit and illicit work, the terms were generally kept short in order to preclude exclusionary effects. Likewise, standardised masterpieces were introduced in order to prevent 'false masters' from entering the trade without having been trained (by simply being registered for the required term without being present on the shop floor), but a degree of flexibility was preserved in order to allow the entrance of prospective masters who had learned specific aspects of the trade only.

In other words, while the agency of manufacturing masters and their guilds explains their efforts in guarding their privileges, they were nevertheless obliged to adapt to the demographic and economic context. In the seventeenth and eighteenth centuries, the manufacturing guilds, moreover, lost a great deal of their credibility and moral authority. After the mid-seventeenth century in particular, guilds turned into juridical institutions with the residual power to certify and grant privileges, but without being a structural element of urban society. While they clung to their privileges, training, like birth, was no longer seen as a means of entering a corporation and achieving a certain status as a member of a group. In line with the more utilitarian worldview of the time, untrained youths mostly aimed at acquiring skills not corporate privileges – and they were

---

[112] De Bie, *Education*, 199.

often no longer registered as apprentices with a guild. To be sure, this does not amount to a return to the situation which had existed before the guilds entered the scene. More likely, both training and the guilds grew more businesslike, bureaucratic and utilitarian over time. The influence of patriarchal forces continued, but training was henceforth subject, above all, to market forces. Or else, it took place in public institutions such as medical colleges, engineering schools and art academies. While partly being rooted in a corporative culture themselves, these institutions heralded an era in which the mysteries of the trade were no longer acquired by becoming member of a corporative household. Learning continued to take place on the shop floor and in the context of a patriarchal household in the nineteenth century, but guilds eventually disappeared for good – leaving vocational and technical training to either the market or public institutions.

9 Apprenticeship in England

Patrick Wallis

In 1766, Sir William Blackstone gave the following definition of apprenticeship in his influential treatise on the English common law:

Another species of servants are called apprentices (from *apprendre*, to learn) and are usually bound for a term of years, by deed indented or indentures, to serve their masters, and be maintained and instructed by them . . . This is usually done to persons of trade, in order to learn their art and mystery.[1]

Blackstone's definition offers a useful starting point for an investigation of apprenticeship in early modern England. Most historical, anthropological or economic analyses of apprenticeship would recognise Blackstone's description of apprenticeship as the exchange of labour services for maintenance and instruction. Apprenticeship was then, as it remains, the primary mode of vocational training, allowing workers to fund their education in general skills by taking a lower wage (in England then, usually just food and lodging). It is a system used for trade – not agriculture. But Blackstone's definition also highlights aspects of apprenticeship that were more specific to England. To him, apprenticeship requires a long term ('of years'), a formal written contract in a specific form ('indentures') and maintenance as well as instruction. Apprentices are servants, but of a particular kind.

That Blackstone discussed apprentices in a commentary on law is also significant. For among the variety of forms of service that existed in England, apprenticeship was understood as a distinct legal practice. Apprenticeship was tied to a particular contractual form and duration. It placed youths in a specific legal position of formal subordination. From the 1560s to the early 1800s, experiences of service sometimes shaded into each other – domestic servants picked up craft skills, apprentices hauled water and swept floors. However, in city halls and guild meetings, in Quarter Sessions and Parliament, the status of apprenticeship was understood to be unique. The reasons for this

---

[1] W. Blackstone, *Commentaries on the Laws of England* (Dublin: John Exshaw, 1766), vol. 1, 414.

arguably had little do with the needs of apprentices or masters, and instead reflected the functions that apprenticeship had been assigned as the basis for exclusive claims to welfare rights, guild membership, citizenship and the right to practise an occupation.

One legacy of the legal significance of English apprenticeship is the enormous volume of records that survive. Apprenticeship was registered, taxed, examined and monitored. Each step left a paper trail. We probably have more information about apprentices in England than in any other pre-modern state. In part because of this, it has a long, rich historiography that has examined a range of issues, from the guilds' ability to protect child labour, to the socialisation of youths and, recently, the efficiency of human capital formation and its contribution to England's distinctive early industrialisation.[2] Thanks to the work of many historians, notably Cliff Webb, large volumes of apprenticeship records are now digitised, allowing us to see how apprenticeship operated in practice. In this chapter, I examine the political economy, scale and distribution, relation to family strategies, openness, and local institutions of apprenticeship. Several broader questions underlie my discussion. Was apprenticeship in England an institution that embedded inequality, redistributing rents to insiders? Was it, alternatively, an unusually efficient system of training? Did guilds somehow sustain apprenticeship? And, throughout, there is the issue of to what extent was English apprenticeship different to that found elsewhere in Europe.

---

[2] The literature on English apprenticeship is extensive, but only two surveys exist: O. J. Dunlop and R. D Denman, *English Apprenticeship and Child Labor* (London: T. F. Unwin, 1912), and J. Lane, *Apprenticeship in England, 1600–1914* (London: University College London Press, 1996). Important studies that have highlighted key themes include: S. R. Smith, 'The London apprentices as seventeenth-century adolescents', *Past and Present* 61 (1973), 149–61; C. W. Brooks, 'Apprenticeship, social mobility, and the middling sort, 1550–1800', in: J. Barry and C. W. Brooks (eds.), *The Middling Sort of People: Culture, Society, and Politics in England, 1550–1800* (Basingstoke: Macmillan, 1994), 52–83; P. Griffiths, *Youth and Authority: Formative Experiences in England, 1560–1640* (Oxford: Clarendon Press, 1996); M. Pelling, 'Apprenticeship, health, and social cohesion in early modern London', *History Workshop Journal* 37 (1994), 33–56; J. Mokyr, *The Enlightened Economy: An Economic History of Britain, 1700–1850* (New Haven, CT: Yale University Press, 2009); M. Kelly, J. Mokyr and C. O'Grada, 'Precocious Albion: A new interpretation of the British Industrial Revolution', *Annual Review of Economics* 6 (2014); J. Humphries, 'English apprenticeship: A neglected factor in the First Industrial Revolution', in: P. David and M. Thomas (eds.), *The Economic Future in Historical Perspective* (Oxford: Oxford University Press, 2003), 73–102; J. Humphries, *Childhood and Child Labour in the British Industrial Revolution* (Cambridge: Cambridge University Press, 2010); N. E. Feldman and K. van der Beek, 'Skill choice and skill complementarity in eighteenth century England', *Explorations in Economic History* 59 (2016), 94–113.

The Framework of Service

In the history of English apprenticeship, one moment stands out: the passing of the Statute of Artificers in 1563.[3] From that date until its repeal in 1814, a completed seven-year apprenticeship was a legal requirement to work in most crafts or trades. No equivalent restriction applied in agriculture. No similar national law existed elsewhere in Europe.

From 1563, the institutional space in which apprenticeship existed was defined by three sets of actors: guilds, town and city governments, and – because of the statute – magistrates. Not all existed in all locations. Independent magistrates were the only relevant authority in rural areas. Guilds operated in many towns and cities in the sixteenth century, but the scale of their activities often declined in the eighteenth century – although the exact chronology of their weakening remains unclear. Urban governments had a long-standing interest in apprenticeship and, outside of London and a few other cities, defined the role of guilds that operated under their sufferance and supervision, while city governors sat as magistrates in their own courts.

To say that the statute invented an English system of apprenticeship would be a mistake. Certainly this was not its intention. The authors of the law aimed to keep labour on the land. To the crown and a Parliament dominated by large landowners, abundant cheap farm labour and social stability were both appealing targets. The statute expanded upon earlier laws that sought to stop the rural poor from becoming urban artisans. Its apprenticeship clauses were designed to limit occupational and geographical mobility. For example, only those with land worth 40 shillings a year could apprentice their children to 'merchants, Mercer, Draper, Goldsmith, Ironmonger, Imbroiderer or Clothier' in corporate towns.[4]

Ironically, the effect of the statute was probably the opposite of Parliament's intentions. By raising a protective barrier around artisanal labour, it increased the incentives to enter a craft or trade. What constituted an apprenticeship was not even closely examined within the statute; instead it generalised the 'custom of London'. The mode of the metropolis was made the manner of the nation. The statute's most visible consequence was fixing the long, seven-year minimum term. This remained the English norm into the nineteenth century. Elsewhere, terms were generally shorter and variable. It also generalised a single

---

[3] See D. Woodward, 'The background to the statute of artificers: The genesis of labour policy, 1558–63', *Economic History Review* 33 (1981), 32–44; and more generally S. Deakin and F. Wilkinson, *The Law of the Labour Market: Industrialization, Employment and Legal Evolution* (Oxford: Oxford University Press, 2005).

[4] 5 Eliz 1, c. 4, S. 28.

form of contract, one narrower and less flexible than the more open, individualised agreements used elsewhere in Europe.

The three most distinctive consequences of the Statute of Artificers lay outside the cities. Firstly, one urban form of apprenticeship now applied nationwide: rural artisans were subject to the same contract and rules as those in Norwich or London. Secondly, a completed apprenticeship became a nationwide qualification. Seven years of service established one's right to work. In contrast, England's guilds and cities had usually demanded that an apprenticeship be served *locally*, to a citizen or freeman, to qualify for guild membership (these rules remained after 1563, limiting the statute's effect in towns, and marked an important difference to much of Europe). Thirdly, the statute put the policing of apprenticeship into the hands of England's magistrates. Justices of the Peace would thereafter judge disputes between masters and apprentices. In theory, at least, the statute created a national skilled labour market supervised by the main local agents of the state.

Within England's towns and cities, the Statute of Artificers did not change apprenticeship much in the short term. City and guild ordinances that had been building up since the thirteenth century anticipated its main contents. London's customs had already become a benchmark for urban apprenticeship elsewhere. No national machinery was created to register apprenticeships and ensure compliance; instead enforcement was left to informers bringing lawsuits to local courts.[5] There is little evidence that the social limitations the statute set on entry to apprenticeship were observed; inflation soon pulled their teeth anyway.[6] It was only from the late seventeenth century onwards, as judges questioned the power of restrictive guild and city by-laws and most guilds lost interest in trade regulation, that the statute became critical to urban artisans' privileges. Journeymen, rather than guilds, increasingly promoted cases under the statute to stop individuals who had not served seven-year apprenticeships from working.[7] At the same time, the scope of the statute was gradually whittled back through narrow judicial interpretations that freed a range of trades from its requirements, as *laissez faire* principles spread through the judiciary.[8]

---

[5] T. K. Derry, 'The enforcement of a seven years apprenticeship under the statute of artificers', D.Phil. thesis, University of Oxford, 1930; M. G Davies, *The Enforcement of English Apprenticeship: A Study in Applied Mercantilism, 1563–1642* (Cambridge, MA: Harvard University Press, 1956).

[6] A single instance of a certificate for ownership of lands is noted by A. L. Merson and A. J. Willis, *A Calendar of Southampton Apprenticeship Registers, 1609–1740*, Southampton Records Series vol. 12 (Southampton: Southampton University Press, 1968), xvii.

[7] Derry, 'Enforcement'.

[8] This process of judicial broadening included recognition of oral contracts, and service without indentures.

Inside incorporated cities, town governments and guilds were the primary bodies involved in apprenticeship. Their efforts focused on two areas: monitoring entry and resolving disputes, which is discussed below. Voluminous records survive from guilds' and cities' systems to register apprenticeships. These records allowed them to check later on claims to access based on service, and to enforce quotas on apprentice taking. At this point, many carried out a simple entry examination, to ensure that only 'suitable' youths entered service. However, the bars to entry they created focused on age, disability, nationality and – very occasionally – literacy. Parallels to modern educational systems break down here: suitability was based on identity not aptitude. For example, London apprentices must be 'Englishmen born', between 14 and 21 when bound and at least 24 when they finished, and not lame or disabled. Only three London guilds, the goldsmiths, barber-surgeons and apothecaries, included a requirement for literacy, the latter in Latin. It is hard to say if these bars were tightly enforced. Their impact would have been small, at any rate. Similarly, the fees that guilds and cities charged for registering apprenticeships were generally low. A period in the fourteenth and early fifteenth centuries in which London guilds deployed high fees to restrict apprenticeship had led to Parliament imposing a statutory limit of 2s 6d in 1530.[9] Thereafter, few guilds demanded more.[10] As in much of Europe, these financial barriers were relatively trivial, equating to less than a week's wages for an unskilled construction worker.

Masters too, faced restrictions from guilds and cities on taking apprentices. These potentially had a bigger effect on the supply of apprenticeship. In cities, masters usually had to be freemen, or freemen's widows, for their apprentices to gain any claim to citizenship or freedom. Most important, though, were guild limits on the numbers of apprentices each could train.

Nearly all guilds set quotas per master on apprentice numbers. Most were low. Only 4 of 22 London guilds surveyed allowed ordinary members more than two apprentices at a time; guild officials usually benefited from an additional spot. The main justification for these rules was to ensure adequate employment for guild members – which, in England, usually included journeymen as well as masters. In 1618, for example, the London clothworkers successfully petitioned the city for its help in limiting apprentices because 'the multitude' bound recently had led to the 'great increase of the number of' clothworkers, creating 'great misery and want' through lack of work.[11] Given that apprentices were concentrated

---

[9] 22 Hen VIII, c. 4.
[10] A few exceptions can be found in Dunlop and Denman, *English Apprenticeship*, 164.
[11] JCC, v. 30, f. 396.

in the workshops of a small share of masters (see below), quotas also lowered inequality, making it harder for masters to use apprentices to expand. While these rules surely affected *which* master apprentices joined – by capping their concentration in certain firms – the sheer volume of apprenticeship that occurred suggests that their main effect was to displace youths into the hands of less desirable masters.

One other distinctive political development affected apprenticeship in early modern England: the passing of the poor laws in 1598 and 1601. England's poor relief system heavily utilised a form of apprenticeship as a welfare strategy. Parishes placed children from poor families into apprenticeships with householders, who would maintain them in exchange for service. The degree to which training was given is unclear. The poor laws envisaged paupers learning 'husbandry and huswifery', and 'menial tasks in the fields' was the lot of most children in the seventeenth century; yet there is also evidence of parishes seeking to ensure youths gained a useful trade.[12] Generally pauper apprentices were younger, around nine or ten years old, and the expectation of menial duties, not learning a skill, means they are not the focus of this chapter.

The poor law had a second implication. Once serving an apprenticeship became one of the 'grounds' for settlement in 1691, apprentices acquired the right to claim relief in the parish in which they trained. This added a further incentive to enter apprenticeship.[13]

The terms of the contract of apprenticeship that were referred to in the Statute of Artificers had developed in London by the thirteenth century.[14] The master promised instruction and subsistence. The apprentice – normally represented by his father or mother – offered service and subordination: he promised to follow orders, avoid taverns, not play at cards or games, spurn fornication and marriage, work hard, and keep his master's secrets. These moral requirements were strongly stated. However, the details of what was to be learned were not specified. Apprentices' ages and the minimum duration were set by city law and, later, the statute. Masters took all their apprentice's earnings, while

---

[12] Contrast S. Hindle, *On the Parish? The Micro-Politics of Poor Relief in Rural England C. 1550–1750* (Oxford: Clarendon Press, 2004) with K. D. M. Snell, *Annals of the Labouring Poor: Social Change and Agrarian England, 1660–1900* (Cambridge: Cambridge University Press, 1985), 278–84. See also K. Honeyman, *Child Workers in England, 1780–1820: Parish Apprentices and the Making of the Early Industrial Labour Force* (Aldershot: Ashgate, 2007); A. Levene, 'Parish apprenticeship and the old Poor Law in London', *Economic History Review* 63/4 (2010), 915–41.

[13] Technically, only 40 days service generated a settlement for an apprentice. However, a completed apprenticeship appears to have been an informal norm applied in many circumstances, particularly in the first half of the eighteenth century.

[14] The best account of medieval apprenticeship is S. R Hovland, 'Apprenticeship in later medieval London, c. 1300–c. 1530', PhD thesis, University of London, 2006.

paying apprentices wages was banned in London – although some apprentices did receive recompense.[15] The contract was written twice on the same sheet and then cut, so each copy could be verified by matching the serrated edge (hence its name 'indenture'). Contracts were transferrable with both parties' agreement (and, where relevant, guild or city approval), allowing apprentices to move masters. By the seventeenth century, contracts were pre-printed, with gaps left for the details.

Contracts were formulaic in England. Usually, only one aspect was adjusted to fit the circumstances of each apprenticeship: the size of the material and financial commitment each party made. Most other aspects, notably duration, were essentially fixed by law. Personalisation took different forms. Some masters promised payments in clothing, cash or tools at the end of the term – Gloucester apprentices in the sixteenth century usually received 'double apparel' on completion, for example – giving apprentices an incentive to complete.[16] Some apprentices' families lowered masters' costs by supplying clothing. This could be a substantial contribution: John Coggs, a stationers' apprentice, went through six pairs of shoes a year, costing almost £2 of his mother's money in 1703–04.[17] A few families placing children in mercantile and trading businesses entered bonds 'for truth', to secure masters against any losses from the apprentice's neglect or dishonesty.

Most famously, apprentices and their families might pay a fee or 'premium' to their master when they started their training. Premiums were negotiated privately, with no guild or city involvement, and were never necessary for apprenticeship; even in the eighteenth century, large numbers of apprentices did not pay fees, as Table 9.1 shows. The timing of trends in fees is unclear. Payments from masters in the form of clothing, cash and tools at the end of apprentices' terms seem to have declined from around 1600 onwards. Apprentices' families may then have become more likely to pay fees: they were frequent enough to attract the eye of the state, which taxed them from 1711.[18]

---

[15] For examples: J. Rule, *Experience of Labour in Eighteenth-Century Industry* (London: Croom Helm, 1981), 104; Humphries, *Childhood and Child Labour*, 276.

[16] J. Barlow, *A Calendar of the Registers of Apprentices of the City of Gloucester, 1595–1700*, Gloucestershire Records Series vol. 14 (Gloucester: Bristol and Gloucestershire Archaeological Society, 2001).

[17] M. Beloff, 'A London apprentice's notebook, 1703–5', *History* 27/105 (1942). Other examples abound, see: Barlow, *Gloucester*, xviii; M. Graham (ed.), *Oxford City Apprentices 1697–1800* (Oxford: Clarendon Press for the Oxford Historical Society, 1987), xxiii; Merson and Willis, *Southampton*; M. Pelling, *The Common Lot: Sickness, Medical Occupations and the Urban Poor in Early Modern England* (London: Longman, 1998), 214–15.

[18] C. Minns and P. Wallis, 'The price of human capital in a pre-industrial economy: Premiums and apprenticeship in 18th-century England', *Explorations in Economic History* 50 (2013), 335–50.

Table 9.1 *London training premiums, companies and selected occupations, 1710–1800*

	Paying premium %	Average £	S.D. £	Median £	P10 £	P90 £	N
(a) Companies							
Apothecaries	84	73	36	63	40	105	585
Blacksmiths	23	11	17	6	3	21	2832
Grocers	53	88	91	60	5	200	705
Plasterers	28	12	15	7	4	20	683
Stationers	46	36	44	20	5	100	4428
Turners	52	13	15	10	4	26	816
Vintners	30	21	36	11	5	30	1628
Clothworkers	36	36	57	20	5	84	5862
All companies	33	36	54	15	5	100	15403
(b) Occupations							
Bookbinder	43	15	14	10	4	30	879
Bookseller	47	90	82	70	11	200	714
Druggist	69	203	112	200	100	315	59
Grocer	64	101	94	92	25	200	200
Haberdasher	79	61	39	50	21	100	119
Instrument maker	59	16	19	10	5	30	299
Plasterer	28	8	4	6	5	15	204
Printer	35	21	20	19	4	40	2691
Stationer	51	79	80	50	10	190	905
Blacksmith	17	7	3	7	3	10	53
Turner	64	12	7	10	5	25	87
Dyer	37	12	10	10	5	20	251
Tailor	56	14	12	10	5	30	100
Butcher	29	12	8	11	5	21	169
Calenderer	14	8	8	5	3	14	545
Watchmaker	57	17	16	15	5	30	194
Engraver	74	33	28	25	10	60	307

Note: The table reports premiums in eight London companies. (a) is grouped by guild; (b) by master's reported occupation. N is the total number of observations, including those with zero premiums. The descriptive statistics (cols 3–7) are for observations with positive premiums. The table reports the standard deviation, and premiums at the tenth and ninetieth percentiles, as well as the mean and median.
Source: Minns and Wallis, 'Price of human capital'.

By altering fees, offering end-payments or negotiating over who paid for maintenance and clothing, masters and apprentices served both to balance supply and demand and provide incentives for completion. In short, within the strictures set by national and local laws, there was an active market for training.[19] But while premiums and payments offered a price mechanism to clear the market for new apprenticeships, the rigidity and length of the required term created a high opportunity cost that, as we will see, stretched the viability of many contracts.

Incidence

Apprenticeship occurred on an extraordinarily large scale in early modern England. It was employed across almost the full range of skilled and semi-skilled non-agricultural occupations. For youths looking to a future in industry, trade or services, apprenticeship was a normal step between family and independence as an adult, just as service in husbandry was a conventional stage in a life in agriculture.[20] But whereas farm service was widely spread, apprenticeship – especially in the sixteenth century – was highly concentrated. Four features stand out about the distribution of apprenticeship: the sheer size and durability of apprenticeship; the centrality of London; the comparatively low levels of apprenticeship in other cities; and the dramatic increase in rural apprenticeship in the eighteenth century. One could say that Parliament's decision to base the Statute of Artificers on the custom of London made sense, given that a big share of apprentices were already subject to those rules.

These key features of the distribution of English apprenticeship are illustrated by Table 9.2, which reports new estimates for the number of youths starting apprenticeships in England. Columns 1 and 2 give estimates for guild or city-registered apprenticeships in towns and cities around 1600 and 1700. For London, I extrapolate from existing guild and city records. For other towns, I use estimates of the number of apprentices per thousand people, calculated from surviving registers, and multiply them by the number of cities in each size category. This is obviously a rough and ready approach. It is also, by definition, an underestimate: urban registers under-record the actual numbers of indentures.[21]

Guild and city records become untenable as the foundation for an estimate in the eighteenth century. Many ceased to register apprenticeships,

[19] Minns and Wallis, 'Price of human capital'; Feldman and van der Beek, 'Skill choice'.

[20] A. Kussmaul, *Servants in Husbandry in Early Modern England* (Cambridge: Cambridge University Press, 1981); P. Laslett, *The World We Have Lost* (London: Methuen, 1965).

[21] An excellent discussion of this for Norwich is given in Pelling, *Common Lot*. See also Barlow, *Gloucester*, xxxi; Merson and Willis, *Southampton*, xvv–xvi, lxxiv.

Table 9.2 *Annual entries to apprenticeship in England, seventeenth–eighteenth centuries*

	Apprentices in incorporated cities		Apprentices paying premiums	
	c. 1600	c. 1700	c. 1710	c. 1790
Urban				
London	3,000–4,000	c. 4,000	1,961	1,019
Towns >10,000	365(162–597)	586 (288–1060)	405	865
Towns 5,000–10,000	484 (293–641)	806 (488–1068)	539	280
Small boroughs	–	–	651	742
Urban subtotal	4,349 (3,455–5,238)	5,392 (4,776–6,128)	3,556	2,906
Rural subtotal	–	–	2,227	3,746
Total	–	–	5,783	6,652
Share of teenage males (%)	8–13	11–14	12	9
Share of teenage males outside agriculture (%)	24–37	21–26	22	15

Note: Columns 1 and 2 are based on the following assumptions. In 1600, aside from London, England had four cities with more than 10,000 inhabitants (Norwich, York, Bristol and Newcastle), and 15 with 5,000–10,000. By 1700, six towns exceeded 10,000 inhabitants, and 25 had 5,000–10,000 (E. A. Wrigley, 'Urban growth and agricultural change: England and the continent in the early modern period', *Journal of Interdisciplinary History* 15 (1985), 686). We calculate the numbers of apprentices per inhabitant at various points between 1600 and 1800 for Boston, Bristol, Coventry, Gloucester, Ipswich, Kings Lynn, Leicester, Lincoln, Liverpool, London, Northampton, Oxford, Southampton and St Albans. For small towns, we find a median of 4.3 apprentices per thousand people and an interquartile range of 2.6–5.7. For large towns, the median is 6.3 (2.8–10.3) apprentices per thousand people. Columns 1 and 2 give the median and interquartile range once again multiplied by the number of towns in each category. Columns 3 and 4 are based on six-year samples of the Stamp Tax Registers (for 1712–17 and 1792–97); part of the underlying data was kindly shared by Karine van der Beek. Urban populations are derived from J. De Vries, *European Urbanization, 1500–1800* (Cambridge, MA: Harvard University Press, 1984) and J. Langton, 'Urban growth and economic change: From the late seventeenth century to 1841', in: P. Clark (ed.) *The Cambridge Urban History of Britain*, vol. 2: *1540-1840* (Cambridge: Cambridge University Press, 2000), table 14.4, 474. The additional category of small boroughs are incorporated towns with a population over 1,000 in 1832. Estimates of 16-year-old males outside agriculture are derived from E. A. Wrigley et al., *English Population History from Family Reconstitution, 1580–1837* (Cambridge: Cambridge University Press, 1997), 614–5, 134. For 1600 we assume 65% of the male population are employed in agriculture (P. Wallis, J. Colson and D. Chilosi, 'Structural change and economic growth in the British economy before the Industrial Revolution, 1500–1800', *Journal of Economic History* 78 (2018), 862–903). For 1700 and 1800, we use Broadberry et al's figures of 46% and 36% of males in agriculture (S. Broadberry, B. M. S. Campbell and B. van Leeuwen, 'When did Britain industrialise? The sectoral distribution of the labour force and labour productivity in Britain, 1381–1851', *Explorations in Economic History* 50 (2013), 24). Estimates of the share of non-agricultural workforce outside towns assume that all urban workers are non-agricultural, and define the urban population as the share living in towns over 5,000 given in Wrigley, 'Urban growth', 688.

while some growing towns, such as Birmingham and Manchester, were not incorporated and so lacked the infrastructure to record apprenticeships. Fortunately, from 1711 records survive from the Stamp Tax, a levy of between 2.5% and 5% on apprenticeship premiums. These records only cover apprenticeships in which the master received a premium. But they extend over the entirety of the country, allowing us to examine rural apprenticeship. Columns 3 and 4 report counts of fee-paying apprentices for the 1710s and 1790s.

Apprenticeship's large scale and enduring popularity is most evident when we compare the numbers who started indentures with the number of teenage males – the population from which they were primarily drawn. In 1600 and 1700, around one in ten teenage males started apprenticeships in a city or town. In the 1790s, 8% of teenage males started fee-paying apprenticeships, compared to 11% at the start of the century.

There is little sign here of sharp cycles in the popularity of apprenticeship over these two centuries. Although historians have long debated the 'decline' of apprenticeship in England, Table 9.2 suggests that apprenticeship remained vigorous through the eighteenth century.[22] It is only in the guilds that apprentice registrations declined steeply, as the ability – and interest – of many guilds in enforcing local limits on economic activity weakened.[23]

Private apprenticeship did not retreat quickly in parallel with the guilds. There was some erosion in its significance: as employment outside agriculture rose in the eighteenth century, premium-paying apprentices fell from 20% to 13% of all youths working in manufacturing or services between the 1710s and the 1790s. But this may overstate developments, as industrialisation meant that some of the new jobs were in low and semi-skilled tasks where apprenticeship had limited relevance.

Individual trades and towns had specific histories that were more varied than this national average suggests. In some trades, loud complaints about unapprenticed workers emerged in the eighteenth century. Calico printers, shearmen and stocking weavers fought for jobs and wages by

[22] The debate is well surveyed in Snell, *Annals*. Later major contributions include L. Schwarz, *London in the Age of Industrialisation: Entrepreneurs, Labour Force and Living Conditions, 1700–1850* (Cambridge: Cambridge University Press, 1992); Humphries, *Childhood and Child Labour*.

[23] The many and growing gaps in guild and urban regulation are charted in Dunlop and Denman, *English Apprenticeship*; S. Kramer, *The English Craft Guilds: Studies in Their Progress and Decline* (New York: Columbia University Press, 1927). See, however, M. Berlin, 'Guilds in decline? London Livery Companies and the rise of a liberal economy, 1600–1800', in: S. R. Epstein and M. Prak (eds.), *Guilds, Innovation, and the European Economy, 1400–1800* (Cambridge: Cambridge University Press, 2008), 316–41.

strengthening or re-establishing apprenticeship.[24] In others trades, journeymen accused masters of recruiting excessive numbers of apprentices as cheap labour. In Spitalfields, rioting by silk weavers in 1719 was blamed on 'the covetousness of both masters and journeymen in taking so many 'prentices for the sake of the money they have with them; not considering whether they should have employment for them'.[25]

It is uncertain how widespread such problems were, however. Few premodern trades were organised in a way that made apprentices central to production, in the way that child workers were to become in textile mills. And as guilds withdrew, journeymen often began campaigns to maintain apprenticeship via closed shops.[26] Moreover, the estimates in Table 9.2 are partial: the Stamp Tax just counted apprentices who paid premiums, and many did not. We thus cannot be sure if overall numbers were changing or just the share paying fees. Nevertheless, the impression of persistence they provide coheres well with Jane Humphries's conclusion that apprenticeship remained commonplace for working-class youths into the early nineteenth century.[27]

London dominated urban apprenticeship in the seventeenth century. The great majority of England's urban apprentices were in London. The city's 3,000–4,000 new apprentices a year around 1600 or 1700 was three to four times the number starting training in all England's other large towns combined. In the late seventeenth century, roughly one in ten of all English teenage males started an apprenticeship in London. This equates to one in five youths working outside agriculture. As E. A. Wrigley noted, London's disproportionate size and rapid growth depended on sucking in youths from across the nation.[28] The impact on the city was particularly acute around 1600, when apprentices supplied around 6% to 8% of the city's population (assuming a 60% survival rate); the social and political importance of apprentices in protest was rooted in this numerical heft.[29]

England's second and third tiers of cities played a much smaller part in apprenticeship. Where London faced a flood, these cities saw a trickle. In Lincoln – population c. 4,000 in 1700 – just 14 new apprentices a year were indentured in the mid-seventeenth century. In Gloucester, a county town with around 5,000 residents, around 40–50 apprentices were indentured each year in the seventeenth century. At least twice as many youths from

---

[24] Rule, *Experience*.   [25] *The Weavers pretences examined* (1719), quoted in ibid., 105
[26] Ibid., 111–12.   [27] Humphries, *Childhood and Child Labour*.
[28] E. A. Wrigley, 'A simple model of London's importance in changing English society and economy, 1650–1750', *Past and Present* 37 (1967), 44–70.
[29] Smith, 'London apprentices'; T. Harris, *London Crowds in the Reign of Charles II: Propaganda and Politics from the Restoration until the Exclusion Crisis* (Cambridge: Cambridge University Press, 1987).

Oxfordshire trained in London as in Oxford.[30] Even Bristol, the country's third largest city, received only 180 apprentices annually around 1600 and about 250 around 1700, when its population reached about 24,000 people. Every year more apprentices were registered in London's larger guilds – the merchant tailors, haberdashers, weavers – than in Bristol. Still, Bristol was relatively important in training: its density of apprentices came close to that of London. Almost 7% of Bristol's population were apprentices in 1600, and around 4% in 1700 (assuming 60% survived). In most towns, apprentices were 1–2% of the population. Apprentices were less important to trade and manufacturing outside London, just as these towns were less important to apprenticeship.

Apprenticeship became less metropolitan, less urban and more geographically diffused in the eighteenth century. London remained the largest centre of training in Britain, but its exceptionality was reduced. In the 1710s, 39% of apprentices paying premiums in England were indentured to London masters. By the 1790s, this had fallen to just 18%. To put this another way, in the 1710s, London received almost four times the number of apprentices that its share of England's population (11%) would predict; in the 1790s, it attracted roughly twice the share its population share (10%) suggested.

Outside London, apprenticeships were distributed widely by the late eighteenth century, as Figure 9.1 shows.[31] Masters in small centres – hamlets, villages, old market centres and new manufacturing towns – were recruiting premium-paying apprentices to a degree not found previously. The rest of England's established towns and cities (those with a population of 5,000 by 1800) took a constant fifth of apprentices. Some of this diffusion of training reflected the transformative effect of industry. In Lancashire, for example, the small hamlet of Hardshaw-within-Windle saw 11 apprentices in the 1790s, up from none in the 1710s, as it was drawn into the manufacturing and coal-mining town of St Helens (whose population would exceed 5,000 in the 1830s).[32] The growth of clockmaking in the area is apparent from their masters' trades: four joined masters who made watches or watch parts; the rest were bound to a surgeon, a draper, a carpenter, a cooper, a saddler and a joiner. Half paid less than £10, and just two paid more than £20 – those bound to the surgeon and the joiner.

---

[30] Counts of Oxfordshire apprentices in surviving London guild records exceed 100 per year on occasion in the seventeenth century; not all guild records survive.

[31] Inevitably, not all locations of masters can be matched to identifiable places. However, the share matched (so far) is the same at 85% of English apprentices for the 1710s and 1790s. We expect this to rise as detailed matching of non-urban places has only been completed for a small sample of counties.

[32] In this paragraph, the 1710s and 1790s refer to six-year samples for 1712–17 and 1792–97, respectively.

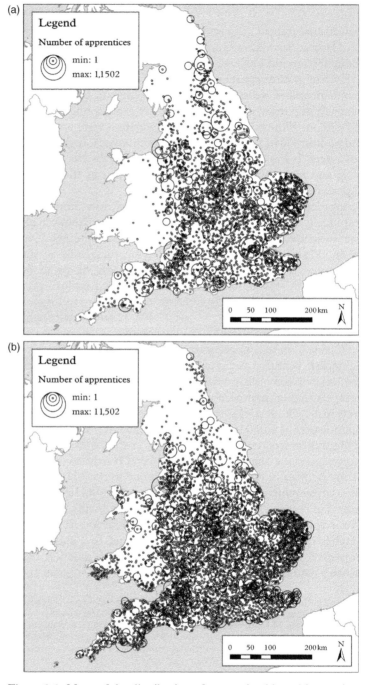

Figure 9.1 Maps of the distribution of apprenticeships with premiums in England and Wales, c. 1710 and c. 1790 (GIStorical Antwerp)

Similarly, Rainhill, a small township in the same county, saw three apprentices in the 1790s, against none in the 1710s.[33] Two made watch parts and one became a saddler.

Yet much of England remained largely untouched by industrialisation in this period, and apprenticeship was increasingly concentrated in these rural backwaters. In Bedfordshire, it was small hamlets such as Old Warden, where the local carpenter Thomas Preston bound a youth for £6, or Ridgmont, where two cordwainers and a wheelwright each took an apprentice (for £5, £10 and £18 respectively) that saw apprentices bound for premiums in the 1790s, yet had seen none in the 1710s.

By the 1790s, it was the largely agricultural counties of Norfolk and Leicestershire that had the highest rates of apprenticeship per person, with 1.26 and 1.09 fee-paying apprentices per thousand inhabitants. Industrial Lancashire ranked thirty-fifth out of 41 English counties with just 0.29 apprentices per thousand.[34] In the Lancashire cotton industry and the woollen manufacturing of the West Riding of Yorkshire, formal indentures in trades such as weaving were rare in the late eighteenth century; that said, these were areas where proto-industry had long relied heavily on training within the family.[35] The five cities with the highest concentrations of apprentices in the 1790s were Exeter, King's Lynn, Cambridge, Ipswich and Norwich. These were not the heartland of industrialisation; they were slow-growing, relatively peripheral places in the East or South where traditional forms of employment and business

---

Caption for Figure 9.1   (cont.)

Source: National Archives, IR1.
Note: The maps plot apprenticeships with premiums in (a) the 1710s and (b) the 1790s where masters are in identifiable locations. Locations are represented by circles weighted by apprentice numbers. For 1710, a six-year sample contained 30,542 indentures; 85.2% were successfully geo-located. For 1790, the six-year sample contained 36,102 indentures; 84.6% were successfully geo-located.

---

[33] 'Radnage–Raithby', in: S. Lewis (ed.), *A Topographical Dictionary of England*, (London, 1848), 630–33, British History Online, www.british-history.ac.uk/topographical-dict/england/pp630-633.
[34] Our data does not distinguish the ridings of Yorkshire.
[35] Derry, 'Enforcement'; D. Bythell, *The Handloom Weavers: A Study in the English Cotton Industry During the Industrial Revolution* (Cambridge: Cambridge University Press, 1969), 36–38, 52–53.

organisation still predominated. Many of the trades youths entered were occupations servicing commercial agriculture: saddlers, blacksmiths, corn dealers and so on.

Because the Stamp Tax only applied to premium-paying apprentices, it is possible that the diffusion of apprenticeship that we see in Table 9.1 and Figure 9.1 reflects changes in the use of premiums, not apprenticeship itself. Perhaps village boys had been bound as often in the 1710s, but without fees? We cannot easily reject this hypothesis without evidence, that has not yet been found, on the frequency of rural apprenticeships without premiums. However, there is little sign that apprentices were paying higher premiums, which we might also expect if demand was outstripping supply, and fee-paying apprenticeship was gradually becoming less common overall.[36]

This expansion in rural apprenticeship was part of a wider rebalancing of apprenticeship in this period. The diminishing importance of London as a source of training implies that more apprenticeships happened elsewhere. Many youths who trained in London would later return home – a quarter of provincial apprentices reappear in their parish of birth's vital records, either marrying, baptising a child or being buried.[37] If fewer youths were making that initial journey, while the numbers working in industry and services was growing, then we would expect more youths to be training in the provinces, as we observe.

One consequence of this shift from London to the provinces was a reversal in the flow of skilled workers. Where skill had once spread outwards from London, as youths apprenticed in the city then migrated, by the mid-nineteenth century the metropolis was stocked with workers who had trained in small towns. In construction, for example, Henry Mayhew suggested that in the 1850s three-quarters of carpenters were 'from the country', having moved to London as journeymen.[38] The decline of guild powers encouraged this. English guild rules had favoured training within the guild; entry for people trained elsewhere was often prohibitively expensive. Now, provincial journeymen became acceptable.

We can see in outline a slow change in other aspects of apprenticeship. Over the seventeenth and eighteenth century, apprentices in London became younger – the age they started fell from nearly 18 years old around

---

[36] Judicial decisions had also removed the requirement for a seven-year apprenticeship to trade in a country village in the mid-eighteenth century (1 Ventr. 51; 2 Keb. 583).

[37] M. Klemp et al., 'Picking winners? The effect of birth order and migration on parental human capital investments in pre-modern England', *European Review of Economic History* 17 (2013), 224.

[38] In E. P. Thompson and M. Yeo (eds.), *The Unknown Mayhew* (London: Merlin Press, 1971), letter LX, 335.

1600 to 15.5 by 1800.[39] (Apprenticeship always came after the age at which children received elementary education in literacy and numeracy.) Terms also became shorter and less varied. Agreements beyond seven years became rare, although they had been relatively common in the sixteenth century.[40] In some trades, by the late eighteenth century, even shorter apprenticeships started to appear – although mainly outside corporate towns.[41] There is a sense in which apprenticeship became more predictable.

One final caveat needs to be stated about the balance of urban and rural apprenticeship. Until the Stamp Tax (and the introduction of settlement examinations, which occurred around the same time) we are almost entirely ignorant of apprenticeships outside corporate towns. Yet these were surely *always* the great majority of apprenticeships.[42] Small towns, villages and the countryside were where the great majority of manufacturing and service work occurred. Without guilds, however, the evidence is scanty. Quarter sessions records, settlement examinations, and diaries and memoirs all suggest that rural apprenticeship was largely consistent with urban norms, but we still know too little about the subject.[43]

Apprenticeship appears ubiquitous taken in the aggregate. Yet the distribution of apprentices across urban households and workshops was highly uneven. Romantic images of the artisanal household with master, wife, journeymen and apprentice as stock characters are deceptive. Many, perhaps most, guild members in London never took apprentices.[44] Forty per cent of the city's freemen apothecaries took no apprentices, for example.[45] Those masters who did take apprentices often had just one or two over their lifetimes. Only a small minority of masters trained multiple apprentices over long careers. As Margaret Pelling showed for Norwich, these large employers often pushed up against guild limits on apprentice numbers.[46]

---

[39] P. Wallis, C. Webb and C. Minns, 'Leaving home and entering service: The age of apprenticeship in early modern London', *Continuity and Change* 25 (2010), 377–404. Even older ages are reported in the 1550s: S. Rappaport, *Worlds within Worlds: Structures of Life in Sixteenth-Century London* (Cambridge: Cambridge University Press, 1989), 295.

[40] For examples from Norwich and Southampton, see Pelling, *Common Lot*, 214; Merson and Willis, *Southampton*, xix.

[41] Snell, *Annals*.   [42] Pelling, *Common Lot*, 119–20.

[43] The fullest discussion remains Snell, *Annals*.

[44] Exact estimates are complicated by the difficulty of matching by name across registers. Estimates from a sample of eight London guilds, suggest at least 40–50% of freemen did not take apprentices.

[45] P. Wallis, 'Medicines for London: The trade, regulation and lifecycle of London apothecaries, c. 1610–c. 1670', D.Phil., University of Oxford, 2002, 170.

[46] Pelling, *Common Lot*, 216–19

Most apprentices were bound to one of the rare masters who taught large numbers. In London, 60% of apprentices joined masters who taught five or more apprentices. Some masters would bind more than 20 over their careers, although they rarely had more than one or two at a time. These larger employers charged higher premiums over time, as their experience and reputation grew; training became part of their business.[47] It was also this group who attracted the ire of the smaller masters and journeymen, for taking too large a share of the trade or preferring cheap apprentices to waged journeymen. Most apprentices would not replicate the success of their master. In Gloucester, for example, only 15% of apprentice shoemakers or weavers would later take apprentices themselves.[48] Training was concentrated, rather than distributed. Only a minority of masters had the volume of work, capacity, reputation and interest to attract numerous apprentices.

Who Was Apprenticed?

One crucial issue for our understanding of early modern apprenticeship is how accessible it was to different people. If access to training was restricted to a specific group, whether by formal rules or informal norms, then it would be socially unjust and economically pernicious. Given that the right to skilled work was tied to completion, apprenticeship would be another institution generating rents for insiders.[49]

At the simplest level, this charge does not appear to hold for apprenticeship in early modern England. Apprenticeship encompassed the children of rich and poor, townsmen and country folk, farmers and merchants. It was an open institution. To a large extent, recruitment on the scale just described necessitated this. Statutory restrictions on who could enter urban crafts seem to have had little effect – and there is little evidence of attempts to enforce them at law.[50] Nor did guilds impose tight social restrictions on entry.

Still, the opportunity to enter an apprenticeship was not evenly spread across society. Apprenticeship came with costs: it removed a pair of productive hands from a household at the age they finally became valuable. It took time and money to arrange: youths needed a stock of clothing

---

[47] Minns and Wallis, 'Price of human capital', 348–49.   [48] Barlow, *Gloucester*, xx.

[49] For the fullest discussion of this, see S. Ogilvie, 'Guilds, efficiency, and social capital: Evidence from German proto-industry', *Economic History Review* 57 (2004), 286–333; S. Ogilvie, 'How does social capital affect women? Guilds and communities in early modern Germany', *American Historical Review* 109 (2004), 325–59; S. Ogilvie, '"Whatever is, is right"? Economic institutions in pre-industrial Europe,' *Economic History Review* 60 (2007), 649–84.

[50] Derry, 'Enforcement', 3–6.

at the very least. These direct financial barriers were probably more important than statute, guild rules or exclusive artisanal norms in defining the prospects of children. Premiums, particularly, were a source of inequality. Fees were lower than has sometimes been thought. As we saw (Table 9.1), median premiums were £5–£10 in most trades. Nonetheless, with unskilled provincial wages hovering around £12 a year, these were difficult sums for poorer families, even with the chance of assistance from parish or charity. One inevitable effect was that poorer children largely ended up in the least prosperous trades.[51] The rich – and well-connected urban children whose parents might escape paying – had an important advantage in the labour market.

Because city and guild registers record the occupations of apprentices' fathers, we can examine the degree of inequality in urban apprenticeship (see Table 9.3). Poverty had a substantial impact. The low share of apprentices whose fathers were described as labourers suggests that movement into (non-pauper) apprenticeship was relatively rare for these families. Labourer might be an under-used label, given that apprentices had some control over the wording of indentures, but a great gulf exists between these figures and the numbers of labourers in the population. In 1688, Gregory King put 43% of the population into his class of 'labourers, cottagers and paupers'; more recent estimates are lower, yet still far in excess of the 4% of apprentices paying premiums in the early eighteenth century who were identified as labourers' children.[52] In London, between 1500 and 1799, only 2% of apprentices were sons of labourers. Higher shares are sometimes observed. In 1650–74, 18% of Lincoln apprentices were labourers' sons. But Gloucester, Liverpool, Bristol and Boston were all similar to London. These are private apprenticeships; the share of labourers' children among pauper apprentices was presumably much higher.

At the other end of the social distribution, sons of gentlemen were relatively numerous: 13% of apprentices across these samples, compared to the 1.4% of the population King estimated. London attracted many – more than 30,000 gentry sons in the seventeenth century alone – but so did Liverpool, with its prosperous merchant houses. Even smaller cities saw substantial numbers. Many merchants and wholesalers came from gentry families. The degree of gentility of these fathers has long been debated. Were they merely socially aspirational large farmers – 'parish gentry', in Christopher Brooks's words? Some probably were, but a

---

[51] Charity funding for apprenticeship was increasingly abundant and important from the early seventeenth century onwards.

[52] Broadberry, 'When did Britain Industrialise', 19; Minns and Wallis, 'Price of human capital', 9.

Table 9.3 Backgrounds of apprentices in English towns and cities, seventeenth–eighteenth centuries

	London 1600–25	Gloucester 1600–25	Boston 1650–75	Lincoln 1650–75	Leicester 1646–48
A. Parental occupation/status					
Gentleman (%)	13.9	6.5	9.9	9.7	0.9
Yeoman (%)	34.7	26.8	12.1	19.4	10.4
Husbandman (%)	7.7	18.8	7.7	8.1	16.5
Labourer (%)	0.7	3.7	9.9	17.7	10.4
Parental sector					
Agriculture (%)	54.5	52.4	30	41.9	31.6
Manufacturing (%)	29.2	37.3	48.6	46.5	55.1
Services (%)	16.3	10.3	21.4	11.6	13.3
	100	100	100	100	100
B. Ties					
Local origin (%)	14.7	27.2		44.4	45.7
Same occupn. (%)		10.9	10.6	26.9	16.8
Father is master (%)	0.2	0	11.2	0	14.5
Father deceased (%)	30.8		21.7	4.4	34.2
N	37,457	616	91	62	115
N guilds	58				

	London 1700–25	Gloucester 1700–25	Boston 1700–25	Lincoln 1750–75	Bristol c. 1690	Liverpool 1700–25	Shrewsbury c. 1690
A. Parental occupation/status							
Gentleman (%)	9.1	4.8	3.2	3.4	8.3	16.4	22.4
Yeoman (%)	8.1	21.8	6.3	3.4	12.8	14.5	5.6
Husbandman (%)	4	0	0	1.5	0.3	17.8	2.4
Labourer (%)	4.2	5.8	10.5	13.1	2.2	0.8	0.8
Parental sector							
Agriculture (%)	19	27.6	23.9	33.5	22.7	42.2	10.4
Manufacturing (%)	51.2	58.5	47.8	46.2	51.1	29.6	68.8
Services (%)	29.7	13.9	28.4	20.4	26.2	28.2	20.8
	100	100	100	100	100	100	100
B. Ties							
Local origin (%)	47.1	52.4	2.7	38.9	45.3	10.3	38.6
Same occupn. (%)	11.1	20.5	6.3	18	19.2	4.7	25.6
Father is master (%)	2.9	0	11.7	0	9.7	1	15.4
Father deceased (%)	22.4		4.9	16		21.4	13.6

Table 9.3 (cont.)

	London 1700–25	Gloucester 1700–25	Boston 1700–25	Lincoln 1750–75	Bristol c. 1690	Liverpool 1700–25	Shrewsbury c. 1690
N	48,669	1037	95	268	2,135	366	125
N guilds	67						5

Note: Panel A reports the reported occupation/status of apprentices' fathers, expressed as a share of all apprentices with relevant information. Rows 5–7 follow Wrigley's Primary, Secondary, Tertiary classification. Panel B reports the share of apprentices with ties, as defined in T. Leunig, C. Minns and P. Wallis, 'Networks in the pre-modern economy: The market for London apprenticeships, 1600–1749', *Journal of Economic History* 71 (2011), 413–43.

Sources: London: C. Webb, *London Apprentices*, 44 vols. (London: Society of Genealogists, 1996–2007); London Livery Companies Online (rollco. org) and Michael Scott kindly shared his transcript of the London Merchant Taylors' registers; Bristol: Bristol Record Office, 04353/2; Gloucester: Barlow, *Gloucester*; Boston and Lincoln were kindly supplied by the Lincoln Family History Society; Leicester: H. Hartopp (ed.), *Register of the Freemen of Leicester, 1196–1770* (Leicester: Corporation of the City of Leicester, 1927); Liverpool: M. Power, F. Lewis and D. Ascott, *Liverpool Community, 1649–1750*, SN: 3882 (Colchester, Essex: UK Data Archive, 1998); Shrewsbury: Shropshire Archives MS6001/126 (glovers); 6001/4263 (mercers); 6001/5837 (tailors); 6001/3360 (weavers); 6001/4583 (smiths).

considerable number can be traced in contemporary lists of armigerous gentlemen.[53] These people had asserted a credible claim to gentility before the officials responsible for defining the status; they include Members of Parliament and Justices of the Peace. The Surrey gentleman Arthur Onslow's eldest son, Richard, became Chancellor of the Exchequer in 1715; his fourth son, Henry, had been apprenticed in the Grocers' Company in 1683.

Wealth aside, some other potential biases had little effect. There was little preference for local children. Instead, apprenticeship was tightly entangled with migration. Roughly speaking, the distance that apprentices travelled grew in proportion to the size of a town's population. London's apprentices, in particular, had often journeyed long distances. This was in part a demographic necessity: the metropolis only supplied 15% of its own apprentices in the early seventeenth century when it was growing most rapidly. Smaller cities, too, depended on apprentice migration. Around 1600, in Southampton and Gloucester, just a third of apprentices were locals.

Nor did masters limit entry to the sons of those already in the trade. Many apprentices came from a background in agriculture, not manufacturing or services. In the first quarter of the seventeenth century, 55% of London apprentices and 52% of Gloucester apprentices were from farming backgrounds, compared to perhaps 60–65% of the population.[54] A century later, 19% of London apprentices, 28% of Gloucester and 25% of Boston apprentices were from farming families. By that stage, agriculture employed around 40% of adult males. Both migrants and youths changing trade tended to pay higher premiums; mobility had its price, probably because of the greater risk of contracts failing early.[55] Yet apprenticeship was, and remained, a well-travelled road between sectors and occupations.

The largest 'missing' group among apprentices were women. This was not because of formal restrictions. Female apprentices were rarely banned in England. Only one London guild, the weavers', is known to have proscribed training 'any mayde damsel or other woeman whatsoever'. Women could become freemen of London and many other cities via apprenticeship.[56] But expectations about gender roles and marriage

---

[53] P. Wallis and C. Webb, 'The education and training of gentry sons in early modern England', *Social History* 36 (2011), 36–53.

[54] To ensure comparability, these figures compare the share of apprentices with fathers identifiable as in agriculture, industry or services to estimates for the male population. Gentry etc. are excluded. See Wallis, Colson and Chilosi, 'Structural change'.

[55] Minns and Wallis, 'Price of human capital'.

[56] Ordinances, Guildhall Library, MS 4647, #12

(the husband's freedom or citizenship superseded his wife's rights, at least in London) lowered the incentive to invest in girls' human capital. Girls placed in pauper apprenticeships usually learned 'housewifery'. Many must have learned trades from their parents. Private apprenticeships of women were rare, however.

In London, roughly 1% of apprentices registered by guilds were female, as were perhaps 5% of apprentices paying premiums in the eighteenth century.[57] Guild records probably underestimate training; as Amy Erickson has suggested, female apprentices were more likely to be bound for shorter terms, as meeting the statutory requirement was less important to them, and so might not be registered.[58] Nonetheless, there can be no doubt that women were far less frequently apprenticed than men. Female apprentices often joined a small number of trades, particularly millinery or another clothing trades, although examples occur in most occupations.[59] In some cases, parents did invest substantial sums; Erickson has tracked a cluster of respectable families apprenticing their daughters to milliners in the 1700s with premiums of £30–£60.[60] Unusually, their contracts named both husband and wife as master, suggesting that it was the mistress who would train them.

Most apprentices were entering different occupations to their father. But for children born into craft or trade families, apprenticeship was less obviously a mechanism for occupational mobility. The most obvious examples are those youths who were bound to their fathers. In London, masters' sons supplied just 2% of apprentices, but they made up 15% in Shrewsbury in the 1690s and in Leicester in the 1650s. That sons entered contracts with their fathers highlights one tension between the Statute of Artificers, which did not recognise any form of skill inheritance for artisans' sons, and that of cities and guilds, which frequently gave masters' sons the right to claim membership by inheritance.[61] By formalising within-family training as an apprenticeship, fathers made the years their sons spent working with them transferrable, should they die or fail in trade, and legally meaningful.

Brooks has argued that the openness of apprenticeship declined in the late seventeenth and eighteenth centuries.[62] This pathway into the urban community narrowed, which contributed to the rise of urban oligarchies.

---

[57] A. L. Erickson, 'Eleanor Mosley and other milliners in the City of London Companies 1700–1750', *History Workshop Journal* 71 (2011), 150
[58] A. L. Erickson, *Women and Property in Early Modern England* (London: Routledge, 1993), 55.
[59] Snell, *Annals*.   [60] Erickson, 'Eleanor Mosley'.
[61] Legal developments in the eighteenth century arguably changed this by recognising time spent working, even without an indenture.
[62] Brooks, 'Apprenticeship'.

Signs of this can be found in the narrowing of migration fields over the seventeenth century. By 1700, for example, Gloucester supplied more than half of its own apprentices; just 6% now travelled more than 25 miles. Similarly, London now gathered almost half of its apprentices from Middlesex. Migrant apprentices were much more likely to come from the south-east, although some did still travel further. The share of freemen entering by patrimony also rose.

On the other hand, there is no evidence that these developments resulted from deliberate decisions by cities or guilds. The freedom of some London guilds did become a more costly proposition, but apprenticeship outside guilds was sustained, and premiums did not rise in real terms, as we would expect if guilds were raising barriers. Increasingly local recruitment may simply reflect the growth of manufacturing outside the old cities, and the slowing of London's breakneck rate of expansion. Better provincial opportunities meant that prospective apprentices no longer needed to travel. Elsewhere in Europe, youths tended to train near their families, allowing parents to support their children, and one imagines that English parents would have favoured this too. Conversely, London was now able to supply more of its own apprentices, and it was increasingly accessible to skilled adult migrants.[63] To see this period as marked by the closing off of the city to outsiders seems an exaggeration, in short.

Apprenticeship and Family Structure

The point, and the desirability, of apprenticeship varied between families, depending on their occupation, wealth, local inheritance system and family size. The choices families made about *which* child to apprentice illustrate this clearly. In gentry families, apprentices were usually younger sons; few eldest sons were apprenticed, as one would expect in a situation in which landed wealth (and status) was transferred through primogeniture. Instead they studied law or spent time at a university. The odds of apprenticeship increased with each step down the birth order, as Figure 9.2 shows. Farming families, headed by yeomen or husbandmen, echoed the gentry's habit of mainly apprenticing younger sons, suggesting that for elder sons inheriting the farm trumped migration into town.[64] Conversely, urban inheritance was often partible and urban resources and networks were already tied to crafts and trade. Hence, for children of the urban middling sort birth order mattered

[63] This may also reflect improving chances of survival for urban children.
[64] Klemp et al., 'Picking winners'.

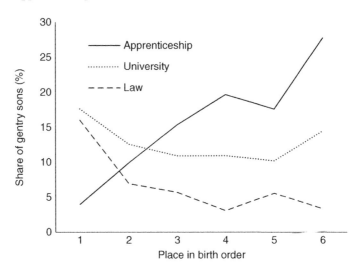

Figure 9.2 The effect of birth order on education and training among British gentry
Source: Wallis and Webb, 'Education and training', 49.
Note: The figure reports the destination of sons in a sample of gentry families, by birth order.

little. In poor families rural norms were reversed: labourers' eldest sons were more likely to be apprenticed, as opportunities were directed towards eldest sons.

Yet individual interest mattered too. That urban families placed children into apprenticeships largely independent of birth position suggests that their ability and enthusiasm played a part in defining who followed what pathway. Certainly, Robert Campbell's advice to parents emphasised the importance of matching the 'Genius and Temper' of children to their career.[65] Ilana Krausman Ben-Amos has shown how youths usually had a voice in choosing their career. Apprenticeships usually started with a month-long trial period to accommodate this. Adam Martindale (b. 1623), for one, returned to school to prepare for university after a few weeks as an apprentice, his father seeing 'which way my mind still went'.[66]

Family breakdown could also push a youth into an apprenticeship, but this was not its usual prompt. High rates of adult mortality meant that

[65] R. Campbell, *The London Tradesman* (London: T. Gardner, 1747), 17.
[66] A. Martindale, 'Diary', in: J. J. Bagley (ed.), *Lancashire Diarists: Three Centuries of Lancashire Lives* (London: Phillimore, 1975).

teenagers frequently lost one or both parents. Apprenticeship offered one way to manage the impact of death on the household. In the small port of Rye, Mayhew found that formal apprenticeship was primarily a way to settle orphans and migrants into stable homes.[67] But apprenticeship was too extensive – and too expensive – to be primarily a mechanism for crisis resolution, and only a minority of children would be orphaned at the right age for apprenticeship to help. In London, Boston, Liverpool, Shrewsbury and Leicester around a quarter of apprentices had lost their father. These are roughly the levels we would expect from adult mortality rates. Only Boston mirrored Rye: 75% of local apprentices had deceased fathers, compared to 28% of migrants. Elsewhere, the difference was small.

Ideally, we would now look at who did *not* become apprentices. How many artisan families trained their sons at home, perhaps lining them up to take over their workshop? How strictly did families stick to the north-west European norm of transferring adolescents to another household? Direct evidence is hard to obtain. Those sons who were not indentured are, generally, almost invisible. One partial indicator is the share of guild members who entered by inheritance, or 'patrimony'. The small share of freemen who entered by patrimony, even among locals, suggests that most urban families did place their children into apprenticeships rather than relying on inherited rights. In Liverpool in the second half of the seventeenth century, only 11% became freemen by inheritance; in London 20–30% of freemen entered the clothworkers', merchant tailors' and apothecaries' guilds by inheritance. Unfortunately, these figures give a clearer indication of the openness of guilds and cities – ex-apprentices made up the vast majority of new freemen and citizens – than of the degree to which families trained their own.

The large scale of apprenticeship migration in England had one further effect: it overwhelmed any reliance on chains of family ties or regional clusters to guide relationships.[68] London, particularly, recruited in such large numbers that most apprentices had no direct connection with their master. The concentration of training with a minority of masters further limited the chance of joining someone known to the family. Masters were themselves likely to have migrated to London, but they usually came from a different place and county to their apprentices. Most apprentices' fathers – 80–90% – were in different trades or sectors, removing the possibility of occupational ties. No doubt apprentices exploited kin ties

---

[67] Thompson and Yeo (eds.), *The Unknown Mayhew*; see also Pelling, 'Apprenticeship', and Pelling, *Common Lot*.

[68] Leunig, Minns and Wallis, 'Networks'. Earlier evidence is surveyed in Pelling, *Common Lot*, 122.

where they existed, but most – 92% in London – joined masters with no obvious family link, judged by surname. Even in smaller cities, apprentices generally trained outside their families: apprentices and masters with different surnames account for 95% of apprentices in Liverpool, 97% in Leicester, 85% in Bristol, 83% in Boston, 95% in Lincoln, 87% in Gloucester and 79% in Shrewsbury.[69] Kin ties increased as apprentices increasingly came from the area. But they were never the norm.

Contracts made with masters outside families' immediate networks often relied on intermediaries to bridge the gap. To give one example, George Bewley travelled from Cumberland to bind himself to Edward Webb, a Dublin linen draper, after a travelling Quaker minister, Gershon Boat, 'proposed to my parents their sending me to Dublin, in which City he thought he could readily provide me a Place'. Boat was true to his word, and soon after his return Webb wrote to Bewley's parents asking for George to be sent over.[70]

Apprenticeship in England was a mechanism to shift out of the family trade, not reinforce it. It was a way to leave places, not stay in them. It was a solvent, in an already fluid society. We know that families took pains to identify good masters, and exploited connections to find opportunities, but the second or third degree ties they might have to masters via intermediaries such as Boat were weak, certainly too weak carry much weight in avoiding abuse or disputes. As Mark Granovetter argued, weak ties are primarily important for information.[71] These two fundamental aspects of English apprenticeship – the extent of migration and the scarcity of informal ties – are entangled with its institutional history and the approach to apprenticeship contracts that developed.

Institutions and the Experience of Service

How apprentices learned their crafts, and their experiences of life in new, often distant households, have left few traces. The one point when they do sometimes come to light is when an apprenticeship broke down. This process of breakdown – and the role of institutions in preventing or resolving disputes, and more generally in enforcing contracts – has attracted scrutiny in recent years, provoked by S. R. Epstein's hypothesis that apprenticeship contract enforcement provided a positive role and

---

[69] These counts include apprentices training with reported kin, such as fathers. Rates excluding reported kin are much lower.

[70] G. Bewley, *A Narrative of the Christian Experiences* (Dublin, 1750), 10–11.

[71] M. Granovetter, 'The strength of weak ties', *American Journal of Sociology* 78 (1973), 1360–80.

justification for guilds.[72] Apprenticeship operated with weakly specified contracts and time-inconsistent investments and payoffs. How might masters ensure that apprentices did not abscond once they were trained, or apprentices avoid being exploited as cheap labour by their masters? Did institutions intervene to help?

In England, at least, the question was ducked. Institutions made relatively few efforts to enforce apprenticeship contracts once the arrangement had been undermined. Enforcement was not impossible. The full force of the law was deployed against recalcitrant workers in the nineteenth century by magistrates and managers. They exploited the master–servant acts to prevent apprentices and other employees quitting.[73] In the sixteenth to eighteenth centuries, however, institutions favoured allowing exit over enforcement.

Doing so acknowledged the basic fluidity of early modern apprenticeship. The impermanence of apprenticeship contracts can be illustrated for London and Bristol in the 1690s, when listings of households allow us to observe the probability that apprentices were absent at different points in their terms.[74] Figure 9.3 shows how apprentices drifted in slowly, often months after the clock had started. After three or four years, many then left – having served periods similar to those set in contracts in France and the Southern Netherlands. Some apprentices left service entirely. Others simply moved to a different master; turnovers were recorded formally for around one in ten apprentices.[75] Those who stayed after the midpoint generally made it to the end. But once their terms were over, they would rapidly leave.

The spur for these premature departures varied. Apprentices might dislike the trade, squabble with their master or be called home to support their family. Some fell in love; others into crime. One apprentice pewterer, John Walmesley, told his master's maid that 'he would not stay ... for that he had no mind to a handicraft trade'.[76] Masters might force out apprentices if they discovered a fault – or simply wanted to avoid the cost of keeping them. Masters' responsibilities included the potentially heavy burden of caring for apprentices who fell sick.[77] Travelling or working in

[72] S. R. Epstein, 'Craft guilds, apprenticeship, and technological change in preindustrial Europe', *Journal of Economic History* 58 (1998), 684–713.

[73] D. Hay and P. Craven, *Masters, Servants, and Magistrates in Britain and the Empire, 1562–1955*, Studies in Legal History (Chapel Hill: University of North Carolina Press, 2004).

[74] C. Minns and P. Wallis, 'Rules and reality: Quantifying the practice of apprenticeship in pre-modern England', *Economic History Review* 65 (2012), 556–79. See also P. Wallis, 'Apprenticeship and training in premodern England', *Journal of Economic History* 68 (2008), 832–61

[75] Minns and Wallis, 'Rules and reality'. See also Barlow, *Gloucester*.

[76] CLRO, MC6/526A.   [77] Pelling, *Common Lot*, 124–28.

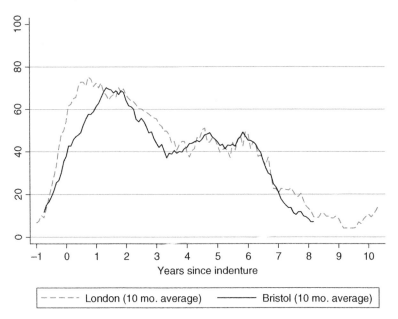

Figure 9.3 Proportion of London and Bristol apprentices resident with their master
Source: Minns and Wallis, 'Rules and reality'.

another household, even another country, to gain experience accounts for another group of apprentices, whose departures were temporary. An apprentice shipwright, Phineas Pett, spent time away assisting two other master shipwrights.[78] For merchants' apprentices, in particular, working as a factor abroad was often specified as part of the apprenticeship – a rare case of the content of training being detailed.

High rates of departure by apprentices – whether quits or transfers – affect the way in which training occurs under apprenticeship.[79] A high risk of apprentices leaving will make masters reluctant to invest much in training. Masters instead will ensure that youths work enough to cover much of their costs as they go; unskilled tasks (sweeping, carrying, watching) allowed this. Premiums offer a different solution, offsetting masters' investment. But we would still expect that instruction would have been

[78] I. K. Ben-Amos, 'Service and the coming of age of young men in seventeenth-century England', *Continuity and Change* 3 (1988), 41–64.
[79] Wallis, 'Apprenticeship and training'.

slower, with apprentices more often left to 'steal with their eyes', than in a situation in which contracts were better enforced.

Exit found its institutional apogee in the Lord Mayor's Court of London.[80] At the centre of England's market for apprenticeship, sitting in the Guildhall of the City of London, notionally headed by the Mayor himself, the Lord Mayor's Court offered a rapid, affordable and accessible way for youths to abandon their indentures and, later, to recover part of their premium. By the later seventeenth century, over one in ten London apprentices used the court. More apprentices were discharged there than existed in other English cities.

Its process was simple. The youth entered a complaint against their master under one of a range of categories (turning them out, insufficient food or training etc.), the master was summoned, and – when he failed to appear, as most did – the apprentice was released from their contract, and allowed to find a new master (without losing the time served) or depart entirely.

The court's formal process concealed a messier reality. The most common plea was that a master had failed to enrol their apprentice's contract with the City Chamberlain within a year. Against this breach of city law (and their freeman's oath), no defence existed. Subsequent lawsuits in which apprentices sought to recover their premiums contain much gorier tales of abuse, neglect and malfeasance on both sides:[81] masters who starved and beat their apprentices; apprentices who lied and stole.

The dry formality of a non-enrolment plea concealed all sins. It also presented a paradox. For a master's failure to fulfil a simple bureaucratic exercise left them with no way to defend any investment in their apprentice. We might reasonably suspect that both sides frequently understood this, and that the right to an easy exit was anticipated in negotiations over an apprenticeship. In effect, these apprenticeship contracts were deliberately unenforceable.

Outside London, no town appears to have operated a court with the same dedicated process as London. To be fair, none had the same concentration of apprentices. Nonetheless, strong echoes of the system appear elsewhere. Enrolment was patchy in most cities where this requirement occurred.[82] Exit was instead managed by magistrates. As

---

[80] P. Wallis, 'Labor, law and training in early modern London: Apprenticeship and the City's institutions', *Journal of British Studies* 51 (2012), 791–819.

[81] These records are discussed in detail in Pelling, 'Apprenticeship'; Griffiths, *Youth and Authority*; Wallis, 'Labor, law and training'.

[82] Barlow, *Gloucester*, xiv. Enrolment was required in Southampton from the fifteenth century, but essentially disappeared by the late seventeenth; it was frequently delayed: Merson and Willis, *Southampton*, xii–xiii, xv.

Blackstone recounted, 'Apprentices to trades may be discharged on rea-sonable cause, either at the request of themselves or masters, at the quarter sessions, or by one justice', followed by 'direct restitution of a rateable share of the money given with the apprentice'.[83] Discharges often concluded those disputes brought before Justices of the Peace; one West Country broad weaver described how 'A difference in opinion arose, and I went to a Magistrate and he released me.'[84] In Gloucester, by the later seventeenth century, youths were being recorded as discharged 'by order of the sessions'.[85] London's distinctive formal system reflected the sheer scale of apprenticeship in the city; it may also have provided an additional incentive for families to concentrate on the metropolis.

That apprenticeship might be ended cleanly and legally did not pre-clude other disciplinary processes.[86] Masters retained and exercised the right to physically punish apprentices – apprentices protested against *excessive* correction, not violence per se. As subordinates within house-holds, apprentices faced the same patriarchal authority as other servants, and children and wives. In London, the city launched repeated campaigns to improve the morality and deference of apprentices, who were enjoined to cut their hair, dress modestly, stay indoors at night and not hunt, play football or dance.[87] Guilds too might discipline apprentices, although examples only occur rarely. In London, the city's Chamberlain heard complaints from masters and regularly prescribed whipping or periods of hard labour in the city's gaols.

The possibility of exit heightened inequalities between apprentices. The Lord Mayor's Court might have been cheap, but it was of most use to those who possessed sufficient familial resources and capital to survive the sacri-fice of the time and money they had sunk into their first apprenticeship. Quitting early was costly; it could damage a youth's reputation.[88] The distribution of the early departures we observe in London and Bristol illustrates this.[89] Wealthy migrant apprentices were more likely to leave; migrant labourers' children were more likely to stay, as were youths with strong local connections. Apprentices who had better outside opportunities were more footloose than those with ties to the community. The price – and the opportunity cost – of exit was not equal for all. When the Essex clergy-man Ralph Josselin's son John quit his apprenticeship in London, it was a

[83] Blackstone, *Commentaries*, vol. 1, 414.   [84] Quoted in Rule, *Experience*, 98.

[85] Barlow, *Gloucester*, xx. See also Graham, *Oxford*, xxiii; Merson and Willis, *Southampton*, xx.

[86] Griffiths, *Youth and Authority*.

[87] LMA, Rep. 554, f. 267v. These efforts are well surveyed in Smith, 'London apprentices'.

[88] Evidence on the cost of an early exit is elegantly presented in Humphries, *Childhood and Child Labour*, 280–282.

[89] Minns and Wallis, 'Rules and reality'.

disappointment to his father, who noted 'sadness in my family, John returned' in his diary. But John could return to his family home, his subsistence assured.[90] One by-product of this was that masters demanded a higher premium from apprentices who were more likely to leave.[91] Inequality was institutionalised in other ways in the eighteenth century, as statute gave Justices of the Peace increasing powers of summary intervention into apprenticeships in which premiums were small or non-existent. Those who had spent substantial sums were only to be dealt with at the full Quarter Sessions.

Cities, magistrates and guilds had a much less clear role in the completion of an apprenticeship than they had in breaking contracts. No English guilds or cities are known to have monitored successful completions. There was no examination or certification waiting for apprentices. Those tests that did exist – fewer than half of London guilds required a 'masterpiece'– applied to individuals seeking guild membership.[92] These were not portable proofs of ability and success. They carried no weight elsewhere, unlike the *Lehrbrief* issued by some Dutch and German guilds.

The link between apprenticeship and the testing of skills was vaguer even than this suggests. First, it is unclear how universally guilds employed examinations of new members even when the rule existed. In London, particularly, freemen often worked – and trained apprentices – in trades that were not governed by their guild, rendering masterpieces moot. How, for instance, should the coopers test a woollen draper? Second, despite guild rules that pressed apprentices to become freemen promptly, many waited for years, working as journeymen without entering the guild. In practice, few guilds were attentive enough to ensure that all journeymen were members – and some explicitly delayed any test until journeymen wished to set up as masters.[93] As a result, most ex-apprentices would never take a mastership test.

Few apprentices would enter their masters' guild or become urban citizens. Rates varied, but in general only around 40% of apprentices became freemen. This was not because of guild barriers. Most imposed relatively low fees; in London, they were capped by law at 3s 4d.[94] Actual charges might be somewhat higher.[95] The most common loophole was for guilds to demand a 'gift', such as the silver spoon worth 13s 4d

[90] A. Macfarlane (ed.), *The Diary of Ralph Josselin, 1616–1683* (Oxford: Oxford University Press, 1976), 120, quoted in Pelling, *Common Lot*, 127.
[91] Minns and Wallis, 'Price of human capital'.   [92] 12 of 26 London guilds surveyed.
[93] The pewterers, framework knitters and clockmakers.
[94] 22 Hen VIII, c. 4. 28 Hen VIII, c. 5 banned additional fees for setting up shop etc.
[95] Company officials might also extort additional fees for services: in 1633, the beadle and porter of the drapers were forbidden to demand fees beyond those allowed by the ordinances for binding or making free. A. H. Johnson, *The History of the Worshipful*

demanded by the apothecaries and wheelwrights.[96] But even fee and spoon together was not a large sum, equating to perhaps ten days wages for an unskilled construction worker. Guild fees in Sheffield's cutlers and Lincoln's tailors were at a similar level. Unusually, moreover, apprentices in London usually paid less than masters' sons who had not been indentured in the guild.

For the remainder of apprentices, their only proof of service was a note from their master or the counterpart of their indentures to indicate that they had finished their term. It demonstrated their freedom from binding contractual obligations and right to work under the statute, not skill. Certification of apprentices' skills was an innovation that emerged as the state began investing in supplementary training for youths in the late nineteenth century.[97] With it, and not coincidentally, the state ensured that its subsidy (via funded technical training) paid off across the whole labour market.

Conclusion

Apprenticeship in early modern England provided the main form of training outside of farming. It was a massive, relatively open and accessible system that may at times have included a majority of youths who were not employed in agriculture, and was widespread in both town and countryside. Paradoxically, it was made more attractive by a national legal framework that had been intended to keep labour on the land, and it remained central to the creation of vocational human capital through to the first Industrial Revolution and beyond. It allowed youths to invest in their own productivity in a period where firms were small and few jobs lasted for long. Working to pay for learning lowered credit constraints and allowed youths to immerse themselves in gaining tacit occupational skills. By accepting high rates of premature exits, and establishing an institutional framework to cancel contracts that were proving unsatisfactory to either party, the English system lowered the risks involved in choosing a master, a city or a career and softened the burden of the exceptionally long

Company of the Drapers of London, 5 vols. (Oxford: Oxford University Press, 1914–22), vol. 3, 192, n.2.

[96] Wallis, 'Medicines'; J. B. Scott, *Short Account of the Worshipful Company of Wheelwrights*, revised ed. (London: Witherby & Co, 1961), 15. The needlemakers charged 10s: *The Worshipful Company of Needlemakers of the City of London* (London: Robson and sons, 1876), 31; the basketmakers' spoon was 10s: H. Bobart (ed.) *Records of the Basketmakers' Company* (London: Dunn, Collin & Co, 1911), 107.

[97] W. W. Knox, 'British apprenticeship, 1800–1914', PhD thesis, University of Edinburgh, 1980; C. More, *Skill and the English Working Class, 1870–1914* (London: Croom Helm, 1980).

terms of service that the Statute of Artificers had created. With few real barriers to entry set by either law or guild regulation, apprenticeship channelled labour from all backgrounds and all regions out of agriculture and into industry and services, and facilitated migration into cities, particularly London, which achieved an extraordinary dominance of urban training; it was a key vector in the extraordinary and precocious process of urbanisation and structural change in England that transformed the nation from an agrarian backwater to an industrial power.

10 Surviving the End of the Guilds: Apprenticeship in Eighteenth- and Nineteenth-Century France

Clare Haru Crowston and Claire Lemercier

Much of what historians know about apprenticeship in eighteenth-century France derives from guild records: statutes and notarised contracts drafted in accordance with those statutes.[1] Our understanding of the outcome of apprenticeship, similarly, derives from guild or police registers that record mastership receptions and the use of apprenticeship as a credential for entry. Reliance on these (abundant and accessible) sources gave rise to the view, still dominant among non-specialists, that guilds strictly controlled vocational training in urban areas and, as a corollary, entry to skilled labour markets. Reception records suggested in turn that guilds rigidly policed the training of would-be masters and thus that apprenticeship was merely the first step towards guild membership. Apprenticeship appeared to be inextricably bound to the corporate system and it has been studied almost exclusively within the horizon of guilds, specifically their regulations, their labour markets, and their reproduction.

In addition to shaping studies of the Ancien Régime, these documentary biases produced a vision of the nineteenth century cast in the shadow of the corporate system. Most historians have long considered, like contemporaries, that apprenticeship did not survive the abolition of the guilds in 1791. Few written contracts exist after 1791 and without the guilds' strict requirements, it has been assumed that apprenticeship withered in the face of the economic and social transformations that occurred in the early nineteenth century. For the nineteenth century, the only obvious sources referring to apprenticeship consist of discursive laments about its decline. Indeed, nostalgia for apprenticeship was expressed earlier and more widely than for any other element of the corporate system. The few

[1] Research for this chapter was funded by an American Council of Learned Societies Collaborative Research Fellowship and Sciences Po ('SAB Learning How'). Information from the sources was entered by the authors, Nicolas Berthelot, Sylvain Brunier, Élodie Charié, Katherine Godwin, Michael Green, and François Lambert.

memoirs of nineteenth-century French workers that mention apprenticeship thus modelled their accounts on Ancien Régime templates.[2]

In contrast, our own research – as well as recent work on other European cities and states – demonstrates how complex the practice of 'apprenticeship' was in the eighteenth century and how nuanced its relationship to the guild system was. This complexity cuts in two directions. First, guild control over apprenticeship, and over the labour market and production in general, while loudly declaimed was in practice challenged in myriad ways across different trades, locales, and forms of employment. Many forms of training existed outside of and across corporate boundaries, particularly for female youths. And yet, even the most apparently informal type of vocational training often existed in a symbiotic relationship with the guild system.

Second, most apprentices who trained within the corporate system – that is with a guild master under the terms of a notarised contract – did not themselves become masters. Apprenticeship as normatively defined and controlled by the guilds thus rarely achieved its ostensible purpose (producing future masters). Guilds themselves relied on multiple forms of reproduction.

For the nineteenth century, even a cursory look at sources closer to actual practices of vocational training shows that apprenticeship had not disappeared, in spite of the collapse of guild regulations. Population censuses reveal that apprenticeship survived as a term frequently used to describe the position of working teenagers. Moreover, other forms of documentation reveal that many of these apprentices entered contracts that retained features of Ancien Régime apprenticeship, such as limited terms of service or the exchange of training, and often lodging, on the master's part for the labour of the apprentice. For example, in Paris, an exhaustive inquiry by the Chamber of Commerce in 1848–51 found approximately 19,000 apprentices, that is 1 for every 17 workers, and probably one for every four teenagers; 6,000 were apprenticed for four years or more, almost 11,000 lived with their masters, and almost 13,000 were not paid.[3]

---

[2] On nostalgia, É. Anheim, 'The history and historiography of guild hierarchies in the Middle Ages', *Annales: Histoire, Sciences Sociales* 68 (2013), 1027–38; C. H. Crowston, 'Du corps des couturières à l'Union de l'Aiguille: Les continuités imaginaires d'un corporatisme au féminin, 1675–1895', in: S. L. Kaplan and P. Minard (eds.), *La France, malade du corporatisme? XVIIIᵉ–XXᵉ siècles* (Paris: Belin, 2004), 197–232. On memoirs, Y. Lequin, 'Apprenticeship in nineteenth-century France: A continuing tradition or a break with the past?', in: S .L. Kaplan and C. J. Koepp (eds.), *Work in France: Representations, Meaning, Organization, and Practice* (Ithaca, NY: Cornell University Press, 1986), 457–74.

[3] *Statistique de l'industrie à Paris résultant de l'enquête faite par la Chambre de Commerce pour les années 1847–1848* (Paris: Guillaumin, 1851). The share of teenagers is our estimate. On the limitations and possible uses of this source, see C. H. Crowston, S. L. Kaplan and

After 1791 apprenticeship offered no specific claim on becoming a master, and, until the twentieth century, no formal credential. Yet many parents, masters, and mistresses still entered into apprenticeship contracts, even if the majority were not written. Why would they do so? Any answer must take into account the normative weight of guild apprenticeship as a template, which certainly survived the abolition of the guilds. It must also, however, acknowledge that the variety of ways in which this template was applied were not an invention of the (liberal or industrialising) nineteenth century, but a continuation of what were already diverse practices under the Ancien Régime.

In this chapter, we first summarise official regulations defining apprenticeship before and after the French Revolution, with a focus on contracts and the related laws. We then describe the diverse types of 'learning and working' that, in the eighteenth and nineteenth century, existed beyond contractually enshrined apprenticeship. Both before and after 1791, most teenagers were not apprentices; apprenticeship was neither the only way to learn a trade, nor a necessary condition to create a business. Yet guild apprenticeship was a crucial template that, at its most basic, provided a model for youths to learn a set of technical skills while simultaneously being socialised and mentored, over a set number of years, in a context infused with paternal (or maternal) connotations.

Finally, we show that, just as many 'apprenticeships' were not standard guild apprenticeships, many guild apprenticeships did not lead to the normative outcome of several years working as a journeyman followed by entry to the guild. Observing the diversity of outcomes of apprenticeship helps us gain a more nuanced understanding of the motivations of the parties involved, especially the parents, in initiating an apprenticeship. It questions the almost exclusive emphasis that has been placed, in the wake of general debates on the economic effects of guilds, on apprenticeship's importance to the transmission of technical skills or social reproduction.[4]

C. Lemercier, 'Les apprentissages parisiens aux XVIIIe et XIXe siècles', *Annales HSS*, 73 (2018).

[4] In trying not to automatically equate apprenticeship with traditional transmission of skills and child labour with modern exploitation, we follow E. van Nederveen Meerkerk and A. Schmidt, 'Between wage labour and vocation: Child labour in Dutch urban industry, 1600–1800', *Journal of Social History* 41 (2008), 717–36. On the economic effect of guilds, see S. R. Epstein, 'Craft guilds in the premodern economy: A discussion', *Economic History Review* 61 (2008), 155–74; S. Ogilvie, 'Rehabilitating the guilds: A reply', *Economic History Review* 61 (2008), 175–82. Similarly, the few historical papers on post-guild apprenticeship mostly frame it against the alleged deskilling caused by the 'industrial revolution', e.g. W. Knox, 'Apprenticeship and de-skilling in Britain, 1850–1914', *International Review of Social History* 31 (1986), 166–84; K. D. M. Snell, 'The

Apprenticeship and the End of the Guilds: An Unlikely Survival

As corporate bodies, Ancien Régime guilds possessed monopoly privileges over well-defined economic sectors with the right to control the entry of new members and the duty to police quality standards and satisfy regular and extraordinary royal fiscal demands. Royal edicts of 1581, 1597, and 1673 required artisans and merchants in all cities where guilds existed to form themselves into corporations and submit statutes for royal approval. In Paris in 1600, there were approximately 85 guilds, which rose to over 110 corporations by the early eighteenth century, in part because of the 1673 edict vigorously promoted by Controller General Jean-Baptiste Colbert. In the 1720s, a contemporary estimate put the number at 32,000 guild masters in a population of approximately 500,000.[5] Between April 1755 and December 1775, as the register of the royal procurator of the Châtelet of Paris, who held jurisdiction over the guilds, shows, almost 28,000 men and women became guild members.[6] Other cities and towns had much smaller corporate systems. In Caen, 69 new masters and mistresses entered a total of 25 different guilds in 1720, and 113 entered 28 guilds in 1748.[7]

Monitoring apprenticeship was a crucial task for guild officers, given the importance of protecting their trade monopolies, policing the labour market, and ensuring the orderly reproduction of the corporation. As a rule, guild statutes required new masters (other than sons of masters and sometimes their sons-in-law and the husbands of masters' widows) to fulfil a set period of apprenticeship, varying from three to eight years. A 1691 royal edict stated that apprenticeships must occur within the framework of a notarised contract underwritten by guild officials. Guilds generally prohibited masters from taking more than one apprentice at a time; they also forbade masters from hiring journeymen who had not completed a formal apprenticeship. In 1755, another royal edict overturned the long-standing corporate practice of forbidding apprentices from becoming masters anywhere but in the city where they had trained. Only the cities of Paris, Rouen, Lyon, and Lille were permitted to

---

apprenticeship system in British history: The fragmentation of a cultural institution', *History of Education* 25 (1996), 303–21.

[5] This figure is based on membership numbers furnished in the 1720s to Jacques Savary des Bruslons by the Parisian guilds; see D. Roche, *The People of Paris: An Essay in Popular Culture in the 18th Century* (Berkeley: University of California Press, 1987), 71. On the organisation of guilds, S. L. Kaplan, *La fin des corporations* (Paris: Fayard, 2001).

[6] Archives nationales de France (henceforth AN) Y 9329–32.

[7] Archives départementales du Calvados 1B2034 and 1B2046.

continue this discriminatory practice; all other guilds had to accept the training credentials of other municipalities.[8]

The relative accessibility of notaries, even for families of modest means, and the legal requirement to use them resulted in the survival of copious apprenticeship contracts in the notarial archives of early modern France. These contracts are both highly routinised, containing a relatively standard set of mutual promises and obligations, as well as enormously variable in the details of age, length, cost, etc. They provide an opportunity to investigate simultaneously what people believed and valued about apprenticeship and how they practised it.

A few key elements of apprenticeship – as enshrined in standardised phrases approved by guilds, sanctioned by the state, and reproduced in notarial manuals and pre-printed contracts – are worth underlining. At the heart of the relationship was the domestic and patriarchal authority exercised by masters, which included the prerogative to use corporal punishment for infractions.

A corollary of this authority was that masters were to act as father figures, treating youths humanely with the conduct appropriate to a paternal relationship, imparting vocational skills, inculcating social control, and extracting obedience. Families entrusted masters with the task of transforming their adolescent children into adults capable of supporting themselves financially and reproducing the social order. Numerous police regulations called on apprentices – like domestic servants – to show deference and obedience.[9] As these observations suggest, mastership was explicitly assumed to be a male role; the unquestioned authority of female guild mistresses over their apprentices in the small number of all-female and mixed guilds underlines the way that corporate privilege could trump gender difference under the Ancien Régime.

Framed by these basic principles, the negotiations between the various parties involved in the contract – parents, youths, masters, guild officials, and municipal and royal authorities – produced tremendous variety. Exhaustive indexes of Parisian notarial archives for 1751 and 1761 show that between 1,800 and 2,100 apprenticeship contracts were signed

---

[8] Arrest du Conseil d'Etat du Roi, 25 March 1755.

[9] The domestic authority of the masters was in keeping with the overall familial structure of guilds, in which sons of masters inherited guild status and journeymen who married masters' widows and daughters often had easier access as well. Another indication of the patriarchal and domestic conception of the masters' authority is the fact that widows of masters could inherit their husband's business, as a form of marital property, but, in France, could not take on new apprentices. Janine Lanza's study of artisanal widows suggests the difficulties women faced in exercising authority over workshops dominated by male journeymen: J. Lanza, *From Wives to Widows in Early Modern Paris: Gender, Economy, and Law* (Aldershot: Ashgate, 2007).

in the city each year. One hundred years earlier, in 1650, there had been fewer than 900 contracts. The vast majority of these apprentices were boys, but a significant minority (approximately 15%) were girls, mostly seamstresses.

A sample of close to 700 contracts from 1761, representing 70 trades, reveals that apprentices were on average 17 years old; however, the youngest were only 12 years old and the oldest in their mid-thirties (standard deviation = 4). The shortest contracts were for three years and the longest for eight, with an average of four years (median = 4). The vast majority of apprentices (over 95%) originated from Paris or the surrounding region, but most lodged with their masters and received food and sometimes clothing. Fully 69% (561 of those with available information) did not pay for apprenticeship; those who did paid a wide range of fees, from 24 to 1,200 livres. The only apprentices paid for their work were roofers, who tended to be much older, given the need for strength and the danger involved.

Apprenticeship contracts were crucial for many reasons: they made explicit the expectation of effective training, humane treatment, and good faith from all parties. They stipulated exactly what the apprentice and his or her family would provide and what they could expect from the master (sometimes down to the precise amount of bread each day). They also served as vital credentials for finished apprentices who wished to enter the skilled labour market and perhaps one day the guild. Once signed by the notary and the guild officials, the master kept the original copy of the contract, the *brevet d'apprentissage*. The moment when he (or she) handed it to the apprentice at the end of the contract was a rite of passage allowing the youth freedom to seek employment as a journeyman or journeywoman.

The importance of guild apprenticeship as a means of social reproduction is underlined by the efforts of charitable institutions to secure apprenticeships for artisans' children whose families were unable to do so. This was particularly common among Parisian parish foundations, who often used charitable endowments to place children with guild masters. For example, the foundation of Saint-Jean-en-Grève parish paid for the apprenticeship of at least 50 youths from 1711 to 1717, divided evenly between boys and girls. The 25 boys entered 14 different trades, from humble cobblers to high-status textile-merchant-manufacturers. Six trained with cobblers and five with shoemakers. Richer trades, including gilders and cloth-makers, received only one or two boys each. Of the 25 girls, 24 were apprenticed to a seamstress; the remaining girl to a linen-worker (another legally constituted female trade).[10]

[10] AN LL 801.

In the second half of the eighteenth century, the parish greatly widened the scope of trades in which girls were indentured, including occupations – such as tapestry-making and embroidery – dominated by male guilds in which female labour was prohibited. These contracts resembled the others in all particulars, except that they tacitly destined the girls for a future of illegal labour. As this demonstrates, the line between normative 'guild apprenticeship' and the types of alternative training discussed below could be imperceptible to contemporary parish elites, masters, and working families.

When the National Assembly abolished guilds in 1791, the fate of apprenticeship was unclear. The law was passed in the context of political attacks on all sorts of associations (trade unions and business associations remained forbidden until 1884). It opened a long period of free entry to almost all occupations and to establishing an independent business. With a few exceptions, such as bakers and butchers in Paris, and goldsmiths across France, the revolutionary government prohibited trades from establishing a *numerus clausus* or any other barrier to entry. Few occupations demanded formal credentials, and the only official requirement for opening a business was the payment of a modest tax (the *patente*). While many attempts were made to re-establish guilds to provide collective representation, training, and socialisation, almost no one seriously considered re-imposing legal barriers to entry.[11]

Despite lamentations over the loss of apprenticeship, the practice of using formal apprenticeship contracts did survive the guilds. For example, in Lyon around 200 notarised contracts were made in 1807. In Laval (Mayenne), a town with 15,000 inhabitants, more contracts were made in 1807 (60) than in 1780 (32).[12] In mid-century Paris, the Chamber of Commerce counted 4,000 written contracts. While on average somewhat shorter than the eighteenth-century norm (around three years), 82 of the 19,000 written or verbal contracts were for 6–9 years. They also began earlier, typically when girls and boys were 13 years old. As in the eighteenth century, most did not involve fees to the master, but a small portion (n = 242) did. In 1848, the Paris labour court for the cloth industries approved the custom of the cloth design firm Laroche to have apprentices create a costly masterwork that was then left to the firm.[13]

---

[11] Kaplan and Minard (eds.), *La France*; M. P. Fitzsimmons, *From Artisan to Worker: Guilds, the French State, and the Organization of Labor, 1776–1821* (Cambridge: Cambridge University Press, 2010).

[12] Archives départementales du Rhône, 3Q/14/18*–19*, 3Q17/26*–28*, 3Q20/12*–13*. Archives départementales de Mayenne, 2C/1628*–30*, 153Q/24*–25*. We thank Gilles Postel-Vinay for sharing pictures of these sources.

[13] *Statistique . . . 1848*; Archives départementales de Paris (henceforth ADP), D1U10/379, 24 November 1848.

These documents prove that apprenticeships, and even notarised contracts, did not completely disappear after 1791. Indeed, the law on industry of 22 germinal an XI (1803) recognised the existence of specific apprenticeship contracts in one of the seven articles on workers that it added to the general law of contracts. Apprentices were thus considered similar to workers, but not identical, because the 1803 law explicitly prohibited contracts lasting more than one year for workers, except for foremen. Workers were essentially subcontractors (or sub-subsubcontractors): the person who hired them supplied the raw materials, but workers frequently used their own tools, and were free to summon auxiliaries as long as they were able to pay them. This was quintessentially true in the context of urban luxury and fashion industries and rural protoindustrial workshops, but also very frequent in the first factories. Sharp divides existed between skilled workers, day labourers, and servants (who possessed only limited citizenship rights).[14]

In this context, it is surprising to find apprenticeship contracts and one might wonder why they survived. The 1803 law only mentioned apprenticeship contracts to state that they could legitimately be broken if a party did not act as promised, if the master abused the apprentice, in the case of misconduct of the apprentice, or if the duration was in excess of 'the ordinary price of apprenticeships'. (All good reasons for breaking contracts in the Ancien Régime courts.) The very fact that nothing was said about the contents of the mutual promises of the parties implied that everybody knew what a contract of apprenticeship was and what type of exchange it entailed. There was no requirement for the contract to be drawn up by a notary, suggesting contractual norms were considered to be disseminated widely enough to eliminate the need for notarial expertise. Through the numerous cases brought before magistrates and labour courts (special courts whose judges were elected skilled workers and heads of workshops), lawyers over time compiled a jurisprudence that complemented this very short law.

This jurisprudence was codified by the law of 22 February 1851, a law specifically devoted to apprenticeship that remained in force with few changes until 1928. The law of 1851 was one of the first in France that limited the discretion of parties in a contract in order to protect the weaker side, albeit in a limited way. The law did not require contracts to be written; there was no limitation on the number of apprentices per master and no exam to test the quality of masters or apprentices. Much of the law

---

[14] A. Cottereau, 'Sens du juste et usages du droit du travail: Une évolution contrastée entre la France et la Grande-Bretagne au XIXe siècle', *Revue d'histoire du XIXe siècle* 33 (2006), 101–20; P. Lefebvre, 'Subordination et "révolutions" du travail et du droit du travail (1776–2010)', *Entreprises et histoire* 57 (2009), 45–78.

consisted of rather vague statements describing an ideal apprenticeship, for example: 'The master must act toward the apprentice as a good father should, watch his conduct and mores, inside and outside the house' (*Le maître doit se conduire envers l'apprenti en bon père de famille, surveiller sa conduite et ses moeurs, soit dans la maison, soit au dehors*). Numerous lawyers and charitable societies later printed model contracts inspired by such stipulations.[15] This law can be read both as the symptom of the survival of an Ancien Régime template and of its adaptation to new situations.

The fact that written contracts were not compulsory made apprenticeship invisible to some contemporaries. When asked about practices in their departments in the late 1870s and early 1880s, many prefects answered that there were no apprenticeships, because there were no contracts. Some added that children certainly learned with their parents. Yet where prefects bothered to look for apprentices, rather than notarised contracts, they found them, and in surprisingly diverse places (often just one or two apprentices per village). For example, 170 contracts, 124 of them verbal, were counted in 1880 in rural Allier. In 1883, in Ille-et-Vilaine, officials reported 1,131 apprentices, scattered across 57 trades, with one significant concentration of 337 slipper-makers (*chaussonniers*).[16]

These cases demonstrate that even though few apprenticeship contracts existed in writing, and apprenticeship offered no formal credential let alone the right to the status of master, large numbers of teenagers were still 'apprentices'. Moreover, their contracts were enforceable. In Paris, around 2,000 cases per year were brought before the labour courts in the late 1850s (for c. 20,000 apprentices); in Lyon, the rate was even higher (it was much lower in most towns). Labour courts, at least in the capital and some other big cities, were an important force in shaping legal and social norms about apprenticeship. And they, like the 1851 law, tended to favour a traditional model: apprenticeship in small workshops, but not so small that the master would not have enough work or expertise; personal teaching by the person who signed the contract; lenient penalties; parent-

---

[15] On laws and jurisprudence, see O. Tholozan, 'Le débat parlementaire de 1851 sur le contrat d'apprentissage ou la liberté contractante acclimatée', *Cahiers de l'IRT* 9 (2001), 207–22; L. Montazel, 'La résolution judiciaire des conflits en matière de contrat d'apprentissage aux XIXe et XXe siècles', in: S. Dauchy, B. Dubois, F. Lekéal and V. Demars-Sion (eds.), *Histoire, justice et travail* (Lille: Centre d'histoire judiciaire, 2005), 277–98; and for a synthesis C. Lemercier, 'Apprentissage', in: A. Stanziani (ed.), *Dictionnaire historique de l'économie-droit, XVIIIe–XXe siècles* (Paris: LGDJ, 2007), 23–34. For examples of lawyers compiling jurisprudence and in effect modelling legal and social norms, Léopold, *Manuel des prud'hommes* (Paris: Patris et cie, Blanchard et cie, 1811); F.-É. Mollot, *Le contrat d'apprentissage expliqué aux maîtres et aux apprentis* (Paris: L. Colas, 1847).

[16] AN F12/4831–33. Specifically in F12/4831: Préfecture de l'Allier, 6 May 1881. In F12/4832: Préfecture d'Ille-et-Vilaine, 22 March 1884.

like moral supervision; not too many domestic duties for the apprentice; and respect for the master. They especially emphasised the need for the apprentice to stay with the master until the end of the contract, by imposing much heavier fines on those who left than eighteenth-century courts had.

Apprenticeships Beyond Guilds: Diversity of Forms of Training, Female Labour, and the Saliency of the Template

If we take as our starting point not the contract, but the acquisition of occupational skill, it becomes clear that a much wider set of possibilities already existed in the Ancien Régime than the apprentice clutching his *brevet d'apprentissage*, signed by notary and guild officials. Across France, many trades were not organised into approved guilds, despite royal edicts. Even in trades for which guilds existed, many skilled artisans worked in rural areas, in privileged manufactures, or in urban enclaves free from guild control, such as the notorious faubourg Saint-Antoine in Paris. Moreover, sworn masters themselves often ignored the rules, by hiring workers without guild-certified training, keeping more than one apprentice, or subcontracting to non-guild workers. Women's labour, most often overlooked by historians whose vision of work remains constrained by guild-generated documentation, constituted a significant portion of the work performed both within the guilds and in the economically vital grey or black-market labour force.[17]

Given the complex ties binding guild masters to multiple varieties of 'illegal' and 'free' labour, it is impossible to draw clear lines between corporate and non-corporate work or to quantify precisely the portion of production and exchange that took place outside the guilds. For the city of Bordeaux, to give one example, a 1762 inquiry revealed that 1,600 masters worked in 40 'sworn trades' (that is guilds that possessed royal letters patent) and roughly 250 in 10 'regulated trades' (corporations recognised by the municipality), leaving the majority,

---

[17] See S. L. Kaplan, 'Réflexions sur la police du monde du travail, 1700–1815', *Revue historique* 261 (1979), 17–77; S. L. Kaplan, 'The character and implications of strife among masters inside the guilds of eighteenth-century Paris', *Journal of Social History* 19 (1986), 631–48; S. L. Kaplan, 'La lutte pour le contrôle du marché du travail à Paris au XVIIIe siècle', *Revue d'histoire moderne et contemporaine* 36 (1989), 361–412; M. Sonenscher, *Work and Wages: Natural Law, Politics and the Eighteenth-Century French Trades* (Cambridge: Cambridge University Press, 1989). More recently, see J. Horn, *Economic Development in Early Modern France: The Privilege of Liberty, 1650–1820* (Cambridge: Cambridge University Press, 2015).

around 2,150, working in 38 'free trades'; illegal workers were not counted.[18] The line between 'incorporated' and 'free' work was blurry; gradations of corporate status existed and workers in even ostensibly 'free' trades sometimes organised into informal associations that were recognised and taxed by the municipality. In the north, and in Paris in particular, corporate organisation was more pervasive. Nevertheless, given the size and importance of the faubourg Saint-Antoine, the city's handful of other free areas, and the importance of illicit labour, the majority of production and exchange in Paris probably took place outside of guild control.

This variability in the forms of labour organisation extended to the multiple varieties of 'apprenticeship' that can be traced in notarial archives and the records of orphanages, charitable schools, and other institutions. Alternative forms of vocational training existed across a broad spectrum. Some were conducted completely outside the guild system, others operated in intense competition with guilds, while still others assumed guild support and assistance for the project of enlarging the circle of skilled and self-sufficient artisans. They all, however, implicitly or explicitly took guild-based apprenticeship as the normative form of trade training, a standard to emulate or a tradition to be rejected. Perversely, the high-quality training associated with 'apprenticeship' in its most formal, corporate manifestation, inspired many non-credentialing, brief, and informal modes of training to seek legitimation by describing the children involved as 'apprentices'.

A first category of 'apprenticeship' absent from the notarial contracts described above consisted of informal training by masters of their own sons, and quite possibly their nephews, cousins, and other family members (with the important caveat that only their sons would be qualified to join the guild). As a rule, guilds exempted masters' sons (and mistresses' daughters in female and mixed-sex guilds) from formal apprenticeship, on the assumption that they would learn from their parent. Jacques-Louis Ménétra, a master glazier's son, briefly learned from his father but then transferred to his uncle's workshop to escape paternal violence. He ended as a guild master, but one bitterly opposed to corporate officialdom. Between 1766 and 1775, 26% of new masters and mistresses in Parisian

---

[18] B. Gallinato, *Les corporations à Bordeaux à la fin de l'Ancien régime* (Bordeaux: Presses universitaires de Bordeaux, 1992), 286. There was no clear rationale for the designation of trades among these categories: butchers, bakers, saddlers, and weavers were 'regulated' trades, and clockmakers, second-hand clothes dealers and barrel-makers were 'free'. In Paris, and many other cities, all these trades belonged to guilds.

guilds were the sons or daughters of guild members (approximately 3,500 individuals, mostly male).[19]

Sharply opposed to these informal training processes in terms of institutional significance was *allouage*, a distinctively French form of training. The *allouage* contract was a notarised document governing vocational training. In practice, these contracts closely resembled apprenticeship: training in the home of the master and requirements for humane treatment and effective education on the one hand, and obedience and hard work on the other, accompanied by a fee from parents to master that varied from very little (often nothing) to quite substantial sums. The decisive difference was that the *allouage* contract provided no formal credential upon completion. A finished *alloué* gained practical skill and possibly social connections, but no claim to guild membership. Not surprisingly, these contracts represent a small minority of training contracts in notarial archives. Our sample from 1761 consists of 677 apprenticeship contracts and 43 *allouage* contracts. Many of the contracts reveal the close conceptual overlap between 'real' apprenticeship and *allouage*, with a number stating that the youth was entering 'apprenticeship in the quality of an *alloué*'.[20]

For masters, *allouage* presented the obvious advantage of allowing them to exceed the guild quotas of one apprentice each. The real question is why parents would go to the expense and trouble of obtaining a notarised contract that denied the possibility of mastership. We can imagine that many of the same motivations that made notarised apprenticeship contracts attractive applied to *allouage*, in particular, obtaining explicit promises, and the possibility of legal recourse for default. We must also conclude that for these parents, the prospect of guild membership seemed if not unimportant, at least unrealistic. It seems safe to assume that these formal contracts represent the tip of a much larger iceberg of informal training arrangements, the vital necessity of obtaining skills outweighing the distant dream of becoming a guild master.

From the sixteenth century onwards, a number of charitable institutions took up the cause of helping poor children acquire craft skills. Parish foundations provided funds and social connections to place children in apprenticeships with Parisian masters. The hôpital de la Trinité instead provided in-house apprenticeships, without a formal contract, to a select group of children who had lost at least one parent (usually the children of guild masters). Hospital administrators recruited journeymen (not

[19] AN Y 9329, Y 9330, Y 9331, and Y 9332; J.-L. Ménétra, *Journal of My Life*, edited by D. Roche (New York: Columbia University Press, 1989).
[20] On *allouage*, S. L. Kaplan, 'L'apprentissage au XVIIIe siècle: le cas de Paris', *Revue d'histoire moderne et contemporaine* 40 (1993), 436–79.

masters) to teach the children a trade; after six years of supplying training the journeyman was entitled to claim membership in his guild. Such journeymen represented 3% of new masters between 1766 and 1775. Finished Trinité apprentices enjoyed the same status as those emanating from the guilds. Gaining access to these parallel systems of training was usually a sign of insider status, a reward for good conduct or faithful service among the established poor, a recognition of social ties in the form of friendship, neighbourhood, and kin, rather than simply a form of oppression or coercion of the destitute.[21]

Girls constituted a major preoccupation of alternative training programmes, given the limited opportunities for girls in guild-controlled apprenticeship. To be sure, roughly 400 girls began apprenticeship with a mistress seamstress each year in the eighteenth century. This was a major outlet for girls to learn transferrable skills in needlework. However, it was far from enough to satisfy demand. Most girls could expect to work in waged labour for 8–10 years, starting around age 16 in order to accrue a small dowry for marriage at age 25 or 26. In the late seventeenth century, several female lay communities formed with the mission of continuing poor girls' education once they had passed the age of schooling in charity schools. In Paris, communities devoted to female vocational training included the Soeurs de la Communauté de Sainte-Geneviève, the Filles de l'Instruction chrétienne, the Filles de Saint-Joseph, the Filles de Sainte-Agnès, and the Filles de Sainte-Anne.

The most important was the Filles de Sainte-Agnès, established in 1678 with four members and 40 or 50 students. The original sisters were a tapestry-maker, two linen-drapers, and a seamstress. By 1729, the community numbered 45 sisters, 40 adult boarders, 35 child boarders, and almost 450 'poor children and external students for instruction and work'. The school was divided into seven classes: two for religious education and five for vocational instruction, with one for linen work, one for embroidery, another for lacemaking, and two for tapestry-making. The community possessed all the equipment and tools necessary, including looms for tapestry-weaving. With a number of sisters devoting their time to administration, cooking, and housekeeping, there would have been less than one mistress for every ten students.

In the mid-eighteenth century, the Filles de Sainte-Agnès earned approximately 2,000 livres per year from the tapestry, lace, linen, and embroidery workshops, which the sisters declared was barely enough to

---

[21] On hôpital de la Trinité and alternative apprenticeship in general, see C. H. Crowston, 'L'apprentissage hors des corporations: Les formations professionnelles alternatives à Paris sous l'Ancien regime', *Annales: Histoire, Sciences Sociales* 60 (2005), 409–41.

cover expenses. As they stated in explaining the low revenue, 'these trades can only be learned by practice and not by theory[,] we thus cannot dispense with undertaking this work to be able to instruct them and form their hands'. Training pupils in large, institutional workshops was far from the guild model, yet the sisters called their charges 'apprentices' and believed their task was – like a guild master – to guide apprentices through hands-on training from initiation to mastery of a trade.[22]

A similar range of forms of training existed in the nineteenth century. Our ambition here is to give an idea of the diversity of situations, not just that of Laroche's pupils producing masterpieces as opposed to flower-makers starved and overworked by the Anfriens (a couple whose work-shop only employed apprentices),[23] but those of teenagers who learned by working generally. This diversity is organised around the same axes as in the eighteenth century: most of the variants that we have listed above had nineteenth-century equivalents.

The most obvious change was the explicit extension of 'apprenticeship' to girls – who had been present, but were in many ways marginalised in guild apprenticeship. The Paris Chamber of Commerce statistics for 1848–51 ostensibly do not provide aggregate numbers of male and female apprentices, but it is possible to establish that one-third were girls. Population censuses allow us to map the occupation of teenagers in other places in the same period (see Table 10.1). Some girls were expli-citly described as apprentices, even in middle-sized towns where appren-ticeship was still mostly male. In Lyon, heavily dominated by the silk industry, female apprentices held a clear majority over males (as did female teenagers, probably due to differences in migration).

The apprenticeship of girls was mostly confined to specific trades, as in the eighteenth century. Female apprentices generally served mistresses, who employed few boys. In Paris in 1860, female apprentices were even more restricted, in terms of trades, than were adult female workers. The ten main trades for each sex employed 44% of adult female workers, but just 32% of adult male workers. While only 42% of male apprentices were engaged in the ten main trades, 78% of girls were concentrated in the top ten. Seamstresses alone trained 22% of female apprentices, while they employed less than 4% of female adult workers.[24]

---

[22] AN S 7047. See C. H. Crowston, 'An industrious revolution in late seventeenth-century Paris', in: M. J. Maynes, B. Søland and C. Benninghaus (eds.), *Secret Gardens, Satanic Mills: Placing Girls in European History, 1750–1960* (Bloomington: Indiana University Press, 2005), 69–82.

[23] ADP, D1U10/385, 23 October 1857. They were condemned by the labour court after complaints by several families.

[24] *Statistique de l'industrie à Paris résultant de l'enquête faite par la Chambre de commerce pour l'année 1860* (Paris: Chambre de commerce, 1864).

Table 10.1 *Occupations of persons aged 13–18 in mid-nineteenth-century French censuses*

Among girls

Place	Apprentices (%)	Young workers (%)	Agriculture (%)	Servants (%)	At school (%)	No occupation (%)	Total N observed
Lyon	20	43	0	9	1	27	759
Caen	1	35	0	11	0	40	618
Dijon	4	25	0	15	0	54	210
Poitiers	7	28	0	21	0	45	1407
Château-Larcher	3	16	32	27	0	22	37
Lusignan	1	14	4	25	0	52	138

Among boys

Place	Apprentices (%)	Young workers (%)	Agriculture (%)	Servants (%)	At school (%)	No occupation (%)	Total N observed
Lyon	15	43	0	1	13	28	565
Caen	5	46	0	7	1	46	684
Dijon	16	24	0	4	4	50	180
Poitiers	15	31	0	11	3	38	1369
Château-Larcher	4	21	46	19	0	10	52
Lusignan	15	14	19	22	0	26	144

Note: For Lyon (Rhône): (total population 177,000), random sample of 50 streets (roughly one-tenth). For Caen (Calvados): (total population 45,000), random sample of 40 streets (roughly one-third). For Dijon (Côte-d'Or): (total population 32,000), random sample of 40 streets (roughly one-third). For Poitiers (Vienne) (total population 29,000), Lusignan (Vienne) (total population 2,500), and Château-Larcher (Vienne) (total population 840), exhaustive studies. Young workers includes youths assigned to specific occupations (artisanal, industrial, shop assistants, etc.). No occupations comprise mostly youths described as son or daughter, and also includes rare 'others' (e.g. day labourers). *Source:* Nominative 1851 census records, except for Caen (1856); photographs of this source are available on the respective departmental archives website.

While the destruction of the guilds (almost all exclusively male) meant that female apprenticeship could be openly discussed and applied in a wider range of occupations than before, gender differences remained. It is likely that new uses of apprenticeship, related to the increased division of labour in urban fashion and luxury trades, disproportionately affected girls. Contemporaries often decried such uses as abuses of the institution. In other words, it is perhaps telling that Laroche apprenticed boys whereas the Anfriens employed girls. The urban *fabriques* in Lyon and Paris are famous for the technical innovations collectively produced by their mobile, skilled workers/entrepreneurs, which allowed them to resist competition from factories for decades.[25] In the nineteenth century, they were also unanimously praised, for example in reports on world expositions, for the taste of even the most modest female worker. Yet the same reports also demonstrated that a very minute division of labour had been the key to the increase in production and in flexibility (allowing rapid changes in fashion) after the end of the guilds. This division of labour implied that some workers, and some apprentices, only wound bobbins of silk, or rolled paper around wire to make the stem of artificial flowers.[26]

Urban *fabriques* did not only employ skilled workers. In Lyon's censuses, 21% of the female apprentices were 'apprentice silk workers' ('apprentice ... worker' was a rare phrasing, indicative of their non-existent prospects of independence) and 34% were apprentice bobbin winders (at best a sub-subcontractor's occupation, always female). Among boys, 28% were apprentice silk workers, but the rest were in a much more diverse range of occupations, often trades that used to have guilds. This probably indicated practices more akin to the Ancien Régime template for boys, whereas for many of the girls, 'apprenticeship' meant that they were hired for a few years to perform simple tasks, in exchange for food and lodging. It does not imply that they learned nothing, but the prospect they would be considered skilled was remote.

What the censuses mostly underline is the large number of teenagers employed in trades whom the census clerk did not describe as apprentices. Given that apprenticeship was not confined to particularly skilled occupations, did they differ from apprentices by something other than name? Censuses cannot tell us who learned what, and it seems a fair guess that, insofar as learning was informal and perhaps 'stolen' from

---

[25] A. Cottereau, 'The fate of collective manufactures in the industrial world: The silk industries of Lyons and London, 1800–1850', in: C. Sabel and J. Zeitlin (eds.), *World of Possibilities: Mass Production and Flexibility in Western Industrialization* (Cambridge: Cambridge University Press, 1997), 75–153; L. Pérez, 'Inventing in a world of guilds: The case of the silk industry in Lyon in the eighteenth century', in: S. R. Epstein and M. Prak (eds.), *Guilds, Innovation, and the European Economy, 1400–1800* (Cambridge: Cambridge University Press, 2008), 232–63.

[26] For example N. Rondot, *Rapport sur les objets de parure, de fantaisie et de goût, fait à la commission française du jury international de l'Exposition universelle de Londres* (Paris: Imprimerie impériale, 1854).

the masters, the two groups were in similar situations.[27] Censuses, however, do provide some clues as to what parents could expect in each situation.

For mid-century Paris, the Chamber of Commerce statistics paint a seemingly clear picture.[28] Apprentices are over-represented in small workshops (with a total of ten workers or less), young workers in larger ones. The few Parisian factories, producing cotton and wool thread, wallpaper, and shawls, stated that they had no apprentices, but many workers under the age of 16. The luxury, fashion, and food trades, as well as most occupations related to wood and metal, listed few young workers and many apprentices. We should not take these contrasts at face value, though, and conclude that the more traditional the industries, the more apprentices they had. Among the myriad luxury and fashion trades that flourished in nineteenth-century Paris, many were never incorporated (apprentices were especially numerous in the faubourg Saint-Antoine, the privileged neighbourhood where guild regulations never applied). Most trades experienced a growing division of labour, so that most workers did not need to master fine skills. Yet they kept, or appropriated, the Ancien Régime template of hiring teenagers for several years, often without fixed wages, in exchange for food and lodging, or food and gratuities – and possibly some training.

What about other cities and towns? In Table 10.1, we generally find many more young workers than apprentices – and from their occupations, it is obvious that not all the former worked in factories, which were anyway scarce. In many trades, there were teenage workers as well as apprentices. In some cases, the term was probably the only difference – which in itself is indicative of the survival of older terminologies. Sometimes, young workers were former apprentices.

Caen illustrates differences in terminology: overall, just 5% of boys were apprentices, whereas 46% were young workers, including 22% of clerks and shop assistants – a much higher proportion than elsewhere. This mostly indicates that teenagers who were learning in shops (of hairdressers, bakers, merchants, etc.) rather than workshops were not called

[27] P. Wallis, 'Apprenticeship and training in premodern England', *Journal of Economic History* 68 (2008), 832–61 usefully summarises discussions on such processes.

[28] *Statistique . . . 1848*. For details about differences across trades, see Crowston, Kaplan and Lemercier, 'Les apprentissages parisiens'. It is difficult to know if the divide between apprentices and young workers was sharper in the capital, or if this is an effect of the sources. Population census lists, which we use for other places, have been lost for Paris. The Chamber of Commerce was actively trying to differentiate apprenticeship from child labour, and to promote the Ancien Régime template (although it was hostile to a restoration of guilds).

Table 10.2 *Median ages of apprentices and young workers in mid-nineteenth-century French censuses*

Place	Female apprentices	Female young workers	Male apprentices	Male young workers
Lyon	15	16	17	17
Poitiers	14	16	15	17
Dijon	14	16	16	17
Caen	15	16	15	16
Lusignan	13	15	15	18
Château-Larcher	17	15	14	15

Sources: see Table 10.1.

apprentices, but *garçon* or *commis*.[29] Their situations probably resembled apprenticeship in many respects, although we do not know whether they had long contracts, but the word was not used. Similarly, young people in agriculture were either styled cultivators, or had life-cycle occupations such as shepherds, but were never called apprentices. They learned by doing, as did teenagers employed in factories, but there was no guild template to reference and the word 'apprentice' was not used.

This leaves us with the many 'young workers' engaged in the same occupations as apprentices. For example, in Lyon there were almost as many apprentices as young workers in occupations that were considered unskilled, such as silk worker and bobbin winder. They worked in similar households, in terms of the gender of the master and the number of people employed and lodged. Some 'young workers' might simply have completed their apprenticeship before reaching 18 – they would be the younger equivalent of Ancien Régime journeymen. Table 10.2 shows somewhat higher median ages among 'young workers', but some were too young to have been apprenticed before.

The main differences between the two categories had to do with the social proximity between teenagers and masters. In Lyon in 1851, 23% of 'young workers' lived and worked with their parents, compared to just 5% of 'apprentices'. It was apparently uncommon to call a son or daughter who worked with a parent an apprentice. It is perhaps obvious that a specific contract was not required to work and learn with a parent, who already had legal authority; it is also consistent with the tradition of the guilds, which considered inheritance and apprenticeship as different paths to the trade.

---

[29] On these variants in several languages, see S. Steffens, 'Le nom de l'apprenti', *Revue belge de philologie et d'histoire* 79 (2001), 591–617.

What censuses show through the large numbers of 'young workers' is partly that many teenagers worked, and presumably trained, with their parents.

In addition, apprentices had specific geographical and social origins.[30] Only 30% of apprentices who subsequently married in Lyon were born there, compared to 60% of young workers. When they married, 45% of apprentices had parents who were alive and living outside Lyon, indicating that the apprentice had migrated alone, not with their family, compared to just 18% of young workers. Although half of young workers did not live with their parents, theirs had generally been a short distance move. Accordingly, 29% of apprentices' parents were farmers, compared to just 8% of young workers' parents; conversely, just 4% of apprentices' parents worked in the silk industry, whereas 12% of the young workers' parents did. Finding a place in a Lyonnais workshop was not possible for any teenager: servants and day labourers were almost absent among the parents of both apprentices and young workers. Geographic and/or social mobility was more common among apprentices. This reflects the fact that migrants more often had long contracts and were mostly paid in kind, whereas local youth could be employed at will. Whatever skills apprentices learned, their contract was, for some, a way to enter the city.

Many teenage girls (and boys in some places) were servants (Table 10.1). In the nineteenth century, there was a shift in the gendering of domestic service; more generally, servants tended to become less well-respected and to come from lower classes.[31] Being a young servant was less a life-cycle occupation and increasingly preparation for a life of service instead. Apprentices' contracts were closer to those of servants than workers, because of the relationship with the master and the duration. However, distinguishing apprenticeship from domestic service was one of the focal points of jurisprudence, especially for girls, whom some masters and mistresses used to tend to their household.

At the other end of the social spectrum, we find teenagers described as pupils or students – a small minority, almost all boys. These were young bourgeois attending high schools. Discussions on technical education had begun before the Revolution and flourished in the nineteenth century, but actual technical schools were few. In addition, most prepared youths for professions, or careers in the higher ranks of public administration or

---

[30] Marriage records were found for 86 apprentices and 103 young workers (on the Lyon municipal archives website). We could not identify a marriage record if the person did not marry in Lyon, or if their name was too common. Those are important biases, but they are the same for our two populations.

[31] R. Sarti, 'Criados, servi, domestiques, Gesinde, servants: For a comparative history of domestic service in Europe (16th–19th centuries)', *Obradoiro de Historia Moderna* 16 (2007), 9–39.

firms, rather than for trades: there were, for example, schools for nautical engineers and accountants. Design schools (first established in the 1760s) were the main exception, but trained only a minority of designers, or artisans in the luxury and fashion industries. According to the promoters of technical schools, masters did not bother to teach because they could exploit apprentices, while parents broke contracts as soon as their children could earn some money. Schools now had to provide what masters had done in the past. When the labour movement began to unite in the 1860s, it adopted a similar position. In France, unlike in England, workers rarely complained about competition from apprentices and never asked for limits on their numbers. Instead, they condemned their exploitation by masters, and deskilling generally. This ultimately led, in the twentieth century, to a new version of apprenticeship, alternating weeks at school and in the workshop; but this only appeared after the 1870 war, when the French turned to German models of education generally. In the nineteenth century, trades were almost never learned at school.[32]

Finally, as in the pre-revolutionary period, one practice blurred borders between schooling, domestic service, and apprenticeship: charity apprenticeships, which religious institutions (hospitals and convents) continued to provide, with an increased focus on orphans or otherwise marginalised children. There were two types of charity apprenticeships. Patronage, on the one hand, furnished a standard apprenticeship in a workshop, supplemented with control from an association, which devised standard contracts and monitored practices. Patronage was essentially an attempt to move market-oriented practices in the direction of the Ancien Régime template.[33]

Alternatively, charity apprenticeships still occurred in workshops established in or around hospitals and convents. For example, in the Lyon census for 1851, we find 19 female 'apprentices', without any indication of trade, aged 8–20 (eight were 11 years or younger), living with seven sisters of the charitable order of Saint-Vincent. These charitable workshops provided children with 'apprenticeships' more often than patronage, but they remained a small minority – especially as girls now had more opportunities to become apprentices in workshops. They made 'apprenticeship' accessible for people who probably would not have found masters otherwise. Yet, as in the eighteenth century, the experience

---

[32] S. Lembré, *Histoire de l'enseignement technique* (Paris: La Découverte, 2016). For examples of promotion of technical schools by an entrepreneur and by workers, see C. Loquet, *L'Apprentissage à l'Atelier de l'Industrie Privée et à l'École* (Rouen : Léon Deshays, 1884); *Séances du Congrès ouvrier de France, session de 1876* (Paris: Fischbacher, 1877), 201–72.

[33] L. R. Berlanstein, 'Growing up as workers in nineteenth-century Paris: The case of the orphans of the Prince Imperial', *French Historical Studies* 11 (1980), 551–76.

described by that label was far from the ideal of acquiring skills through one-to-one mentoring.

For nineteenth-century teenagers, apprenticeship was part of a continuum of ways of learning, working – and leaving. No more than before the Revolution was it the only way to learn skills, even artisanal skills. The widespread use of apprenticeship contracts was an oddity in a context of commercial labour relations, in which most workers had short contracts and faced no legal barrier to becoming entrepreneurs. The Ancien Régime template had clearly survived, partly for symbolic reasons – with many contemporaries actually believing that all past apprenticeships had followed guild rules. Long contracts paid in kind also offered practical opportunities for some masters as well as some parents.

What was Apprenticeship Used For? Becoming a Master, and Other Outcomes

Could apprenticeship open genuine prospects of upward mobility, especially of becoming an entrepreneur? According to many in the nineteenth century, whereas apprentices could become masters in the eighteenth century, their modern followers would at best earn a living as semi-skilled workers. Our results question both the bright vision of the Ancien Régime and the grim assessment of nineteenth-century apprenticeships.

From the early modern period through the nineteenth century, many apprentices did not complete their training; France is no exception to the European pattern. For the Ancien Régime, we used the well-kept registers of the *Grande Fabrique* of Lyon (the guild covering the city's large and prosperous silk industry) to track premature termination of training. Corporate officers recorded children's entry into apprenticeship, often noting the outcome of the contracts in the margins. We analysed three registers, from the late 1680s to the late 1760s, containing information on 5,281 apprentices. They indicate that 18% of contracts were cancelled. Cancellation was most common in the 1680s, occurring in 24% of apprenticeships, mostly because the apprentice had quit (rather than being dismissed by the master). Another 1.2% of apprentices died. In addition, 10–15% of apprentices would interrupt their contract. Of that group, around a third in the 1740s and a quarter in the 1760s would later restart. Another third later cancelled their contracts (of whom a small number had restarted first). We do not know what happened to the final third of apprentices who interrupted. Perhaps they returned to apprenticeship without informing the guild; perhaps they stayed away. Finally,

27% of apprentices in the 1680s, and 25% in the later period were transferred to a different master during their contracts.[34]

Most of the cancellations happened during the first three years of the contract in the 1740s, and the first two years in the 1760s, but exits continued throughout the term. There is no clear clustering of departures either at the start or end of the contract. This implies a mix of motivations among apprentices and masters: from resolving a poor initial match to quitting after having learned enough. The notion of a two-stage model of apprenticeship, in which the later period was seen by masters as crucial because only then could they benefit from profitable labour from the apprentice, is not borne out by these registers.[35]

In the nineteenth century, there were no such registers. As contracts were generally unwritten, it is even possible that the duration was not always strictly determined at the start (although the law and model contracts advised this). Yet the number of unfinished apprenticeships that reached the courts, at least in the main cities, suggest a share of exits as high as in Ancien Régime Lyon. As mentioned, one-tenth of Parisian apprenticeships gave birth to a labour court case in the late 1850s. Many of these resulted in reconciliation between the parties. When judgments were issued, most ended the apprenticeship, sometimes because the master was deemed too violent or insufficiently skilled. However, more than 70% of cases were brought by masters and mistresses seeking damages because their apprentice had left prematurely. In a sample of 319 cases in 1848–85, 38% of early exits happened during the first year, 37% in the second year, and 25% came afterwards.[36]

The frequency of early exits helps explain another striking continuity from the eighteenth to the nineteenth century: very few apprentices went on to become masters or mistresses of their trades. If we compare the names of youths who commenced an apprenticeship or an *allouage* in Paris in 1761 with the lists of individuals entering a guild from January 1766 to December 1775, the number of matches is surprisingly low. Of 1,404 apprentices and 89 *alloués* in 1761 (as well 23 apprentices who moved to new masters by notarial contract that year), only 194 individuals can be said with certainty to have become masters in the

[34] The guild's rules on apprenticeship are set out in J. Godart, *L'ouvrier en soie: Monographie du tisseur lyonnais*, part 1: *La réglementation du travail* (Lyon: Bernoux et Cumin and Rousseau, 1899), 100–33. Our data come from Lyon Municipal Archives, HH 597, HH601, HH602. We thank Patrick Wallis for his work on these registers. For more detailed results, see R. Schalk, P. Wallis, C. Crowston and C. Lemercier, 'Failure or flexibility? Exits from apprenticeship training in pre-modern Europe', *Journal of Interdisciplinary History* 48 (2017), 131–58.

[35] On this notion, see Wallis, 'Apprenticeship'.

[36] Crowston, Kaplan and Lemercier, 'Les apprentissages parisiens'.

trades in which they began training. The rate extends from a minimum of 13% to a potential maximum of around 20%. A comparison of 1751 apprentices with guild records from 1755 to 1775 produces similar results.

Among those who became masters and mistresses, a handful were *alloués*, suggesting that this gloomily exclusionary contract did not necessarily foreclose entry to mastership. In total, apprentices in fewer than 50 of the 106 trades appearing in contracts in 1761 became guild masters. For those who became masters, the time necessary to achieve mastership varied widely, from 5 to 15 years.

The *Grande Fabrique* of Lyon saw similar outcomes. Between 1769 and 1773, 281 of 777 new masters qualified by apprenticeship and another 116 former apprentices qualified via another route, an average of 79 - per year. Between 1763 and 1765, the latest years in which these former apprentices could have started training, 1,126 new apprenticeships were registered, an average of 375 per year. If these rates are broadly representative, then around 21% (79/375) of youths who started apprenticeships became masters. Given that at least 18% of apprentices cancelled their contracts, this implies that up to 61% of those who started apprenticeships in silk weaving spent their lives as journeymen – either in Lyon or elsewhere – or changed their trade or place, and that a minimum of 26% (21/82) of those who qualified as journeymen became masters.

Apprenticeship played different roles in the reproduction of different trades. In Paris, for example, among apprentice grocers (*épiciers*), 8 out of the 15 apprentices who began in 1761 became masters, as did 7 of 13 distillers and beverage sellers (*limonadiers-distillateurs*) and 6 of 11 small grain dealers (*grainiers-grainières*, a mixed-sex guild). By contrast, only 8 of 121 apprentice pastry-makers, 6 of 80 apprentice shoemakers, and 2 of 31 apprentice printers became masters. Most apprentices did not become masters, but those in some trades had a much better chance than others.

For women, the questions of continuity or rupture and 'success' and 'failure' are even more complicated. Among seamstresses, an average of slightly more than 400 girls began an apprenticeship each year in mid-eighteenth century Paris. In the same period, approximately 110 women entered the guild via apprenticeship each year (of a total of around 140 new mistresses). This means that one in four apprentice seamstresses became mistresses, slightly more than we found for Parisian apprentices in all trades who entered apprenticeship in 1761.[37]

---

[37] C. H. Crowston, *Fabricating Women: The Seamstresses of Old Regime France, 1675–1791* (Durham, NC: Duke University Press, 2001), 326–28.

We have found marriage records for 86 of the apprentices observed in Lyon in 1851, and 103 of the 'young workers'. Those who married in Lyon arguably had the most linear trajectories, yet just half of each group remained in the trade they had entered as teenagers. Broadly speaking, locals and those with more bourgeois origins were more likely to have changed occupation, while those who had migrated to Lyon on their own stayed in the same trade more often. Those with better local connections, or more family resources, often used them in order to *not* become entrepreneurs or workers in the trade they first joined.

We cannot reconstruct similar trajectories for Parisian apprentices in the nineteenth century (the records were destroyed), but figures published by the Chamber of Commerce for 1848 and 1860 show similarly diverse outcomes across trades. They allow us to compare the numbers of apprentices, masters, well-paid workers, and standard workers for a finely grained set of trades (more than 300 were recorded). If we assume that these numbers did not change quickly, we can estimate the likelihood of an apprentice becoming a master or mistress or a well-paid worker in the same trade.[38]

Extreme cases are easily found. For example, in 1860, 20 engravers on cameo and fine stones employed 60 (male) apprentices on 3–5-year contracts: each year, 12–20 apprentices would complete their training. It appears very unlikely that most would open their own workshop in Paris. Similar ratios of 2–3 apprentices per master were found in larger trades, such as the fine jewellers (1,417 apprentices in 738 workshops). These apprentices were also not likely to become well-paid workers: there were just 24 men making more than 6 francs per day in cameo engraving and 852 in fine jewellery. In such trades, it is likely that former apprentices were either hired as standard workers, with no skill premium, or left the trade or city.

However, other trades had numbers of apprentices that were commensurate with those of masters and well-paid workers: a smooth ascent from apprentice to master could have been a reality in such cases. The 253 industrial designers had 209 well-paid male workers and 103 male apprentices (called 'apprentice-pupils'), mostly with three or four-year contracts. With one apprentice finishing each year for every ten workshops, at least some had the chance to take over from their master. In 1860, this trade was also noticeable for the low proportion of apprentices living with their master (11%), hinting at mostly Parisian origins. The Laroche workshop, where apprentices produced masterpieces, was part

---

[38] *Statistique ... 1848; Statistique ... 1860.*

of this trade: all the more reasons for parents to believe in the Ancien Régime myth.

These findings raise questions about the expectations and aspirations of new apprentices and their families. Why go to the trouble of arranging a formal apprenticeship, when a youth had such a small chance of becoming a master? One possible answer is the limited information available to families contracting apprenticeships, a particular problem for non-locals and non-artisans. In England, manuals existed from the 1720s that offered advice on the costs involved in establishing a business in different trades and the obstacles one might face. Similar manuals only began to appear in the later nineteenth century in France,[39] meaning that parents may have lacked an understanding of the potential to become a master. However, it is unlikely that information shortages alone can account for the massive numbers of children entering apprenticeships that were unlikely to lead to independent mastership through the eighteenth and nineteenth centuries.

Our study suggests, instead, that the terms 'failure' and 'success' are inadequate to understand the relationship between apprenticeship and guild membership. Given the expense and risk of establishing a business, the freedom of life as a skilled journeyman – which included the ability to travel in search of economic opportunity – may have been appealing to many youths from modest backgrounds. The high rate of non-ascension to guild membership suggests that most families knew in advance that the prospect of guild membership was highly uncertain. With only one or two in ten becoming masters in many trades, these parents looked to apprenticeship for its other advantages: vocational skills, contacts and know-how to obtain future employment, and a coming-of-age process that readied the youth for the world. Another important factor was that large trades were also those in which parents could most easily (and often more cheaply) locate a master willing to take on their children. Cost aside, the social capital necessary to obtain a master for apprenticeship in one of the mercantile guilds meant that those children were poised for success from the outset. Thus, in drawing broad conclusions we must also keep in mind that the horizon of expectations and aspirations varied greatly between children with sharply unequal forms of capital.

Finally, it is likely that parents knew that some skills could be transferred to other occupations – something the Ancien Régime template entirely ignored. An apprenticeship contract, even in the nineteenth century, was predicated on the master teaching his or her trade to the

---

[39] One of the pioneers was H. Leneveux, *Manuel d'apprentissage, guide pour le choix d'un état industriel* (Paris: Passard, 1855).

apprentice: the only occupation mentioned was the master's. Yet the division of labour within even small workshops meant that many apprentices received training from a worker rather than the master. While this was seen as a problem in nineteenth-century jurisprudence, it could instead represent an opportunity. Some skills learned with a worker were probably transferable from one trade to another. For example, mechanics were listed in 43 of the 105 main trades in the 1860 Parisian statistics: the increased prevalence of machines made this a transferable skill *par excellence*. Similarly, 29 non-generic male occupations (e.g. fitters, engravers, gilders) and four female ones (polishers, silver polishers, gilders, piercers) were listed in ten separate trades or more. It is also plausible that, even in the eighteenth century, some seemingly unlikely career moves were made possible because specific, transferable skills, rather than 'the trade', had been learned – and some parents, knowing this, could have chosen trades that offered such advantages.[40]

Conclusion

From the Ancien Régime to the twenty-first century, a vision of apprenticeship as a privileged form of social production prevailed, which saw it as a stable system that served to reproduce a given social and economic world. This chapter has challenged this vision of apprenticeship and corporate institutions by demonstrating the great diversity in outcomes of apprenticeship and, by extension, the multiple aspirations and expectations that teenagers and their families brought to vocational training. This analysis repositions apprenticeship not as the determinant of the outcome of children's lives, but instead as one choice among several, and as one step in a long series of life stages, each of which had their own strategy, choice, and constraints.

This chapter has also demonstrated the variety of forms of apprenticeship from the Ancien Régime through the nineteenth century, emphasising the durability of the guild template for apprenticeship, even while many other forms of training existed, many of which laid claim to the term 'apprenticeship' despite important divergences from the basic framework enshrined by the guilds. In so doing, this chapter has provided the first examination of nineteenth-century apprenticeship based on records derived from practice. As we have seen, the patterns that emerged in the nineteenth century were often similar to those of the Ancien Régime:

[40] On jurisprudence, see e.g. L. Guibourg and L. André, *Le Code ouvrier, exposé pratique de la législation et de la jurisprudence réglant le travail et les intérêts des ouvriers et apprentis* (Paris: Marescq aîné, 1895). *Statistique ... 1860* lists occupations within each trade, giving an idea of the division of labour.

although the laws had almost completely changed, the ways to learn a trade were quite similar, as were the varieties of expectations leading to, and outcomes emanating from, vocational training. Moreover, in both periods, the range of possible trajectories was also similarly shaped by gender and by the range of social resources available to the youths.

The template of guild apprenticeship was very much present in the minds of social reformers, judges, and probably parents and masters/ mistresses themselves in the nineteenth century. Ironically, however, this template referred to Ancien Régime apprenticeship as it had existed in theory, but not necessarily in practice.

However, by 1880 apprenticeships were becoming rare, and, where they still existed, shorter. Reformers, who were increasingly worried about social and economic production and reproduction, tried to revive the guild template by infusing it with some school teaching, which ultimately gave birth to the law of 1928.[41] This law arguably revived apprenticeship as a specific contract, and its monitoring by trade associations, which were once more legal. But it had become very different from the guild template: apprentices were entitled to wages, spent a lot of time in schools, and could be employed by a large firm. A precise exploration of these late-nineteenth-century transitions is beyond the scope of this chapter. Their timing is, however, a good indicator of the fact that the Ancien Régime template of apprenticeship, and the diverse trajectories that it allowed, had survived as long as French economic growth had been mostly driven by 'flexible specialisation', not large firms.

---

[41] On debates at that time, see S. Lembré, 'La "crise" de l'apprentissage: De l'échec à la loi (fin XIXe siècle-années vingt)', in: N. Coquery and M. de Oliveira (eds.), *L'échec a-t-il des vertus économiques?* (Paris: CHEFF, 2015), 309–18.

Conclusion: Apprenticeship in Europe – A Survey

Maarten Prak and Patrick Wallis

The previous chapters have discussed local and national apprenticeship arrangements. In many places, the authors of these chapters highlighted local or national peculiarities. For good reasons, because in many areas the variation is striking at first sight. Still, reading the chapters together suggests that there was, nonetheless, something of a template for apprenticeship in Europe that applied in most places and could therefore be seen as the model on which individuals and organisations built their own specific set of rules and practices. In the following pages we seek to establish the outlines of that template.[1]

Firstly, and perhaps most importantly, all European countries had a system of regulated apprenticeships. By regulated we mean that it was embedded in established rules and in institutions that applied and monitored the application of those rules. Some of the rules were consolidated in laws and other formal regulations, others were, perhaps, more conventions. Apprentices everywhere possessed a recognised status in the eyes of the community and the state. Their agreement with their master distinguished them from other servants and employees. Completing training meant acquiring some form of rights in the labour market: apprenticeship combined an element of licensing or certification with the transmission of human capital. Such a system does not seem to have existed in other parts of the world.

The European apprenticeship system was already long in existence by the start of the seventeenth century and we must therefore assume that it was a medieval 'invention'. Under this system very impressive numbers of youngsters were trained and educated. For England, between 11% and 14% of male teenagers were apprentices, in the Dutch Republic every year an estimated 13,800 youngsters started their apprenticeship, and apprentices made up around 4% of the urban population. Paris in the mid-nineteenth century had around 19,000 apprentices and 1 in every 17 workers was an apprentice. Apprenticeship, in other words, was a major dimension of growing up in pre-modern Europe, and getting an

---

[1] Unless stated otherwise, all the data quoted in this Conclusion come from the preceding chapters and have not been referenced.

education. Remarkably, in many towns and cities local orphanages or poor-law providers ensured apprenticeships for their wards. Almost everywhere, apprentices started in their mid-teens. In Finland the legal minimum age for starting an apprenticeship was 14, but this also seems to have been the normal age in places where there was no legal constraint in place. By implication, during their late teens and early twenties youths of both sexes often lived outside their parental home – for domestic service, exceptionally for higher education, but in a great many cases to serve as an apprenticeship.

In many urban centres the number of apprentices was regulated. This happened, however, at the level of individual masters, not of the system as a whole, and masters in non-guilded trades and the countryside remained unaffected. Normally, guild masters would only be allowed to take on one or two youngsters at a time. This was a constraint on popular masters but not necessarily on the system as a whole, because most masters trained very few apprentices throughout their career, or none at all. The system, in other words, was never used to capacity; although it might have affected the quality of training if the best masters were limited in their capacity to accept new pupils. This suggests that these limitations were not only designed to limit the inflow of new skilled labourers.

Apprentices came from a wide range of backgrounds. Most importantly, the chapters in this book do not support the claim, still regularly made, that guilds managed to restrict access to their trade to the sons, daughters and sons-in-law of the established masters. Relatives of the established masters were a minority among apprentices almost everywhere. It may be surmised that this is a reflection of the registration process that ignored such apprenticeships, but in several places these kin apprenticeships were registered and these records show a significant but nonetheless limited percentage of kin. In Turin, in 1792, such apprenticeships varied between 5% and 27% of all apprenticeships, with only the local bakers showing a higher rate at 35%. Among the London apprentices whose fathers worked in industry, the great majority of youngsters were nonetheless trained in a different trade. Migration, on the other hand, was a common feature of apprenticeship. In places like London migrant apprentices were even a clear majority, but even when this was not the case, their numbers usually equalled those of the sons (and daughters) of masters in training.

Apprenticeships were usually open to non-kin, but such openness did not apply to females. In most places, the percentage of registered female apprentices remained well below 10%. In Venice, among around 6,000 apprenticeship contracts, less than 1% related to a female, and in London a similar percentage applied. This is one area where the family provided the main alternative, because there are hints that the numerous skilled females in, for instance, the various textile trades, were trained informally. France and Turin provide the most significant exceptions to this pattern and this suggests that absolutism, by restricting guilds' agency over access, was beneficial for the gender balance in apprenticeship. This conclusion would require, however, a more systematic investigation before it can be accepted. Such an investigation will have to take into account that the volume of female apprenticeships remained small in places where guild restrictions were relaxed or even absent.

This brings us to the legal and organisational framework of apprenticeship. The state regulated apprenticeship in some countries, but by no means everywhere. In Venice such regulation went back to the fourteenth century. In England the famous Statute of Artificers was introduced in the sixteenth century and in France royal legislation of apprenticeship also started in the sixteenth century. Finland applied Swedish legislation. In the Low Countries and the Holy Roman Empire, on the other hand, national legislation, insofar as there was any, ignored apprenticeship and left it to local and regional authorities.

In many places this implied that craft guilds were a source of rules for urban apprenticeships, although by no means for all of them. Some trades were not incorporated, for example, nor was much work in manufacturing and services outside urban centres, although proto-industrial guilds did control some large-scale rural trades, especially in textiles. Setting the rules did not automatically mean that guilds also organised apprenticeships. Their involvement was most encompassing in the Holy Roman Empire, the Low Countries and England. In these countries apprenticeship contracts drawn up outside guild oversight were either unusual in guild-governed trades, as in the Low Countries and the German lands, or limited in scope, as in England. In France, Spain and the Italian peninsula on the other hand, apprenticeships were regulated by notarial contracts, which were usually still subject to guild approval. Formally, therefore, the guilds were only indirectly involved in the regulation and monitoring of apprenticeships in the Mediterranean countries. Nonetheless, guild apprenticeship provided the default model. Most of the chapters in this book demonstrate that guilds were not as deeply involved in apprenticeship as was previously assumed and that S. R. Epstein's claim that 'the primary purpose of craft guilds was to provide adequate skills training through formal apprenticeship' should therefore be considered an overstatement.[2] At the same time, the guild template remained the benchmark for apprenticeships everywhere.

---

[2] S. R. Epstein, 'Craft guilds, apprenticeship, and technological change in pre-industrial Europe', *Journal of Economic History* 53 (1998), 685.

If guilds were less important than historians once assumed, the civic institutions of Europe's towns and cities appear to have been consistently more important than has been recognised. Specific tribunals or legal processes existed in many of the main centres of training. These urban courts provided a solution to some of the major tensions that were generated by apprenticeship. It looks as if most apprentices lived with their masters and were therefore part of the master's household. The authority of the master, and the willingness of the apprentice to obey him (or her), was often explicitly confirmed in the contract. At the same time, a significant minority of apprentices, in the order of a quarter to a third, stayed with their own relatives. Clearly, this was only feasible for local youngsters. This arrangement of adolescents moving in with the master inevitably was the source of numerous conflicts, and urban institutions everywhere had to deal with such conflicts. The approach they took was rarely to reinforce the rights of masters over apprentices. Instead, urban courts offered arbitration, and exit if necessary.

That enforcement was in the hands of courts and city tribunals rather than guilds seems surprising if we think of apprenticeship as a system run under the supervision of the occupation to reproduce a closed professional grouping. However, it makes sense if instead we understand it as an exchange that was fundamentally structured by a legal contract. As one contract among the many made within these economies, it fell to the courts – more or less specialised – to hear and settle controversies. And as a contract drawn up between two parties who had starkly unequal voices within the guild, it made little sense for the apprentice and their family to look to the guild's officers for fair and equal treatment if they had a problem with their master. Finally, we must recognise that many contracts were not made within guilds, and for those individuals it was only ever general courts that could offer a source of recourse.

Even if guilds often did not regulate the details of individual apprenticeships, they often contributed to the production of the 'paper trail' that would help apprentices to demonstrate that they had completed their training. Perhaps most importantly, this happened by registering apprentices in ledgers maintained, and therefore implicitly also certified, by the guild. In Finland, France and the Dutch Republic apprentices received a formal document as proof of the completion of their training. In England they received the master's half of the indenture paper when they had finished. In Venice the *Giustizia Vecchia* kept records of all apprentices, whereas in the Southern Netherlands and in Madrid journeymen had to produce a trial piece to demonstrate their skills, and this was supplemented by guild registration. One way or another, the apprentice would be able to demonstrate completion of the training period.

Not all apprentices who started actually finished their apprenticeship. Although there was much variation, all systems seem to have lost a third or more of the initial crop of apprentices somewhere during the 2–7 years that an apprenticeship would take. Some apprentices died or ran away, others switched trade, but many also seem to have been satisfied with only partial training. What happened to those who left, we do not know. Likewise, there is at this point no obvious reason why German crafts seem to have been much better at retaining their apprentices than those of other countries.

One incentive for leaving or staying was probably financial. This is the area where we see the greatest amount of variation, not only between locations but also between individual crafts and even individual apprentices. Staying with the master usually implied payment for food and lodging. Sometimes this was compensated by the labour services that the apprentice was supplying to the business. Premiums would also depend on the master's reputation, as a craftsman or as a teacher. A minority of apprentices received wages, often increasing as he (or she) became more experienced. There is evidence of a trade-off between wages and the length of the apprenticeship. Long apprenticeships implied a greater labour contribution and could entail higher wages. Short apprenticeships, on the other hand, might require a higher premium.

Only a minority of apprentices who completed their training subsequently established themselves as independent masters in their own right. For England a figure of 40% is reported, but many apprentices left their unusually long (seven years) apprenticeship early so the percentage may have actually been significantly lower. For France the reported percentage is 20, in the Dutch Republic in the order of a third. This strongly suggests that it would be wrong to define the success of apprenticeship exclusively in terms of the attainment of master status. Parents and teenagers must have been aware that mastership was not the predetermined outcome of an apprenticeship. A future as journeyman must have been acceptable as well. Unfortunately, journeymen in pre-modern societies are a poorly known group.

In many European towns and countries the traditional apprenticeship system was under pressure during the eighteenth century. Apprenticeship became scarcer at the same time as alternatives were emerging, such as drawing academies. Around 1800, the fallout of the French Revolution created a huge shock to the apprenticeship system. The abolition of the guilds, in particular, seems to have opened up more training positions, while at the same time concerns were raised about the quality of training in this unregulated environment. Everywhere, however, the guild template of apprenticeship continued to be the standard against which alternatives were measured. In a surprising number of places that template continued to be used as a format for shaping apprenticeships. In this sense, the particular pre-modern form of skills training remained relevant into the modern period. However, with the emergence of organised labour unions, apprenticeship acquired a new status in economic organisation, as the focus of a crucial debate in politics and political economy about efficiency and equity in labour markets. Political settlements over the support and status that was to be given to apprenticeship were made in different forms across Europe between expansive central states, employers' organisations and unions. While apprenticeship remained tied to entry to skilled labour in many parts of Europe, it acquired a new connection to formal educational institutions with the shift to adding part-time technical education alongside workshop practice. This constituted a fundamental reorganisation of apprenticeship as a mechanism for training. At the same time, the rise of large firms provided a new framework of incentives for workers, who might now seek long-lasting careers, and gave employers a fresh motivation for investing in training.

Two 'big ideas' have been launched in the literature about European apprenticeship, one about comparisons between Europe and Asia, the other about comparative advantages within Europe. The latter is the easier to deal with on the basis of the chapters in this volume.

Joel Mokyr and others have suggested that English apprenticeship created a workforce that was exceptionally well trained. This high level of skills education would be one of the reasons why England was home to the remarkable sequence of technological innovations that helped launch the Industrial Revolution. The role of craftsmen in the early Industrial Revolution has indeed been re-evaluated in the recent literature.[3] Contemporaries were much impressed by the quality of the English workforce, and their testimonies to this effect should be taken seriously.[4]

Our evidence suggests that England was exceptional in two areas, and those two areas alone: apprenticeship in England was governed by national legislation, creating a broad framework for skills education that applied throughout the country, and that legislation stipulated unusually long and uniform terms of apprenticeship. However, we should bear in

---

[3] R. C. Allen, *The British Industrial Revolution in Global Perspective* (Cambridge: Cambridge University Press, 2009), 265–66; M. C. Jacob, *The First Knowledge Economy: Human Capital and the European Economy, 1750–1850* (Cambridge: Cambridge University Press, 2014), 12.

[4] J. Humphries, 'English apprenticeship: A neglected factor in the first Industrial Revolution', in: P. A. David and M. Thomas (eds.), *The Economic Future in Historical Perspective* (Oxford: Oxford University Press, 2003), 73–102; J. Mokyr, *The Enlightened Economy: An Economic History of Britain, 1700–1850* (New Haven, CT: Yale University Press, 2009), ch. 6.

mind that the majority of English apprentices did not complete the seven years of training prescribed in the law. This was only necessary for those who became masters and were seeking full membership of the guild. Many continental guilds, moreover, expected additional training from prospective masters, either through a period of travel as was required in the German-speaking world, or through some other sort of post-apprenticeship experience. We have not been able to demonstrate unequivocally that English masters had gone through a longer period of training than their competitors on the continent, before they settled down and opened their own businesses.

The second argument has been articulated most comprehensively by Jan Luiten van Zanden, but was also proposed by Epstein.[5] These authors argue that guild apprenticeships gave early modern Europe a head start over other continents in the area of human capital. The ready supply of skilled labour diminished the skill premium in Europe, making its indus-tries more competitive. Because most European youths were apprentices outside their parental household, they were also forced to become acquainted with new information and mindsets. This was especially true for mobile apprentices, who might be exposed to multiple ways of making certain objects. As a result, European industry became more innovative, even if many of these innovations occurred randomly, rather than as the result of systematic R&D. In the absence of equivalent studies of training in other regions of the world, this debate cannot be settled, but the chapters in this volume contribute to this debate by suggesting that it is the intersection of state and skill – particularly given recent evidence on the thinness of the rule of law in other regions – and the openness of labour markets that this then sustained that may have been a critical factor in Europe. In short, while apprenticeship could be an instrument of exclusion, in pre-modern Europe it was shaped into an institution of inclusion.

Three points stand out from this survey. First, if we consider who became apprentices in Europe then it is the scale, openness and breadth of training that stand out. Apprenticeship was a mechanism for social, geographic and occupational mobility across Europe. Family resources still mattered for a youth's future, to be sure, but the general effect of apprenticeship was to lubricate labour markets and ease spatial and social

---

[5] J. L. van Zanden, *The Long Road to the Industrial Revolution: The European Economy in a Global Perspective, 1000–1800* (Leiden: Brill, 2009), ch. 5; S. R. Epstein, 'Transferring technical knowledge and innovating in Europe, c. 1200–c. 1800', in: M. Prak and J. L. van Zanden (eds.), *Technology, Skills and the Pre-Modern Economy in the East and the West* (Leiden: Brill, 2013), 65–66.

mobility by providing a framework in which the risks involved were reduced.

Second, the operation of apprenticeship in the heartland of Europe's commercial and manufacturing sectors – its large cities – was rooted less in the guilds and more in urban and national provision of legal institutions that created a space to sustain contracts. Formal enforcement is only ever directly important to a minority of contracts of any kind; informal sanctions of reputation and private resolution will always be the first and easiest way to settle issues. But the law courts of the cities and the magistrates of the states of Europe sustained a rule of law for apprentices and masters that allowed exchanges to operate over a long duration and with the involvement of substantial financial and in-kind benefits. They were tied together by legal contracts; this allowed them to seek legal solutions.

Third, the long-term fortunes of apprenticeship look somewhat different to the traditional association of declining guilds with declining apprenticeship around 1800. Although only a few of the chapters cover the post-1800 period, we can see several commonalities in the evidence they present on this issue. Decline was not contingent on the abolition of guilds (where that occurred), but was a slower process. Removing guild regulations did allow apprenticeship to shift in structure in regulated trades – terms were adjusted, younger children entered places. But the fall in numbers reflected shifts in labour markets, particularly the growing size of firms and greater opportunities in expanding urban centres, and changing patterns of production that were a result of both the effect of new technologies and greater division of labour. Some of these processes had long been visible in the more developed parts of Europe.

Index